D0984183

DEMOCRATIC COMMUNITY

NOMOS

XXXV

NOMOS

Harvard University Press

The Liberal Arts Press

Atherton Press

Aldine-Atherton Press

Lieber-Atherton Press

New York University Press

NOMOS XXXV

Yearbook of the American Society for Political and Legal Philosophy

DEMOCRATIC COMMUNITY

Edited by

John W. Chapman, *University of Pittsburgh*

and

Ian Shapiro, *Yale University*

NEW YORK UNIVERSITY PRESS   *New York and London*

NEW YORK UNIVERSITY PRESS
New York and London

Democratic Community: NOMOS XXXV
edited by John W. Chapman and Ian Shapiro
Copyright © 1993 by New York University
Manufactured in the United States of America

Library of Congress Cataloging-in-Publication Data
Democratic community / edited by John W. Chapman and Ian Shapiro.
    p.   cm. — (Nomos ; 35)
  Includes bibliographical references and index.
  ISBN 0-8147-1497-8
    1. Democracy. 2. Community. 3. Liberalism. I. Chapman, John
William, 1923–   . II. Shapiro, Ian. III. Series.
JC423.D4417 1993
321.8—dc20   92-40158
                          CIP

New York University Press books are printed on acid-free paper,
and their binding materials are chosen for strength and durability.

c 10 9 8 7 6 5 4 3 2 1

CONTENTS

vii

This thirty-fifth volume of NOMOS began with presentations and commentaries delivered at the meeting of The American Society for Political and Legal Philosophy, held in conjunction with the annual meeting of the American Political Science Association in San Francisco, September 1990. We are grateful to our new editor, Ian Shapiro of Yale University, for having organized the program.

The topic for the meeting, "Democratic Community," was inspired by Christopher J. Berry's *The Idea of a Democratic Community,* published in 1989. I prevailed upon our president, Joel Feinberg, to make this selection by exercising my prerogative as editor of my final volume of NOMOS. I thought the matter both timely and important, which are the criteria our Society has always applied in choosing topics for consideration.

On a personal note, I wish to thank the Society for presenting me, through our officers, with a splendid Tiffany ship's clock for "devoted service." It looks just great on our mantle. You may wish to know, or perhaps you may not, that it runs perfectly on a Japanese quartz movement about the size of a small matchbox.

J. W. C.

CONTRIBUTORS

RICHARD J. ARNESON
Philosophy, University of California, San Diego

JEAN BAECHLER
Philosophy, University of Paris—Sorbonne (Paris IV)

CHRISTOPHER J. BERRY
Political Science, University of Glasgow

ROBERT A. DAHL
Political Science, Yale University

MARTIN P. GOLDING
Law and Philosophy, Duke University

CAROL C. GOULD
Philosophy, Stevens Institute of Technology

AMY GUTMANN
Political Science, Princeton University

JANE MANSBRIDGE
Political Science, Northwestern University

KENNETH MINOGUE
Political Science, London School of Economics

ROBERT C. POST
Law, University of California, Berkeley

DAVID A. J. RICHARDS
Law, New York University

GERALD N. ROSENBERG
Political Science, University of Chicago

BRUCE K. RUTHERFORD
Political Science, Yale University

ALAN RYAN
Political Science, Princeton University

CARMEN SIRIANNI
Sociology, Brandeis University

INTRODUCTION

JOHN W. CHAPMAN AND IAN SHAPIRO

Over the past two decades many Western political thinkers have been preoccupied with the confrontation between liberalism, institutionalized as modern welfare capitalism, and various communitarian philosophies of life. Some of these are deeply communalist and would transcend liberalism into participatory, non-competitive, essentially cooperative and solidaristic ways of living. Lurking beneath the surface of the liberal/communitarian debate, therefore, are assumptions and arguments about democracy. Often deeply implicit and seldom explored systematically, they set the terms of discussion in the present volume.

At the heart of liberalism is the idea of an equal right to freedom as exercised by autonomous individuals. In action this right generates the "competitive collaboration"[1] displayed in all the realms of life from science and the university through business and industry to the military. Given that we are ambivalent creatures, both individuated and social, and we are both differentiated and unequal in our abilities, in action the equal right to freedom produces inequalities in income, wealth, and authority, about which some have become increasingly uncomfortable. The "democratic communitarians" experience our world, in the words of Christopher J. Berry, as "excessively individualistic" and "insufficiently democratic." Our ambivalence dooms, or perhaps exhilarates, us to indissoluble tension between liberty and equality, between individualism and communalism. Hence it is no accident that in contemporary political theory, radical, individualistic liberals, such as David Gauthier and Robert Nozick, stand against radical communitarians like C. B. Macpherson and Roberto Mangabeira Unger, the latter of whom would have us discover our true social selves through the absolute democracy of life in "organic groups." In this connection, notice Gauthier's remark that his conception of the just society "provides a framework for community but is not communal."[2] As is to be expected, behind the great debate lie divergent views as to who we are and can be.

Whereas liberals, including John Rawls in our own day, have always insisted on the supremacy of freedom and autonomy, communitarians have come to think that an almost fetishistic addiction to freedom, without regard for its differential worth in our inegalitarian society, lies at the core of most that is wrong with the modern world. Even the liberal Jean Baechler would seem to subscribe to this diagnosis, at least in part. He says that "a democratic regime encourages individuation to the point of turning at times into the most extreme form of individualism."[3] According to the communitarians, unless the virtues and demands of community can gain precedence over individualistic aims and opportunism, at least some if not most of the time, the social and cultural ingredients of a viable political and economic order cannot flourish. And the more thoroughly communal among them would push on to a social order controlled by a monolithic conception of the good. The proposed forms vary, but their proponents all share a motivating sense, however, that unbridled individualism is self-destructive.

Could it be that moral individualism, the greatest of all Western discoveries about the self, inevitably degenerates into fecklessness and so self-destructs? Here critics of liberalism commonly call attention to our national failure to save and invest, to the rise in alienation exhibited by the urban underclass, to the excesses of 1980s yuppiedom, to outrageous executive earnings, to the closing of libraries, to opportunistic behavior on the part of university faculties and administrations, and to the breakdown of such civil institutions as the nuclear family. Are we in the grip of an *après moi le déluge* mentality? These are often cited as frightening signs of ill health; consequences of both a public and a private ethos in which wildly individualized gratifications have been permitted to displace devotion to our communities—national, professional, and local. America appears to have suffered a ghastly collapse of morale.

Fortunately, by the late 1980s the debate between liberals and communitarians seemed to be losing much of its doctrinaire character. Most liberals had backed away from libertarianism, and most communitarians embraced pluralism to some degree, conceding the necessity of substantial areas of individual freedom and choice. The interesting questions were revealed to be not *whether community?*, but rather *what sort of community?* And not *whether individual freedom?*, but rather *which freedoms, guaranteed by what constraints, at what cost, and to whom?*

Nevertheless, because we are dealing with genuinely divergent philosophies of life, important issues, having mainly to do with inequalities and fundamental moral attitudes, still remain contested. Notice a recent clash between the liberal-conservative Roger Scruton and communitarian Steven Lukes. According to Scruton, with reference to liberalism,

> Lukes proposes a rival morality, combining liberal values with a concern for the disadvantaged, in the manner of John Rawls's *Theory of Justice*. This "political morality" of the Left is animated by a "militantly rectifying spirit"; it is "anti-individualist" and promises to return us to "reciprocal and solidaristic ways of living."[4]

Scruton also takes strong exception to Lukes's description of the Soviet catastrophe as "our century's heroic social experiment of 'real socialism.'"[5] Here we catch a whiff of what Kenneth Minogue castigates as the "normativist" attitude toward life.

Both liberals and communitarians would perhaps do well to attend to Robert E. Lane's recently published *The Market Experience*.[6] It has something for each. Among other things, Lane reports that what people really care about is satisfying, self-directed work.[7] And they do not much care about equality,[8] feeling that all get pretty much what they deserve from the market.[9] With specific reference to communitarianism, Lane points out that affiliative motives and attitudes may well be a serious threat to productivity.[10] Disturbing also is Lane's conclusion that in our market driven society people in their guise as consumers dominate themselves as producers. Evidently we care more about having than doing.[11] This lends some substance to C. B. Macpherson's charge against the "neo-classical liberals," namely, "Chapman, Rawls, and Berlin," that they are willing to treat people as "consumers," rather than as "doers" and "exerters."[12]

In NOMOS XXXIV, *Virtue,* our contributors deal with the question: What virtues does a good society require and sustain? The present volume not only deals with fundamental issues that divide liberals and communitarians, it is concerned also with the structure of communities, the roles of freedom and democratic institutions in sustaining one another, and on the place of a democratic civil society in a democratic polity. The volume contains theoretical analyses of these and related questions, but several of our authors also explore their implications in concrete contexts. We have included considerations of freedom of speech in American jurisprudence, and of the tensions between markets and democracy as they operate in practice. Islamic fundamentalism's complex relations with polities are examined in an innovative way, and several of our contributors consider the significance, for the theory of democratic community, of the history of the women's movement and of feminist political theory more generally.

We begin with foundational matters. Part I presents three advocates of the liberal philosophy of life, understood in a classical or neo-classical manner. In effect, Jean Baechler, Kenneth Minogue, and Christopher J. Berry offer vantage points from which the reader may wish to appraise the ongoing argument between liberals and communitarians. None has much sympathy for the communitarian project. As is the case with pleasure, they seem to say, fraternity and fellow-feeling are not values at which we may take direct aim. The principles of "89" got it straight in putting "fraternity" in third place.

In an appropriately Cartesian manner, Jean Baechler presents definitions of the individual, the group, and democracy. These clear, distinct, and interdependent ideas generate a model that he thinks has important substantive implications. According to Baechler, the democratic polity seeks peace through justice, is inherently pluralistic, and naturally distinguishes between the public and the private. Unlike authoritarian and charismatic regimes, democratic ones are based on "consensual and calculated" obedience. To work, a democracy needs real persons, "upright and resolute" individuals. Baechler thinks the liberal democratic way of life is best conceived in terms of multiple markets, or "agories," as he calls them. Agories are the key democratic institutions, and the more fluid they are, the more democracy will be respected and valued. But common interests cannot be spontaneously realized through agorical mechanisms. "Common interests cannot be defined and realized but in common, that is, in public within the realm of the polity as such."

For communitarians inclined toward some kind of democratized "market socialism," perhaps the most important conclusions that Baechler defends have to do with the economy. "A market is neither more nor less than a permanent mechanism of quasi-direct democracy where, by their decision to buy, the clients accept or reject supply candidates, and delegate some of the suppliers to fulfill economic functions." Conceptions of "self-management" are naive and endanger democracy. Furthermore, "capitalism and its central institutions are the most perfect expression of and most in agreement with the unwritten law of democracy as applied to the economic order." As one reads Baechler, one cannot help but recall Raymond Aron's dictum that "democracy means competition!" Competitive politics and competitive economics, combined with community in the shape of virtuous devotion to common interests, are the hallmarks of Baechler's good society.

Kenneth Minogue writes in the spirit of Michael Oakeshott and Friedrich von Hayek. His conception of "normativism" invokes their respective analyses of "rationalism" and "constructivism." Indeed, normativism is nothing other than "imperialistic rationalism." Our basic trouble is that the concept of justice has "expanded" from the commutative and procedural to the substantive and "social." This expansion poses a deadly danger to freedom, to moral "identity" and integrity. Minogue affirms that "the moral life can be nothing else but an open ended dialogue between disparate types of human response to the world." However, "the basic aim of the normative reconstruction of society is equalization." This is to go directly against the grain of human nature. For "man is a comparative animal" and desires to excel, as Hobbes made clear long ago. Moreover, "inequality is built into the very structure of a moral identity." Minogue is working with a conception of human nature quite foreign to the cooperative and politicized creature that lives in the communitarian world. Minogue's philosophy of life points toward what Oakeshott calls "civil association," not toward building a deindividualized and equalized "community."

Christopher Berry defines the aim of the democratic communitarians as "the preservative transcendence of liberalism." For them the truly democratic way of life is affiliative and cooperative rather than competitive, and yet presumably free. Rather than hold to ambivalent "competitive collaboration" in our basic institutions, they would democratize them all, including industry and the home. According to Berry, this effort to "transcend" liberal individualism often leads communitarians to elevate "community" above discrete persons whose decisions, projects, and beliefs must be afforded respect. He says that communitarians face the challenge of transcending liberalism without thereby becoming illiberal. And Berry contends that this cannot be done. Crucial to his argument is his analysis of the communitarian concept of "shared understandings." These are said to be the outcome of cooperative rather than competitive activities. But the very idea of "shared understanding" is ambiguous. It may be a "product," as in the case of a compromise or mutual accommodation among people, in which case liberal individualism is not "transcended." Or it may take the form of a "discovery" that people make about themselves, a discovery in which they are transformed into the social and cooperative beings they really are. In this perspective, life in a "democratic community" would call forth our communal nature, presently obscured by liberal capitalist democracy. This is a vain hope if we are, indeed, ambivalent creatures, to whom "competitive collaboration" comes naturally.

In Part II we begin a descent from the heights of moral and political theory to the plains of everyday reality. Now things look somewhat different. Alan Ryan seeks to change the terms of the liberal-communitarian dispute by arguing that what is at issue has all too often been misconceived. If we look to intellectual history we see immediately that in practice many paradigmatic liberals have been communitarians in some respects, and many cultivators of community have also been liberals. Ryan claims that the contemporary debate has conflated epistemological, psychological, and moral issues. If these are properly distinguished, he says, it becomes clear that no one great and general issue is at stake, although the concerns that divide liberals from communitarians are interconnected.

Once the conceptual ground-clearing has been accomplished, Ryan goes on to paint a "liberal community" with its distinctive social, economic, and political attachments, and to explore several related tensions between liberty and community. "A viable community is cherished for the sake of the liberty and self-development of the individuals" who compose it. Yet occasions do arise, notably war, in which the community can be preserved only by measures that cannot but impair freedoms.

Martin Golding criticizes Ryan's conception of the relation between theories of the self and methodologies of social inquiry, on the one hand, and moral and political commitments on the other. He argues that we should expect to meet both liberal communitarians and communitarian liberals, but that their mixed philosophical commitments do not result from conceptual incoherence. Rather, disputes between liberals and communitarians reflect disagreements concerning their conceptions of the self and the nature of social bonds. This claim is illustrated by reference to the legal debate on freedom of association.

Amy Gutmann's chapter addresses the gap between the ideals and practices of American democracy. To locate this gap she says we must first get clear about our ideals. The first, populist, ideal contains a dilemma about what to do when majorities legitimately enter upon undemocratic courses of action. Proponents of the second, liberal, ideal avoid the populist paradox by emphasizing the need to protect personal freedom from majority or minority tyranny. The third ideal, which she calls "deliberative democracy," reconciles populism and liberalism by giving autonomy, conceived as the freedom of all to participate in shaping their political lives, pride of place. As she puts it, "unlike populism and negative liberalism, deliberative democracy articulates a compelling conception of the person as self-governing."

Moreover, "the absence of deliberation offers a key to interpreting the malaise of American democracy." Gutmann is calling
for a more liberal form of democracy and a more democratic
brand of liberalism. "Deliberative democracy seeks to maximize
the scope of self-determination for interdependent individuals."

Part III deals with the idea of democratic community and
American constitutionalism. Robert Post supplies concrete content to the debate between liberal democrats and communitarians by examining how they are played out in American First
Amendment jurisprudence. According to Post, for the past sixty
years our constitutional law has dealt with democratic community as a complex dialectic between two distinct and antagonistic
forms of social organization. He says the law advances "community" when it attempts to organize social life on the principle
that people are socially embedded and dependent. The law advances what he calls "responsive democracy" when it takes as its
organizing principle the postulate that persons are autonomous
and independent. He maintains that although these principles
frequently point to conflicting ways of deciding specific cases,
nevertheless in a plausible general jurisprudence they may be
reconcilable and perhaps even, in the end, interdependent.

Richard Arneson is critical of Post for granting too much to
the communitarian critique of liberalism. As Arneson views
them, communitarians dispute the liberals' claim that the state
should promote justice while remaining neutral on questions
about the good life. The right is not independent of the good,
Arneson concedes, and then he goes on to argue that a utilitarian
conception of the good should be incorporated in liberal doctrine
to defuse its critics on this point. Hence, contrary to Post's analysis, Arneson concludes that liberalism and communitarianism
are not inherently in tension. To say that the conflict between
"responsive democracy" and "community" in judicial treatment
of free speech resists resolution is to concede too much, Arneson
thinks, to the communitarian philosophy of life.

Like Kenneth Minogue and Robert Post, Gerald Rosenberg
believes that the tensions in democratic communities cannot usefully be understood or evaluated in abstract terms. However,
Rosenberg does not think that Post's move to legal practice is
sufficient to resolve the matter. In his view, the study of de-

mocracy, community, the courts, and the law must take account of the political, social, and economic environments in which they are embedded. This forces us to attend to the ways in which race, class, and gender structure our daily life. Using this more thoroughly empirical approach, Rosenberg makes a case for the truth of a less sanguine view than Post's of American courts and constitutional law, and of the meaning of democratic community in practice.

In Part IV, as if heeding Rosenberg's methodological advice, Robert Dahl, Carmen Sirianni, and Bruce Rutherford all take us on empirical explorations of the tensions and conflicts that arise in different settings. Dahl undertakes to demonstrate that democracy is incompatible with both centralized command and unregulated market economies. In command economies, politicians can and do use their control of economic resources to reward their supporters and punish their opponents. In market systems the injured invariably organize to force the government either to institute regulation or to crack down on dissidents. For those harmed by unregulated markets to accept this outcome as for the greater social good, they would have to be moved by a strong feeling of public virtue. Market society's emphasis on economic individualism does not promote this kind of virtue. In any nation, the mix of government intervention and free markets will vary in response to changes in the economy and in political culture. Democracies, however, will never be compatible with either command or free-market economies.

Carmen Sirianni is concerned with democratization of the internal structure of civil society. His vehicle is a case study of the feminist movement in American politics since the 1960s. This has been centrally occupied with redefining the democratic community in a more participatory manner. In the late 1960s and early 1970s, the movement attempted to achieve this by linking its members' ideas about an "ethic of care" to the radically egalitarian ideal of participatory democracy advocated by student political activists. In pursuing practical goals, however, feminists encountered many of the same problems that the students had before them. Sirianni's analysis reveals a profound paradox that any civil-society centered theory of participatory democracy must confront. This derives from the fact that increased participation in any sphere of social life incurs the expense of decreased participation in others. Sirianni delves into some of the complexities of these opportunity costs, and suggests some creative ways of thinking about and coping with them.

Bruce Rutherford's chapter deals with the role that may be played by undemocratic groups in building a democratic civil society. Undemocratic organizations, for example, the Catholic Church and Eurocommunist parties, have facilitated democracy in some settings. May not the kind of undemocratic Islamic group that most democrats fear, in particular the Muslim Brotherhood of Egypt, have similar consequences? Its ideology, goals, and internal organization are quite hostile to democracy. Yet Rutherford's analysis of Egyptian politics since 1971 shows that the Brotherhood has advanced democratization in several respects. It has helped to disperse power, widen political participation, and strengthen democratic values. The pressures of Egyptian politics have also led the Brotherhood to modify its ideology in democratic directions. These findings indicate Islam is not monolithic and that Islamic organizations may play a more constructive role in democratizing a society than previously believed. Rutherford lends new support to the Tocquevillian hypothesis that an internally undemocratic civil society can help to sustain a democratic political order at least in some circumstances.

Having moved from the theory to the practice of democratic community, in Jane Mansbridge's chapter, which leads off Part V, we begin a return journey. She looks into the implications of a wide array of feminist arguments for democratic political theory. She argues that democracies need a sense of community to help develop their citizens' faculties, solve collective action problems, and legitimate democratic institutions. Community is in tension with individualism, thus most polities must find ways of strengthening communal ties while protecting the individual from communal oppression. Women's experiences, traditionally neglected by political philosophers, help to meet both these challenges. These highlight undervalued components of community such as autonomy, nonvoluntary obligation, our moral emotions, particularity, and persuasion based on common interests. They also unmask underestimated threats to individual autonomy in the realms of subtle and private power where the taking of unfair advantage is located.

According to Carol Gould, although Mansbridge provides a useful account of feminism's contributions to democratic theory, she does not render explicit just how these contributions can be expressed in a theory of democratic community. Gould affirms that the first contribution, the critique of power and domination, leads both to a norm of reciprocity and to an emphasis on individual rights that are necessary for political agency. Feminism's second contribution, that familial or mothering relations may serve as a model for political activity, does have some exemplary implications for democratic politics but also has the potential to distort conceptions of care and democratic community. Gould advocates instead a synthesis of women's historical experience with the male concerns and values that have hitherto dominated public life. This fusion would integrate care with justice and individuality with community.

Our final contributor, David Richards, is less sympathetic to the spirit of Mansbridge's enterprise than is Carol Gould. Indeed, Richards questions the implications that Mansbridge draws from the feminist literature. He points out that she distinguishes three contributions of feminism to the theory and practice of democratic community: (1) mothering as an alternative ethical ideal; (2) gender hierarchy as a model for unjust subjugation; and (3) the stark injustice of gratuitous gendering. Yet he doubts Mansbridge's suggestion that these feminist insights impose a new normative theory. Rather, Richards holds these insights merely demand a somewhat different interpretation of the enduring values of liberal political theory. His conclusion reminds us once again that destinations usually turn out to be new beginnings.

NOTES

1. For more on the principle of "competitive collaboration," see John W. Chapman, ed., *The Western University on Trial* (Berkeley: University of California Press, 1983), pp. 5–6.

2. David Gauthier, *Morals by Agreement* (Oxford: Clarendon Press, 1986), p. 339.

3. Jean Baechler, "Individual, Group, and Democracy," chap. 1 in this volume, p. 24.

4. Roger Scruton, "What is Right? A Reply to Steven Lukes," *Times Literary Supplement*, 3 April 1992, p. 12.

5. Ibid.

6. Robert E. Lane, *The Market Experience* (Cambridge: Cambridge University Press, 1991).

7. Ibid., pp. 6, 235, 383.

8. Ibid., pp. 475–76, 602.

9. Ibid.

10. Ibid., p. 602.

11. Ibid., pp. 32, 601, 609.

12. C. B. Macpherson, *Democratic Theory: Essays in Retrieval* (Oxford: Clarendon Press, 1973), pp. vii, 94.

PART I

LIBERALISM AND COMMUNITARIANISM

1

INDIVIDUAL, GROUP, AND DEMOCRACY

JEAN BAECHLER

TRANSLATED BY SUZANNE STEWART

The three terms in the title may be considered the very essence of modernity and of the problems that face modern man. Since at least the 17th century, the question of "good political regime" has been raised in Europe. To the extent that experiences have accumulated, that reflections have deepened, and that institutions have become more clearly defined, this question has received an increasingly democratic answer. A first set of problems is given by the difficulty one encounters when trying to lend an unambiguous definition to democracy. A second set of problems arises in connection with the actor and the beneficiary of a good regime. The solution appears straightforward: the individual. But what is an individual? Furthermore, it is obvious that human societies are not simply made up of individuals, but also of groups, a fact that generates a third set of problems: What are groups? And to complicate matters even further, each of the terms evokes the other two and is related to them in problematic ways. If one views the problem from the point of view of the "individual," one will inevitably raise the question, on the one hand, of the individual's relations to groups and, on the other hand, of his or her position toward democracy. To a great extent, the starting point for Auguste Comte's reflections was precisely the danger that democratic individualism poses for groups, as well as the consequent risks of dissolution and anomie. If one focuses on groups, one cannot escape questions about the place that individuals occupy in these groups, nor questions about the role that democracy plays in a group. The entire "socialist" current may be considered a multiform development of these speculations. If, finally, one views the question from the standpoint of democracy, one inevitably comes up against its relations to the groups that make up society, and to the individuals that make up groups. The "anarchist" positions, which have not ceased to flourish since at least the 19th century, seem to start off from this point. The debates about "self-management" in Europe during the fifties and sixties are an expression of this trend, as also, it seems, are the current arguments about "democratic community" in the United States.

The problems are real. It would be pretentious to want to solve them in a trice. It is rather possible to delineate them more precisely, in a such way as to allow for a distinction between legitimate and illegitimate solutions. One possible entry into such an endeavor is a definition of the very terms of the problems and of the relations between them, a definition that should be as rigorous as possible. It is only after this intellectually ascetic inquiry that one may draw conclusions regarding the place of groups in democracy and of democracy within groups.

I. The Individual, the Group, Democracy: Definitions

Nothing is more indispensable than a definition of the concepts one employs, and few endeavors are as dangerous, because a definition does not hold except as a particular element within the general body of a theory. One thus runs the risk of proposing definitions to one's interlocutors who adhere to different theories. One must, nevertheless, take this risk, by progressing from what is more certain to what is less.

1. The Individual

Nothing seems less problematic than the individual: The individual is you and I, everyone knows that. Without doubt, you and I are individuals, and yet the term is as devoid of meaning as if we referred to ourselves as "man" or "living being." A butterfly, too, is an individual, as is an ant, a mountain, a galaxy, or all that exists. All beings are individuals, and vice versa: The nominalist position is correct and seems unassailable. But let us look at it more closely. Let us take a clearly identifiable individual, one whom we will name Pierre. This singular Pierre who exists incontestably in his irreducible singularity, is in fact the focal point of an infinity of determinations, whose singular status is at least problematic. Pierre is a man, in the sense that he is neither a lion nor a dolphin, and in the sense that he is not a woman. He may further be defined as a mammal, a vertebrate, an animal, a living being. In other words, according to the Naturalist, Pierre is the representative of a specific species among the kingdom of the living. By virtue of this fact, his individuality is destabilized and is almost dissolved in its specificity. Pierre may also become ill. Insofar as he is ill, and from the point of view of the doctor, his individuality tends to dissolve itself in the symptomology of his illness: He will be seen as tuberculous or cancerous. Pierre may also love and be loved, and may form a couple together with another individual. His individuality increases and becomes more defined because it is he personally who is loved. Yet this individuality is not as broad as within a Christian or a Buddhist perspective where the individual as person is in charge of his or her salvation or deliverance, and it does not matter what the conception of the person may be, a reflection of his or her creator or a precarious and insignificant agregate.

One need not add further examples because a first conclusion can already be drawn. The human individual is the geometric locus of an indefinite number of determinations, which each in turn may be defined along a scale that moves from the greatest generality to the greatest particularity. Let us clarify such a conclusion by the introduction of a more technical vocabulary. By "order of activities" or more simply put, by "order," I designate a domain of human activities that is delineated by appropriate goals and the appropriate means for attaining these goals. One may distinguish between orders that are political, religious, economic, pedagogical, of leisure, technical, ethical, psychological, and so forth. Viewed from within each order, the individual is at first the final actor of the activity of which he or she takes charge. Within the political order, the individual is a citizen; within the economic, an economic agent; a child to be educated in the pedagogic order, and so forth. This is, of course, a very simplified description. Economic agents may be workers of varying degrees of skill—they may be peasants, capitalists, or entrepreneurs. Such details are not, however, crucial to our argument.

The concept of the individual as geometric locus of determinations by different orders must itself be qualified by two important points. The first concerns the determinations themselves. Each determination is so arranged as to include a complete scale that ranges from the singular to the general. Let us assume Pierre to be religious. His religiosity—which we will assume to be both authentic and genuine—will necessarily involve metaphysical concerns, concerns that lend the religious order its specificity; it will involve a particular interpretation of this concern, be it Christian, Buddhist, Jewish, or Muslim; it will involve a religious practice that is influenced by historical time, by the group to which one belongs, by the country, by intellectual background; it will involve a personal experience of such a practice. We have not mentioned but a few elements of this range, and one could easily come up with more. The points between the two poles of the singular and the general have an objective reality that has access to consciousness, be it to that of the actors themselves, to exterior observers, or to both.

The second qualification concerns the ways in which actors deal with the determinations that affect them. A further range or scale may be sketched between two extremes. At one extreme one would find the individual who has deliberately become conscious of the determinations and their singular, particular, and general manifestations, and who cultivates them all with the most scrupulous respect for their multiple definition. In relation to such an ideal—impossible as are all ideals—individuals would be fully and simultaneously citizens/economic agents/believers/ethical subjects as representative of a civilization/members of a collectivity/themselves. At the other extreme, one would find individuals who are engulfed by one exclusive determination, captives of their singularity and lived by an idiosyncratic psychological formation. An anomalous cohort of drug-addicts, marginals, religious fanatics, virtual or real tyrants, misers and coveters, and so forth pass by. Between these two extremes, one would encounter all those human types that make up average and middling humanity.

To make the argument complete, one must introduce one last source of differentiation. Individuals tend to be formed closer to the pole of the ideal person or alternatively to that of unidimensionality, depending on an infinite number of factors, such as those of culture, historical time, political regime, social position, representation, or educational background. One should approach the problem of modern individualism from within such a perspective, both as a problem in its own right and in comparison to other cultures, that is, cultures that have defended positions often very different from our own.

2. Groups

An initial definition of groups may begin as that of the union of at least two individuals. This definition is insufficient because two individuals who meet in the street and exchange a few words do not make up a group, and even less does a gathering of individuals who attend a neighborhood or village market. One must specify that the union of at least two individuals is motivated and justified by the intention of attaining together one or more agreed-upon objectives. A group is defined as an organized and instituted set of individuals who are united in order to attain a common goal.

This simple and little contestable definition requires additional refinement. The first concerns goals. We return to our "orders" and may now lend them greater substance. An order is a domain of human activities defined by the ends pursued. The economic order has as its goal the satisfaction of human needs and desires, while bearing in mind the scarcity of resources. The religious order has as its end the bliss that would fulfill the deficit of being that affects all beings to the degree that they are not at one with the Being. The political order has as its end peace and justice, peace through justice. I am aware of the audacity and the incongruity of making such large statements without accompanying them with decisive supportive arguments. Perhaps my excuse is that not everything can be said, whereas what has been said must suffice for present purposes. In effect, one will easily agree with my conclusion, namely that groups are defined by the ends they pursue. More specifically, a group is the means to achieving determined ends, which implies that one finds economic groups (e.g., enterprises, workshops, stores), religious groups, (e.g., churches, sects, monasteries, fraternities), scientific groups (e.g., laboratories, universities, seminaries, journals), and so forth. Let us look more closely at political groups, because we will later return to our present comments about them.

The political group *par excellence* may be called a polity. The polity is a group where together its members try not to suppress the conflicts that arise inevitably among them, but to prevent these conflicts from degenerating into violence. This is accomplished by mechanisms that permit the allocation to each member of what is owed to him or her, that permit the definition of rules of the game, the punishment of those who break the rules, the regulation of litigations. In a word, the polity is a group of attempted peace-making through the imposition of justice in its various meanings. Until now, individuals, who at any moment represent the species, have never been united into one single polity, and therefore there are always at least two polities. By definition, therefore, they do not make up one single group of peace-making through justice, so two or X number of polities define a system of action where conflicts may always degenerate into violence and into war. To sum up, a polity is internally a group of attempted peace-making and externally a group of potential war.

The plurality of polities already exhibit a second characteristic that may be applied to groups in general. They are in the plural. This plural structure flows from all our preceding remarks, along two radically different axes. On the one hand, each order has its group or groups. Biology and pedagogy have the family, of which there are a number of possible types, as the proper group through which to pursue their goals. The economic order has its own, as do the religious, the political, the one of leisure, and all other orders. The plurality of ends and the diversity of means required to meet these ends ensure that, even in minuscule societies like the bands of the Pygmies or those of the Eskimoes, the association can never be reduced to one single group. The second axis along which groups multiply is that of the orders taken one by one. Even in societies of reduced size, it is rare that the number of groups within one order is reduced to uniqueness. Even the polity, whose uniquity would seem to result from its very definition, becomes more or less differentiated depending on whether its structure is more or less centralized or federal. Even within a centralized polity such as the ancient Greek city, political sub-groups do form, such as demes, tribes, or phratries. The irreducible plurality of groups raises the problem of their competition and their coexistence. A third and last specification concerns the relations between groups and individuals. Groups are not amorphous collections of an arbitrary set of individuals, they are units of collective action. Groups are formed by individuals to attain together specific ends. They must assign to themselves these ends because they are human beings defined by their belonging to a particular species, and they must unite because these ends cannot be attained unless they join together. This common-sense proposition leads to conclusions that are not indifferent, even if they are banal. Individuals should only enter into groups to contribute to the pursuit of ends that justify the existence of these groups. From this point of view, the individual should lend himself to the group, but not dissolve there. But, on the other hand, adherence to a group is affected in its intensity by the personality of the individual. My point is that if, in principle, a group should never be anything for the individual but a society with limited responsibilities, it may always become a community where the individual dissolves her- or himself to the point of losing individuality. In the opposite direction, an individual may live in a group and forget the ends that justify its existence, and pursue there personal goals that bear no relation to the collective goals.

It is easy to establish a connection with the definition of the individual proposed in the preceding section. The accomplished person, the one who perfectly embodies the concept of the individual conformed to the nature of things, participates in all the groups necessary for the pursuit of ends that he or she has assigned to him- or herself. The individual participates in these groups and respects the proper finality of each group, but participates in them without dissolving into them. At the other extreme, one encounters those atrophied images of individuals who have either dissolved themselves to the point of indistinction within one exclusive group, or of individuals who avail themselves of groups for their own personal ends, or of individuals incapable of entering into a group at all and confined within their individuality, without being able to pursue any end whatsoever.

3. Democracy

It is not easy to arrive at a plausible and acceptable definition of democracy in a few words. Let us, nevertheless, give it a try. The best point of departure is probably the political order. We have defined it as an order of activity centred on the goals of peace and justice. To lend such a definition greater specificity, one must successively introduce human freedom, in the sense of a non-programmed species who must invent its humanity; the plurality of possible realizations of this freedom, and the conflicts that necessarily follow; and human sociality that entails that individuals and groups, who will not fail to oppose conflicts, are condemned to live together. In a word, a free, conflictual, and social human species must confront the concrete problem of making individuals and groups live together without killing each other. The general solution may be found in the definition of polities, where there exist different procedures that allow for the peaceful resolution of conflicts through the application of justice. One may agree to call "political regime" the ensemble of institutions that define and organize these procedures.

At least two regimes are possible, one that is able to put into place and make function those procedures that lead to peace and justice, and another that fails. Furthermore, there are all those intermediary forms that succeed or fail to varying degrees. The decisive factor that makes a regime either successful or a failure is power, because peace and justice have either more or less chance of success, depending on the definition and the distribution of power. One may define power as the potential ability of an individual or a group to impose its will on other individuals or groups. More accurately, power is the probability of eliciting obedience from others. Now, there are three sources of obedience, namely fear, admiration, and reckoning. From this, one may distinguish between three basic regimes of power. Let us call tyrannical or autocratic a regime where a power imposes its will by force, and encounters a form of obedience that is based in fear; hierocratic a regime where an authority presents itself as the vicar of a transcendental principle, and where this authority is recognized as such by its subjects, who bow before it out of respect both for the transcendental principle and for its vicar; and democratic a government where the subjects reckon that they have an interest in obeying qualified people who can lead them to success through collective endeavors.

The source of obedience at the foundation of the democratic regime—or of whatever one may call such a government, because it is not here a question of words but of substance—suffices to delineate its central character: By nature and by definition, in a democracy each position of power is rooted in those who accept to obey and do so because they assume it is in their interest to obey. In other words, in a democracy, all relations of power are founded on delegation that is consented to by the subjects. We will hold to this basic proposition, reserving the possibility of drawing from it some useful consequences for later developments. For the time being, let us simply make two comments. The first will content itself with simply raising a major problem. If it is true that the essence of the political is to pursue peace by justice, could one show that "good political government," which brings about the realization of the end of the political, is a democratic government, defined as consensual and calculated obedience? If the answer to this question is positive, and if the proof holds, one escapes political relativism completely and reaches a theoretical position that reconciles the rational analysis of political facts and the rational justification of political values.

The second remark returns us to the other two terms of our triad. Democracy defined as consensual obedience and delegated power has as its privileged interlocutor the individual, and indeed, more accurately, the individual as person, as pointed out earlier. This statement is self-evident because only free individuals can agree to obey other free individuals who are chosen by them. The conclusion is supported by the different types of democracy that one may encounter. In the tribal world, one generally meets democracies where the social actors are lineages, and where each lineage is represented by an elder. One may speak of a "deaconal democracy" where the elders, in the name of the segment they represent, obey and delegate on an individual basis. Within an aristocracy, power is held by those who are well-born; within an oligarchy, by those who are rich; within a perfect democracy, by all social participants. The tight bonds that unite democracy and individuality work in both directions. Democratic regime encourages individuation to the point of turning at times into the most extreme form of individualism. Conversely, a democratic regime cannot become established and last until upright and resolute individuals are capable of controlling power and preventing it from turning into a hierocratic regime or into an autocracy. Democracy needs persons but it may produce ectoplasms. But democracy and the individual are not confined to a dialogue between the two. By necessity, individuals unite into groups to attain their ends. A two-part question arises from this: In a well-shaped democracy that has as its actors individuals who are defined as persons, what should the role of groups be in democracy, and how should democracy be realized within groups?

II. The Role of Groups within Democracy

We have chosen to argue at the level of principles—where one seeks to establish how things should be, in conformity with their nature and their ends, and not how they are, deformed and taken off course by history, by constraints, by corruptions, and by perversions. The problems that arise for groups in a democracy may be reduced to three: What rules of access can and should groups legitimately impose on individuals? What is the root of the distinction between public and private? How should one conceive of relations between groups?

1. Rules of Access

These rules stem directly from consideration of the two definitions given earlier: Individuals are free and groups are founded to achieve certain ends that would otherwise be impossible for an isolated individual to attain. Let us set aside a more precise definition of freedom for later consideration. For now, it is enough to understand as "free" individuals who may decide for themselves whether or not to join some group or another of their choice in their social environment. This is even better expressed in a negative manner, by saying that individuals are free insofar as they are not forced to enter into a group, either because of an irresistable compulsion, or by an exterior will.

The first rule states that *nobody is free to enter*. It is not enough, for individuals, to have the desire or the interest to enter a group, be it political, economic, religious, or athletic, for the group to open its doors to them. This rule follows from the very raison d'être of groups. They are founded and exist because the human condition and the nature of things are such that people generally need to be in the plural—starting from two to possibly all of humanity—to achieve the ends they are prevailed upon to pursue. Consequently, members of a group must be able to justify their place in the group by making a positive contribution toward the pursuit of the ends of the group. It is not enough that applicants demand entry, it is also necessary that they in turn can promote the group's progress in achieving its ends.

This obvious conclusion leads to two important corollaries. The first states that the required qualifications of the applicants must conform to the nature of the ends, while ignoring all external considerations. Within an economic group, most commonly referred to as an enterprise, the criteria of selection must be strictly economic: "Does the hiring of X contribute or not to the growth of profit?" The enterprise must neglect all arguments regarding sex, race, age, and citizenship, unless it is possible to show that such an argument is relevant: In a plant producing secret armaments, the question of citizenship may be justified because of the fear of espionage. The second corollary defines the judges who are to pronounce on the qualifications of the applicant. These judges are already accepted members of the group, who must make a decision by taking the group's ends into consideration. In a word, each acceptance into any group within a democracy is equivalent to a form of cooptation. What remains, one may ask, of the liberty of the individual? The essential—one's right of application to any group and, in principle at least, the guarantee that this application will be examined with the utmost justice.

The second rule states *the freedom not to enter*. This statement entails nothing but the concrete application of the freedom of the individual, which consists, among other things, in the freedom of choice. No individual accepted into the pool of legitimate applicants to established groups—this clumsy and awkward formulation cannot be made more precise until the following paragraph—can be forced to enter into a group, to get married, to practice a sport, to work for a given corporation, to practice a given faith. Individuals may choose not to enter, but at their own risk and peril. One may decide not to enter a polity. But just as, following the first rule, no polity has any obligation to accept a new citizen, so the logical consequence of refusing to enter a polity is to find oneself outside it, and, by definition, within a space where all forms of aggression are permitted, and from which there is no refuge. Within the purest imaginable democracy, this rule will surely be transgressed at one point, and this transgression is not at all harmless. No one has ever had the chance of using one's freedom not to enter life, and no one will ever have it. One may state that individuals exercise their freedom *a posteriori* by confirming their will to live by the sole fact of not committing suicide. The argument has its merits, but does not completely eliminate the difficulty, because between accepting life with joy and committing suicide, there exist an infinity of nuances ranging from discomfort to existential unhappiness.

The third rule states the *freedom to leave*. It is a direct consequence of the second rule. Thus are founded the democratic rights or liberties to, for example, divorce, emigrate, or to change religion. It is possible for this freedom to enter into contradiction with the rules of any given group. A religious group, for example, may consider marriage indissoluable, and the reasons for this rule may be dogmatic or scriptural. The group may prohibit divorce to its members, as members, but not as citizens of a democracy. In other words, this group has the right to exclude the divorced from its ranks, but it does not have the right to impose or to try to impose its beliefs beyond its own sphere, for example, by usurping political power to obtain legislation that would veto divorce completely. It is possible that the group of believers may coincide exactly with those who would be affected by such legislation. In this case, no individual would feel his or her freedom to have been curtailed. Nevertheless, democracy is not being respected and freedom is abolished, even if there is no one around to enjoy it.

2. The Public and the Private

To establish this fundamental distinction, one must begin with the individual in a democracy. The individual, we believe to have shown, is the site of many determinations. One must not begin with the individual in general, who remains indeterminate, but with the individual-in-a-democracy. The individual's distinctive trait is that he or she is the source of all delegations of power. From this, one may deduce three "democratic determinations" of individuals. They are free, insofar as they can delegate or not delegate; they reckon—one used to say, "rationally"—because they decide to obey or not to obey on the basis of considerations of well-understood interests; they are end-oriented, because their interests are defined by the ends they pursue.

Let us continue by retaining the word "interest" because it is convenient despite its unfortunate utilitarian and economic connotations. One will have understood that for us "interest" signifies indifferently the ends proposed to the actors by all orders, whether this interest involves money, mystical fusion with God, scientific theory, love, or pleasure. We find here individuals who are free, end-oriented, and reckoning, and who pursue interests. Let us call "singular" an interest that is endorsed by an actor within a unit of activities, that is to say, within a unique combination of means and ends. Each actor, even if one imagines him or her confined to the pole of the most undifferentiated individuality, has a number of singular interests. Because the individual cannot achieve them all at one time, he or she is forced to impose on them a certain order of preference; let us call "particular" that order of preference. The choice of an order is free and the reasons for a determinate choice are innumerable. On the other hand, an order is not fixed except in one instant, and may vary from moment to moment because motives as well as constraints change. Men are free and capable of inventing their own humanity, and in stating such a truism, I want to make the point that the range of particular interests is virtually infinite in its diversity. The realization of this virtuality depends on factors connected to number, civilization, economy, technical issues and science, thus to all the orders in varying degrees.

To eliminate a common and serious confusion right away, it may be appropriate to introduce a distinction here. Every individual pursues a particular interest. He or she does so, and cannot but do so because he or she is an actor in the theater of life. Conversely, it follows from this that every particular interest is borne by an actor. But, as we have seen, an actor can be an "individual" or a "collectivity" if this actor presents her- or himself on the scene as a group collectively pursuing an objective. Consequently, every group, insofar as it is an actor, pursues a particular interest, which may be individual or collective. The only difference between these two types is that an individual interest is more diverse because out of necessity the individual participates in many orders, whereas a collective interest is more unilateral because groups are constituted within the framework of different orders.

One will better grasp the usefulness and pertinence of this distinction by introducing the idea of "common" interest. By definition, an interest is common when it shows itself in *each* particular interest, be it individual or collective. To return to our terminology, one may define a common interest as a singular interest that is shared by—or should be shared by—all particular interests. What are the concrete interests that would correspond to such a definition? A priori, it would be useful to look in the area of the common conditions for the realization of any given interest, be it singular or particular, individual or collective. Without looking too far, one comes upon at least three interests that correspond to the stated criteria. It is in the interest of each that it be guaranteed the best possible security in relation to all external polities; that rules of the game be defined within the framework of the polity, allowing the interests to attempt their realization without the need to revert to violence and civil war; and that those be punished who transgress the rules of the game.

From this we can derive the sought-after definitions, and identify the private with the sphere of particular, individual, and collective interests, and the public with that of common interests. We can now also reconnect what was left open before, and specify that the public and common interests coincide exactly with the framework of the polity: The polity is by definition and by nature the group that makes a distinction between, on the one hand, internal gradual peace-making by stating the rules of the game and by punishing those who break the rules, and, on the other hand, the external insecurity brought on by virtual war. However, there is no reason why particular and private interests should coincide with the polity, for they may express themselves in the transpolitical arena, be that arena economic (the world market), religious (a church with a universalist calling), or scientific (the community of scientists), or anything else (the Olympic Games, for instance, which should be conceived as a transpolitical private institution, as they were envisioned by their modern founder Pierre de Coubertin). Let us define "citizens" as distinct from "members of society." Citizens are actors, the individual actors in contemporary democracies, as well as representatives of groups—lineages or guilds—in earlier democracies, and they participate in the public arena through the definition and realization of common interests. Members make up the private sphere and private groups where they have particular interests to pursue. Every citizen is a member of society, but every member participant is not necessarily a citizen: A polity may accept some foreigners in its midst, as it may also exclude from citizenship other members according to criteria of age, sex, or criminal record.

3. Relations among Groups

One may define what they should be in a democracy by starting from the particular interests and the common interests, and by looking for the democratic mechanisms of their realization. Particular interests are multiform, diverse, divergent, and contradictory. Chances for spontaneous harmony are nil; on the contrary, human conflictuality is nourished precisely by this cacophonic dispersion of interests. All interests are, however, legitimate. We touch on a subtle point, one that has given rise to serious confusions, dangerous for democracy.

One must distinguish between political legitimacy and the legitimacy according to each individual order. Political legitimacy is defined, for the interests, by their respect for the rules of the game, that is, rules of custom and of law. The first rule of the game is not to resort to violence to realize oneself, but to accept instead a peaceful mediation with other interests. According to this political principle of legitimacy, any citizen and member of society may believe that 2 + 2 equals 5, and then try to persuade others of this through words, writing, and image. This citizen may do so legitimately as long as he or she neither resorts to violence and ruse to impose these views, nor prohibits the expression of different views. Arithmetically, this position is illegitimate, because it is false. If we generalize from this example, we can state a proposition that is not false at all: Each particular interest must be appraised on the one hand according to its political legitimacy, and on the other hand according to its conformity with the ends of the order where it manifests itself. When one affirms that, within a democracy, freedom of thought is analytically inscribed in the concept of citizen, one states a truth, on the condition that one does not draw the absurd conclusion that all opinions are valid and that all of them must be shielded from criticism.

How may one reconcile the political legitimacy of particular interests and their conflictual dispersion? The solution is admirable for its simplicity and elegance. It is necessary and sufficient to organize social spaces that are protected from violence and ruse, to open them up to all politically legitimate interests and let these interests come together within a context of permanent multilateral negotiations. From these negotiations will result instant points of equilibrium that are in a state of permanent change. Let us call this equilibrium that of "average" interests. Average interests result by aggregation and composition from particular interests. Because an individual interest generally has little chance of realizing itself in isolation, it is more often collective interests that meet to define the average interests. One normally calls these regulated social spaces "markets." Unfortunately, in modern languages the word has received a connotation that is too economic not to be troublesome, in contradistinction to the Greek agora or the Latin forum. This is why I have proposed a convenient and obvious neologism: *agory*.

Agories are multiple, there are at least as many of them as there are orders; and for one given order, a number of agories may coexist. For example, within the demographic order, the agories where partners meet to form couples, are superimposed onto "demographic isolates" adding up to about a total of a thousand persons. Democratic agories must be strictly private, because they deal with particular interests, and there is no reason why they should be confined to the polity: One can do business with and get married to a stranger.

Common interests are of such a remarkable character that, although they figure within each particular interest, in principle at least, they cannot be spontaneously realized through agorical mechanisms. To leave everyone with the trouble of defining the rules of the game means to make it impossible to define the rules of the game. To entrust to everyone the care of ensuring external security, is to condemn oneself to succumbing to an enemy who is better organized. To leave to everyone the possibility of defining a crime or an offence, to search for and arrest the presumed culprit, to judge and to condemn this person, is to give to everyone the right of life and death over everyone else. Common interests cannot be defined and realized but in common, that is to say, in public, within the framework of the polity as such. An obvious difficulty arises immediately. If everyone agrees that one must ensure defense, that one must promulgate laws and punish those who break the laws, such agreement ceases as soon as it is a question of leaving behind these ethereal generalities, and of lending them a specific content. Freedom and human diversity combined with the uncertitude of the issues dealt with lead to the fact that common interests inevitably give rise to diverging interpretations. They are politically legitimate, and have the right to express themselves and try to be realized. However, common interests must be realized immediately, for fear of consequently compromising all particular interests. The difficulty is eliminated solely by the organization in public of rhetorical and dialectical—in the Aristotelean sense—contests among the interpretations, in such a way as to enlighten citizens and to allow them to choose between those interpretations that seem to promise the greatest chances of effectively realizing the common interests. Just as the private agories are the space where particular interests are reconciled, so the public arena is the space where citizens define and try to realize common interests.

III. Democracy within the Group

All the previous analyses lead to a distinction between the polity and all other groups because the polity has a special status and a decisive role to play. The difference stands out with particular sharpness when one tries to define the democratic rules as they are applied in the polity as opposed to all other groups.

1. The Democratic Polity

The points that should be made and clarified here would be too numerous if one made any claims to exhausting the subject matter. Actually, that which one normally understands as "democracy" or "democratic regime" is limited almost exclusively to the democratic organization and institutionalization of the polity, omitting here that democracy affects all groups, be they private or public, as well as all individuals, be they citizens or members of society. We too have omitted until now and will continue to neglect dealing with democracy within the transpolitical framework, because this poses specific problems and because one cannot speak of everything. If one chooses the democratic problems to be discussed according to the debates and concerns of the day, then it seems that one must concentrate on three points where democracy is applied to the polity: the structure of the polity, the choice of leaders, and the idea of the Rechtsstaat.

The *structure of the polity* raises the least problems at the level of principles. Its conceptual definition as group of gradual peacemaking toward the inside and of virtual war toward the outside does not prejudge its internal structure. To move to the most essential point directly, one can locate the most extreme possible solutions and determine in which direction a pure and perfect democracy should tend. Two poles may be defined. At one extreme—let us call it the "unitary" pole—the polity is conceived as a homogeneous and isotropic group where common interests are defined and pursued by a unified common center, whose decisions and actions directly affect and engage all citizens. At the other extreme—let us call this one the "federal" pole—the structure of the polity takes on a polycentric and pyramidal shape. At the lower level of the pyramid, a high number of political sub-groups takes charge of the common interests of the local population. At a higher level, a more comprehensive center occupies itself with the common interests of a number of local group-polities. And so forth, until at the top of the pyramid, we find a center that is concerned with the common interests of the whole. Arguments regarding cost, efficiency, and stability allow one to conclude that the number of levels should be three or four. Below that number, the federation turns or reverts to the unitary model; above it, the system regulates itself with difficulty. Two characteristics of the federal structure merit special attention. On the one hand, the pyramidal structure must be conceived as ascending rather than descending, in the sense that a higher level of political integration comes about only in order to deal with those common interests that remain insoluble at a lower level. On the other hand, each level must be in direct contact with all the citizens affected by the interests dealt with at that level, and must not delegate functions from level to level. If, for example, the highest level takes charge of war and peace, something that seems logical, all citizens of the entire polity must directly contribute to the defense budget through personal contributions. This excludes a solution that would consist of feeding the budget through transfers that are agreed-upon by lower levels because this would give to each sub-center a power of veto that would compromise the effectiveness of defense. The first principle is usually called "principle of subsidiarity". The second could be named "principle of immediacy."

It does not seem useful to argue long in favor of the federal structure. All considerations of efficiency, flexibility, proximity on the part of the interested parties, participation in the running of public affairs, control over the leaders by the citizens, in one word, all such considerations speak in its favor, even if—and in human affairs this goes without saying—there are always problems and occasions for corruption. One can indicate only two of them: inevitable conflicts regarding the areas of competence between federal levels, and the numerous risks of encroachment of the public over the private at all levels.

Rather than trying to define the mechanisms by which leaders are chosen—elections, drawings by lot, cooptation—a subject that is too banal when taken in a general sense and too technical when one enters into the labyrinth of all the details, it might instead be appropriate to dissipate two confusions or illusions that are particularly tenacious and dangerous: "direct democracy" and "representational democracy." We have left the public sphere as soon as the totality of citizens has made a statement regarding the interpretation of the common interest to be pursued. Citizens may make this statement as a corporate group, following a public palaver or a public meeting, as it may happen within towns and cities. Yet numbers may forbid such a direct solution and force citizens to vote on programs. Or else, they can agree to delegate a more restricted group from their midst to be in charge of permanently following the destiny of common interests. To whom does the realization of common interests fall? To the totality of citizens as a body, evidently. Though dictated by the very concept of the public, obvious constraints of number, of competence, of time, of taste make this solution technically impossible. Even in the tiny polities of hunters and gatherers, spontaneous delegation of executive power intervenes, as do delegations of legislative and judiciary power. In effect, these three powers always exist, even if only in embryonic form, in all democratic polities, for the good reason that they are implied by the concept and nature of common interests: security, rules of the game, the punishment of those who break the rules.

Within this general scheme, "direct democracy" has no other meaning except that citizens as a body may deliberate, decide, and act as a body. As soon as the "as a body" becomes impossible, mechanisms of delegation intervene, by which one should understand the temporary, circumscribed, and reversible delegation by and under the control of citizens, of the ability to deliberate, decide, and act, a delegation given to members of the polity, according to legitimate and legal mechanisms. The constraints that lead to delegation most affect action, that requires a unified point of view, rapidity of decision making, and the firmness of will, whereas deliberation and decision making better adapt themselves to the ups and downs of assemblies. This is, by the way, a strong argument for a federal structure, which facilitates the organization of committees where the citizens can deliberate and decide in common, even if they must resign themselves to delegate power in order to act. In sum, direct democracy understood in the sense of a democracy without delegations of power, has never existed and can never exist.

As to representation, it is a tyrannical fraud, if one understands by it the delegation by citizens of their very consent to obey, that is, the decision that a reduced body of citizens chosen by the citizens is considered an adequate substitute, and is thus entitled to replace citizens as the origin and source of power. Citizens have no substitutes, because they are persons who only define reality: The polity is a body of citizens taken one by one, as individuals united to attain together peace and justice. They may delegate the trouble of contributing toward the realization of these ends, they may not, however, without changing the political regime, abdicate their sovereignty to anyone, where by sovereignty one must understand the citizen as defined by freedom, end-orientation, and reckoning.

The concept of Rechtsstaat makes sense only if the distinction between legitimacy and legality makes sense. If, in effect, it is enough that a polity promulgate laws according to recognized procedures, then all polities, tautologically speaking, are Rechtsstaats. One does not get out of this tautology except under three conditions. The first is through the concept of "unwritten law" that defines the basic principles of a "good regime," not at all as arbitrary axioms, but as natural realities. Otherwise stated, the idea of a Rechtsstaat implies the idea of "natural right" in the Aristotelean and Thomist sense. The second condition is the translation of unwritten law into customs and written laws according to procedures that maximize the chances of an as truthful as possible translation. Legislators must be so defined and the processes of producing laws so conceived that the citizens can be reasonably guaranteed that these laws will be legitimate. The third condition is the presence of an institution—a supreme court or a constitutional court—that must ensure the legality of

laws, that is to say, their conformity to written law. Written laws
are legitimate if they conform to the unwritten law. Their legality
is their conformity to the written law or to custom.

2. *Private Democratic Groups*

By nature and by definition, all groups other than the polity are
private and are in charge of particular interests. Let us recall
also that arbitration between groups and between particular interests falls, in a democracy, to the agories. The agories *are* democratic institutions, and the more fluid they are, the more
democracy will be respected. Conversely, each attempt at controlling and organizing the agories, be it through private coalitions or, more probably, through public initiatives with private
pressure groups behind them, each such attempt is directly antidemocratic. It may be legal, but it is never legitimate.

Let us leave behind the question of democracy between
groups, and concentrate on two problems connected to the question of democracy within a group. The first concerns the delegation of power. This does not pose a problem in all private
groups, whose members are united to attain collective ends. This
is the case in sports associations and religious associations. There,
delegation takes place by bearing in mind the realization of objectives that are fixed by the group and defined by the relation
to the ends followed. There are circumstances in which institutions that, although inherited from a nondemocratic past,
nevertheless have proven their efficiency and their compatibility
with a democratic environment, and therefore deserve to be kept
as long as they satisfy the members of the group. This is the case
of the Catholic Church, where, aside from the institutions of the
pope and the monasteries, delegation by the body of the faithful
is unknown. More delicate is the democratic status of other
groups, whose function it is not to be at the service of their
members, but at that of citizens and members of society in general. The economic order is the primary example of such a case.
The place of economic activities in a modern democracy is a
given, so one must not be surprised by the profusion and per-
serverance of misunderstandings on this subject.

To try and dispel them, one may take three logically related approaches: the relations of the economic group or enterprise with citizens/members; the internal organization of power in the enterprise; the internal organization and the freedom of the members of the enterprise. By a forgetfulness that is only too systematic not to pose a problem that merits a response, the majority of ideologues and even many economists completely ignore the fact that the enterprise is exclusively at the service of citizens and of members insofar as they demand those goods and services destined to satisfy their needs and desires. Enterprises, which may be as small as the shop of the cobbler or of the grocer, exist only because, beyond a certain threshold of needs and desires, demanders no longer can or want to satisfy them on their own. Demanders then delegate the responsibility and the problem of producing goods and services to some of them, calculating that, in doing so, they will have more, of better quality and at lower cost, it being absurd for a rational being to want less, of worse quality and at a higher price. No one knows in advance who is capable of combining scarce resources in such a way as to realize this end, that is, to supply whatever satisfies demand. The democratic solution is obviated and has been so for a long time. It is necessary and sufficient to allow persons to present themselves as "supply candidates", to manage to gather the necessary factors of production, to present themselves with their supply on an economic agory—one may here retain the usual word of market—to face clients who will or will not buy their products. A market is neither more nor less than a permanent mechanism of quasi-direct democracy where, by their decision to buy, the clients accept or reject supply candidates, and delegate some of these suppliers to fulfill economic functions on a basis that is temporary (limited by the time of acquisition), circumscribed (by a specific good or service), and reversible (the act of acquisition does not imply another act of acquisition). They do this in the same way as they would delegate others to fulfill political or leisure functions.

Insofar as the supplier/entrepreneur acts alone, "economic democracy" is realized through exchanges and sharings on markets that should be as regulated and fluid as possible. Confusions begin as soon as the suppliers elicit outside help to satisfy demand, as soon as they appeal to outside capital, as soon as there

is a disjunction between property and management, in short, as
soon as the large modern capitalist enterprises appear and multiply. The confusions disappear as soon as one agrees to distinguish between internal and external relations.

Regarding external relations, the democratic principle requires, on the one hand, the sovereignty of the client in his
decisions to buy, and on the other hand, and most importantly,
that the resources used by the supplier are not wasted. Citizens
want more for less, because this is the very end of the economy:
to get the most from scarce resources. Reasoning and experience
show that waste is minimized and efficiency maximized when
fluctuations in demand most immediately affect management.
Such a positive relation is obtained most surely, both when the
manager is the owner and when a group of shareholders has a
personal and direct interest in closely controlling management
and in taking account of market indications as reflected in the
stock-market prices of the shares they hold. Regarding external
relations, and we say this without looking for paradox and even
less for provocation, it appears even to the most scrupulous
democrat that capitalism and its central institutions are the most
perfect expression of and most in agreement with the unwritten
law of democracy as applied to the economic order.

Regarding internal relations, the capitalist enterprise unites
human beings, a fact that subordinates it to two constraints, if
the enterprise is to be democratic: It must be efficient and it
must respect the freedom of those who constitute it. It is not by
coincidence that the requirements of efficiency and freedom
converge, because both have the same relation to the nature of
things. It remains true that the constraints and habits of the past
have masked this convergence for a good century and a half. If
we had the time, we could show how all contemporary developments of the enterprise are simultaneously justified by efficiency and by freedom. Let us content ourselves with sketching
such a demonstration, as it relates to the question of freedom.

A definition of freedom is difficult and controversial, probably
because its concept and its reality inevitably blend three distinct
aspects. One may clarify things a little if one begins with that
which freedom opposes. One may spot three contradictories to
freedom. In one, subjects are deprived of all choice, they are

subjugated to the necessity, be it exterior or imposed by will, of a single choice. In a second, subjects have all decisions imposed on them from the outside, without an autonomous sphere for themselves. In the third, subjects have no part in the decision-making process that affects them. In positive terms, freedom signifies choice, autonomy, and participation in decision making.

Applied to the enterprise, these three definitions of freedom lead to a form of organization that is as decentralized as possible, to the greatest elasticity, to the widest circulation of information, to the most consistent participation by everyone in the definition of tasks, and so forth. In fact and even in its details, modern management is the translation of the definitions of freedom to the specific environment of the economic enterprise, established to confront competitors and clients on a market. The internal structure is a space of freedom, subjugated to the constraints of the exterior, both inscribing themselves in the proper ends of the economic. One must measure against this standard the naive conceptions of self-management, and the danger they pose for democracy. In trying to apply to the enterprise the heresies of direct democracy or of representational democracy, they no doubt corrupt both democracy and economic efficiency, which is too much.

Conclusion

If conducted with the utmost care and justice, an analysis such as that outlined here may serve several ends. One would be purely cognitive. Our outline describes a model. A model, in the social sciences, can have several uses. By proposing a mental reproduction that simplifies reality, it becomes possible to locate in this same reality the primary and the secondary, the same and the other; in short, it allows for the resolution of the infinite complexity of human histories into intelligible ensembles. A model proposes also a standard of measurement of reality in relation to an ideal to locate and explain the dislocations that never fail to appear. It allows us, in other words, to envision reality in evolutionary terms, as the progressive, contingent, and imperfect emergence of an intelligible structure, in this instance of a certain way to enable people to live together. Finally, a model favors historical explanation, by dividing such an explanation into two moments, the first belonging to the definition of the necessary and sufficient conditions for realizing the model, the second to the demonstration of how and why the conditions have been effectively united in a given historical context.

A model may also aid practice. A model of democracy allows us initially to convince citizens of a truth that they have a presentiment of, namely to know that in political matters, as everywhere else, there is truth and falsehood, that one cannot say and do whatever one pleases without thereby exposing oneself to fallacious miscalculations. A model authorizes citizens to distinguish two varieties of falsehood. The first is directly and overtly antidemocratic; it is made up of all reactionary ideologies that "react" by negation to modernity in general and democracy in particular. This variety is encountered more often in Europe, thanks to memories that are more or less true to a nondemocratic past. The second variety resembles all those democratic heresies, all those ideologies that retain a fair amount of the healthy doctrine, but that in isolating it from its context and developing it unilaterally, leave orthodoxy behind and tip the model over into non-democracy. Finally, and this may be most useful, a model allows citizens to determine what remains to be done, in view of today's realities, so that tomorrow these realities may be even more true to the nature of good government, which is something men have always desired.

2

IDEAL COMMUNITIES AND THE PROBLEM OF MORAL IDENTITY

KENNETH MINOGUE

My aim is to make certain critical points about normativism, which is the belief that moral and political philosophy should *demonstrate* the basic practical rules for distributing goods so as to constitute a just society. Any modern theory of a perfect community is normativist in this sense. The main argument purports that the normativist has a seriously inadequate view of the moral life. In ignoring the fact that human beings are not merely rational agents, and social beings, but also, and quite distinctively, sustainers of moral identities, normativism has, for all its dazzling technical sophistication, banalised our understanding of both moral and political life. I preface this argument, however, with some more general remarks about normativism and political philosophy.

I

Everyone agrees, as a recent survey by Will Kymlicka puts it, that there has been an "explosion of interest in the traditional

I should like to express my gratitude to the Social Philosophy and Policy Center at Bowling Green Ohio, for providing the leisure and facilities for writing this chapter.

aim of defining the one true theory of justice."[1] Kymlicka is referring, of course, to the vast growth of normative political philosophy that has followed in the wake of *A Theory of Justice* by John Rawls. This "explosion" is all the more remarkable if one remembers the positivist domination of political studies in the middle of the century. The history of this revived normativism is an interesting one, and some of it can be related to the fortunes of Marxism during this period. In Marxist terms, normative political theory is a type of utopianism. Radical political thinkers, denied the project of revolution by the collapse of Marxism, have resigned themselves to designing paper utopias.

There is however a striking difference between these two intellectual tendencies. Marxism was a kind of poetry of human productivity. It made a hero out of the producer and was notably indifferent to, indeed contemptuous of, distribution and distributors. The objective correlate of this socialist disdain for distribution was the pile of badly made commodities rotting and rusting at the railway sidings of twentieth-century command economies. Prestige came from busting norms; no one in such a Marxist society got much out of moving commodities from the producer to the consumer.

Normative political philosophy is distributive prose rather than the poetry of production. It seems to be as indifferent to production as old-fashioned socialists were to distribution. Indeed, the whole of justice turns into the problem of how to distribute goods and losses without any very direct relation to law and order or even constitutionality.[2] To mark its new role, the term "justice" is commonly partnered by "social," and social justice is what happens when all basic goods, which may notionally include individual talents and skills, are centrally distributed in accordance with a rational scheme. In actual societies, of course, people acquire goods in large part by working in pursuit of their interests to earn them. The normativist tends to resent the fact that self-interest is the major distributive mechanism in liberal democratic society, identifying it with irrationalism and the rule of greed. The basic aim of much normativism is to replace self-interest by central distribution: command consumerism. In doing for themselves what should be done for them by society, individuals threaten, according to the normativist, what we can only call the "domination" of justice.

The basic question we may ask is: Why is there no conservative version of normative political philosophy? Elaboration of this question requires us briefly to consider both philosophy and conservatism. Philosophy is a reflective understanding of the whole, and normativism, as a body of theory that can find no place for one of the major tendencies of the Western political tradition, is obviously leaving something out. Normativism is practical theory designed to change the world. It is unmistakably a form of imperialistic rationalism, exhibiting the academic will to power that breaks out in many twentieth-century forms. Consider from another field the remark: "Unless the ideals expressed in great works of literature and art . . . can and do become politically empowered, there seems to be no point in teaching them."[3] Philosophy, however, is not concerned with power; it does not even begin until we take the next step and reflect on both changes in power, and on what is being set up for change. Whereas conservatism begins with the present condition of the world, normativism begins with the materials for a political foundation, usually principles supposedly derived from human rationality. The conservative position is represented by the story of the Irishman who, asked how to get to a certain town, replied: "Oh, if I wanted to get *there*, I wouldn't start from here." All political failure may be attributed to trying to arrive at a destination that is impossible to reach from where you actually are, and one sure fact of political life is that no one ever starts out from behind-the-veilville. The first premise of normativism is setting out in the Year Zero from a bare and characterless place. The place we have actually left behind has emerged out of our character and our desires, and many of us are attached to it: About the place to which we go, we know only that some academic theorists believe it to be just. Will it be lovable or livable? Only experience can tell.

The issue of whether we are dealing with theory or practice, with philosophy or politics, is thus unavoidable. If we are dealing with philosophy, the appropriate question is whether what we are told enhances our understanding; if we are dealing with practical politics, then serious questions of feasibility cannot be avoided. We may bring the charge against normativism that by straddling this issue it has the best of both worlds. In resembling philosophy, it can treat questions of feasibility with disdain, and enjoy the prestige of seeming to emanate from the ultimate authority of reason itself. It may be going a little far to say of normativism, as Stanley Baldwin remarked of the press baron Lord Northcliff, that it enjoys "power without responsibility— the prerogative of the harlot down the ages," but the frequent cleansing of hands by theorists whenever theoretical principles end in political disaster, as in many recent versions of socialism and anticolonialism, makes it relevant to point out that those who seek to change the world are in some degree responsible for what results. Understanding and recommending are differ- ent lines of work, and political theorists need to be clear about which line they are in.

A recommendation to change the world, such as advancing a norm, can only be part of a complex situation that also includes the norm-proposer. Precisely because the postulation of such a norm is thus partial, it is not to be identified with a philosophical argument that seeks to understand the total situation, including also that of the norm-proposer. This point is not affected by how abstract the norm may be. Philosophy begins at one self- conscious remove beyond the practical business of recommend- ing, concerning itself perhaps with the character of norms, or of the activity of recommending, or the abstract features of the complex situation within which this recommending arises. It can do nothing else except interpret the world, and therefore it would be entirely irrelevant to ask how its propositions are to be implemented; there is nothing there to implement. If, on the other hand, we are recommending a norm, we are engaged in practical business, and we may legitimately be asked to come clean about the means that might be employed in the imple- mentation of the norm. When, as in the case of much normative theorising, the policy to be implemented requires immense pow- ers to be exercised over society by a notional Distributor, Allo- cator, or Compensator, then we may legitimately make the initial point that the promised social justice seems likely to cost us our freedom. Such Enlightenment looks as if its old partner Despotism is hanging around in the background. But this clarification of what is involved in normative theorising cannot easily be pressed if normativists hide behind a philosophical remoteness from practice.

Clearly only a despotic power could actualize the dream that lurks behind the *telos* of social justice. Our liberal instincts are hostile to such a power. But there is a more profound objection to the project: It replaces the adventure of the moral life with a process of compulsory socialisation. Hegel reports Epicurus as repudiating communism among his followers on the grounds that it showed a deplorable lack of faith in friendship.[4] The moral life can only happen when certain desirabilities are left to the judgement of individuals freely associating together. A society in which social control, or therapy, or the end of supposedly alienating systems had socialised the entire community to a point where moral rules were necessarily rather than contingently followed would be the end of morality no less than the end of history.

Such a terminus—and normative proposals are in principle the arrival at perfect conditions that would not, indeed must not, respond to changes in taste or popular judgement—would also be the abolition of human beings in the present imperfect form that we know them. A human being is someone who has no option but to respond in his or her strivings to the conditionalities of success: such things as hard work, luck, common sense, intelligence, prudence, attractiveness, and so on. Each person makes the best of his or her equipment in these respects, and happiness in the recognition and reward of success in doing so, success being entirely dependent on circumstance and, as the Irishman insists, starting points. Now normativism is the proposal to abolish these conditionalities as the determinants of happiness. Nothing is more striking than the way in which justice has expanded, in the Platonic manner, from its basic habitation in constitutions, in the law, and in property rights, into every area of life, even the most private.

This movement of thought, by which socialisation as a process swallows up morality as a human activity, reveals a puzzling tension in the normativist project. That project is to derive the basic constitution of a just society from the exiguous materials of an abstract deliberating agent. "The theory of justice" as John Rawls remarks "is a part, perhaps the most significant part, of the theory of rational choice."[5] Foundations ought to be of the simplest, because the more extensive and complicated they are, the more impossible it will be to derive them from the inevitably simple postulates of a timeless rational human creature. Yet the foundational project exhibits the titanic ambition to put on unassailable foundations a scheme of justice that is no less than a complete blueprint of social life.

So titanic an ambition flickers intermittently in normative writings, even though careful writers like John Rawls take care to distance themselves from the ultimate possible claim:

> I do not claim for the principles of justice proposed that they are necessary truths or derivable from such truths. A conception of justice cannot be deduced from self-evident premises or conditions on principles (*sic*); instead, its justification is a matter of the mutual support of many considerations, of everything fitting together in one coherent view.[6]

"Everything fitting together into one coherent view" is what governments actually try to achieve, but they have the problem of actuality to deal with, and know that they must sometimes achieve coherence by exclusion. There are features of the world (luck, inheritance) that must largely be excluded from governmental intervention, partly because even governments must recognise limits. Normativists are unimpressed by such restraint, and bring whatever they choose within their ambit by denigrating it as irrational. One significant denigratory device is the term "arbitrary," as when Rawls remarks that his two principles "express the result of leaving aside those aspects of the social world that seem arbitrary from a moral point of view."[7]

This remark is deservedly famous, partly because the expression "a moral point of view" seems arbitrary. There are many moral points of view, including some invocations of religious providence that would deny that any human circumstance is "arbitrary." Controversy has raged over the project of taking natural talents as subject to redistribution, an idea taken up with enthusiasm by various normativists:

> Because talents are undeserved (writes Kymlicka) it is not a denial
> of natural equality for the government to consider people's talents
> as part of their circumstances, and hence as a possible ground
> for claims to compensation.[8]

Normative thought is often a determined assault on the very idea of desert, thus nothing would seem to be safe against the redistributive government here envisaged. The principle is clearly a thin end of the wedge you could cut your throat on. With marvelous insouciance, the normative political theorist is advocating a government that might despoil its citizens of absolutely anything on which its eyes might alight.

The reason why normativism finds itself on this particularly vertiginous slippery slope is the Rawlsian tendency, in spite of half-disclaimers, to see nothing between necessity and chance. Marxism sought to rescue people who were conceived of as the victims of a system called capitalism; justice as fairness wishes to rescue them, not from a system, because the more sophisticated normativists have at least learned that human life is not determined by systems, but by chance *conceived as if it were a system,* and a system little less deplorable than capitalism, patriarchy, and all the other gnostic systems in which we are supposedly imprisoned.

A sounder view of the matter is to recognise that everything in our social world is contingent[9] and human life can be nothing else but a contingent response to contingent circumstance. It is impossible to imagine in practice any distribution of goods between competing claimants of which one could not possibly say: "it's unjust." Contrariwise it is never easy to be certain that any particular advantage or talent is undeserved. A "talent" is an abstract thing, and what it amounts to concretely depends on virtues that the individual brings to its cultivation. No doubt we all find it easy to make confident judgements about the arbitrary character of some talents or advantages (Salieri or Mozart, perhaps) but even here we do not always agree. When it comes to the immense variations of ordinary human life the attempt to determine what should be redistributed could be nothing short of nightmarish.[10]

What I am commenting on as normativism is clearly a shifting target. The thing called "normative political philosophy" is a miscellaneous endeavor. Much of it consists of conceptual analysis, of technical exploration of abstract models, of probing the presuppositions of various forms of political activity. Mixed up with these endeavours, however, will be found the project of philosophically generating a timeless set of principles that could not be changed because any change would merely be irrational. Nozickian rights and the Hayekian liberal economy are normative in this sense, but the norms they propose are at least limited in scope. The core of what I am calling "normativism" takes the form of a theory of social justice in which the conditions of all members of society will be equalised by the operations of a single Redistributor. Theories of this kind have been criticised on the grounds that they replace democracy, indeed politics itself, by the rule of experts. They have also been criticized for the unreality of the human beings they assume. My concern is particularly with the question of human nature, and especially the moral life.

II

Homo normativus is a two-dimensional creature. The inescapable self-consciousness of the human condition has been abstracted out, or, where that is implausible, self-consciousness has been assimilated to the individual policy science of normative thought as a type of constraint.

The actual moral life we experience has two elements: first, the desires of a complex organism pursuing goals; and second, the constraints to which such a creature responds, or fails to respond: physical, for example, such as gravity, distance, time, and our own strength; and also legal, moral, social, and so forth. We weave our way in and out of these constraints, sometimes violating sometimes transcending them, in an attempt to live life as a sequence of satisfactions, the continuous enjoyment of which Hobbes described as felicity. This two-dimensional creature is the one studied in behavioural psychology and much of the social sciences. It is intellectually attractive as a simplified model because it can be the basis of an experimental science. Economic man and rational choosers are alike abstractions of this kind.

Being rational, this creature can trade off satisfactions, decide on values, or bring them to a single market of preferences, adopt strategies and face up to more or less moral conflicts about whether or not to be a free rider. Such a creature is a natural utilitarian, but he can also be equipped with rights, which are classes of immunity from specific kinds of frustration. He can even be given duties, though their derivation is likely to be shaky. But the basic point about this calculating organism is that it is such a pre-eminently *theorisable* animal.

Human beings, however, are actually three-dimensional. Most normative theorising reduces, and much entirely omits, this dimension of self-consciousness. All the world, as Shakespeare observed, is a stage, but *homo normativus* is a desperately untheatrical and unplayful creature. It is not at all a tautology to observe that action involves acting. In another part of the intellectual forest (in literary studies, and sociology, for example), it is taken for granted that human experience is *also* the never-ending presentation of a self both to oneself and to the world. Hobbes recognised the fact that this form of self-consciousness never ends in telling the story of the passion for suicide that came over the maidens of a city in ancient Greece, a problem cured by one that supposed about these maidens that "they did not contemne also their honour" and therefore advised that any that thus hanged themselves should hang out naked.[11]

The human agent, then, is engaged not only in the pursuit of ends but also in the sustaining of an identity—*being* someone, as it were. Such an identity is extremely complex; it is certainly subject to cultural differences. In India, caste is often a vital component of identity, whereas in China wives, elder brothers, and others in the Confucian cast of types used to be accorded known duties. In our own civilisation, the distinguishing out of morality from these more social identities means that a central component of the identity that we sustain is moral. We wish to exhibit identities that will be recognised as courageous, sensitive, heroic, kindly, and so forth, whereas we generally wish to avoid being recognised as cowardly, deceitful, thieving, and so on. From an external point of view, this moral identity is referred to in terms of honor, respectability, name, and reputation ("who steals my purse, steals trash" as Iago rightly remarked, going on to emphasise what a disaster it is for someone to be the victim of calumny). From an internal point of view this identity is the content of the self, and it is recognised reflexively as self-respect and self-esteem, things impossible to animals and to any entity lacking self-consciousness. It is the self to which Polonius thought Laertes ought to be true, and it is what was referred to by the framers of the American Declaration of Independence when they pledged to their desperate resolve not only their lives and fortunes but also an additional thing that they described as their "Sacred Honour." It would be interesting to work out a contemporary translation for such an expression; if as I suspect, there is no corresponding term, much is revealed about the evolution of modern ethics.

We cannot, of course, regard these identities as invariably admirable. Children at school work hard, we may paradoxically suggest, to avoid the label of "swot," and it is said that some Black children in American schools are discouraged from attending excessively to their books for fear of the charge of "acting white."

It will be obvious that these identities are in constant flux as new tastes and fashionable descriptions contort the cultural landscape. Admirations and contempts emerge from hidden undercurrents of our communal life, and morality is no less subject to fashion than dress. In our own world, a general drift away from moral, toward social, political, and other cultural categories has created a new landscape of sensibility. Recent identities include racist, sexist, Japan-basher, insensitive, caring, and so on, and these are social and intellectual rather than substantively moral. For many reasons, some we shall come to, we cannot simply identify such selves—selves constituted, that is to say, in terms of sustaining the admirable and eschewing the contemptible—with moral integrity. The fact that there are immense differences in what people admire and despise is only one of the reasons.

Any serious account of human life and conduct must include a concern with moral identity, even if only because this element of identity can at a moment's notice overturn every calculation of rational agency, as in cases of self-sacrifice, for example. Moral identity, however, seldom appears in the decor of normative political theory, except occasionally in the form of special constraints. Yet all those optimisers, preference orderers, rights bearers, calculators of expected utilities, selectors of cooperative or noncooperative strategies, free riders, and so on are also involved in the game of sustaining a moral identity, which is to say that they share in the burdens and delights of self-construction. Normative theory, in other words, gives us only half the picture. And yet it is out of this half of the picture that serious practical proposals for the entire transformation of society are advanced.

How do we explain the normativist preference for dealing with a mere human caricature? One basic reason is perfectly clear: Any technology of policy requires the postulation of a two-dimensional calculator whose decisions emerge by replicable steps from rational considerations. I do not wish to deny, of course, that these models of human behaviour may be of great intellectual interest, and indeed they are sometimes quite reliable predictors of what people actually do, for the richness of our rhetoric of moral identity is such that any optimiser can, with just a little ingenuity, find a satisfactory identity consonant with what he or she wants to do anyway. Error only begins when whole schemes of society are predicated on a two-dimensional organism mistaken for a complete specification of human life. This arises from the Platonic idea that a just society is composed of human material animated by the correct idea, and two-dimensional creatures are essentially the mere matter of some harmonising ideal. The activity of government as normatively conceived emerges from this matrix as a technical rather than political matter of making the preferences coherent by an appropriate set of rational constraints.

This kind of rationalism assumes that the right calculation can eventually solve the problem of moral philosophy. It is the search for the Leibnizian *Calculons!* Actual moral life is not calculated but created. Self-consciousness submerges calculation beneath drama and dialogue. One aspect of the moral life is our propensity to admire and to denigrate, and much of our moral vocabulary is employed in these judgements. This aspect of morality is quite distinct from moral calculation, and the managerial calculation that normativists see as the business of a just government cannot escape the unpredicatable operation of forms of admiration and denigration that they cannot even recognise without forfeiting the power of abstraction on which the projects depends. To reduce our moral repertoire to the idea of justice is to impoverish it. Conflict between the two aspects of the moral life often converges dramatically on the idea of self-interest, because the reflexivity of that term hints that, by contrast with preferences, needs, constraints, and the rest of the calculable vocabulary, some recognition at least is being given to a side of the moral life commonly invisible to the normativist. This hint of reflexivity, however, is enough to bring out the passionate hatred the rationalist feels for anything that escapes his rationalisings. Self-interest is for many normativists precisely that which constitutes the problem of social order, and the solution is to find some way, either the imposition of constraints or the seductions of a co-operative strategy, by which self-interested people can be suitably domesticated to the imperatives of social justice. The self-interest which in modern political philosophy is a complex concept including, among other things, duties to ourselves, is brutally debased by being identified with selfishness. This vulgarisation is sometimes retrospectively attributed to the philosophers of past time—Hobbes and Hume, for example. Hobbes is sometimes saddled with the doctrine that all men are selfish, something that this rather cynical philosopher, who certainly believed that most men are in fact most of the time pursuers of the main chance, nevertheless took care to exclude from his actual philosophy. The problem of the free rider that modern normativists often identify with self-interest appears in Hobbes in the form of a specific belief: the "foole" who has said in his heart there is no such thing as justice. Hume correspondingly talks of the "sensible knave."

Bad behavior understood as a self-interested failure to co-operate cannot be fully understood in terms of two-dimensional human beings; indeed, it cannot even be properly conceived. What alone can be understood in these limited terms is co-operation or its absence, selfishness or altruism, where altruism is simply a different preference set from that of people who are characterised as selfish. Altruists are people who are thought to require less manipulation to be fitted into a social project than those who are self-interested; they are naturally cooperative. But what makes their behavior moral? Moral predicates emerge from conduct exhibiting certain sorts of motive or moral identity. Normative theory is therefore dependent for whatever moral quality it can claim on a feature of moral reality that it cannot recognise on pain of subverting the merely managerial project by which it is inspired. Normativism signals its awareness of this difficulty by replacing the term "moral" wherever possible with "social," so conveying a moral aura without a real moral content.

III

The question of moral identity arises most insistently not in discussions of justice where, as we have seen, it can often be ignored, but in the understanding of freedom. Isaiah Berlin's famous discussion of liberty sets up the positive sense of liberty as a derivative of Stoic thought that posits two selves. A higher self animated by reason regulates the lower self constituted of contingent desires and aversions. Berlin rejects this account in favour of negative liberty, a view he thinks less susceptible to totalitarian manipulation.[12] The merely desiring self, whose freedom is nothing but the avoidance of frustration, is identical with the two-dimensional creature we find in normative political theory. But many theorists of liberty have argued that this disposes of the baby as well as the bathwater. It fails to distinguish between trivial desires and appetites on the one hand, and our moral valuations on the other. The most notable exponent of this important revision has been Charles Taylor. We human beings, he observes, "are not only subjects of first-order desires, but of second-order desires, desires about desires."[13] This formulation echoes a basically Christian sense of individuality as a coherence of desires, a view that rejects the Platonism of Reasons and the Passions, but from my point of view in this chapter, it does not distinguish sufficiently between desires and aversions on the one hand, and moral identity on the other. By characterising both these quite distinct levels in terms of "desire," Taylor leaves the door half open to the simplicities of rational choice. In a later work, Taylor provides a masterly exploration of the whole theme, using the basic idea of a framework of evaluation: "We are all framed by what we see as universally valid commitments... and also by what we understand as particular identifications... our identity is deeper and more many-sided than any of our possible articulations of it."[14]

Normative theory must be understood as part of a much wider intellectual project in our civilisation that seeks not merely to ignore but actually to break down the moral identities that block the creation of an entirely harmonious social order. To theorise mankind in these limited terms is in part an attempt to persuade us that human beings are, indeed, nothing else but rational organisms. One road to happiness can plausibly be constructed by clearing the ground of the moral identities that stand in the way of pure self-expression. These moral identities are the moral and cultural inheritance of a Christian civilisation, and although we for the most part inherit them from our familial milieu, we also select and choose among them as part of the expression of our individuality. They are often at war with our inclinations. It is notorious that there is often a gap, even in the private life of consenting adults, between the fantasies people entertain and the conduct in which they engage. In this and many other ways, moral identity can be presented as repressive of natural inclinations and a cause of neurosis; when this theory is linked to political ideology, repression is taken to be the basic cause of unhappiness, and explained in terms of systematic oppression.

For over a century now, great efforts have been made to break down the gap between natural inclination and moral inhibition, to weaken many forms of guilt and shame so that inhibition and repression may be destroyed. The grand drama of this movement has been the conflict between the muscular uplift of the concept of duty and self-improvement as understood in earlier centuries, and the attack on that moral concept by Freud and his therapeutic successors. The idea of liberation, so central to the self-understanding of our century, generally ends up as the destruction of some set of moral identities. Feminism, for example, in many of its versions seeks to destroy the specific moral identity involved in being a "lady." But if these complex moral identities should be destroyed, and human beings should achieve a condition of unrepressed and uninhibited nature, would they not descend into irremediable conflict and self-destruction? No doubt they would, unless they could be managed in such a way as to become socially co-operative in a manner rationally determined by a central co-ordinating institution acting in the name of social justice. The broad movement is away from hero, lady, gentleman, worshiper, lone individualist, fastidious carer for one's own soul, and so forth, toward such social identities as worker, comrade, sister, carer, sharer, and so forth. The problem of social order has always been identified, both at a traditional and at a rationalist level, as self-consciousness, *alias* pride, *alias* alienation, *alias* inauthenticity.

These concepts are ways of picking out individuality as causing the problem of conflict and disorder. They are ways of rejecting Western civilisation that has evolved a form of civil society in which a rule-governed individuality has actually been constructed out of the tendencies to self-expression that traditional societies find so disruptive. No doubt these individual moral identities do then work imperfectly, because they *are* moral rather than socially engineered components. They certainly generate competition and sometimes conflict. Normativism is the attempt to remedy such deficiencies (if that is what they are) by going back to a rationalised version of traditional society.

Co-operation in rational choice theory results from a calculation in which a preference for long-term advantage overrides impulses toward immediate or mistrustful individual maximisation. This structure of calculation can in actuality be imposed only by an external balancer of considerations. The balancer might claim to derive from reason a set of principles of just distribution and this alone, in spite of familiar difficulties of actualisation, might be thought to guarantee co-operation. It is essential to this harmonising work, however, that individuals should agree in their basic valuations; no eccentric moral identities can be allowed to intrude on the process.

We arrive at a characterisation of normativism that brings it remarkably close to totalitarianism, for it is the attempt to impose upon a whole population a single basic moral identity, that of "worker" or "optimiser," or "comrade," for example. Such an identity is both comprehensive and compulsory, just like the roles to which people are bound in traditional societies. The essence of the matter can most easily be grasped by looking to grotesque extremes. A Nazi society is one in which the idea of the leader is transmitted without resistance from top to bottom, and the notionally spontaneous comradeship of a communist society incorporates the same Platonic dream. Resistance to the idea might come from shame, honor, absolute sense of right and wrong, a sense of ugliness, indecorum, or indecency, religious commitment, conception of moral integrity, scientific craftsmanship, or any of the vast number of other sensibilities that constitute the moral identities of modern human beings. The self-interest constantly attacked in the normativist tradition is an individual's claim to make his or her own judgments about what he or she should do, and thus constitutes a general characterisation of all types of resistance.

One of the most powerful ways of undermining individual moral identity has been to elevate the term "society" from its simple descriptive sense of a vast network of relations in any particular state, to a system of influences acting on individuals as if it were an agent. Understood in this causal role, society becomes the formal generator of all the evils in need of reform, and politics turns into the project of replacing a bad "society" by a good one, thus creating a true community. Social technology replaces morality and promises to solve the human condition understood as a problem. Moral responsibility, eroded by this new idea of society, is never allowed to reappear, and the idea of social justice comes to stand for a set of human beings transmuted into the happy unself-consciousness of the ant or the bee.

It must be recognised, of course, that it is not merely normativists who attempt to give an account of the moral life in terms of the strivings of an intelligent organism, and perhaps the popularity of this view illustrates Bernard Williams' remark that the prevailing fault of moral philosophy is to impose on ethical life some immensely simple model, whether it be of the concepts that we actually use or of moral rules by which we should be guided.[15] Sidney Hook, for example, discussing human rights, asks about the basis of obligation, and suggests that among theories of obligation

> the least inadequate of them is the view that obligation is derived from the reflective judgement that some shared goal, purpose or need—some shared interest, want, or feeling—requires the functioning presence of these rights. Without some common nature or some community of feeling, the sense of obligation could hardly develop; the assertion of rights would have no binding or driving emotional force.[16]

Again, a strikingly two-dimensional view of the moral life is the argument that "moral obligations are desire-dependent in the sense that one can be under a moral obligation to do x only if there is some desire or purpose that one has that x would fulfill."[17] This is to assume that the desire for a particular end is the same *kind* of thing as the determination to sustain a specific moral identity. Hook's phrase "reflective judgement" is a quick bow in the direction of recognising a self-conscious moral identity but he only succeeds in describing what human beings have in common with animals. Kant may have gone too far in splitting the moral and natural worlds asunder, but he did at least recognise what is specifically moral in human life, and that cannot be done in policy terms with components thought to arise merely from natural desires. An ingenious attempt to recognise these complexities is to be found in Loren Lomasky's view of human beings as pursuers of projects, though I do not think it succeeds. Some projects, we learn

> are directed at becoming and remaining a certain sort of person. One may commit oneself to carrying out one's promises and avoiding lies not simply because of consequential considerations establishing the generally optimistic tendency of that practice, but because one wishes to be a man of one's word.[18]

No doubt identities may indeed become objects of policy in this way, however eccentric these aims may seem, but ends of this kind cannot escape the element of self-consciousness concerned with *how* one pursues *that* end. A person will still make distinctions at a higher level about the kind of person he or she is *in* pursuing this end. Some states of moral character, he or she might also remember in doing so, cannot be achieved by direct means, and some cannot be achieved by willing at all.[19]

The sustaining of a complex identity, including a moral identity, is a self-conscious dimension of human agency that rational choice theory cannot accommodate. It is necessarily fatal to any attempt to create utopias out of the abstractions of individual policy. Utopias are a genre of political writing that necessarily involves a static and changeless set of moral identities. Normativism is the attempt to screen out history, contingency, and irrationality from the understanding of human life, partly because of the intellectual attractions of simplification, and partly because these complications are impediments to the rationalist projects of the philosopher-bureaucrat. But in fact human history is partly the story of whole new clusters of moral identity sweeping civilisations and transforming the understanding of human life. Christianity was one, diffusing such unlikely virtues as humility and turning the other cheek. So too was the spread of the ideal of chivalric knighthood throughout Europe from its origins in Provence, leaving in its wake many variant ideals and virtues, including the English idea of the gentleman, which floated down into wider social classes. These admirations created whole literary genres and transformed the position of women, but they were in no sense the result of any kind of rational choice. The spread of Protestantism is another example of a "transvaluation of values" that swept across the flat plains of policy calculation and transformed the human condition. None of these things was predictable or calculable, and they reveal that, for all the usefulness of understanding human life as the rational pursuit of interests under constraints, the moral life can be nothing else but an open-ended dialogue between disparate types of human response to the world.

A dialogue of this kind emerges out of history and tradition, and we are thus in a position to give one part of our answer to our original question: Why are there no conservative versions of normative theory? The answer is that the disposition of conservatives is to cherish and protect the historic identities of which human beings are constituted—the memories, legends, language, culture, and so on of the people to whom they belong. Normatively, however, all of these things are seen as reflections

of the injustices we inherit, and the business of the critical re-
former is to replace them with his or her new scheme of social
justice.

IV

Those who construe human life as a kind of game implicitly
recognise identity conditions. *Homo ludens*[20] is a self-conscious
creature whose competition with others allows him to explore
his own dispositions and talents. For two-dimensional man, by
contrast, a competitive game can only be the attempt to achieve
the satisfaction of winning, whereas losing is merely failure to
achieve a goal, to be identified with frustration. He can play
games (by contrast with animals) in the sense that he understands
the rules of a game, but what he is doing is a game only in the
sense used in games theory, that is, no game at all, but merely
conflict over benefits. It is only along this dimension that the
slogan "winning isn't the main thing, it's the only thing" takes
on the rebarbative character of an axiom of behavior. It is only
when the dimension of moral identity is recognised that the point
of playing a game, including the game of life, is seen to be not
whether we win but how we play.

Once we are clear on this point, a number of things fall easily
into place—the basic Marxist misunderstanding of a modern
economy, for example. Two-dimensional man can only recognise
two types of relations between human beings: conflict and co-
operation. What then is the position of competition? From a
policy point of view, it generates losers; people fail, and as political philosophers who take this view know, from Plato to John
Rawls, failure generates discontent and envy—what Rawls calls
"particular" envy. Rawls does indeed recognise some forms of
moral identity, and takes self-respect to be a primary good, but
he takes it purely in policy terms. We cannot continue in our
endeavours when "plagued by failure and self-doubt."[21] The
ideal society is maximally cooperative, indeed society (which for
Rawls includes the economy), is actually defined as social co-
operation. In fact, of course, competition itself involves an important cooperative element: It is a game played according to
shared rules, and an opponent helps to bring the best out in his

or her competitor. It seems that the more preoccupied people become with justice, the harder it becomes for them to distinguish between an opponent or a competitor on the one hand, and an enemy on the other.

Furthermore, failure, which normativists seek to make impossible, is vital to sanity. It is the best clue we have to reality. It gives us our bearings throughout life, tells us what we are capable of, teaches us the Irishman's lesson of starting from where we are, and reveals to us what constitutes in our own lives an achievement—which in many areas may well be something very easy for other people.

Clarity on this point further exhibits one of the most significant aspects of distorting abstraction found in normative thought: It assumes for all human beings a standard starting point for a movement toward the same abstract goal. Homogenised in this way, human beings are assumed to recognise exactly the same things as being advantageous and disadvantageous, the same thing as privilege or lack of privilege. With a kind of insouciant dogmatism, the normativist takes it for granted that certain abstract conditions are unambiguously advantageous, others disadvantageous. In fact, there is nothing in human life whose value is not significantly determined by circumstances. Poverty has its victims, but so too do education, wealth, and political enthusiasm. The point is crisply made by the American novelist Willa Cather comparing the first generation of immigrant daughters in America who had to work to support their families with the next generation who had the benefits of education:

> Those girls had grown up in the first bitter-hard times, and had got little schooling themselves. But the younger brothers and sisters, for whom they made such sacrifices and who have had "advantages," never seem to me, when I meet them now, half as interesting or as well educated.[22]

This is an observation many people have made in one form or another. If true, as I believe it is, what explains it? Part of the explanation is that in facing up to frustration and hardship, the first generation developed a certain pride in their own responses that gave them a conspicuous kind of moral identity;

and this did not happen to the next generation, beneficiaries of an effortless flow of benefits directed toward satisfactions not actually chosen. We might try generalising the point: The people who came out best experienced the less controlled environment. Normativism is an attempt at the maximum possible control of the environment.

Control of the social environment according to projects of social justice involves supplying unconditionally a range of benefits supposedly necessary for the pursuit of a range of satisfactions. What cannot be planned for is the valuation the recipients will put on those benefits, or the moral identities that will emerge over time as they are received. Sometimes, indeed, this barely recognised nettle is grasped by normative theorists in the assertion that such benefits will generate self-esteem in the receiving selves, but this is to ignore one of the major features of our civilisation: the disposition to value much more highly what one has achieved for oneself than what has fallen into one's lap. This widespread belief in desert—no doubt intermixed with much illusion but a real feature of our moral life for all that—is part of our moral individualism. The organic individuality which in other civilisations is subordinated to a traditional pattern is among us drawn out, made significant, and incorporated in an order made by rules rather than roles. No doubt we are all imitative beings, but the creativity of our civilisation comes from transcending rather than succumbing to what are popularly called "role-models."

According to the normativist understanding, part of the population fails to share in this individualism as the result of injustice and oppression. These things are typically understood as deprivations of standard benefits and advantages that are available to the better off elements in the community. This project is a complete misunderstanding of the actual character of both individualism and freedom.

It misunderstands individualism by identifying it with the content of individual desires and satisfactions. But the real location of individualism is in the moral identities we cherish, and the point here is whatever is revealed *in* pursuing the objects we pursue. Quite what that revelation is responds to the immense complexities of the rhetoric of everyday life but it is entirely decisive. Further, such identities may as easily be institutional as individual. A historian of the American Civil War describes the Union Army in the following terms:

> Under everything else, they were fighting not for the Union nor for freedom nor for anything else that carried a great name, but simply for the figure which they would finally make in their own eyes. They were about to go into a great fight, and their pride as soldiers might be the decisive factor in it.[23]

War is supremely an area that is inexplicable without this concern with moral identity, and it may well be significant that the twentieth century tends to find it baffling and irrational. But the same incomprehension is no less obvious in the understanding of economic matters. Thus the greater visibility of monetary transactions in the world economy of the 1980s provoked a wave of moral criticism of economic actors as exhibiting the vices of greed and selfishness. In terms of our argument, this is to make the mistake of thinking that the only significance of entrepreneurial activity is to acquire and appropriate an increasing availability of satisfactions. The mistake is a complex one, and another of its roots is the failure by many intellectuals to be able to make the distinction between conflict and competition. This particular error is endemic among those who use Aristotle as a stick with which to beat the modern world: They believe there is a bundle of resources adequate to the living of a decent and admirable life, and anyone who acts to increase his or her resources beyond that point is guilty of the vice of greed. Assailed by this multiple set of confusions, a whole dimension of moral understanding collapsed in the course of the 1980s, to the point where an American newspaper columnist could solemnly write: "Greed is a vice I cannot afford."

An individual in Western moral terms is thus a self-understanding organism pursuing self-chosen goals in terms of some cherished moral identity, and it is because the West is populated by such people that it has embarked on the unpredictable adventure of modernity. It has done so under the banner of freedom, and freedom itself requires the invocation of moral identity for its explanation no less than does individualism.

The swiftest way to make this point is to invoke the familiar socialist example of paradigmatic unfreedom: the worker in a one company town. Leaving aside certain unrealities (the possibility of emigration, the fact that even in such towns there will be shops, houses to clean, and so on.) we have here someone whose "choice set" (as they say in these circles) is down to a single option.[24] Such a person is the very model of unfreedom in a capitalist society. Freedom however refers not only to the choices people make but also to the spirit in which they make them. We exhibit virtues and vices by doing whatever we do cheerfully, courageously, sullenly, unwillingly, heroically, proudly, and so on, and in this way we transform our lives and respond to our circumstances. We can exhibit such virtues no less in prison camps or humble occupations than in the full amplitude of the middle-class comfort of which the average normativist is thinking. Such normativists are descendents of the kind of schoolteacher who used to whip his pupils into action by inducing a dread of ending up in things called "dead-end jobs."[25] The truth is that "impoverished choice sets" in the external world, and lack of virtue and imagination in our own characters can both limit our possibilities, but freedom is not the condition of an abstract self confronting a finite and calculable set of possibilities. If it were, human beings would have no history. Freedom is, rather, the way in which a complex entity exhibits or enacts[26] its identity by responding to the endlessly changing possibilities offered by the world. The attempt to treat this element of the human condition as an administrative problem to be solved by an allocation of rights and primary goods is a remarkable example of imperial overstretch by an alliance between philosophy and bureaucracy.

The normativist project is, of course, an impossibility, and the reason it is so brings us to the heart of the matter. The basic aim of the normative reconstruction of society is equalisation. Thus Kymlicka cites Ronald Dworkin in support of the view that "every plausible political theory has the same ultimate value, which is equality."[27] The normative project of equlisation is as radical as imagination can devise and does not stop, of course, at a little progressive taxation: human talents and differences are also to be equalised or at least compensated for, to the extent that current technology (medical, bureaucratic etc.) allows. Equalisation directly collides with reality the moment we realise that the moral identities we sustain often result from a conviction of our superiority to others who fail the standards we reach. And when, indeed, we ourselves fail the standards, we feel guilt or shame about doing so. Superiority or inferiority, competence or incompetence, these are the polarities between which our moral identity lies, as Machiavelli and Hobbes recognised in talking of glory; many writers discuss them in terms of pride and honor. Man is a comparative animal, and we find our sense of ourselves in constantly and often painfully estimating our performances in relation to those of others; and when we find ourselves preeminent in some admirable respect, it is a great pleasure.

A dislike of this pleasure may well be the main reason that the normativist wishes to abolish this moral experience: The pleasure some take in their own sense of glory infallibly involves pain for others being judged in terms of it. The dimension of moral identity must thus be excluded from human experience as the normativist seeks to transform it for two reasons. First, being dramatic rather than deductive, it is not subject to such technical manipulations as calculation; and second, it is inherently self-conscious and inegalitarian. Inequality is built into the very structure of a moral identity. It follows that the normativist project of creating a society out of two-dimensional man must involve the death of man projected a century ago by Nietzsche, and rather joyously espoused in this century by Foucault and his followers, among many others. It was also the project of the communist society envisaged by Marx and is central to all ideological systems of thought. But it is a project that has only recently appeared in the remote calm of academic political theory.

It may seem that in this somewhat pessimistic conclusion I am forgetting that *homines normativi* will all enjoy the equal liberty to implement life plans of their own choosing. It seems clear, however, that they will be domesticated creatures. I am reminded of what used to be the condition of guest workers in the mines of southern Africa. They lived in hostels in which their needs and welfare were entirely taken care of, and some element of their wages was sent home to support absent families. The money they then received as wages was pocket money, in one sense the freest kind of money there is, money that can be spent on any pleasure, or any life plan the spender can conceive. But in fact, of course, their lives and their limits had already been determined for them, and nothing they chose mattered very much. They were the archetypal inhabitants of a socially just world because they could come to no serious harm. Their choices were trivial choices that had no consequences. Similarly, moral responsibility in a society built on philosophically prefabricated abstract norms is pocket money moral responsibility.

NOTES

1. Will Kymlicka, *Contemporary Political Philosophy: An Introduction*, Oxford: Clarendon, 1990. He goes on to remark about this explosion of interest that experience might seem to show the ambition "wholly implausible." He himself, however, thinks that an agreement on foundations is ultimately possible.

2. It is notable that in the Kymlicka survey of what purports to be an introduction to contemporary political philosophy, there is no place even in the index for democracy, law, authority, or constitutionality.

3. Patrick Branklinger, *Crusoe's Footsteps: Cultural Studies in Britain and America*, London: Routledge, 1990. See the review of this book by Wendy Steiner in the *Times Literary Supplement*, 25 Jan. 1991.

4. Hegel, *Philosophy of Right*, ed. T. M. Knox, Oxford: Clarendon, 1952, p. 43.

5. John Rawls, *A Theory of Justice*, Cambridge: Harvard University Press, 1971, p. 16.

6. Rawls, *A Theory of Justice*, p. 21.

7. Rawls, *A Theory of Justice*, p. 15.

8. Kymlicka, *Contemporary Political Philosophy*, p. 106.

9. Cf. Michael Oakeshott's treatment of the necessary, contingent and the fortuitous in *On History*, Oxford: Blackwell, 1983, pp. 45–96.

10. For a subtle discussion in general terms of the problems of relating normative theory to the real world, see Christopher T. Wornell, "Problems in the Application of Political Philosophy to Law," *Michigan Law Review*, Vol. 86, pp. 123–155.

11. *Leviathan*, Penguin ed., Harmondsworth: Penguin, 1968, ch. 8, pp. 142–143.

12. Isaiah Berlin, *Four Essays on Liberty*, London: Oxford University Press, 1969, p. 131.

13. "What's Wrong with Negative Liberty?" in David Miller, ed.,

Liberty: Oxford Readings in Politics and Government, Oxford: Oxford University Press, 1991, p. 152.

14. Charles Taylor, *Sources of the Self: The Making of Modern Identity,* Cambridge: Cambridge University Press, 1989, p. 29.

15. Bernard Williams, *Ethics and the Limits of Philosophy,* London: Fontana, 1985.

16. Sidney Hook, *The Paradoxes of Freedom,* Berkeley: University of California Press, 1962, p. 4.

17. David O. Brink, *Moral Realism and the Foundations of Ethics,* Cambridge: Cambridge University Press, 1989, p. 18, n. 5, and ch. 3.

18. Loren Lomasky, *Persons, Rights and the Moral Community,* Oxford: Oxford University Press, 1987, p. 26.

19. Cf. Jon Elster, *Sour Grapes,* Cambridge: Cambridge University Press, 1983, p. 56.

20. See for example J. H. Huizinga, *Homo Ludens,* London: Routledge & Kegan Paul, 1949.

21. Rawls, *A Theory of Justice,* p. 440.

22. Willa Cather, *My Antonia,* New York: Heritage Press, 1967, p. 127.

23. Bruce Catton, *This Hallowed Ground,* New York: Doubleday, 1955, p. 360.

24. See the discussion in "Chance, Choice and Justice" by Brian Barry, for example, published in the collection of essays *Democracy, Power and Justice: Essays in Political Theory,* Oxford: Clarendon, 1989. This was a public lecture given at the London School of Economics, 25 April 1990.

25. See for example Charles Murray's account of people responding imaginatively to what are conventionally regarded as boring jobs in *In Pursuit of Happiness and Good Government,* New York: Simon & Schuster, 1988. One is reminded of people of great talent who have found certain kinds of fulfillment in simple tasks—Wittgenstein in life, the hero of Somerset Maugham's *Razor's Edge,* London: Heinemann, 1949, in fiction. Stendhal's heroes seem to find both freedom and fulfillment only by being imprisoned, but they are perhaps an extreme example.

26. This term refers to Michael Oakeshott's distinction between self-disclosure and self-enactment in *On Human Conduct,* Oxford: Clarendon, 1975. This is much the most brilliant contemporary account of the distinction I am developing in this chapter.

27. Kymlicka, *Contemporary Political Philosophy,* p. 4.

3

SHARED UNDERSTANDING AND THE DEMOCRATIC WAY OF LIFE

CHRISTOPHER J. BERRY

In a book of that title I coined the term "the idea of a democratic community" to encapsulate, and interrogate, a significant strain in contemporary political speculation.[1] I sought to capture the essence of this by presenting this "idea" as, in a Hegelian dialectical sense, the preservative transcendence of liberalism.

According to my presentation, supporters of the idea understand liberalism as the theoretical counterpart to the practice of contemporary capitalist democracies and criticise it for being excessively individualistic and insufficiently democratic. For these reasons they insist, on my gloss, that it must be transcended. But to transcend is not to reject root and branch and there is, and here is the Hegelian provenance that I am attributing to the idea, an acknowledgement on their part that liberalism contains genuine "goods" that must be preserved. It is being true to the idea if, as a working shorthand, we identify the core of these goods as a notion of self-legislation—individuals are both loci and sources of value whose decisions, actions, beliefs, and so on must be respected by other individuals. For the democratic communitarians, the goods acknowledged in this way constitute a positive principle worthy of preservation. But the acknowledgment also serves a defensive function by circumscribing the requisite idea of community. They require this circumscription because they are aware that communitarianism can easily be made to appear authoritarian or anti-liberal. This authoritarian reading follows if the community is accorded some superior or ultimate value that, accordingly, can permit the interests of its individual members, their capacity as self-legislators, to be over-ridden in the name of the community's greater good. To forestall that potential danger the supporters of the idea insist that the communitarianism they support must be qualified as "democratic."

Here I pursue the assumption implicit in this manoeuvre, namely, that democratising the community solves the problem of any apparent illiberalism.

We can identify two ways in which, in principle, a solution could be found. However, these differ fundamentally. The first looks on democracy as a procedure. The way to organise a community so that it does not act illiberally is to ensure, by means of what we might term an external control, the presence of certain democratic processes or institutions. This emphasis on procedure or method aligns this first way with Schumpeter's analysis of democracy, or at least accords with a conclusion that he draws.[2]

The distinctive character of the second is perhaps best captured as rejection of the Schumpeterian account. Instead of a conception of democracy as a set of neutral processes and institutions it is put forward as a value in its own right.[3] Democracy is not viewed as an external control policing the proper (non-illiberal) operation of a community but as integral to that normatively loaded operation. A community that is democratic necessarily embodies values that will solve the problem of illiberal authoritarianism. On this second conception the ideas and values that democracy of itself possesses necessarily imply a distinctive conception of community. The two are internally connected.

Of these two ways, the second best meets the aspirations of the advocates of a democratic community. Because, thanks to the internal conceptual linkage between democracy and community, it follows that not only is democracy integral to a proper community but also that a true, authentic (proper) democracy embodies the values of community; only through this fusion can liberalism be *aufgehoben*. Accordingly, I focus on this second way, using the first solution, democracy as a procedure, as a foil. My strategy is to utilise a notion of "shared understanding" and relate these two different solutions, these two models of democracy, to a systematic ambiguity in that notion.

COMMUNITY AND CO-OPERATION

Some preliminary analysis is necessary before the notion of "shared understanding" can be analyzed. In my book two key features of a "transcendent" community were identified: the idea of community enjoys a conceptual priority to that of the choosing or will-full individual and, second, the goods associated with community express themselves non-competitively.

Alasdair MacIntyre conveys the idea of a noncompetitive community in his conception of a "practice."[4] Inherent in any practice, he argues, are certain standards. These standards constitute "internal goods." Practices are non-competitive in the sense that for one individual to achieve the inherent standard, or the "excellence" characteristic of a practice, is without prejudice to the same achievement by others. Not all of MacIntyre's examples are free of ambiguity, but his claim that Turner transformed seascape painting to the enrichment of the whole relevant community captures what seems to be the core of this argument. In contrast, goods that are "external" to a practice are competitive. Here there are winners and losers; I can enjoy greater status, can carry more prestige, can be wealthier than you.[5]

In MacIntyre's terms, therefore, to attain its aim the democratic community must embody a standard of excellence. I think it fair to infer from the writings of the democratic communitarians that they think the most appropriate excellence to be that constituted by the democratic way of life itself. That is to say by living such a life the individual is involved in a co-operative rather than a competitive activity. I elaborate on this later but, for the moment, we can note that because it is a "way of life" this is also to say that it is not some instrumental means to an individually determined end. Rather, as characteristic of a community, it enjoys the status of a conceptually prior mode of being. Only through, and in virtue of, membership of a community can individuals come to know themselves as individuals. And, in consequence, only in and through that membership are they able to conceive of themselves as, for example, bearers of rights or as competitors for external goods.

CITIZENSHIP AS A WAY OF BEING

The basic question that now arises for these authors is, what sort of excellence does a democratic way of life, the democratic community, embody? The notion of citizenship, or what MacIntyre calls "the moral community of citizens,"[6] seems best to serve the ends of the democratic communitarians. One writer who develops this theme is Michael Walzer. To Walzer the good of community is "conceivably the most important good."[7] Walzer goes on to draw a connection between communal membership or citizenship and self-respect. This connection is especially relevant to our purposes.

Self-respect is not competitive. Walzer's argument to that end is similar to that propounded by MacIntyre in his account of internal goods. In contrast to self-esteem, Walzer argues that self-respect is a good that everyone can enjoy because individuals judge themselves with reference to a common standard, not with reference to other people.[8] What is definitive of a democratic community (what Walzer calls "a society of citizens")[9] is that it possesses a general standard or "one norm of proper regard for the entire population of citizens."[10] This norm makes possible, he claims, a kind of self-respect the enjoyment of which is independent of any particular social position. For Walzer self-respect is a matter of measuring up to conceptually prior shared norms/standards.[11] In a democratic community "measuring up" to these standards is not a competitive question of pass or fail but "rather a way of being in the community."[12] We now approach what will be the key term in our analysis because Walzer draws the consequence that these standards comprise "shared understandings."[13]

Walzer emphasises that this sharing of understandings is a co-operative rather than a competitive activity.[14] In attaining and enjoying *my* self-respect as a citizen, I am consolidating *your* citizenship not confining it. Yet I remain, and here in our terms we can identify the preservative dimension to the transcendence, a self-legislator in the sense that in the community I am a free, responsible participating member.[15] This co-operative, consolidatory citizen self-respect means, to Walzer, that "every citizen is a potential participant, a politician."[16] This last phrase will repay further analysis. We can start by taking seriously, perhaps more so than Walzer himself does, the reference to "potential."

DEMOCRACY AND LEGITIMACY

If we interpret this reference along Aristotelian lines then the democratic community can be understood as the realization of our "natures" as political animals (as Walzer remarks "every citizen" possesses this potential). This understanding, common among democratic communitarians, rests on identifying the "political" with the "democratic." This identification is not simply a conflation of a species with the genus but the adoption of a prescriptive perspective. What this adoption amounts to is the claim that democracy is the only legitimate politics. Hence the *democratic* community can preserve while transcending precisely because this preservation is retaining (indeed for its adherents is, more properly, enhancing) *the* principle of legitimacy.[17] This is to be expected once democracy, along the lines of the second model identified earlier, is understood as inherently a normative principle.

Once again recourse to Aristotelian principles can help clarify what is at stake. For Aristotle the nature of a thing (say, a knife) lay in its function or end (*telos*) and that thing can perform its function well or ill (a good knife is a sharp knife). The evaluative criterion is not something superadded to the definition but is internally connected to it. Similarly, if—following Walzer that there is a universal potential for citizenship—political activity or participation realizes the *telos* of humanity then failure to engage in that activity is "unnatural," just as it is unnatural to use a knife to eat soup. This carries with it a powerful corollary, and one commonly drawn by radical democratic communitarians, such as Bachrach, namely, lack of participation or apathy cannot be a genuine choice but is, rather, an expression of alienation or privatisation, a privation from the democratic "way of life" or communal "way of being." The conclusion is drawn that non-transcended liberal democracies with their apathetic electorates possess no more than an impoverished legitimacy. Full legitimacy can only be found in a democratic community where the universal political potential of each citizen is realised. This explains, too, why the advocates of that community regard themselves as enhancing and entrenching democracy beyond its formalistic, etiolated character in liberalism.

The criticism of liberalism has a further dimension. One of the cardinal tenets of liberalism is to keep politics "in its place" and to regard it as an activity of limited application. In contrast, for its advocates, one of the benchmarks of a democratic community is that it extends the scope of politics and, given the aforementioned argument, this extension ipso facto extends the democratic arena. This throws added light on the notion that the "excellence" at the heart of the democratic community is involvement in the democratic "way of life."

A "way of life" in general, we can presume, is constituted positively by a set of values, principles, or habits that permeates a range of institutions and interactions and in so doing invests them with an identity or definitive coherence. This coherence gives to a way of life that co-operative character emphasised by the democratic communitarians. Negatively it is not something indulged in either instrumentally or discretely. The Christian way of life, for example, is not something reserved for church attendance on Sundays to be judged socially respectable but a set of values, and so forth judged to be inherently worthy or to manifest an ideal character, an "excellence," that pervades every day of the week. Analogously the democratic way of life encompasses more than the periodic business of government and elections; it is a continuing community-wide concern. Hence democracy, as understood by the democratic communitarians, is held to be applicable to the operation of all the basic social institutions. The workplace is a special focus of attention and industrial democracy, the overcoming of divisive capitalist relations of production, would be a central feature of any democratic community. Closely allied is the strong advocacy by democratic communitarians of some form of "market socialism."[18] Democracy is also applicable in the home. Indeed feminist thinking provides a good illustration of this entire chain of reasoning.[19]

DEMOCRATISATION OF THE COMMUNITY

We are now in a position to deal directly with our initial question, in what way, for its advocates, does the democratisation of a community exempt it from the charge of illiberality?

In the light of the earlier analysis two possible answers can be rejected. First, the very fact that democratic procedures exist is sufficient to guarantee the retention of the positive aspects of liberalism. But this Schumpeterian view of democracy as "merely" a method is unacceptable. If procedures were indeed sufficient then the whole idea of a democratic community as a preservative transcendence of liberalism would be redundant. Moreover, as liberals like Berlin have openly admitted, a liberal and a democratic society are not necessarily conterminous.[20] To its critics a Schumpeterian democracy underwrites a political elitism that, in practice, can sustain an authoritarian, that is, undemocratic, community. Simply to allow the community a democratic voting procedure (Schumpeter's "competitive struggle") can result in, at best, an indifference to a minority's interests and, at worst, a violation of them.

The most favoured liberal response to this danger, and the second answer, is to entrench the minority's interests by investing them with the status of "rights." What now characterises a democracy is the presence of institutions that guarantee to all individuals therein the enjoyment of certain indefeasible rights. These rights can, in Dworkin's phrase, "trump" any potential illiberality in a community's conduct.[21] This solution, however, will not find favour with the advocates of a democratic community; *this* is not what they have in mind. The basic reason for this disfavour is that this answer embodies a major ingredient in liberalism that has to be transcended. As we observed in passing earlier, to communitarians this recourse to rights rests on a false prioritisation. The idea of individuals as ipso facto possessors of rights only makes sense in terms of some supposed extra-communal circumstance, a Lockean State of Nature for example, within which "rights" enjoy some special status.[22]

Relatedly, because of this false prioritisation, rights are consistent with only an attenuated, individualistic, or atomistic (liberal) conception of community. At the root of this equation of rights with atomism lies Marx's argument in the "Jewish Question," though in point of fact Marx's own argument there is largely definitional. In that essay Marx had aligned the idea of "rights" (of man) with egoism, with a view of man as separated from community.[23] These egoistic individuals, preoccupied with their own private interests, look on other, similarly constituted, individuals as potential competitors. Given, then, that the notion of rights offends both principles of community, its priority and non-competitiveness, it is clear that this answer, too, must be rejected.

In contrast, the democratic community will rely less on institutional, external (because prior) safeguards like rights and far more on participatory activity that is necessarily integral to communal membership. We saw that this activity is interpreted as joint-involvement in common endeavours and, as such, is co-operative rather than competitive. We also noticed that it was in the interpretation of this involvement that my pivotal notion of "shared understandings" emerged. Recall that for Walzer these understandings constitute the standard of excellence, or "one norm of proper regard," of a democratic community. The notion is, however, open to two different readings: the sharing can be regarded as a *product* or as a *discovery*. I argue that this difference is crucial because it undermines the attempt to transcend liberalism while preserving its acknowledged merits.

PRODUCTION OF SHARED UNDERSTANDING

On the first of these readings shared understanding is produced by means of debate or discussion. Because Walzer seems to adopt this reading I confine myself to linking production of shared understanding with discussion. Making the move, on which we have already commented, Walzer declares democracy to be *"the political way* of allocating power."[24] This is the way to legitimate its use. He then proceeds to declare that what "counts" in a democracy is "argument among citizens." Although some citizens are likely to be more persuasive than others there is no "dictatorship of the articulate"[25] because all citizens are still equal. The basis of this equality is two-fold. First, because sources of inequality like power or wealth will be denied any place then the relation between citizens reposes on argument alone. Second, there are no exclusions because all citizens (ideally should) participate. Significantly, Walzer goes on to remark that the decisions that emerge from this argument/discussion "may well reflect a multitude of compromises."[26]

Clearly a connection can be made between the ideas of a compromise and a shared understanding. What is less clear is whether the notion of "community" that follows from that connection is able to perform the crucial role of preserving while transcending liberalism. The lack of clarity stems from the fact that in a compromise what occurs is a mutual accommodation between individuals but, and this is the crux, this remains between *individuals*. A conclusion akin to that arrived at earlier in the case of rights can now be drawn; if shared understanding means mutual accommodation arrived at as a compromise among individuals, then liberalism has not been transcended. This failure occurs because the relations between individuals remain "external." The operant model is that of striking a deal, or contract, after a process of bargaining. Through this process, or debate, a mutually agreeable outcome is achieved or shared understanding is produced: I want X and wish to pay £20, you want to sell X and wish to obtain £40, we agree, or compromise, on £30 and, in so doing, we each realise our own individual objectives.

The alternative reading of shared understanding-as-discovery rejects this contractarian model. Before turning to a analysis of this alternative I wish to elaborate on the notion of compromise. This elaboration is prompted by a plausible response to the argument put forward in the previous paragraph: That is, my particular example oversimplifies the issue and, in that way, misinterprets Walzer. The example, it might be charged, elides an important difference between a debate or discussion and a contract. The latter involves only an external interconnection, whereas in the former "change" takes place in the discussants. Building on this difference it could now be argued that compromise *produced* by discussion does transcend individualism and preserve the desiderated idea of community. However, as my elaboration now demonstrates, the most defensible version of this argument relies implicitly on the "discovery" and not on the "production" of shared understanding. This implicit reliance has the significant consequence that, contrary to the aim of the argument, the notion of "compromise" remains individualistic.

We can start this demonstration by pursuing the idea that discussion produces a "change." Many advocates of a democratic community talk of political participation, itself of course a pervasive community-wide activity, as a process of education at the heart of which lies the transformation of the participants. Benjamin Barber is typical. He writes,

> In a strong democratic community . . . the individual members are transformed, through their participation in common seeing and common work, into citizens . . . that community cannot remain an association of strangers because its activities transform men and their interests.[27]

Clearly we need some account of this transformation. For all its eloquence Barber's text is not helpful. More assistance is provided by Peter Bachrach.

Bachrach believes that personal involvement in the participatory process may "significantly change one's attitude, perspective and value priorities."[28] The effects of participation, and here is the reinforcing tie with the idea of community, leads, he argues, to our development as "social beings." Bachrach's argument rests on this notion of "development." However, *this* argument reposes on a reading of shared understanding not as the product of debate but as a discovery. Bachrach states that participation is valuable because it enables "the individual to discover his real needs."[29] And these real needs are themselves discovered through "the intervening discovery of himself as a social human being."

The explanatory weight of "development" in Bachrach's account rests on the Aristotelian idea that we are creatures of the polis. We are naturally communitarian beings (Significantly, perhaps, the nearest that Barber gets to an explanation is when he resorts, against the grain of his argument, to this vocabulary).[30] What is discovered, namely, our "social being" is no accident but the realization of an imperative or unfolding of a potential. What is discovered cannot be an open question. Bachrach lends support to this interpretation when he immediately goes on to claim that this development-through-participation is the development of an individual's "real interests."

The fact that this idea of development implicitly forecloses questions makes clear its divergence from the first reading of shared understanding. The Millian emphasis on debate that was seemingly adopted by Walzer is a recognition that there are no definitive answers. The best that can be achieved—a "best" with substantial normative power—is for a shared understanding to emerge out of the multiplicity and variety of voices in the debate.

To spell this out in ideal terms: in debate I learn to appreciate your concerns as you learn to appreciate mine. Through this educative process we each come to realize that the other is not being capricious or obstructive or suffering from delusion. This appreciation and realization on both our parts means each has some understanding of the other. We share something. In this way our mutual accommodation can indeed be viewed as something more than an external bargain or contract (I pay £30). But it does not follow that this reading of a shared understanding apes Bachrach's. There is a difference because this sharing is compatible with continuing substantive disagreement; *pace* Barber[31] it is compatible with remaining strangers (I won't pay more than £20 and you won't sell for less than £40). This conforms to the liberal principle of tolerance. A Muslim and a Christian can share an understanding of the importance of belief and ritual to the religious but not share the understanding that Christ is the Son of God. The former can be the object of a compromise, for example, uniform application of any laws concerning blasphemy or religious education, whereas the latter cannot.

Because this last example refers to *communities*, Muslim and Christian, it might seem to be beside the point. But this would be a mistake. The issue at stake is the claim that a democratic community will not be illiberal and a test case of that is its ability/capacity to accommodate *within it* the pluralism that this example represents. The first reading of "shared understanding" as a product of discussion brings out that the essence of the understanding produced in that manner is an agreement to differ.

Two points follow from this conclusion. First, this reading with its recognition of the possibility of disagreement and the contingent character of compromise presupposes an individualistic or liberal reading of community[32] rather than the concept of community presupposed by the idea of measuring up noncompetitively to a conceptually prior way of being. Second, this agreement to differ is what a democratic community, as the preservative transcendence of the liberal model, also has to incorporate.

DISCOVERY OF SHARED UNDERSTANDING

We now turn to the second reading, shared understanding as something discovered. As implied by Barber's notion of "transformation" and Bachrach's account of "development," the crux of this interpretation is that shared understandings have a profound effect on the sharers. He claims that "the way of life" in the democratic community is not something incidental but is rather integral to the attainment of the "identity" of the members of that community. To exploit the analogy with Christianity once more, participants in the Christian way of life understand themselves, and are understood by others, in terms of that participation; this is how they know "who they are." Michael Sandel refers to this as a "constitutive" rather than "instrumental" conception of community.[33] He claims that the latter can consistently underpin only a liberal conception of community, wherein individuals interact in pursuit of their own private ends, as in making a contract. To MacIntyre, similarly, the liberal individualist understanding of community is "simply" that of an " rena in which individuals pursue their own self-chosen conception of the good life."[34] By contrast, involvement or participation in a constitutive community is not an instrumental means to an end but involvement in "a way of life" wherein "identity is bound."[35]

That which constitutes identity is not made or produced, it is "discovered."[36] As the notion of discovery entails, this constitutive identity is conceptually prior to the sentiments and dispositions of the individuals in it: Our self-knowledge is inseparable from our knowledge of ourselves as members of "our" community. In a fundamental sense we are not self-constituting but are constituted in and through our shared membership of, and participation in, community. As Charles Taylor puts it "we are what we are in virtue of participating in the larger life of our society."[37]

Walzer adopts a similar argument in his account of self-respect that we referred to earlier. Self-respect is not a matter of will, or instrumental choice, but of membership of a group or community. Membership is by definition something shared, it is not something of itself competitive. It embodies a standard or "excellence."[38] In a later essay he says that social, that is, non-competitive, goods, like, most plausibly, grace and knowledge "are distributed in accordance with shared understandings of what they are and what they are for."[39] Walzer, therefore, appears to adopt not only the first reading of "shared understanding" but also the second. I return to that observation.

An apparently obvious objection now presents itself. This second reading provides an idea of community that transcends the individualism of the liberal version but seems less well equipped to handle the key issue that this community must be democratic if it is to preserve as well as transcend. The reason for this is simple. To be constitutive the community wherein shared understanding/identity is discovered need not be democratic.

Feminist theory provides an apt illustration. In a patriarchal community women are liable to discover that their rightful place is in the home. A woman who accordingly identifies herself as a "housewife" could be described, in Sandel's terms, as attaining, through her participation in a prior form of life, a "mode of self-understanding."[40] Or, in MacIntyre's terms, her identity could be described as being derived from the story of the community of which she is inevitably and ineluctably a part.[41] Yet for the feminist the fact that this community is patriarchal is sufficient to deprive it of legitimacy. And in line with an earlier argument this deprivation means that no patriarchal community can be properly labelled "democratic."

Nonetheless the point that underlies this objection might be thought to be of limited effect because it ignores the fact that what constitutes the prior way of living is a *democratic* community. Barber, for example, is insistent that he is an advocate of "strong democracy" and is at pains to distinguish that from what he calls "unitary democracy." He rejects the latter because of its "activist totalism," a situation where everyone is thought of as some sort of "blood brother" in an "organic community."[42] This manoeuvre is typical. Sandel is careful to insert the qualifier "partly" when he talks of community constituting identity and distinguishes the "encumbered" which he accepts, from the "radically situated" self.[43]

Underlying these manoeuvres is the basic argument that the ideas of genuine democracy and community are internally related. This relation means that the objection can be countered more positively. In line with the "idea" of a democratic community not only will the individualism of liberal democracy be transcended by a recognition that democratic values truly express themselves in a co-operative, or internally coherent, way of life but also the liberal principle of free discussion will be preserved. In other words the first reading of "shared understanding" is included. And in virtue of this inclusion what is discovered is a *democratic* community. The outcome is that there are not two *different* readings of "shared understanding." Rather the readings complement each other. That both readings can be detected in Walzer, and others,[44] is, therefore, unexceptionable.

I want to take exception and resist this counter-proposal. There are indeed *two* readings because the role that debate or argument plays in each case is different. Where discussion *produces* shared understanding it is an interactive process whereby divergent views come to some mutually agreeable compromise. Where discussion *discovers* shared understanding it is, at best, a process of incorporating partial aspects of the one truth. Whereas on the first reading it is possible for no compromise to be struck, for a failure to share understandings to occur, on the second reading a shared understanding is always in principle possible. This is because we are, essentially, not rivals but co-partners in a common undertaking. In the terminology used by Bachrach, my "real interest" as a social being cannot *ex hypothesi* clash with your real interest. As a consequence, issues that are left open by the former understanding could be foreclosed in the latter. For example, the former might permit, under safeguards arrived at as a compromise, access to entertainment and literature that the latter would prohibit as pornography, because it was inimical in fact to our real interests or the community's well-being.[45]

A similar outcome is also reached if the crucial link between identity and the discovery of a shared understanding is the point of reference. Discussion that relates to questions of identity has a different quality than that which concerns itself with finding compromises. This difference can be usefully elaborated by means of a brief return to the principle of tolerance. Tolerance is not a question of identity: One can only tolerate that which is in some respect divergent from oneself and recognised to be so. Integral to that recognition is the shared understanding that is produced when each appreciates that he or she can remain a stranger to the other. But once shared understanding is a question of identity then substantive divergence is intolerable; schizophrenia is a suitable case for treatment. Less tendentiously, members of the democratic community cannot remain strangers. The understanding shared between strangers is different from that shared between friends just as the role of discussion is different. In the former case discussion rests on an acknowledgement of their mutually independent status. Only on that basis is a genuine compromise possible. In the latter case discussion rests on complicity, on a recognition of their interdependent status.

Hence if Walzer, and the others, do, as part of their subscription to the idea of a democratic community, uphold both readings of shared understanding then these differences between the readings reveal a basic disparity, rather than a dialectically subsumable complementarity. To the extent that they wish to transcend liberal individualism they should regard shared understanding as a voyage of discovery, but to the extent to which they wish to preserve the pluralism that the liberal good of self-legislation seemingly entails they should regard shared understanding as an object of production. Contrary to the pretensions of the "idea" they cannot do both.

Models of Democracy and Shared Understanding

In conclusion I return to the two models of democracy outlined at the outset. More particularly, I wish to relate the differences between these models to the difference between the two readings of shared understanding. The relation that I sketch, and that is all that is warranted by the foregoing, is the weaker one of affinity rather than a stronger one of necessity.

On the first model democracy consists of certain procedures and institutions. The first reading of shared understanding can be accommodated in this model because it would require the presence of procedures and institutions necessary to sustain free discussion and the ever-present possibility of disagreement. Democracy can be judged superior to other forms of political organisation because it is the most effective instrument to sustain discussion and the freedom to differ and so produce shared understanding. The value accorded to democracy is instrumentalist; it is valued in virtue of something other than itself. Like all instrumentalist evaluations it is open to replacement either because another instrument can attain a desired end more effectively (for example, ensuring the independence of the Supreme Court by appointing Justices for life or, even, taking the head of State out of politics by means of a hereditary monarchy) or because the area under consideration is inappropriately controlled by democratic procedures, for example, that between teacher and pupil. Given that free discussion is the definitive feature of a liberal society then a liberal will favour democracy in as much as it fosters that feature.

If, alternatively, shared understanding is read as a discovery then this first instrumentalist model would be out of place. Democracy is not an instrument to discover shared understanding because that implies that what is being discovered is something other than itself. Democracy is favoured on the second reading because it is self-discovery.

When we turn directly to the second model we can appreciate why this second reading of shared understanding is there more at home. On the second model, democracy is itself invested with inherent value. The second reading can be accommodated in this model because of its insistence that the non-competitive communal relations discovered embody these inherent values. The point of these values is that democracy is properly described as a way of living, not a set of instrumental procedures that serves, inter alia, to produce those compromises indicative of the first reading of shared understanding. In C. B. Macpherson's typical version, democracy is a community understood as "an equal society in which everybody can be fully human."[46] It follows from this conception that my humanity is not some external good in competition with your humanity and democracy is the political system that embodies that fundamental value as we discover an understanding that we share. Additionally, because that value is communitarian, then it means that the connection between democracy and community is internal.

Although this conception of a democratic community transcends the competitiveness built into liberalism—the wariness of others consequent on accepting that it is prudent, in Hume's terms, to presume everyone to be a knave[47]—its preservative pretensions are less secure. The insecurity is the obverse of its successful transcendence. Just because communality is placed ahead of a now derivative individualism it means that the key liberal "good" of self-legislation is delimited to discovering its "self" in that prior way of life. In other words, the sole way that the preservativeness can be sustained is by arguing that the self that legislates is only truly constituted in a democratic community.

The liberal, however, would detect here a presumptive premise to the effect that there is a Good in which the self's real interests inhere. More precisely, the issue is the extent to which citizenship can meaningfully constitute a way of life. What appears to be central to the idea of a democratic community is the idea that being a citizen is indeed significantly analogous to being a Christian. As a way of living Christianity is a substantive state of affairs and for the liberal this is properly accommodated at a sub-state level through group, that is, church, membership. Moreover because these groups are not co-extensive with the state then the necessarily voluntary membership thereof allows a diversity of "ways." To regard citizenship as more than the enjoyment of formal rights and as a question of identity is to run the risk of confusing democracy with the "church" or "nation" or the like: This confusion would not be possible if democracy were seen as a set of procedures and institutions.

The upshot is that the democratic community can only be exempted from illiberalism because it interprets democracy in such a way that, in virtue of the values it possesses, it is true by definition that the essential liberal value of self-legislation is retained. This exemption, however, is bought at the price of making democratic values conterminous with the "good life." Yet clarity is surely enhanced by curtailing democracy's normative pretensions. A democratic state of affairs is not always the best of all possible worlds.

NOTES

1. C. J. Berry, *The Idea of a Democratic Community* (Hemel Hempstead: Harvester-Wheatsheaf; New York: St. Martin's, 1989). I take the liberty, on occasion, of drawing on this earlier discussion in what follows.

2. J. Schumpeter, *Capitalism, Socialism and Democracy* (London: Allen & Unwin, 1961), p. 242. Schumpeter's own account, which exploits the notion that the rationality of individuals diminishes when they forsake the familiar and enter the political arena, as well as his generally ill-informed view of what he calls "classical theory," can be safely ignored in the present context.

3. Cf. for example, "Democracy is more than a mere means for the achievement of basic values. Rather, it is the best and proper institutional embodiment that gives expression to the values of life and of equal positive freedom. Therefore, democratic decisions have an ethical status which must be taken very seriously." C. Gould, *Rethinking Democracy* (Cambridge: Cambridge University Press, 1988), p. 281.

4. A. MacIntyre, *After Virtue,* Second Edition (hereafter *AV*) (London: Duckworth, 1985), p. 187.

5. MacIntyre, *AV,* p. 190. Cf. A. MacIntyre, *Whose Justice? Which Rationality?* (hereafter *WJWR*) (London: Duckworth, 1988), where he contrasts "goods of excellence" and "goods of effectiveness," the latter being tied to external rewards, pp. 32ff.

6. MacIntyre, *AV,* p. 254.

7. M. Walzer, *Spheres of Justice* (hereafter *SJ*) (Oxford: Blackwell, 1983), p. 29.

8. Walzer, *SJ,* p. 275.

9. Walzer, *SJ,* p. 276.

10. Walzer, *SJ,* p. 277.

11. Walzer, *SJ,* p. 278.

12. Walzer, *SJ,* p. 279.

13. Walzer, *SJ,* p. 313. To fasten on to this phrase is not to go against

the grain of Walzer's argument; he uses it elsewhere in the book (e.g., pp. 29, 151) and in a later article that draws on the book ("Liberalism and the Art of Separation," *Political Theory* 12 [1984], 315–30). Nor is the phrase confined to Walzer; other communitarians employ it. Cf. M. Sandel, *Liberalism and the Limits of Justice* (Cambridge: Cambridge University Press, 1982): "Community must be constitutive of the shared self-understandings of the participants" (p. 173); C. Taylor, "Atomism" in A. Kontos (ed.) *Powers, Possessions and Freedom* (Toronto: Toronto University Press, 1979): "Our identity is always partly defined in conversation with others or through the common understanding which underlies the practices of our society" (p. 60); MacIntyre: "A community whose primary bond is a shared understanding both of the good for man and for the good of that community and where individuals identify their interests with reference to those goods" (*AV* p. 250).

14. Walzer, *SJ*, p. 278.

15. Walzer, *SJ*, p. 279.

16. Walzer, *SJ*, p. 310. Cf. B. Barber, *Strong Democracy* (Berkeley: University of California Press, 1984): "Universality of participation—every citizen his own politician—is essential" (p. 152).

17. Barber, for example, writes, "given that humans are social by nature" then citizenship is "the only legitimate form that man's natural dependency can take" (Barber, *Strong Democracy*, p. 217).

18. Cf. inter alia C. Pateman, *Participation and Democratic Theory* (Cambridge: Cambridge University Press, 1970); P. Green, *Retrieving Democracy* (London: Methuen, 1985); D. Miller, *Market, State and Community* (Oxford: Clarendon Press, 1989). Walzer comments that democratic values "can't stop at the factory gates" (Walzer, *SJ* p. 298).

19. The underlying premise, basic to much subsequent feminist writing was stated by Kate Millett who stipulated, "the term 'politics' shall refer to power-structured social relationships, arrangements whereby one group of persons is controlled by another" (*Sexual Politics* [London: Virago, 1973], p. 23). When this is applied to the relation of men to women, when that is seen as a power-relation, the typical, restrictive, liberal view that equates power with the political/legal system is undercut. The liberal principle of non-interference in the personal lives of its citizens is not, as pretended, a neutral principle but a political matter. It is an exercise of power by and on behalf of men that establishes and countenances the domestic servitude of women. But because the only legitimate politics is democratic politics, such servitude is illegitimate. Accordingly, feminists seek a legitimate politics of sex whereby women, inter alia, will have democratic control over their bodies and lives. Only a democratic community will achieve that goal.

20. I. Berlin, *Four Essays on Liberty* (London: Oxford University of Press, 1969), p. 130.

21. R. Dworkin, *Taking Rights Seriously* (London: Duckworth, 1977), p. xi. Cf. "The nerve of a claim of right . . . is that an individual is entitled to protection against the majority even at the cost of the general interest" (p. 146). Of course liberals can differ amongst themselves as to how absolute they make these rights.

22. Cf. P. Selznick, "From the perspective of community . . . rights are derivative and secondary." "The Idea of a Communitarian Morality," *California Law Review* 75 (1987), 454.

23. K. Marx, "On the Jewish Question" in G. Benton (tr.) *Early Writings* (Harmondsworth: Penguin, 1975), p. 229.

24. Walzer, *SJ*, p. 304 (Walzer's emphasis).

25. W. Kymlicka, "Liberal Individualism and Liberal Neutrality," *Ethics* 99 (1989), 900.

26. Walzer, *SJ*, p. 304.

27. Barber, *Strong Democracy*, p. 232. Cf. C. Pateman, *Participation and Democratic Theory*, pp. 42–43.

28. P. Bachrach, "Interests, Participation and Democratic Theory" in J. R. Pennock & J. W. Chapman (eds.) *Participation in Politics*, NOMOS XVI (New York: New York University Press, 1975), p. 51.

29. Bachrach, *Participation in Politics*, p. 40.

30. Cf. "Man is a developmental animal—a creature with a compound and evolving telos whose ultimate destiny depends on how he interacts with those who share the same destiny" (Barber, *Strong Democracy*, p. 215).

31. Cf. A. Oldfield who writes that the relation between citizens is a "relationship between people who know each other, they are not strangers." *Citizenship and Community* (London: Routledge, 1990), p. 22.

32. Cf. B. Ackerman, "Liberal community is instead [of appeals to love, sympathy and the common interest] grounded on the simple desire to communicate." "What is Neutral about Neutrality?" (*Ethics* 93 [1983], 375).

33. Sandel, *Liberalism and the Limits of Justice*, p. 143.

34. MacIntyre, *AV*, p. 195.

35. Sandel, *Liberalism and the Limits of Justice*, p. 161. Cf. Selznick who identifies "belonging" or our participation as "implicated selves" as the central value of a communitarian morality ("The Idea of Communitarian Morality," pp. 454, 460).

36. Sandel, *Liberalism and the Limits of Justice*, p. 22; MacIntyre, *WJWR*, p. 88.

37. C. Taylor, *Hegel and Modern Society* (Cambridge: Cambridge University Press, 1979), p. 88.

38. Walzer, *SJ,* pp. 278, 275.

39. Walzer, *Political Theory,* p. 321

40. Sandel, *Liberalism and the Limits of Justice,* p. 161.

41. MacIntyre, *AV,* p. 221

42. Barber, *Strong Democracy,* p. 222.

43. Sandel, *Liberalism and the Limits of Justice,* p. 21.

44. Cf. Taylor "Atomism," as quoted in n. 12 supra. MacIntyre stresses the role of debate and conflict in *WJWR* though he still wants to distinguish "non-rational persuasion" (the first of our readings) from "rational argument" (the second reading). The former is characteristic of liberalism with its denial of any justifiable theory of human good, whereas the latter operates from the presumption that conflict can be resolved by deciding which of a set of premises is true (p. 343). Also Gould who associates shared understanding with compromise as part of a disposition to reciprocity in the democratic personality while regarding "social reciprocity" as shared understanding going beyond intrumentalism and as undergirding the extension of democracy throughout society (*Rethinking Democracy,* pp. 75–77, 290–91).

45. This example is not entirely fanciful. Two city councils in the U.S. did pass ordinances against pornography on the grounds that it restricts women in particular (though presumably not exclusively) from "full exercise of citizenship and participation in public life." (quoted in R. Langton, "Whose Right? R. Dworkin, Women and Pornographers" *Philosophy and Public Affairs* 19 [1990], 336). Those ordinances were subsequently vetoed on grounds of free speech (contrary to the First Amendment). Cf. E. Cook, "Unwholesome Appetites" *The Listener* 13 (December 1990).

46. C. B. Macpherson, *Democratic Theory: Essays in Retrieval* (Oxford: Clarendon Press, 1973), p. 33.

47. D. Hume, "Of the Independency of Parliament" (1741) in *Essays; Moral, Political and Literary* (Oxford: Oxford University Press, 1963), p. 40.

PART II

LIBERTY, AUTONOMY, AND DEMOCRATIC COMMUNITY

4

THE LIBERAL COMMUNITY

ALAN RYAN

What follows is not meant to be the last word on the "liberal-communitarian debate."[1] It is, however, an attempt to change the terms of that debate.[2] My strategy is simple. Part I argues that the conflict between liberalism and communitarianism that the "debate" supposes is a figment of the imagination; many paradigmatic liberals have been communitarians, and many paradigmatic communitarians have been liberals.[3] A sample is offered, biased to my purposes. Though the sample is biased, I emphasize some illiberal-sounding remarks of Green and Hobhouse in order not to cheat. Part II argues that epistemological, methodological, psychological, and moral issues have been muddled together, and when they are unmuddled, it emerges that there is no one *general* issue at stake. Nonetheless, the various issues I uncover are connected, and I say something about how they are connected. Part III offers a sketch of a liberal community, and its social, economic, and political attachments, and finds several tensions that could properly be called tensions between liberty and community. In this part, I also say a little about community and democracy, though hardly enough to satisfy even myself.

I

An under-noticed feature of the so-called "liberal-communitarian debate" is its resemblance to two late nineteenth-century debates.[4] The first debate was over the empiricist conception of the self; the second over the idea of the social contract. One episode in the first debate was the assault launched by the English Idealists on their utilitarian predecessors; one episode in the second was Durkheim's assault on anyone who denied the autonomy of sociology. The implications of these arguments concern us in Part II. Here we need only notice that Durkheim and most of the Idealists were unequivocal political liberals, whereas one of their main targets, J. S. Mill, was not backward in recognizing the claims of community.[5] It is, of course, commonplace that turn-of-the-century British "New Liberalism," which coincided with Durkheim's hey-day and with the last years of the Hegelian revival, was communitarian in both its politics and its epistemology.[6]

In the second half of the nineteenth century, Idealist critics of Mill and Bentham attacked what they called "one-sided" or extreme individualism, a term sometimes replaced by "atomism." This was not primarily a political criticism; in economics Bosanquet was more of an individualist than Mill, and it is a fine call whether Green was not also.[7] The crux was epistemological, or metaphysical, though it carried moral consequences. The battlefield was conceptions of the self. The best brief statement of the Idealist case came in one of F. H. Bradley's footnotes: "Mr Bain collects that the mind is a collection. Has he ever thought who collects Mr Bain?"[8] To put it more lengthily, the Idealist target was what has come to be known as the "punctual" or "serial" view of the self. If a person was merely a succession of instants of consciousness, together with some cumulative memory of those instants, there could be no genuine personal identity.

Mill was a tempting target, directly or through his follower Alexander Bain. Mill's analysis of the external world in terms of "permanent possibilities of sensation" invited the question, If a sensing self creates the identity of external objects, what provides the sensing self with *its* unity?[9] Idealists thought these questions unanswerable in an empiricist and associationist framework.

Their criticisms mirrored Kant's criticisms of Hume, and when they edited Hume, Green and Grose made much of Hume's avowed incapacity to find his *self* within, but distinct from, the flow of sensory experience.[10] The connection with political issues was indirect. The Idealist view was *not* that Mill's political and social views were simply wrong, but that even their merits showed up the defects of their metaphysical (or psychological) supports. Bradley was unusual among the English Idealists in thinking Mill's liberalism was mischievous, but Bradley's arguments against it were independent of his arguments against Mill's conception of personal identity. *Ethical Studies* was unkind to all Mill's opinions, but even Bradley did not suggest that the wickedness of Mill's politics followed deductively from the incoherence of his view of the self. The case was more broad brush. Mill's system was incoherent in its foundations and its superstructure. Green, Ritchie, Caird, and liberal Idealists were no kinder about Mill's metaphysics, but shared most of his political ideals.[11] Green was even ready to agree that utilitarianism had done much for moral progress, at any rate when it was detached from a hedonistic theory of motivation.

No liberal Idealist deplored the ideals of *On Liberty*. Liberal Idealists, too, thought a morally serious agent must keep his or her life permanently under review, assessing it by the ideals of autonomy, rationality, and openness to the claims of novel experience. When Mill insisted that his defence of individual liberty was not a defence of "mere selfishness," they believed him. They knew that when Mill based the doctrines of *On Liberty* on "the utility of man as a progressive being" he espoused a wholly congenial vision of the unity of a well lived life. They complained that such ideas were impossible to ground in Mill's atomistic psychology, not that Mill did not believe in them, nor that they were worthless. Where they differed with him, it was because they were more nearly orthodox Christians than Mill and did not see religion as a threat to liveliness and variety. This, and their belief—perhaps the same belief—in the ultimate rationality of the universe certainly gave their views a different coloring from Mill's. Bradley's demand that we must live life as a whole, and make of ourselves a more perfect whole, displayed an optimism about the attainability of harmony that Mill did not share, as did Green's account of the way individual good shared in the goodness of the world as a whole.

Otherwise, the Idealists' *idée maîtresse* owed as much to Aristotle as to Hegel—to describe someone as happy or unhappy, vicious or virtuous, involves the appraisal of long run dispositions and experiences. *Something,* as already suggested, carries over from the metaphysical disagreement; Mill was quicker to look for disagreement between one individual and another, and slower to look for conciliation than T. H. Green, say. There are ways in which Green did and Mill did not think that the highest good was a common good. Further than that it is impossible to go. They were at one in their view that moral analysis looks at life in the long term and on a holistic basis. Take Mill's emphasis on character; in the *System of Logic,* Mill tackles the Owenite argument that because our characters are the product of education and our actions the product of our characters, our actions are not under our own control.[12] Mill replies that we can make our actions our own by making our *character* our own. It is not the plausibility of Mill's answer that is at issue, but the readiness with which Mill invokes the idea of character.

Utilitarianism offers another striking instance. When Mill considers the objection that persons whose decisions are based on self-interest cannot act *morally,* he replies that we create a moral character that tides us over the temptations of self-interest. The plausibility of this reply is again not at issue, merely the way Mill appeals to the work of a fixed moral character in explaining how distinctively moral motivation squares with his hedonic theory.[13] A last example is provided by Mill's account of punishment and guilt in his *Examination of Hamilton:* There he writes of the criminal momentarily succumbing to temptation and being reproached for the rest of his life by the better self that deplores his bad behavior. "After the temptation has been yielded to, the desiring "I" will come to an end, but the conscience-stricken "I" may endure to the end of life." Again, the issue is not whether such a self can emerge from Mill's raw materials, but what his conception of moral agency, responsibility, and character is.[14]

This does not settle the question of how "communitarian" Mill was. It shows that his conception of moral agency was not dictated by the "punctual" or "abstract" conception of the self that recent writers have deplored, but that is only the first step.[15] The second step is to recognize that he insisted that we develop our fixed and persistent characters because we are embedded in our social relations; indeed we can hardly think of ourselves apart from them. This deep social connection develops the conscience, as we internalize the known or assumed disapproval of others for actions that damage their interests. Mill was also anticommunitarian, but in such a way that only someone who was so impressed by the capacity of society to make itself felt *within* its members' souls could be.[16] Far from ignoring the reality of community, Mill was so impressed with the community's power over its members that he devoted *On Liberty* to ways of holding that power in check, not by destroying it or denying its existence but by teaching his readers when they ought and when they ought not to deploy that power.

The third step is to notice that later liberal writers, such as L. T. Hobhouse in Britain and John Dewey in the United States, had no doubt they were defending liberalism even if it was a communitarian liberalism. They were liberals because they justified political and social action in terms of liberty, rather than simple welfare. T. H. Green claimed that the wage laborer was to all intents and purposes a slave, and in need of liberation, whereas Hobhouse defended the nascent modern welfare state as an essential support to *freedom*.[17] The romantic prose aside, Bertrand Russell's *Principles of Social Reconstruction,* although overtly committed to guild socialism, is in the same vein.[18] Neither Green, nor Mill, nor Hobhouse, nor Russell thought a simple opposition between individualist and communitarian social theories reflected a conflict between liberalism and communitarianism.

Several things explain the appearance, and often the reality, of conflict in this field. First, T. H. Green (and Hobhouse and Dewey) said things that seem illiberal to the last degree. Green famously insisted that we could not have rights against the State because the State was the precondition of our moral identity and existence.[19] He analyzed an individual right in terms of "a capacity for contributing to the common good," and Hobhouse followed him. John Dewey explained rights in almost identical terms. According to Bradley, " "Have I a right?" means "Am I in this the expression of law?" " No present-day American reader can help flinching at the thought that we have no rights against the State, and no one who thinks of rights as "trumps" can help flinching at the claim that rights are to be explained in terms of our duty to promote the common good. To some extent, these anxieties can be palliated: The State against which one can have no rights is not an actual government, but the ideal embodied in the community's social and legal arrangements. The claim that we have no rights against this entity is less illiberal than tautological. Nor is such a theory of rights indefensible. If one supposes, as John Rawls does, that rights can only be claimed by rational agents who interact with similar agents in a network of rights and duties, one is half way to the Green–Hobhouse view. I think the view is wrong to leave out the way rights protect interests regardless of a capacity to contribute to anything. Still, it is not indefensible.

The other contributor to these deceptive appearances is the rise of sociology during the last half of the nineteenth century. Durkheim sometimes seemed to think sociology had shown that there was simply no such thing as an individual. If there was no individual, it would be hard to make sense of liberalism's concern for individual liberty. Durkheim's unrelenting emphasis on the priority of society over its members, on the coerciveness of social facts, and his hostility to using psychological and biological considerations in explaining social behavior can easily make one think that Durkheim must have been a political collectivist and authoritarian. The truth is quite otherwise.

Durkheim's conception of the imperative power of morality relied on his view of the connection between the *conscience collective* and the individual conscience. Unless so linked, an individual's moral views would not be moral views, but personal whims or tastes, which is echoed in the arguments employed by Charles Taylor in his recent work.[20] But, Durkheim never suggested that the *conscience collective* is or must be or ought to be employed on behalf of authoritarian or conservative moral sentiments. Modern morality regards the individual as sacred and treats his or her projects as demanding moral respect. The difference between Durkheim and other moral theorists lies in Durkheim's understanding of how morality is dictated, not in his view of its content. The principle of respect for persons that Kant enunciated and on which Dworkin bases his liberalism is the dictate, not of the noumenal self but of the *conscience collective*.

Mill and Durkheim did not see eye to eye on everything, but they agreed on more issues in social theory than one might expect. Mill agreed wholeheartedly that society had to be a felt unity if society was to exercise moral authority and governments were to be able to draw on that authority.[21] He quoted Coleridge to this effect when he wrote his famous essay on him, lifted the passage bodily for the *System of Logic,* and treated it as the intuitive statement of a fundamental truth of political sociology.[22] In his treatment of representative government, Mill anticipates Durkheim's enthusiasm for secondary associations as schools of public spirit, drops his father's suspicion of "sinister interests," and treats local government and local forms of organization as training grounds where individuals develop public spirit by performing public tasks.[23]

Even on the methodological front, Mill and Durkheim shared antipathies. Durkheim was fiercely hostile to any appeals to social contract. It was absurd to think society could be constructed by a contract between individuals. The very idea of a binding contract presupposed a social setting where *pacta servanda sunt* was already accepted. But utilitarians had always thought contract theory absurd. Mill agreed it might be useful to think of our duties to society in a quasi-contractual way; we receive the protection of society and owe a return for that help. Before conceding even as little as this, he insisted that no good purpose is served by explaining rights in terms of a social contract.[24]

Durkheim and Hobhouse wrote very different sociology, and had very different moral styles, but it would be hard to separate them on the issues that defined the "new liberal" position. Both agreed that the modern world's conviction of the importance of the individual was essentially a moral conviction. Both agreed that it involved individual liberty understood both positively and negatively. *La carrière ouverte aux talents* meant that individuals ought not to be shoe-horned into traditional occupations and statuses *and* that a positive effort was required to find them occupations in which their abilities would be employed to the advantage of society at large, and where the combined economic

and psychological rewards for conscientiously doing their job
would be and would be *felt* to be a just return for their contribution.[25] Unrestricted laissez-faire capitalism was a poor background for this ambition; the anomic distribution of success and
failure unrelated to merit and contribution that characterized a
regime of boom and slump was morally intolerable, and state
intervention was required to bring some order to it. On the other
hand, the individualism of their moral positions meant that neither thought the state should literally own and run any substantial portion of industry or commerce. Like many others of their
kind, Hobhouse and Durkheim were welfare state liberals, hard
to separate from moderate socialists, not wholly at odds with
Christian democracy, but entirely opposed to traditional conservatism or Marxian socialism.

II

Liberal views have always had a communitarian component, and
many liberals have launched their liberalism from a basis in
communitarian sociological theory. The so-called liberal-communitarian debate cannot be what its name implies, a debate
between liberals and communitarians. I suggest there are at least
four different debates, of which two are not liberal-
communitarian debates at all, although two might be so described, but not entirely perspicuously. Nothing hangs on the
labels offered here, but for present purposes we can distinguish
first, an argument about accounts of the self that could be called
"atomist-holist," second, an argument about sociological and
moral enquiry that could be called "holist-individualist," third,
an argument about substantial moral commitments that might
be called "collectivist-individualist," and lastly, an argument
about social, moral, and political change that might be called
"traditionalist-innovative." The last two will be glossed as a conflict between communitarianism and liberalism by those who
think liberalism must be both individualist and innovative and
that any invocation of communal values is necessarily collectivist
and traditionalist. On any account, only the first two issues are
genuinely dichotomous. The last two cry out for resolution by
"more or less." None of the four is so conceptually intertwined

with any other that there are relations of implication between a stand on one issue and another; but there are affinities stronger than merely accidental connection between them.[26]

As pointed out in the first section of this chapter, the relation between conceptions of the self and society on the one hand and substantial moral and political positions on the other is indeterminate. Most of us have views, however inchoate, about human nature and social structure, and we use them to justify our moral and political views. But it is an open question as to how far our views about social nature and human nature demand philosophical justification or imply a definite social theory. Certainly we have to believe that people possess whatever characteristics it takes if they are to be suited by the social values we are defending, socialist, conservative, or liberal as they may be. But we may hold views about what features people have and about what suits them without being able to say much about why they are in fact like that, let alone being able to say why they *must* be like that.

Thus it is not an objection to John Rawls's account of justice that we cannot imagine what it would be *like* to be one of the individuals placed behind the "veil of ignorance." An individual who knew neither where he or she was, nor what sex he or she was, nor what abilities or tastes he or she possessed would find it hard to give sense to being anyone in particular. "The rational actor" who features in theories of rational choice, and his cousin, "rational economic man" are in the same boat. Orthodox economic theory has prospered by adopting this austere notion of the rational actor, even though it is as hard to imagine what it would be like to *be* one as to imagine life behind Rawls's veil of ignorance. Empirical remoteness is not an objection to a theory. We make sense of economically rational man by treating his behaviour as a limit case, and we can make sense of the abstraction from our present identities required by Rawls's theory by treating that as a limit case of what we do when we set aside self-interest and consider what is fair. To attack Rawls's procedure we must show not that it embodies a counter-intuitive conception of personal identity, but that a procedure successful in economic analysis is unsuccessful in moral and political argument.

The claim that abstraction is misguided leads us to the second of our four kinds of argument, the defence of holistic approaches to social and moral theory. Here Michael Sandel's objections to Rawls's approach in *A Theory of Justice* bite as they do not when the subject is personal identity, though the fact is obscured by the way Sandel moves from criticisms of what he calls "deontological liberalism" to criticisms of liberalism *sans phrase*. The arguments for holistic and "unabstract" moral theory are many and varied, but the possibilities are readily illustrated. Bernard Williams's *Ethics and the Limits of Philosophy* criticizes Kant's search for a demonstratively true moral theory that is rationally rather than morally compelling, and binding on agents who share few of our human characteristics. Kant's error was not that he believed in a "noumenal self," but that he failed to see that ethics has a history, that moral considerations apply to embodied creatures with particular hopes, beliefs, and aspirations, and that ethical demands cannot provide reasons for action for creatures too radically different from ourselves. The message is that we must start *in media res*. We must recall the ways in which we differ from the members of other, earlier cultures; we must, in a manner of speaking, employ Aristotle's understanding of ethical argument without Aristotle's finite and local conception of human nature.[27]

One could call this "anti-abstractionism" rather than "holism," except that what underlies the attack on abstraction is the claim that individuals do not invent morality by legislation *ex nihilo* but by striking out from the commitments they find in the language and life of their own social setting. This idea reappears in the recent work of Charles Taylor, whose *Sources of the Self* is an ornament of communitarian liberalism.[28] Taylor recognizes the difference between holism as a methodological commitment and collectivism as an ideological commitment, and argues for the sanctity of the individual *via* a historical phenomenology whose form is Hegelian, though its exposition is blessedly less portentous than the master's own. Taylor claims that we must accept some form of liberalism; social and conceptual change, mutually interwoven, have made it true that our best reasoning yields a liberal account of the tasks of the individual and the social setting in which to pursue them.

Taylor's political allegiances are not implied in his methodology. The conservative or socialist may share Taylor's tastes in moral reasoning but that *reading the same record* teaches a different lesson. Political agreement can by the same token coexist with methodological disagreement. Durkheim's account of the division of labor in modern society and its moral implications is methodologically and politically close to Taylor's, for both believe that what is revealed by the appropriate moral inquiry is what it is that forms the moral ideals of the modern individual. Both eschew the state of nature inhabited by the heroes of *A Theory of Justice* and the passengers on Bruce Ackerman's spaceship.[29] That is how holistic liberals differ from contractarians.

One last point. The criticism to which *A Theory of Justice* was subjected inspired its author to further explanations and reformulations. Those reformulations move the discussion of the positive doctrines of *A Theory of Justice* onto the terrain occupied by Williams and Taylor. Rawls now says that the conception of the self implicit in the book is "political not metaphysical"; he did not commit himself to any theory of personal identity, but only to whatever would best illustrate the conception of justice to which "we" subscribe.[30] The idea that a theory of justice should seek an "overlapping consensus," again, is a recommendation especially apt to anyone working in the unabstract, holistic, contextual way Rawls's critics commend. To build liberalism on a presumption of ignorance about the good is in the abstract very odd advice. Decoded, it turns out to be a reminder not to think a liberal regime will be sustained in the contemporary United States by a mass commitment to the ideal character portrayed in Mill's essay *On Liberty*.

A certain briskness in pressing on may be excused by the need to leave methodology for substantial moral and political issues.[31] These are even more slippery than those already encountered, because the number of ways of being a moral and political collectivist is certainly large but probably indeterminate. I split off an analytical issue that preoccupies some theorists, most notably Charles Taylor, then take two collectivist claims, one for the importance of certain sorts of collective *entity*, the other for the superiority of goods provided and enjoyed in common to goods provided and enjoyed privately. I wish to inspect the claim that some goods are misunderstood if they are not understood as *essentially* collective. Taylor suggests as an example the experience of an audience listening to an orchestra giving a live performance, where the orchestra's consciousness of the audience and its response to the audience enter into the quality of what we experience. It is not the experience of an aggregate of individual goods.

What is at stake is obscure. Taylor contrasts the provision to a large number of people of some good that each values self-interestedly, such as garbage collection by the municipality of Montreal, and common goods like concert going. His invocation of self-interest clouds the issue. There is nothing unself-interested about listening to a concert. The distinction seems to lie between an instrumental and non-instrumental view of the presence of one's companions; six of us may pool resources to hire a taxi, while each wishing we could hire it for ourselves alone, and this is different from wishing to be part of an appreciative audience, where everyone else's presence and pleasure is an element in one's own. But if that is all that is at stake, a moral and political individualist may set as high a value as you like on such goods.[32]

We can now turn to positive collectivism. Its first element is the view that some collective entities, such as the state, or the local community, or the family, or the church are the proper objects of one's ultimate loyalty, and certain virtues such as submission to their authority, or a deep understanding of their purposes and natures, are the greatest virtues. Hegel understood the Greek *polis* to embody a claim of this sort. The individual was submerged in the political and social life of his own city, his virtue a matter of his contribution to the city's life. There was an immediate identity of individual and community.[33] The deeds of great individuals were the stuff of Greek poetry and history, but they were not following what we think of as individual moral projects; they were fulfilling roles already laid down by and implicit in the nature of the social or political whole to which they belonged.

The second element is the view that collectively provided and enjoyed benefits are to be esteemed more highly than individually enjoyed benefits. Public health care may be held to be intrinsically superior to private health care because one thing that unites the human race is the common hazard of ill health and eventual death. Because society exists to unite our resources in the face of the hazards of nature, common provision by a national health service is an apt expression of a determination to tackle a common fate. The individual receives medical attention, but also an assurance that he or she is valued by the community, that he or she will continue to be cared for regardless of his or her ability to pay, and so on. Those who provide help make just such morally reassuring gestures as well as providing treatment.

It is easy to see how the argument must proceed. The individualist who repudiates the argument from the value of a collective entity may insist that the state in particular should not be an object of loyalty, because it is violent, and thrives on the human disposition to find enemies. Or the individualist may agree that we owe it some non-instrumental loyalty, but argue that it is more often worth only an instrumental loyalty, to be rationally valued for its aid to non-state-related individual virtues, such as kindliness, imagination, and intellectual curiosity, and thus to other collective entities such as churches, universities, and clubs. The individualist who repudiates collective goods may in the extreme regard collective activities with a sort of fastidious loathing as Nietzsche sometimes seems to have done, or not see their point, as Edward Bellamy did not when he preferred piped music to concert going.[34] He may more moderately argue only that there is no *general* reason to prefer collective goods to private, individual goods. Its collective qualities may make concert going attractive in just the way it is, say, but the only question about health care is whether people get decent treatment at a non-exorbitant cost. Private insurance and national health services are to be compared strictly instrumentally.

Now we can broach the fourth of my dichotomies. Rarely will this be an all-or-nothing struggle between those who insist on the absolute subjection of the individual's moral judgment and imagination to the traditions embedded in his or her community's existing understanding of their moral and political condition, and those who insist on every individual's absolute obligation to think out afresh every item of their moral system. Nor is it necessary that an insistence on the role of tradition is tied to a community that bears that tradition. Still, most writers who insist on the role of tradition insist also on submission to the community's understanding of that tradition, or to community practices in which the tradition is embedded.

Enthusiasts for tradition change their minds, too. Alasdair MacIntyre now makes more of tradition's role as *tradition* than he does of its relation to any particular community that embodies it or to which it gives substance. The "Thomist tradition" in Catholic thought is more strongly recommended by its intellectual power and its ability to absorb the merits and correct the demerits of other systems of thought than by its embodiment in the community of the Catholic faithful.[35] This is a more intellectualist and less communitarian defence than one found in *After Virtue,* where it was their qualities as communities that commended Benedictine monasteries or Icelandic settlements of the Norse sagas.[36]

Ideals of moral and political innovation on the one hand and ideals of faithful submission to tradition on the other do not divide the terrain neatly, and do not align at all with positions on the nature of personal identity or on the sociological analysis of ethical systems. What is involved in moral innovation and inventiveness may be as cautiously spelled out as it was by Mill or as recklessly demanded as it was by Nietzsche; equally, submission may be demanded with all the blandishments of Edmund Burke or at the point of the sword by Hobbes. For Burke, submission flows gently from an acknowledgment of our sociability, for Hobbes the demand comes most urgently from our need to escape from a war of all against all.

The most dramatic demands for moral innovation, Nietzschean or Sartrean, are beset by paradox. They need as a background a general belief in the fixity and permanence of our identities that Taylor makes so much play with, but have to claim that it is an illusion we subscribe to out of cowardice. Anyone with a more moderate taste for change, a respect for innovation, and a taste for an expanded moral imagination, can agree that our selves are at any given moment more or less fixed. They need only observe that our present selves can always be the starting place for the process of becoming something else. If the method and prescription are not confused with each other, the most that ontological or methodological considerations can tell us is how hard it will be to behave in one way rather than another, or how to find out how hard it may be. Only if the prescriptions are smuggled back into the ontological or methodological considerations—as they often are—can ontological or methodological theses foreclose our moral and political options.[37]

The "communitarian liberals" on whose existence I have been insisting think that it is possible to draw on tradition but to innovate too. They are not radical innovators in the way Sartre and Nietzsche are, but they insist that human nature is open-ended, moral and political discoveries yet to be made, and the existence of some fixed points on the moral compass does not preclude the existence of open options. Liberal innovators will generally be interested in innovations in novel individual aspirations. They may not be interested only in these. Among the options not foreclosed are varieties of common good and kinds of association not yet widespread. Individual innovation is not limited to experiments in solitary or self-centered activities. The string quartet was an invention; so was the democratization of concert going, and both are "collective" activities. Nor are all calls for innovation calls for liberal innovation. *After Virtue* ends with an appeal to its readers to create a community not yet born but latent in the insights of Trotsky and St. Benedict.[38] When we distinguish between the upholders of tradition and enthusiasts for invention, we must remember that this dichotomy, too, will not lie neatly on top of the others we have been looking at.

III

My last task is to ask what one can sensibly say about the liberal community. I cannot deal with the view that the term "liberal" has become so degraded by political controversy, and so indeterminate in its application to Britain, Europe, and the United States that nothing at all can be said about liberalism, nor with the view that we must distinguish between a (good) narrowly circumscribed political theory and a (bad) larger theory of life. It is not that nothing can be said for and against these views, merely that it cannot be said here. My object is only to show how distinctively liberal aspirations may be defended by someone who has absorbed everything the Idealists usefully said against their predecessors, and everything Durkheim usefully said against earlier social theorists.

The theorist who has absorbed these things, but believes like Mill that mankind is so much a social animal that he needs to be given some breathing space, or who believes like Russell that unbridled laissez-faire won't do, but that *Brave New World* is worse, will want to argue for a non-stifling communitarianism. This is not the "dialogical" openness of Bruce Ackerman's liberal society, nor the rationalism of Jürgen Habermas's system.[39] It is a looser, less philosophically ambitious ideal, content to look for no more precision than the subject allows. For all that, it is more eager to proselytize than Richard Rorty's aphilosophical defence of "late capitalist bourgeois liberalism"—or whatever tongue in cheek characterization he presently prefers—and hopeful that it is possible to lurch less violently between the extremes of abstractness and localism than John Rawls's successive characterizations of his view of justice have done.

According to the communitarian claim, we each need *some* complicated emotional, moral, and intellectual support from those we live among. The liberal claim holds that this support should be support for an individuality that goes beyond the fulfillment of a social role. It has many aspects. One is what Charles Taylor labeled "expressivism," the German romantics' ideal of a distinctive character whose expression is akin to the expression of the artist's capacities and vision in his art. A second, more austere thought makes each of us responsible for our own existence, and indicates that we must be scrupulous about the burdens we impose on others. This is not just the desire to stay off the welfare rolls that animates so many neo-conservatives. It is a fastidiousness about demanding from others more than a fair share of their time, attention, and resources and a positive ambition to make one's own way in the world.

A third, more relaxed aspect says we are entitled to pursue the harmless pleasures and interests that the variety of human nature has handed out to us. Mill's essay *On Liberty* is a hymn to expressivism combined with a casual defence of the third view, and a strong dose of the second. Mill's critics have complained of his elitism, arguing that this first ideal demands too much from those who have nothing very individual to express. Yet, the third view bulks as large as any and is emphatically unelitist. Mill says that a man needs a warehouse full of clothes if he is to find a jacket that fits him, and how much more so a whole life. The image is not an elevated one, and is not supposed to be. Still, the point is not to defend or criticize *On Liberty*. It is to ask what the connection is between these ideas about the individual's moral and social fate and an appeal to community. The answer is self-evident. Unlike Rawls and Dworkin, the communitarian liberal insists that liberalism needs a community of liberals to flourish.

Writers who merely demand toleration for harmless activities do not demand as much as this. They will be content if they can secure the majority's indifference. But liberalism has historically demanded much more, for it is clear that reliance on indifference is dangerous. Toleration for the odd pleasures and weird pursuits of others must rest on something more secure than indifference, or it will not last the first outbreak of ill temper and dislike. Without a public opinion committed to the belief in a *right* to toleration, toleration is insecure. Dworkin's attempt to provide what is needed by invoking the state's duty of neutrality is not as unhelpful as it may seem, because he distinguishes so sharply between the *State's* duty to remain neutral between ideals of the good life and the liberty we all have as private persons to defend such ideals as and when we can. Still, something has to motivate the demand for neutrality, and it is hard to see what it can be other than a full blown defence of the liberal vision of what members of the same society owe one another by way both of assistance and forbearance.

Such a community would be united in defending the negative liberties of its members. The most ambitious vision of a liberal community would go further and hope for a community where we each tried to sustain the positive individuality of our fellow citizens. We might turn Charles Taylor's image of the orchestral concert to a different purpose. We shan't divide the audience from the performers, but will think of a community as simultaneously audience and orchestra. Each member contributes to the *Gesamtkunstwerk* that we hope we can make of our social interactions. For some purposes, deciding on the town drainage system, for example, this will be a hopelessly overblown and high falutin' image, but for many it will not. Such an image is not the property of liberals alone. The liberal character of any such vision comes in its taste for innovation (the orchestra does not stick to the standards but improvises, divides into chamber groups, experiments with mixtures of old and new, and so on). This terrain is one on which familiar political divisions are visible. The grimly Hobbesian variety of conservative thinks we have too little time left over from keeping *homo homini lupus* under control to engage in social play; the disciples of de Maistre try to beat us into a submissive recognition of our irreparable sinfulness; the Marxian doesn't repudiate the aspiration but insists that between us and its realization lies the long haul of proletarian revolution.

This is the aestheticist version of a communitarian liberalism, attractive to Schillerians and enthusiasts for the more romantic facets of Mill's work, and perhaps catching something of what Richard Rorty defends by celebration rather than cerebration.[40] This chapter is less concerned to argue for it than to place it in the intellectual landscape, along with the practicalities of the maintenance of a society in which persons are as far as possible self-maintaining, career-pursuing, self-respecting citizens, and the maintenance of whatever combination of barriers and positive support it takes to preserve toleration and the rule of law.

I return to three dry, familiar, central issues. The first is the relation of community to liberty in the economic realm. The role of private property is a central issue. Too rigid an insistence on the sanctity of property takes us back to the kind of contractarianism that Durkheim denounced as morally and explanatorily inadequate; too casual an acceptance of the need to curtail property rights for the sake of public benefits threatens security, innovation, and the motivation to be a self-maintaining member of society. To Durkheim it seemed obvious that property was both sacred and in need of collective supervision. An argument in favor of the style of argument offered here represents this as an argument *within* liberalism as well as one between liberals and others. The economic equality that Charles Taylor defends in *Sources of the Self* may or may not be as important to modern liberalism as he thinks, but it is clear why it may be, and clear how this view recapitulates the old view that the emancipation of property from traditional and familial constraints was once a needed spur to progress and individuality while the later manifestations of a regime of unfettered ownership and absolute freedom of contract threatened to produce new forms of slavery.

Because the liberal conception of community sees common provision as an aid to individual freedom, the defence of economic equality is not based on considerations of solidarity whether proletarian or other. Rather, a degree of economic equality and some collective control of the economy are nowadays required to ensure general access to education and employment, and to ensure that average wages will keep body and soul together and provide for a decent family life, especially if the family is to produce the kind of individual the liberal wants society to foster. Conversely, the importance of *la carrière ouverte aux talents* is enough to make the liberal prefer a market to a command economy, to prefer a private property-based economy to a collectivized economy, and to demand no more equality than is consistent with giving people an incentive to seek employment, and to better their condition. It would be foolish to pretend that this yields a determinate result. But if we cast the argument in this way, tensions within the liberal vision are clearly distinct from tensions between liberalism and alternatives. Different facets of individual freedom may come into conflict, may be accorded different degrees of priority on different occasions, but those "intra-liberal" arguments are different from arguments between defenders of individual liberty on the one hand and enthusiasts for unthinking integration on the other, and different again from arguments between defenders of individual liberty and enthusiasts for revolutionary solidarity, the historical mission of the proletariat, or whatever.

Second, the politics of communitarian liberalism unsurprisingly turn out to be the politics of a pluralistic representative democracy. The reasoning behind this has two facets. One lies in the considerations eloquently brought out by John Rawls. To exclude anyone from the process of decision making in their society is inconsistent with self-respect we seek for each individual. Nobody has a natural title to rule, and nobody can expect to rule except by way of the consent of his fellows. This is the

principled argument for representative democracy. According
to the pragmatic argument, the diversity, and changeability of
our ambitions, as well as our ordinary self-interested desires, can
hardly be accommodated in any other system for legitimating
our rulers. Both reasons depart quite drastically from some obvious alternatives, such as the thought that in the economic class
conflict the superior resources of time, money, and organizational skill enjoyed by the possessing classes will infallibly reduce
the laboring classes to poverty unless they can devise a political
system to counterbalance those advantages.

Third, consider the question of constitutional restraints upon
government and society. Within our framework, there will have
to be *de jure* or *de facto* some analogue to what Rawls secures by
talking of the priority of the right over the good. This is not the
place for a long discussion of the comparative merits of written
constitutions and unwritten conventions. The considerations
that lead to a stress on both individuality and community are
enshrined in famous essays in advocacy such as Locke's *Letter on
Toleration* and in famous documents such as the U.S. Constitution. The communitarian liberal is unlike John Rawls in setting
more store by social and political action than Rawls does. Where
Rawls sees politics in essentially *coercive* terms, and wishes to keep
government at bay in all sensitive areas, the communitarian can
see government as more creative, but still think that in many
areas—religious allegiance and sexual preference being two obvious ones—the community may properly foster a respect for
taking such matters seriously, but must not require any particular
choice from the individual.[41] It is otiose to repeat the demonstration that this will still allow a good deal of dissension internal
to liberal theory, while drawing a clear line between liberals and
their opponents and critics.

In conclusion, two things need to be said. First, this has been
an arms-length account of its subject matter. No one could take
an interest in the topic without some sympathy toward the intellectual and political leanings involved. Still, it has been the
intention of this chapter to lay out a view in such a way that it
can readily be assaulted. My own understanding of democracy,
for instance, is closer to the "domesticated class warfare" conception of democracy than to the liberal view. Second, it is time

to make good on my opening paragraph. Having denied the existence of any general "liberal-communitarian" conflict, I agreed that within communitarian forms of liberalism tensions arose that could be seen in that light. This section ought to have revealed how such a conflict arises. A viable community is cherished for the sake of the liberty and self-development of the individuals composing that community; yet, occasions must arise when the community must be preserved by measures that frustrate the freedom and self-development for which we value it. A nation at war curtails its subjects' civil liberties. A nation at peace may preserve the peace by means that violate an ideal right to free expression. Not all liberal societies would allow a Nazi procession to march through a Jewish neighborhood.[42] Affirmative action is an issue that reveals an inescapable tension between trying to establish a community outlook that is genuinely favorable to *la carrière ouverte aux talents* and a regard for the liberty of employers and employees to strike whatever bargains they can. These tensions are part of the messiness and incompleteness of political and social life, not to be deplored nor swept out of the way by conceptual cleverness. I claim that a good liberal can be a good communitarian, not that he will find life simple.

NOTES

1. I acknowledge with pleasure the criticism of the first version of this chapter that I received from Nancy Rosenblum, Martin Golding, and Ian Shapiro. I have paid them what I hope is the compliment of silently amending my text where they have shown it to be unclear, but I have not restructured my argument nor altered contentious claims. Our readers and I will learn more if I offer my critics a good fat target, than if I beat a premature retreat.

2. It thus follows Alan Ryan, "Communitarianism: The Good, The Bad, and The Muddly," *Dissent,* Summer 1989; and Charles Taylor, "Cross-Purposes: The Liberal Communitarian Debate" in *Liberalism and the Moral Life,* ed. Nancy Rosenblum, Cambridge, Harvard University Press, 1989, pp. 159–82. Supervising Dr Mimi Bick's D. Phil dissertation, on "The Liberal-Communitarian Debate: A Defense of Holistic Individualism," University of Oxford, 1987, taught me a great deal.

For an excellent overview of the subject, see Will Kymlicka, *Community, Individuality and Culture,* Oxford, Clarendon Press, 1989.

3. Taylor's view that "the heirs of Mill" have forgotten the legacy of Humboldt is, on this view, quite wrong. Rather, recent American liberals have forgotten the legacy of Mill. Taylor, "Cross-Purposes," p. 163.

4. But see L. A. Siedentop, "Two Liberal Traditions" in *The Idea of Freedom,* ed. Alan Ryan, Oxford, Oxford University Press, 1979, pp. 153–74, on the sociologically sophisticated character of French liberalism early in the nineteenth century too. The Oxford D. Phil dissertation of my former student Avital Simchoni, "The Social and Political Thought of the English Idealists," University of Oxford, 1980, is uniquely illuminating on the politics of the English Idealists.

5. John Stuart Mill, "Coleridge," in *The Collected Works of John Stuart Mill,* ed. John M. Robson, Toronto, University of Toronto Press, 1969, vol X, pp. 117–63.

6. L. T. Hobhouse, *Liberalism,* London, Longman, Green and Co, 1911; Stefan Collini, *Liberalism and Sociology,* Cambridge, Cambridge University Press, 1979.

7. Bernard Bosanquet, *The Philosophical Theory of the State,* London, Macmillan, 1958 [1899], pp. 59–62; T. H. Green, *The Principles of Political Obligation,* in *The Philosophical Works of Thomas Hill Green,* ed. R. L. Nettleship, London, Macmillan, 1894, vol II, pp. 522–23.

8. F. H. Bradley, *Ethical Studies,* Oxford, Oxford University Press, 1976 [1874], p. 39n.

9. John Stuart Mill, *An Examination of Sir William Hamilton's Philosophy,* in *The Collected Works of John Stuart Mill,* ed. John M. Robson, Toronto, University of Toronto Press, 1979, Vol IX, chs XII, XIII; Bradley, *Ethical Studies,* pp. 36–41.

10. Green, *Philosophical Works,* vol I, pp. 297–98.

11. Green, *Principles of Political Obligation,* pp. 512–1; conversely, Bosanquet, *Philosophical Theory of the State,* pp. 61–65, shows a more conservative Idealist agreeing with some of *On Liberty,* disagreeing with much else, and always claiming that Mill's foundations are flawed.

12. John Stuart Mill, *A System of Logic,* Book VI, ch ii, sec 3, in *The Collected Works of John Stuart Mill,* ed. John M. Robson, Toronto, University of Toronto Press, 1974, vol VIII, pp. 840–41.

13. John Stuart Mill, "Utilitarianism," in *The Collected Works,* vol X, pp. 215–16, 228, 238.

14. Mill, *Examination of Hamilton,* ch XXVI, p. 452.

15. Though it bulks larger than that for Michael Sandel, *Liberalism and the Limits of Justice,* Cambridge, Cambridge University Press, 1982, pp. 1–11.

16. As I argued in Alan Ryan, *The Philosophy of John Stuart Mill*, London, Macmillan, 1970, ch XIII.

17. Hobhouse, *Liberalism*, pp. 54–55; T. H. Green, "Liberal Legislation and Freedom of Contract," in *The Philosophical Works*, vol III, pp. 365–86.

18. Bertrand Russell, *The Principles of Social Reconstruction*, London, Allen and Unwin, 1916, pp. 11–13.

19. Green, *Principles of Political Obligation*, pp. 451–54.

20. Charles Taylor, *The Sources of the Self*, Cambridge, Harvard University Press, 1989, part I.

21. Mill, "Coleridge," pp. 134–36.

22. Mill, *System of Logic*, pp. 919–20.

23. John Stuart Mill, *Considerations on Representative Government*, in *The Collected Works of John Stuart Mill*, ed. John M. Robson, Toronto, Toronto University Press, 1977, vol XIX, pp. 535–39.

24. John Stuart Mill, *Liberty*, in *The Collected Works of John Stuart Mill*, ed. John M. Robson, Toronto, Toronto University Press, 1977, vol XVIII, p. 276.

25. Emile Durkheim, *Professional Ethics and Civic Morals*, London, Routledge and Kegan Paul, 1957; Steven Lukes, *Emile Durkheim*, London, Allen Lane, 1973, pp. 264–76.

26. The detachability of commitment from method leads Richard Rorty to recommend that we just dispense with philosophical "foundations"; even he admits that we shall find it helpful to engage in the philosophical "articulation" of our commitments. Richard Rorty, "The Priority of Democracy to Philosophy," in Richard Rorty, *Philosophical Papers*, Cambridge, Cambridge University Press, 1991, vol I, p. 178.

27. Bernard Williams, *Ethics and the Limits of Philosophy*, London, Fontana, 1985, ch 10.

28. Taylor, *Sources of the Self*, pp. 495ff.

29. Bruce Ackerman, *Social Justice in the Liberal State*, New Haven, Yale University Press, 1980, ch 2.

30. John Rawls, "A Theory of Justice, Political Not Metaphysical," *Philosophy and Public Affairs*, 14(1985), pp. 215–35.

31. Dr Bick relies on three paired distinctions, between "ontology and advocacy" as a general organizing distinction, and then between "atomists" and "holists" in ontology and between "individualists" and "collectivists" in advocacy. I am uneasy about ontology, so I stick with the distinction between methodological-cum-conceptual issues on the one hand and prescriptive issues on the other. There is, I hope, nothing much at stake here.

32. Taylor, "Cross-Purposes," p. 169.

33. G. W. F. Hegel, *The Philosophy of History,* New York, Dover Books, 1956, pp. 266–68.

34. Edward Bellamy, *Looking Backward,* New York, Modern Library, 1951, pp. 90–91.

35. Alasdair MacIntyre, *Three Rival Versions of Moral Enquiry,* London, Duckworth, 1990, makes much of authority, and thus of those who exercise it, but less of the community of the faithful who sustain that authority.

36. Alasdair MacIntyre, *After Virtue,* London, Duckworth, 1981, pp. 114–21.

37. Charles Taylor's "Neutrality in Political Science" argues that social, political, and psychological theories have a "value slope" because they point out the ways in which people get what they want; he agrees, of course, that the critic may say they want the wrong things, or get what they want at too high a price (in *The Philosophy of Social Explanation,* ed. Alan Ryan, Oxford, Oxford University Press, 1973, pp. 75–77).

38. MacIntyre, *After Virtue,* pp. 243–45.

39. Ackerman, *Social Justice in the Liberal State,* pp. 3–9; Jurgen Habermas, *Toward a Rational Society,* Boston, Beacon Press, 1970, ch 4; Richard Rorty, "Postmodernist Bourgeois Liberalism," in *Philosophical Papers,* vol I, pp. 197–202.

40. Richard Rorty, *Contingency, Irony, and Solidarity,* Cambridge, Cambridge University Press, 1988.

41. This would, in my view, allow an approach to abortion that was sensitive to moral convictions—for example, by forbidding abortion based on sex selection, by providing plenty of room for those who conscientiously objected to performing abortions to keep well away from the whole business—while allowing ready access to abortion in cases of hardship. It would not be very hospitable to treating the issue as a clash between a mother's right to choose and a foetus' right to life. Cf. Mary Ann Glendon, *Abortion and Divorce in Western Law,* Cambridge, Harvard University Press, 1987.

42. The British *Public Order Acts* allow the police to prevent marches and demonstrations that pose a threat to the peace, and allow local authorities to impose restrictions, amounting to prohibition, on such demonstrations in a way that U.S. courts would find unconstitutional. Geoffrey Robertson, *Freedom, The Individual and the Law,* Harmondsworth, Penguin Books, 1990, pp. 66–76.

5

COMMUNITIES AND THE LIBERAL COMMUNITY: SOME COMMENTS AND QUESTIONS

MARTIN P. GOLDING

Ryan's chapter, "The Liberal Community," encompasses a great deal of subject matter for discussion. Here, I can only briefly consider two rather substantial issues: first, the relation of theories of the self and methodologies of social inquiry to moral and political commitments; and second, the concept of community and constitutional restraints in the liberal community.

Ryan's general thesis suggests that the liberal-communitarian conflict has been misconceived; it is in fact "a figment of the imagination." He distinguishes four matters that have been involved. These are (1) a debate between atomist and holist theories of the self and (2) a debate over the methodology of social and moral inquiry, which divides along holistic (or anti-abstractionist) and individualist lines. For reasons to be mentioned shortly, Ryan maintains that these two matters are not communitarian-liberal debates at all. The metaphysics of the self and the methodology of inquiry are indeterminate with respect to liberalism versus communitarianism, he argues.

The other matters are (3) a debate between collectivist and

individualist substantive moral commitments; and finally (4) a debate between traditionalist and innovativist attitudes regarding social, moral, and political change. According to Ryan, these two issues "will be glossed as a conflict between communitarianism and liberalism by those who think liberalism must be both individualist and innovative and that any invocation of communal values is necessarily collectivist and traditionalist." As he suggests, the conflict on these issues may be a matter of degree rather than all-or-nothing.

In the last part of his chapter, Ryan develops, at "arms length" he says, the idea of a liberal community in terms of a liberalism that has absorbed, as it apparently can do without difficulty, both the Idealists' critique of the notion of the "punctual" self propounded by some older liberals and the Durkheimian critique of an atomistic social methodology. This notion of a liberal community, Ryan allows, is beset by various tensions internal to liberalism itself.

One striking thing about Ryan's chapter is that no definition is presented of the terms "liberalism" and "communitarianism." Perhaps it is too late in the day for that. We do get the suggestion that modern liberals are committed to an ideal of equality as well as to liberty, where "equality," I think, stands for some greater or lesser degree of equalization of welfare as well as for equality of civil rights. That there are tensions internal to liberalism is therefore hardly surprising. Yet, many varieties of communitarianism also accept these values, and their commitment to some equalization of welfare is expressed in their endorsement of the problematic idea of positive freedom. I suspect that as liberalism became welfare liberalism, it became more amenable to holistic notions of the self and holistic methodologies of social inquiry. Why should that be? What is the connection between these holisms and political ideology?

Ryan points to cases. T. H. Green has a holist theory of the self and is disposed toward the social program of liberalism; Durkheim has a holist methodology and is a political liberal; Mill, the paragon of liberalism if anyone is, leans toward the communitarian or holist side of the line in his emphasis on character and the "internal culture of the individual." Other examples of line-crossing are also given. Ryan's purpose in presenting information of this sort is to establish that the metaphysics of the self and individualist and holist approaches to social inquiry do not directly translate into a conflict between liberalism and communitarianism, and these theories are indeterminate with respect to liberal and communitarian ideologies. This claim can be interpreted to mean that the parties to the dispute are simply confused if they think that accounts of the nature of the self and social bonds provide a basis or foundation for their political ideologies and social programs; political ideologies and social programs are matters of *commitment,* to which all talk of foundations is entirely irrelevant.

But this understanding does not seem to be Ryan's own position. Nor does it represent the views of most, if not all, of the writers he mentions. These writers, liberal communitarians and communitarian or welfare liberals, if I may use these labels, are anxious to attack individualistic accounts of self and society. And they are anxious to do so not merely for the sake of theoretical accuracy but also because of the laissez-faire politics these individualistic accounts are taken to support: hence, for instance, T. H. Green's assault on the proposition that the object of action is always a pleasurable future state of the individual agent; hence, also, John Stuart Mill's move away from the "older liberalism" of his father, James, and Jeremy Bentham, partly because of dissatisfaction with their account of the human mind. As to the question of social bonds, one might conjecture that the trend toward socialism in the later editions of the *Principles of Political Economy* is accompanied by an increasingly holistic understanding of social inquiry. But whether this is so is a question that I leave to Ryan, who is an expert on the subject.

Ryan's own view is not that communitarianism and liberalism are the products of political leaps of faith. For he holds that the affinities between political commitments and theories of self and society are "stronger than merely accidental connection." Plainly, given the way in which each outlook may contain elements of the other, as Ryan shows to be possible, it will be difficult to detect *particular* disagreements on the nature of the self and social bonds. Still, I think that when we find disagreements between communitarians and liberals or insider disagreements, it remains plausible to look for theoretical disagreements down below. As much as Mill absorbs notions of the self and society held by communitarians, his views on these matters are not likely to be identical to T. H. Green's.

It is often said that communitarianism represents a kind of nostalgia for *Gemeinschaft,* nostalgia for a lost "sense of community," nostalgia for a past that was destroyed by the rampant individualism and materialism of industrial capitalism, that is, nostalgia for an imaginary past. I don't know to what extent, if any, Durkheim's distinction between organic and mechanical solidarity and his notion of anomic suicide were driven by any such nostalgia, though he was much concerned with social changes that had been taking place and did think that his notions of solidarity and anomie were morally significant. It cannot be doubted that Ferdinand Tonnies's holistic ideal-type concepts of *Gemeinschaft* and *Gesellschaft* are intended as methodological categories. But it should be noticed that these concepts had their origins in critical reflection on Hobbes's atomistic and individualistic approach to social bonds. Once it is seen, however, that actual social groups display various combinations of Gemeinschaft-like and Gesellschaft-like characteristics, the ground is cut from under the Hobbesian political philosophy. It is not just the methodologies alone that have moral and political significance, but also the results that they purportedly enable us to reach.

Can we locate where the non-accidental affinities between theories of self and methodologies of social bonds, on the one side, and political philosophies, on the other, get cashed out? It seems to me that we can, and it is precisely where the parties to the debate think it is, namely, in theories of the good, personal, and common. Holistic accounts of self and society forge a connection between the two that is more than instrumental, for they also are accounts of how we identify ourselves and therefore find fulfillment. This is why holism and communitarianism go hand in hand. Atomistic accounts of self and society supply a different view of the constitution of the self and undergird a different understanding of the relation between the personal and the common good. The truth probably lies somewhere between the extremes, so it is not surprising that we get liberal communitarians and communitarian or welfare liberals. It also would not be surprising if the positions should suffer from some degree of incoherence.

Ryan does not discuss in detail the notion that is so dear to the hearts of communitarians, namely, the idea of community. Despite his reference to such collective entities as churches, universities, and clubs, if I do not mistake the tenor of his exposition, he identifies the community with the state or with that amorphous thing, society-at-large, an identification that is found in the more authoritarian and corporatist varieties of communitarianism. But Ryan also alludes to the possibility of kinds of association that are not yet existent or widespread, and the same allusion is made regarding kinds of common good. These tantalizing allusions enable us to raise an important question about the character of Ryan's liberal community.

The fact is, there are many kinds of association and community and kinds of common good that already are existent and widespread, and they have implications for the communitarianism-liberalism debate. These implications are important if we accept Ryan's suggestion that the debate be glossed as a dispute between collectivist views of community and individualist views of liberalism.

Perhaps the most important implication is the bearing of the idea of community on the nature of common goods. If it is plausible to maintain, as I think it is in many cases, that each community has a good connected with it (much like a good that is inherent to a particular activity)—I use the word "good" here in a noncommendatory sense—then the question arises as to whether there are kinds of goods that are not simply reducible to the good or interest of each of its members. Part of the reason for wanting to make that reduction is the dread of hypostatizing groups, a dread that is typical of both methodological individualists (or atomists) and individualistic liberals. But the character of a community's good will depend on the kind of relation of community its members are in.

These points may be developed by noting that human beings stand to each other in many kinds of relation, which run the gamut from near to distant, short-term to long-term, affectionate to indifferent to antagonistic, voluntary to ascriptive, and so on, in various degrees and combinations. Out of the elements of these arrays of relations, we can construct many kinds of community. Each of us, I take it, is a member of more than one community and of communities of different kinds; for instance, close, affectionate, and long-term as well as impersonal and long-term.

Now if the members of a community should become involved in a conflict and a neutral third party were called on to resolve it, various processes would be available. These processes range from adjudication and arbitration at one end, through mediation and conciliation, to therapeutic integration at the other. In determining the most suitable process, the type of community will be a crucial consideration. For instance, in a labor-management dispute, the parties generally are in a relation that is partly antagonistic and of long-term dependency, and for such a conflict mediation usually will be the most suitable. There is a kind of common good here, one that requires a trade-off between interests, that the mediator will try to help the parties to achieve. In the case of a family dispute, to give one more example, the least suitable process appears to be that of adjudication, a win-or-lose affair. Adjudication tends to exacerbate family conflict and destroy any residual "sense of community." Adjudication, which is our courtroom method for resolving conflict, seems most suitable in disputes between strangers, which is in fact the way judges tend to regard the parties even if they are members of the same family. If there is a sort of community that holds between the stranger-litigants, the common good to which it is connected will have to be located elsewhere than in the adjudicatory zero-sum outcome.

The previous remarks are intended to present a way of generating models by which it may be explored whether the various kinds of common good are simply reducible to the personal good or interest of a community's members, and they strongly suggest, I think, that the question itself is too simplistic. And they also suggest that we need not go very far in order to acknowledge that many kinds of community and association already exist.

The importance of the latter point resides in the question of the degree of deference or protection that should be accorded to the various kinds of communities by the wider society or state.

This question goes to the heart of the issue of freedom of association and the public-private issue in some of its aspects. Some communitarians have stressed the significance of *communities* and of the institutions of community as providing the individual with a buffer against the state, while also noting that it is in communities, and not the wider society, that we live most of the time and find our fulfillment. These communitarians have stressed the importance of communities for which the terms "sense of community" and "loyalty" sit well: communities of mutual aid, such as the family, and communities of memory, with their distinctive traditions. These communities often call on their members to make great sacrifices and are quite different from Ryan's association of individuals who pool resources to to hire a taxi to get home. This sort of communitarian faces the difficulty of finding a common good that can serve as a basis for common action in a pluralistic society, a society of a plurality of communities and not just a melting pot of individuals who have been amalgamated into a unitary group.

A parallel problem seems to arise for the "constitution" of Ryan's "liberal community." Although he regards its politics as the politics of pluralistic representative democracy, which requires that no one be excluded from decision making, it is not clear how it will conceive a common good other than as one that is instrumental to the personal good of the represented parties. (It is also not clear to me how Ryan's remarks on the liberal's recognition of certain collective goods bear on the issue.) But the question I wish to raise now is how the communitarian liberal will deal with the various sorts of community whose existence we have acknowledged. Is this going to be another debate that is internal to liberalism itself and not a communitarian-liberal debate?

Recall that Mill defends experiments in living in terms of individual expression and self-development. My question is raised at the communal level: How much deference should the liberal community accord to community variety, to the different ethnic and religious communities, for instance, and to private associations, which Alexis de Tocqueville found to be so characteristic of America? The answer to this question is the true measure of a commitment to pluralism and diversity because, as stated earlier, most of us, even solitary academics, live out our lives not as lovable English eccentrics but rather in communities and associations, and find our identity and fulfillment in them. I am not sure how either individualistic and communitarian liberals sort themselves out on the matter, but I suspect that both kinds will be rather suspicious of particularistic communitarian claims. Communities bring people together, but they also divide them. Hence, in part, the requirement that the liberal state be neutral on ideals of the good life and secular with respect to religion. I cannot go into these topics now, except to say that secularism can easily lapse into a sectarianism of its own and it is impossible for the state to be neutral on many of the most divisive value questions. It is one thing for the American Bar Association to take a neutral stand on abortion and quite another for the state to do so.

It might be mentioned here that in consonance with Rousseau's conception of fraternity and its opposition to "exclusive attachments," in 1789 the French National Assembly dissolved all trade guilds, corporations, and unions; and in continuation of this antagonism the Code Pénal of 1810 criminally proscribed all associations, except mercantile partnerships, of more than twenty persons unless specifically authorized by the government. (This antagonistic attitude apparently impeded the development of company law in France.) In 1791 the National Assembly granted the Jews of France complete civic rights; but it exacted a price for emancipation. Deputy Clermont-Tonnere, a key proponent of Jewish rights, reassured the opposition that his intentions were to make Jews Frenchmen first, yet enable them to practice their religion: "The Jews should be denied everything as a nation but granted everything as individuals." In all this we find two elements, holistic fraternity or communitarianism and a push for assimilationist equality. I suppose that Ryan's liberal communitarians will reject both, but I am not sure about what they will accept. In a discussion of multiethnic societies, in a different context, Nathan Glazer points out that responses to that situation by a nation (for instance, on the questions of an official national language and bi-lingual education) will depend on whether it sees the different groups as remaining "permanent and distinct constituents of a federated society" or whether it sees these groups as "ideally integrating into, and eventually assimilating, into a common society."[1] Extending Glazer's remarks to the diversity of communities, I wonder how the liberal community sees itself, what its vision of society is.

In the United States these issues have come to a head in "freedom of association" cases. Two sorts of freedom of association have been recognized by the Supreme Court: intimate association and expressive association, as they have come to be called. The former is connected to the idea of privacy in one of its aspects and generally is restricted to familial relations, as in the contraception case, *Griswold v. Connecticut.*[2] Expressive association is tied to free speech, and it sees the freedom of association as an instrument to that right, as way of amplifying one's own microphone, so to speak. The classic case is *N.A.A.C.P. v. Alabama,* which is strewn with references to the freedom of association.[3] The underlying principle seems to be that whatever a person can pursue as an individual, freedom of association ensures that he can pursue it with others. This instrumentalist-individualist analysis, however, will not fit some of the kinds of community and association considered earlier.

A third kind of freedom of association claim, one whose constitutional status has been more problematic, is more germane to our subject. This is a claim to associational exclusivity, to the right of an association to preserve its integrity as it sees it, by excluding certain classes of individuals from membership in the group. (It is important to stress that the private realm whose existence is being asserted is a realm of *social* life and that the associational interest is not always reducible to individual interests taken distributively.) In a number of fairly recent cases the associational claim has been rejected on the grounds that the groups in question were not genuinely private or that a compelling state interest in eliminating sex-discrimination overrode the claim to exclusive association.[4] Thus far, Chief Justice Rehnquist has been most explicit in rejecting a general right to "social association" and in confining the freedom of association to expressive and intimate association, which is perhaps what should be expected from an individualist-instrumentalist liberal.

But there are many *dicta* that suggest a broader view. In the xenophobic phase that persisted after the First World War, the state of Nebraska enacted a statute that prohibited the teaching of foreign languages before the eighth grade. *Meyer v. Nebraska* invalidated this law as applied to non-public schools. One of the considerations adduced by the notorious Justice McReynolds in his opinion for the Court indicated that the state has no power to "foster a homogeneous people."[5] Very similar considerations are adduced by McReynolds, again writing for the Court, in *Pierce v. Society of Sisters,* which invalidated a state ban on all private education, a ban motivated by anti-Catholic sentiments.[6] These opinions are still cited as good law. Justice Brennan, for instance, cites the former in his dissent in *Bowen v. Gilliard,* where he states: "If we are far removed from the Platonic republic [where no intermediate forms of association stand between the individual and the State], it is because our commitment to diversity and decentralized human relationships has made us attentive to the danger of Government intrusion on private life."[7] Finally, let me quote some words from Justice Douglas's dissenting opinion in *Moose Lodge No. 107 v. Irvis:*

> My view of the First Amendment and the related guarantees of the Bill of Rights is that they create a zone of privacy which precludes government from interfering with private clubs or groups. The associational rights which our system honors permit all white, all black, all brown and all yellow clubs to be formed. They also permit all Catholic, all Jewish, or all agnostic clubs to be established. Government may not tell a man or woman who his or her associates must be.[8]

These considerations and statements, then, seem to evince a broader view of a general right of "social association" than that of the present Chief Justice's.

But shall we also say that it is liberal community's view? If we take the broader communitarian line that I have been suggesting, a line that emphasizes communities and not just the community, a line that recognizes the importance of cultural diversity, then where does the liberal community stand on the matter? What are the constitutional restraints in the liberal community? These questions are in desperate need of answers today.

NOTES

1. Nathan Glazer, "Individual Rights against Group Rights," in E. amenka and A. E.-S. Tay (eds.), *Human Rights* (Port Melbourne, Australia: Edward Arnold, 1978), p. 98. Glazer's analysis is concerned with affirmative action and quota programs in which an individual who did not personally suffer from discrimination becomes entitled to certain benefits because he or she is a member of a group that historically suffered discrimination.

2. 381 U.S. 479 (1965).

3. 357 U.S. 449 (1958).

4. *Roberts v. U.S. Jaycees,* 468 U.S. 609 (1984); *Rotary International v. Rotary Club,* 481 U.S. 537 (1987); *N.Y. State Club Assoc v. City of New York,* 487 U.S. 1 (1988).

5. 262 U.S. 390 (1923), at 402.

6. 286 U.S. 510 (1925).

7. 483 U.S. 587 (1987), at 632.

8. 407 U.S. 163 (1972), at 179.

6

THE DISHARMONY OF DEMOCRACY

AMY GUTMANN

Does it make sense to be disappointed about the condition of democratic politics in the United States yet enthusiastic about democratic developments elsewhere in the world? I cheer Czechoslovakia on as it moves in a democratic direction. At the same time, I criticize party politics, public education, commercial television, and the general condition of our politics. The problem does not appear to be privatization, capitalism, minority or majority tyranny, but something about democratic political activity itself. Presidential campaigns specialize in 10-second sound bites intended to short-circuit thinking about the issues. Supreme Court justices win confirmation by distancing themselves from their past record and refusing to discuss even the general principles that are likely to inform their future decisions. State governments extoll the rewards of gambling and encourage the opposite of any work ethic. The Pennsylvania State Lottery claims, "It pays to play every day." The New York State Lottery advertises the dreams of ordinary people to live like aristocrats. These are only a few among the many disappointments of American democracy.

Is disappointment in American democracy justifiable? After all, with all its flaws, the United States is far more successful than any country in Central or Eastern Europe judged by the democratic standards—universal suffrage, competitive elections, freedoms of speech, press, and association—that are invoked to commend political developments there. In this chapter, I wish to examine the ideal of democracy to determine the extent to which it justifies these judgments, and is itself justified. In Section 1, I begin with the ideal of populist democracy, which values popular rule and those conditions, such as universal suffrage, competitive elections, freedoms of political speech, press, and association, that are necessary to ensure popular rule over time. Populist democracy can explain our enthusiasm for developments abroad, and can also supply a credible basis for criticizing American politics whenever majorities threaten the conditions of popular rule (for example, by restricting political speech) or minorities restrict popular rule for reasons other than the preservation of democracy. But the ideal of populist democracy does not comprehend criticisms directed at the quality of democratic decisions and decision making.

Is it simply a mistake to expect an ideal of democracy to provide a perspective for criticizing the quality of democratic decisions and decision making? To answer this question, we must look beyond populist democracy. In Section 2, I evaluate a liberal critique of populist democracy, because liberalism provides a commonly used platform for criticizing the quality of democratic decisions and decision making. If the liberal platform is adequate for comprehending our criticisms of democracy in America, then we need not look further. The understanding of liberalism as protective of personal (or "negative") freedom, freedom from interference in one's personal life, does not capture our criticisms of democracy in America. The criticisms levelled by liberalism, at least on this "negative" understanding, apply with even greater force to the fledgling democracies of Central and Eastern Europe. These do not adequately account for our disappointments in the condition of democracy in America.

An ideal of democracy that is more inclusive and critical than both populist democracy and negative liberalism, what I call "deliberative democracy," can better account for our disappointments. In Section 3, I begin to develop the case for deliberative democracy by describing the ideal, and distinguishing it from both populist democracy and negative liberalism. The criticisms of democracy generated by populist democracy and negative liberalism are incomplete, because they are inadequate political ideals. Popular rule and personal freedom are valuable, but their value is better accounted for, and qualified by, deliberative democracy.

The tension between populist democracy and negative liberalism, the external disharmony of populist democracy, helps account for the project of deliberative democracy. Democracy is valuable not simply because it expresses the will of a majority of the people, but because it expresses and supports individual autonomy under conditions of interdependence. Deliberative democracy goes a long way toward reconciling democracy with liberalism by allying itself with autonomy, understood as self-determination through deliberation. Deliberative democracy is committed to expressing and supporting the autonomy of all persons in collective decision making. This commitment makes sense of our dissatisfactions with American democracy, better sense than either populist democracy or liberalism can.

Americans, as Ronald Dworkin reminds us, have typically understood democracy to embrace more liberal values than populist democracy admits.[1] But the content of this understanding is unclear. It is not obvious how best to reconcile democracy and liberalism, or whether a complete reconciliation is possible. Section 4 appraises the success of deliberative democracy in reconciling democracy with liberalism. The reconciliation depends on the inclusiveness of autonomy, on autonomy embracing distinctively liberal as well as democratic values. The price of reconciliation is disharmony among the goods internal to democracy. Well-informed and reasonable people dissent from collective judgments that arise from the exercise of everyone's political freedom. This disharmony, unlike that of populist democracy and the disharmony that Samuel Huntington associates with American democracy, is morally inescapable.[2]

1

The outcry for democracy in Eastern Europe lends support to the view that democracy is valued first and foremost in opposition to political rule by a self-appointed, unaccountable, and tyrannical minority. Movements for democracy there and around the world demand policies and institutions that secure freedom of speech, press, and association, freedom from arbitrary arrest, the right to organize oppositional parties, and the right to vote in genuinely competitive elections. These demands form the core of a common ideal of democracy, "populist democracy" or simply "democracy." Populist democracy is a political system of popular rule that places no constraints on the substance of popularly supported outcomes *except* those that are required by the democratic procedure of popular rule itself.[3] These exceptions, political freedoms, for example, are as essential to the theoretical ideal of populist democracy as they are to democratic practice.

What outcomes are required by the ideal of popular rule itself? Few if democracy is understood, along Schumpeterian lines, as a *minimalist procedure* with little or no substantive value, "that institutional arrangement for arriving at political decisions in which individuals acquire the power to decide by means of a competitive struggle for the people's vote."[4] By Schumpeter's own standards, Russia today is democratic and Stalinist Russia would have been democratic if members of the Communist Party could vote. Insisting on *procedural minimalism* entails forsaking democracy as an ideal.[5] The call for democratic reforms in the former Soviet Union today becomes meaningless. Our enthusiasm for the democratization of Czechoslovakia makes little more sense. From Schumpeter's definition to the conclusion that only a fool or a fanatic would sacrifice any significant values to democracy is a small step. But the conclusion says less about the limited value of democracy than about the inadequacy of a minimalist understanding of democracy as *merely* a political procedure. The value of democracy is limited, but its limits can only be understood in light of a more robust and substantive understanding of democracy.

Contemporary political theorists who see democracy as a political procedure move miles away from minimalism, toward an *ideal* of democracy as popular rule. Insisting that democracy be understood as a political *procedure* of popular rule, Brian Barry explicitly builds the following constraints into democracy:

(1) free speech, press, and association "necessary for the formation, expression, and aggregation of political preferences,"[6]

(2) the rule of law, as contrasted to the arbitrary will of public officials,
(3) formal voting equality, but not equality of actual influence on outcomes. "If there are two constituencies each of which returns one representative, the value of a vote is obviously unequal if one constituency contains more votes than another."[7]

Barry does not add inclusive enfranchisement as a constraint on grounds that the ideal of popular rule itself cannot determine what territory, or who, should constitute a polity when political boundaries are disputed.[8] Accepting this important limitation, we can still, following Robert Dahl, include a fourth constraint on outcomes that is presumed by populist democracy *under those conditions where boundaries are not disputed:*

(4) extension of citizenship to "all adult members of the association except transients and persons proved to be mentally defective."[9]

This fourth constraint avoids the absurdity of calling Stalinist Russia or the former Soviet Union today democratic. At the same time, this standard of inclusiveness does not pretend to determine the boundaries of a democratic Soviet Union, Czechoslovakia, or any other democracy in the face of competing nationalist claims to sovereignty.

These four constraints are outcomes required by democracy understood as an ideal of popular rule, but they are not guaranteed by any procedure of popular rule.[10] A practically inevitable tension exists between any actual procedure of popular rule and the corresponding *ideal* of populist democracy. The ideal requires outcomes—unmanipulated political preferences, the rule of law, formal voting equality, and inclusive citizenship—that can, and do, conflict with the actual popular will as revealed by any procedure designed for the sake of popular rule.

In cases of conflict, some democrats say that the popular will is not a democratic will, even by populist standards. They draw attention to the substance of the democratic ideal. And they are, strictly speaking, correct to do so. But this way of speaking may also be misleading. Whichever way democrats resolve the conflict between popular rule and its conditions, democratic losses remain. Democrats value popular rule. Their ideal is a political community in which all adults have public standing as political equals to share in shaping the future of their society. Any constraints on popular rule constitute losses even if, all things considered, the losses should be taken. In light of the conflict, democrats must concede either that some degree of unpopular rule, such as judicial review, is justified for the sake of achieving outcomes unsupported by popular will, or that a truly democratic will, a popular will that supports the outcomes that make it democratic, is unlikely to be fully realized, or both.

Populist democracy is not paradoxical in the sense famously claimed by Richard Wollheim, but it is nonetheless paradoxical.[11] No paradox is generated by my voting against deer hunting because I think a ban is the best alternative available, and my accepting hunting as the policy that should be implemented once a majority chooses it, using legitimate democratic procedures. After all is said and done, I may still believe the majority wrong, but they have a right to implement the policy so long as it does not violate the aforementioned conditions of democracy, those necessary for sustaining popular rule. Here there is no paradox, just a difference between what I believe constitutes a correct policy on its merits, and what I believe is legitimate for a democratic community to implement in light of the results of democratic procedures. The paradox of populist democracy lies elsewhere, in the tension between popular will and the conditions of maintaining popular will over time. When a majority chooses to restrict freedom of political speech by punishing symbolic speech (flag burning, for example), populist democrats are in a bind. On the one hand, they should oppose the restrictions on free speech because the popular will in this case is undemocratic. It is inconsistent with the maintenance of popular will. On the other hand, they should also support the restrictions on free speech because they are also undemocratic; any attempt by a minority to overturn the restrictions is a genuine restriction on popular will at this time, and therefore undemocratic.

Some democratic theorists who otherwise accept the populist definition of democracy resist acknowledging this paradox by enlisting two strategies, reminiscent of Rousseau, for supposedly

transcending the tension between popular rule and its preconditions. One strategy is theoretical, the other practical. The first
consists in distinguishing popular will from the will of the majority, where popular will roughly corresponds to Rousseau's
general will, and the will of the majority to Rousseau's will of
all. In those instances where the outcomes dictated by democratic
standards are opposed by majority will, the Rousseauian concludes that the people were asking the wrong question. Instead
of considering the common good, they were thinking of their
own interest. Rousseauians conclude that the collective will so
revealed is not properly speaking a popular or democratic will
at all.

The questions people ask when voting should influence how
we interpret the results. But we cannot assume that whenever a
majority supports a democratically prohibited outcome, the
source of the problem is asking the wrong question. Majorities
may sometimes give the wrong answer to the right question,
believing that the common good requires restrictions on freedom
of speech, press, and association that violate the conditions of
democracy.

Whenever popular rule supports an outcome that violates
democratic standards, populist democracy is paradoxical. Democrats who deny the paradox often make a false inference from
a true definition: Because a popular will is not necessarily a
democratic will, nothing of democratic value is sacrificed when
popular will is constrained for the sake of achieving democratically required outcomes. The sacrifice in popular rule is a significant democratic loss, even if it is a loss that the democratic
ideal itself justifies, or at least excuses. The justification does not
obliterate the loss. Populist democrats who defend judicial review
need not, and should not, do so unambivalently. By the standards
of populist democracy, our society would be better were judicial
review unnecessary.

The second strategy for avoiding the paradox challenges the
practical necessity of judicial review and other constraints on
popular rule. This does not come naturally to Americans, but
should be taken seriously. Judging by democratic standards,
many countries have done as well, or almost as well, without

judicial review as the United States has done with it. Jeremy Waldron points out that alternatives to judicial review—checks and balances, separation of powers—are prominent even in the American tradition.[12] Rather than avoiding the paradox of populist democracy, however, these Madisonian institutions are themselves means of constraining popular rule, and justifying the constraint by invoking other values, such as personal freedom, that are not adequately safeguarded by populist democracy.

What about the non-institutional alternative, which John Stuart Mill emphasized, of educating public opinion to respect individual liberty?[13] Waldron points out that the success of Mill's project would permit democracy to do without constraints on popular rule. It would. But neither Mill nor anyone else has yet succeeded in educating public opinion continually to respect the conditions of democracy, and to imagine success in the foreseeable future is hard. The internal disharmony in populist democracy, the source of the paradox, remains.

To recognize this internal disharmony is not to recommend some other form of government. It need not even entail recommending institutional constraints on popular will, unless the minority in control of the constraining institutions is predictably more reliable than the majority. The internal disharmony of democracy helps explain why democrats, although reluctant to constrain popular will, ambivalently support constraints when they appear necessary, for example, to protect political speech. The ambivalence stems not only from the paradox but also from the *substantive aspiration* of the democratic ideal, although it makes no guarantees that the people can govern themselves as a "self-determining" political community without constraint. Popular rule, not free speech, is the core value of populist democracy. Democracy has multiple defenses. Where majority rule would not honor free speech, for example, democrats can consistently support judicial review or other institutional constraints. But none escapes the paradox so long as any constraint on popular will is necessary to preserve popular will over time.

Finding reasonable ways of defending populist democracy is easier than deciding just how to defend it. In most situations of possible conflict between popular will and its conditions, democrats are divided about the value of judicial review, other institutional constraints, public education, procedural reforms, or prevailing popular will as the best way of honoring the democratic ideal. Some democrats ally themselves with liberals on particular issues, others with conservatives. Disagreements among democrats and their conflicting alliances over the issue of whether to regulate hard-core pornography, for example, reflect the paradox of populist democracy. If rule by the people is the ideal, and something along the lines we have considered previously constitutes the requirements of that rule, then democracy both defends and criticizes popular rule where the majority would choose to violate the conditions of its own legitimacy. Populist democracy lacks a standard by which to resolve this contradiction among its own values. Deliberative democracy, I argue later, avoids this paradox.

2

Liberalism, on a common understanding, also avoids this paradox, and obviously so. Like populist democracy, negative liberalism is a political doctrine, not a complete philosophy of life. Whereas democracy's overriding value is popular rule, liberalism's overriding aim is "to secure the political conditions that are necessary for the exercise of personal freedom."[14] I call this conception "negative liberalism" because it emphasizes the value of freedom from interference. (Positive liberalism, by contrast, also values the freedom of individuals to govern themselves in society, which is not strictly speaking a negative liberty at all.) Whenever I speak simply of liberalism, I refer to negative liberalism as Judith Shklar characterizes it: "Apart from prohibiting interference with the freedom of others, liberalism does not have any particular positive doctrines about how people are to conduct their lives or what personal choices they are to make."[15] Neither does negative liberalism have any particular positive doctrine about how people should make collective decisions.

Liberalism prohibits collective choices from interfering with personal freedom. Democracy promises that they reflect popular will. Two competing ends cannot simultaneously be maximized.

Democracy and liberalism part company when collective choices threaten to interfere with personal freedom, or personal freedom threatens to interfere with collective choice.[16]

The tension is easily overlooked because it is intermittent, for two reasons that explain the convergence of liberal and democratic ideals. Liberalism is committed to protecting not all freedoms but personal freedom. Liberalism is therefore at peace with popularly sanctioned constraints on non-personal freedoms. Corporate freedom, for example, is not absolutely protected by liberalism. Protection of corporate freedom is a matter of public policy, not moral principle, and therefore up to democracy to decide.[17] Second, democracy is committed not only to processes that reflect popular will but also to outcomes that secure popular will. Those outcomes—including freedoms of speech, press, and association necessary for the formation, expression, and aggregation of political preferences, hereafter called "political freedoms"—are also among the personal freedoms that liberalism is committed to protecting. Democracy therefore defends freedom of *political* speech, press, and association, which are necessary conditions of popular rule. But liberalism gives priority to freedom of speech, press, and association whether or not these freedoms are conditions of popular rule. Negative liberalism avoids the paradox of populist democracy by subordinating the value of popular rule to that of personal freedom. Personal freedoms have priority for liberalism because they are personal freedoms, not because they are conditions of democracy. In politics, where results count more than reasons, negative liberalism and populist democracy are often allies in supporting those freedoms that are necessary conditions of popular rule.

When confronted with a conflict between popular rule and those personal freedoms that are not part of political freedom, negative liberalism and populist democracy diverge in results as well as reasons.[18] Populist democracy cedes to communities the authority to determine whether and how to regulate personal freedom so as to carry out popularly sanctioned policies. A paradigm case is hard-core pornography that intends no political message. The particular personal freedom at issue is, at least arguably, unnecessary for the formation, expression, or aggre-

gation of political preferences. Democrats have a principled reason to defend popularly sanctioned restrictions on hard-core
pornography that liberals have a principled reason to oppose.
Democrats may of course oppose such restrictions on grounds
that restrictive legislation gives government an opening to regulate pornographic speech that is part of political freedom. But
the slippery slope argument will not always apply, or suffice as
a reason to restrict popular will. In cases where the government
can be trusted to respect the democratically mandated line or
where the risk of over-reach is small, democrats and liberals will
be at loggerheads, disputing the value of community standards
versus free speech, where community standards are articulated
by a democratic decision that finds the speech in question harmful to the interests of members of the community.

The most illuminating cases are those where the finding that
the speech may harm the interests of members of a community
is credible, where restricting speech does not clearly interfere
with political freedom, and where available evidence and argument are insufficient to resolve the disagreement between
democrats and liberals. Consider a state legislature that passes
a law against "harassment by personal vilification," modelled on
a rule recently passed by Stanford University. The law restricts
speech that (1) is "intended to insult or stigmatize an individual
or a small number of individuals on the basis of their sex, race,
color, handicap, religious, sexual orientation, or national and
ethnic origin"; (2) is addressed "directly to the individual or
individuals whom it insults or stigmatizes"; and (3) "make[s] use
of 'fighting words' or non-verbal symbols," defined as words or
pictures that "are commonly understood to convey direct and
visceral hatred or contempt for human beings."[19] Should this be
upheld?

Cass Sunstein has made a strong case that it should, comparing
the law to a ban on obscene telephone calls, which restricts personal freedom but clearly does not restrict political freedom.[20]
Suppose enough evidence and argument supports a credible
democratic defense of the harassment legislation, but not
enough to answer all reasonable doubts. Placing the burden of
proof on restricting popular will leads a democrat in doubt to
defend the legislation, whereas a liberal in doubt is likely to

oppose it because liberalism places the burden on restricting personal freedom. Democrats and liberals can agree about what is at stake while disagreeing both in principle and practice about the proper resolution.

Populist democracy's uneasy alliance with negative liberalism therefore does not depend on its embracing the corrupted understanding of individual freedom famously elaborated by Isaiah Berlin.[21] On that understanding, which Berlin associates with the defense of democracy, positive freedom is identified with self-mastery, and is used to justify an authority exercising control over individuals in the name of their "higher" or "true" self. Populist democracy does not claim that popular will constitutes a higher or truer self that defines people's best interests. It claims rather that the most legitimate way to govern collective life is by popular rule, granting that the outcome will sometimes be mistaken, so long as it does not violate the conditions of popular rule itself. Popular rule is the most legitimate way to govern a society because other ways, in addition to making mistakes, deny adults equal political standing in making the laws, or choosing and holding accountable the representatives who make the laws that govern their collective life.[22]

Without claiming that it constitutes a higher form of freedom or that it elevates individuals to some higher level of being, democracy can oppose the absolute priority that liberalism attaches to personal freedom over popular rule. In the face of reasonable disagreement over the value of personal freedom relative to other goods, democrats say that majorities rather than minorities should decide. In situations of reasonable disagreement, democrats give more weight to the legitimacy of political decisions, the moral matter of who should decide and how, than to their justification, the moral matter of what should be decided on the merits.[23]

Liberals wonder why democrats place so much value on popular rule when in practice each of us has so little chance of affecting the outcome of any decision. Would reasonable people not choose an expanded realm of personal freedom instead of one mere voice, or vote, among so many in making decisions? At most, only a small minority of people relishes political activity; many people choose not even to vote. In practice, for a majority of people, the democratic choice constitutes a loss of personal freedom with no corresponding gain, indeed perhaps yet another loss in the unwelcome pressure to engage in politics for the sake of protecting one's personal freedom.

Populist democrats have two closely related responses. First, they argue that liberals misconstrue the policy trade-off as between personal freedom and political voice. The trade-off on the policy level is between personal freedom and other social goods that are often more valuable to individuals, for example, the value of being protected by seat belts or prescription drugs. Populist democracy does not offer a theoretical settlement of the substantive policy issue of whether personal freedom is more or less valuable than such protections, and rightly so. What it offers, the democrat's second response, is a procedure to decide issues that by their very nature must be collectively decided. In controversial cases where freedoms essential to personal dignity are not at stake, most people have good reason to rely on popular rule. The liberal alternative on the procedural level, democrats argue, is worse; it entails alienating authority to decide controversial issues from a majority of competent adults to a minority. If the right outcome is uncertain, moral competence is broadly distributed, and most citizens are affected by the decision, why should the opinion of a minority rule?

Liberals may reply that some minorities, judges, for example, are more likely by virtue of their institutional roles to make decisions on the basis of principle rather than preference.[24] While agreeing that principle is the proper basis, at least where personal freedom is at stake, democrats dispute the claim that judges make better principled decisions than democratically elected legislators.[25] The historical record of judicial review in the United States stands open to this democratic challenge.

Populist democrats cannot dispute, however, that majoritarian decision making legitimates the sacrifice of personal freedom to popular will, a sacrifice that liberalism on principle opposes. Democrats cannot rely on liberalism's lack of a general procedural alternative to popular rule to justify, or even legitimate, the sacrifice of personal freedom to popular rule.

That reasonable people disagree on the merits of a case may be grounds for deferring to popular rule, but only if we are also satisfied that the merits of the case have been thoroughly and intelligently considered by the public and their representatives. If the democratic process, or democratic society more generally, is unconducive to deliberation, then it is doubtful that popular rule has as much to recommend it as populist democrats claim. Granted that moral competence, at least the capacity for moral competence, is broadly distributed, it is surely reasonable to ask: What's so great about popular rule if the people do not deliberate? Perhaps minority rule is a worse alternative, but are these our only options? Liberals are not committed to defending minority rule. They are committed to defending personal freedom in the face of either minority or majority tyranny. Liberals lack a procedural alternative. But in the face of restrictions on personal freedom, they pose an important challenge to populist democracy: Why should we give absolute priority to popular rule without any assurances that democracy lives up to a standard that would render popular rule more than an assertion of will?

Liberalism, Shklar argues, is "monogamously, faithfully, and permanently married to democracy—but it is a marriage of convenience."[26] The marriage is convenient because negative liberalism values populist democracy only insofar as it protects personal freedom, particularly freedom from an oppressive state. The marriage endures because neither liberalism nor democracy can find a more compatible political partner.

What this otherwise apt metaphor misses are the marital disputes over the terms of the contract. Liberal democratic politics is about the protection of personal freedom *and* the carrying out of popular will. When the two ends conflict, the partners dispute the terms of the contract, making the marriage appear more like a tempestuous affair. Alternatively, over the course of time, adapting themselves to the absence of more acceptable partners, they may set aside their differences and seek a more fully compatible identity. Leaving the marital metaphor behind, I now turn to assessing the attempt at reconciliation on the part of democracy, the development of an ideal of deliberative democracy.

3

Populist democracy lacks the resources to resolve the tension between popular rule and its conditions. Its principled commitment to popular rule entails the paradox of restricting popular will in order to defend it. Negative liberalism unjustifiably resolves the tension by denying the value of popular rule except as an instrument for securing negative liberty. Populist democracy places too few qualifications on the value of popular rule; negative liberalism places too many. Deliberative democracy, a more demanding and inclusive ideal, offers a way of resolving the tension both within populist democracy and between it and negative liberalism. It does so not by avoiding hard choices or assuming that democracy includes everything that is worth valuing, but rather by pushing the defense of democracy a step further and offering an answer to the question unposed by populism, "Why should we value popular will?" and to the question unposed by negative liberalism, "Why should we value personal freedom?"

Deliberative democracy offers the answer that we value popular will and personal freedom to the extent that the exercise of popular will and personal freedom reflect or express the autonomy of people, where autonomy is understood as self-government, the willingness and ability to shape one's private or public life through deliberation, informed reflection, evaluation, and persuasion that allies rhetoric to reason. Deliberative democracy uses popular rule to express and support the autonomy of all. Popular rule is valued as a means of expressing and supporting the autonomy of persons, their ability to deliberate together on matters of public concern and to abide by the results of their deliberations.

An autonomous person is self-governing where self-government requires that people engage in deliberation in shaping the many dimensions of their lives, personal and political. Whereas populist democracy assumes that the expression of popular will is an overriding good, deliberative democracy argues that the primary value of popular rule lies in its encouragement or expression of the broadest possible degree of public deliberation, not in its mere expression of popular will. Popular rule

is less valuable to the extent that it is unaccompanied by deliberation. Whereas negative liberalism assumes that freedom from
interference is the highest public good, deliberative democracy
argues that personal freedom, like political freedom, increases
in value to the extent that its exercise reflects or encourages
autonomy, our ability to shape our lives in accordance with well-
considered judgments.

Unlike populism and negative liberalism, deliberative democracy articulates a compelling conception of people as self-
governing, who reflect, evaluate, and decide issues on the basis
of the broad range of relevant considerations that are available
for their consideration in a society where every adult is treated
as an autonomous person, and thereby granted political standing
as an equal citizen. Accompanying this conception is an ideal of
politics where people routinely relate to one another not merely
by asserting their will or fighting for their predetermined interests, but by influencing each other through the publicly valued
use of reasoned argument, evidence, evaluation, and persuasion
that enlists reasons in its cause. In a deliberative democracy,
people collectively shape their own politics through persuasive
argument. Persuasion is of course a form of power; it is the most
defensible form of *political* power because it is the most consistent
with respecting the autonomy of persons, their capacity for self-
government.[27]

Autonomy is not self-sufficiency. Autonomy, as Arthur Kuflik
points out, "is perfectly compatible with a 'division of moral
labor.' . . . Indeed, in a complex world it is difficult to believe that
anyone is always the best judge of every possible matter."[28] Autonomy is compatible with *delegating* authority over one's life,
but not with *alienating* it. Democratic citizens may delegate many
policy decisions to politicians and other officials. Not only is
autonomy consistent with our delegating many important matters to people who, for a variety of reasons, are in a better
position to judge the merits of those matters, autonomy may
even *require* delegation of some matters to them. We must, however, always be able to justify our decision to delegate or not. As
importantly, we must be prepared to hold accountable those to
whom we delegate. Failures to hold officials accountable for the
decisions they make in our name or refusals to be held account-

able violate a primary political demand of autonomy and, by extension, of deliberative democracy. Recurrent failures of accountability should lead us to question whether our political and social institutions are adequate for supporting autonomy.

An autonomous person wants to evaluate choices in life, including the choice of delegating decisions, and live life in accordance with these evaluations. The desire to live such a life is a matter of autonomous character; the ability is also a matter of information, education, will power, and good fortune. By its very nature, autonomy cannot be given to people; it must be claimed. But political practices and institutions can encourage or discourage autonomy, render autonomy impossible or within our grasp. A deliberative democracy supports those political practices and institutions that encourage autonomy and put it within reach of every educable adult.

The challenge to deliberative democracy from the more common political positions we have considered might go as follows: That democracy can express popular will or suppress individual freedom is obvious. But how can any form of democracy claim to express and support the autonomy of persons? Critics understandably suspect that calling democracy deliberative is a smoke screen for restricting *individual* freedom. Democracy limits the opportunity of all of us to live under laws of our own individual choosing. In this sense, democracy seems to undermine rather than express or support autonomy. If autonomy is understood individualistically, as all individuals legislating by themselves for themselves, then democracy's relation to autonomy is at best instrumental. The most limited form of government, one that maximized the number of decisions left to individual choice, might do better.

Autonomy, however, has a broader, more political dimension that is lost by taking the social context of individual choice for granted, and focusing only on the control individuals have over those life choices that they can make by themselves for themselves, free from interference. Many of the most important, along with the most trivial, of our life choices are influenced and constrained by social context, over which political authority has the greatest control. If we are excluded from that authority, then we lack autonomy in an important dimension of our lives.

Part of freedom, especially as experienced by people who are deprived of it, is the freedom to share in shaping one's political context. In a representative democracy, this aspect of autonomy entails the political freedoms necessary to share as an equal in electing one's representatives and in holding them and other officials accountable for their actions. To limit these political freedoms is to limit the scope of moral autonomy.[29] It is also to deprive people of dignity as self-governing beings.

The political dimension of autonomy requires that officials who make decisions that influence and constrain the choices of citizens are accountable to us. Because my individual choices are influenced and constrained by political choices, autonomy in the realm of individual choice presupposes autonomy in the political realm, which in turn presupposes democracy. Democracy provides all adults with a share in political authority, thereby encouraging us to exercise our autonomy by holding officials accountable, and it also expresses our autonomy by publicly recognizing our political standing.

Because autonomy requires that we deliberate, it presupposes a distinctive kind of democracy, a system of popular rule that encourages citizens to think about political decisions. Accountability, not direct participation, is the key to deliberative democracy. Accountability is a form of active political engagement, but it does not require continual and direct involvement in politics; it is fully compatible with the division of labor between professional politicians and citizens that is characteristic of representative democracy. Whereas participatory democracy points toward a polity in which all actively participate in making decisions, deliberative democracy takes account of the burden of political action and the advantages of a division of labor. Deliberative democracy insists on ongoing accountability, not direct participation in politics. Those who act on our behalf must be accountable to us, and we must hold them to account. The challenge posed by deliberative democracy to American politics is to create institutions and cultivate a political culture that encourages political understanding, interest, and discussion that accountability demands.

Although an autonomous citizen need not actively participate in politics, she must be prepared to hold those people who do actively participate accountable for the decisions made in her name.[30] Deliberative democracy underscores the importance of political institutions that facilitate accountability to an adequately informed public, institutions that range from radically improved public schools that teach deliberation to radically reformed debates among political candidates that are structured in ways that discourage evasion of issues. Institutions that shield officials from public scrutiny and poorly educated, ill-informed citizens are anathema to autonomy. So are practices of deception and evasion by public officials that institutional reforms cannot legislate away. Deliberative democracy must rely partly on public commitment, bolstered by institutions that require, reward, or at least make room for, open and informed political discussion.

Deliberation holds out the prospect for a more defensible democratic order. Deliberative democracy values popular rule to the degree that it manifests or supports autonomy in politics, not simply for its expression of majority or plurality will. If people are poorly educated or uninformed, if politicians evade issues, if political or cultural institutions discourage deliberation, and citizens therefore do not deliberate, then popular rule loses a great deal of its value. The aim of deliberative democracy is not popular rule, but autonomy, thus no inherent tension exists between popular rule and those conditions necessary to support autonomy *as long as it is possible to design recognizably democratic political institutions that further autonomy.* The test of a democratic institution is not direct participation by all but effective accountability of those who make decisions to those who do not.

Deliberative democracy therefore offers a significantly different perspective on judicial review than populist democracy, a perspective that is not inherently paradoxical. Democratic political institutions may include a judicial system, with appointed judges, authorized to overturn majoritarian legislative decisions provided that judicial review (1) is a *delegation* of popular authority, not an *alienation* of it, and (2) aids in principled public deliberation over issues involving individual rights. Judges must of course account to the public for their decisions; a critical element in the democratic justification of judicial review is the willingness and ability of judges to offer a public account of their reasons for deciding cases. Without such an account open to assessment by citizens, judicial review would in effect be an alienation rather than a delegation of democratic authority. Recent nominees to the Supreme Court deserve criticism for their refusal to discuss their judicial philosophy, regardless of their motivation, because their refusal demands that citizens and their elected representatives alienate rather than delegate their authority.

Autonomy exercised in the political domain, like autonomy exercised in the realm of individual choice, is compatible with delegations of authority. Where autonomy recommends delegation, it also requires that citizens be willing and able to *justify* their delegation. If citizens are unwilling or unable to justify judicial review *and* judicial review is a condition of autonomy, then deliberative democracy falls short of its own standards, alerting us to the tension that may arise between the actual exercise of autonomy by individuals and the political conditions of autonomy, such as those that facilitate thorough deliberation on complex issues.

This tension between autonomy and its conditions captures the central disharmony of democracy as reflected in increasingly common criticisms of American democracy, including those that introduced this chapter. Because autonomy depends on deliberation, the conditions of autonomy may require us to criticize features of the political process that are compatible with popular rule but not with deliberative government. Deliberative democracy alerts us to the way that American electoral processes discourage deliberation. It opposes practices, exemplified by Admiral Poindexter's defense of presidential deniability in the Iran-Contra affair and Judge Clarence Thomas's refusal to discuss his judicial philosophy, that shield the political actions and understandings of officials from public scrutiny. Deliberative democracy is critical of schools and television for their failures to motivate children to become active learners, to think critically about their lives, and to know enough, and care enough, about politics to hold officials accountable. Deliberative democracy moves beyond the issue of the popularity of state lotteries to question the quality of decision making and the legitimacy of deceptive advertising. In these cases and others, deliberative democracy requires more than popular consent to political practices. A fully democratic practice must be deliberative.

The absence of deliberation offers a key to interpreting the malaise of American democracy. It also helps explain how, without radically shifting our standards, we can be enthusiastic about democratic developments in Czechoslovakia yet critical of political developments at home. Recent processes of democratization in Czechoslovakia have conspicuously encouraged citizens to develop their self-governing capacities. Many transitions from autocratic to democratic politics have the effect of temporarily raising the level of deliberation over issues.

By contrast, many aspects of democratic politics in the United States tend to neglect, or downright discourage, the exercise of autonomy. The absence of public funding for most electoral campaigns means that politicians must spend a large proportion of their time raising money rather than thinking and talking about public policies. The mass media show flagrant disregard for the quality of political discussion and encourage politicians to speak in shorter than ever sound bites. Presidential debates in recent years have been structured by the candidates themselves to avoid extended discussion of controversial issues.

The point of deliberative democracy is not to convert democratic politics into a series of boring university seminars. Public deliberation can be simultaneously entertaining and enlightening, although the combination does not come naturally, as academics should be among the first to recognize. Yet presidential debates would be *less* boring were they structured to be more challenging and illuminating of the candidates' positions on issues. The American public was extremely critical of the 1988 presidential campaign for its deceptive tactics and studied avoidance of issues. Deliberative democracy does not recommend substituting education for politics, but does generally demand truth telling rather than deception, confrontation rather than deflection of the issues, and revelation rather than disguise of the inner workings of government.

Any acceptable democratic resolution to the undeliberative character of American politics must be consistent with the public representation of adults as autonomous members of a self-governing society. But deliberative democracy cannot rely merely on this constitutive or expressive relation of democracy to autonomy. Necessary conditions for supporting autonomy in American politics include improving institutions of public accountability and education, and establishing political practices that, unlike our present electoral system, encourage people, both inside and outside government, to deliberate about politics.

To what extent can deliberative democracy make good on its promise of combining the conditions of autonomy with a recognizable democratic politics, one in which delegations of democratic authority both support autonomy and are autonomously approved by the public? An answer, I think, depends on whether it is the case that democratic institutions, especially those that require officials to account publicly for their actions, are more likely to support deliberation than nondemocratic institutions, which permit officials to act unaccountably in the name of the people. All theorists of deliberative democracy, most famously John Stuart Mill,[31] affirm the critical substantive assumption that public accountability, which at minimum offers citizens a chance either to punish the rascals or vote them out of office, encourages deliberation about public issues that affect people's lives. If the assumption is false, we have no prospect that deliberative democracy can make good on its promise of supporting autonomy through democracy. If the assumption is true, then the justification of deliberative democracy is stronger, and its internal coherence greater, than that of populist democracy or negative liberalism. Although I cannot explore the credibility of this assumption in any depth in this chapter, it may be worth noting that many of the conditions of autonomy, unlike those of popular rule, are realizable by improving the processes of popular rule rather than by placing constraints on that rule. The recourse of deliberative democracy is not *un*popular rule, but institutional reforms that foster accountability and the deliberative capacities of citizens. To the extent that those reforms can be implemented within a recognizably democratic system, the present tension of deliberative democracy between autonomy and its conditions may someday be overcome, even though that day is not in sight.

Deliberative democracy draws our attention to a disharmony that both populist democracy and negative liberalism obscure, a disharmony that accompanies the life of an autonomous person, and may account for the skepticism of some thoughtful people to the ideal of autonomy. In politics, as in personal life, autonomy requires reasoned choice among conflicting and incommensurable values. This choice, as many people gather from experience, can sometimes be agonizing. Although deliberative democracy avoids the paradox of populist democracy, it does not dissolve all conflicts among values. The political institutions and practices of a deliberative democracy are designed to help citizens make well-informed decisions about their collective life, enlisting their critical capacities in making political choices. But deliberation does not guarantee that any single deliberator or community of deliberators will converge upon a singularly correct resolution to a difficult problem, especially in cases that have several attractive alternatives each of which entails the sacrifice of some important value.

Although deliberative democracy is a substantive political and moral theory, committed to fostering autonomy, it does not offer a calculus of choice. It is compatible with the belief that rational deliberation can, at least in theory, yield uniquely correct answers to all political questions, but it does not presuppose this belief. In practice, under conditions of imperfect information and understanding, deliberation often does not yield knowledge of uniquely correct resolutions to political controversies. Deliberative democracy is therefore bound to be disharmonious both because individual citizens face hard political choices without any assurance of finding clear-cut resolutions, and because the conclusions of a community of deliberators are likely to differ when confronted with a difficult issue like abortion. The more political life encourages autonomy, the more agonizing decisions may become. But the level of political acrimony and violence is likely to decrease as citizens learn to respect each other as deliberative, rather than merely willful or self-interested, beings.[32]

Deliberative democracy legitimates the collective judgment resulting from deliberative procedures, even if deliberation does not yield a uniquely correct resolution to a political controversy (What process could produce a uniquely correct resolution?), or even if the collective judgment is at odds with the judgment of some citizens, so long as all citizens have equal standing in the deliberations. Our autonomy is violated when an unaccountable elite spares us the work of deciding among competing values, not when the decision goes against our best judgment provided that the decision makers offer good reasons for their position against our opposition.

Self-governance entails personal agonies and political arguments over how best to live with fundamental conflict, where collective deliberation is the only legitimate basis for making controversial decisions that are binding upon all. But our deliberations never close the case on what constitutes the most justified policy. Deliberative democracy defends autonomy, or self-governance, as the ideal that should guide us in coping with fundamental conflict of values and the indeterminacy of judgment under conditions of imperfect information and human imperfection. Autonomy makes a virtue out of the necessity of this disharmony.

4

Can democracy reconcile itself with liberalism? Deliberative democracy suggests the possibility of a more liberal form of democracy than populist democracy and a more democratic form of liberalism than negative liberalism. In so doing, it addresses the challenge of liberal critics that the sovereignty of an unenlightened, self-interested citizenry "could easily destroy that of individuals."[33] Properly understood, autonomy does not threaten tyranny over individuals but rather safeguards our most valued personal and political freedoms.

A simple story suggests that the marriage of liberalism and democracy is not merely one of convenience, that democracy has more than an instrumental relation to liberalism and liberalism entails more than a defense of negative liberty. The story takes off from a cartoon that appeared in *The New Yorker* just about the time when Central and Eastern Europe were erupting. A nondescript dictator addresses a sea of disgruntled people who have taken to the streets to protest his authoritarian rule. "If I had known how badly you wanted democracy," he declares, "I would have given it to you ages ago."

A benevolent dictator can give people all the personal freedom they want. He can grant them freedoms of speech, press, religion, and non-political association, freedom from arbitrary arrests and seizures, due process, the right to fair trials, even the right to bear arms. Granted, this is a most unlikely scenario. But it is meant only as a thought experiment to suggest that something rightly called individual freedom still would be missing from an *undemocratic* liberal state, something that deliberative democracy supplies. What would be missing is not protection of *personal* freedom or *popular* rule per se, but rather the freedom of adults to share in discussing and determining either directly or through institutions of accountability the *public* policies of their society, in all those cases where the liberal standard of personal freedom does not uniquely determine a set of policies. Without institutions that support public deliberation and accountability on matters of political importance, members of a society are *politically* unfree, and their lack of political freedom decreases their *personal* freedom in direct, discernible ways.

This democratic argument applies to a vast array of policy choices, including taxation, trade policy, environmental protection, zoning, work place safety, education, national defense, and health care. Political decisions in these and many other areas have a direct effect on the range and nature of people's personal choices: their disposable income, the prices they pay for goods, the quality of air they breathe and water they drink, the safety of their work places and the products they use, the availability of drugs, the location of their homes, the safety of their work places, the quality of their children's education, the lure of military service, and the affordability of health care. The list could be much longer.

Equally important for understanding the convergence of democracy and liberalism is the fact that political decisions in these areas also directly influence the way people identify, understand, and evaluate their choices. Consider the decision faced by many Americans of whether to spend some part of their income on gambling, before and after the institution of state lotteries. State lotteries not only offer people new choices, they also suggest, by way of advertising, fantasies people may never have had before. A typical advertisement for the New York State Lottery, for example, relates a secretary's dream of hiring a chauffeur instead of using public transportation. Deliberative democracy asks not merely whether political decisions result from processes and institutions that are formally democratic, but also whether democratic processes and institutions foster public understanding and discussion of policy alternatives and how they are likely to affect people's lives.

Deliberative democracy addresses liberalism's first and foremost concern with protecting personal freedom by demonstrating that in the vast realm where collective choice is unavoidable, democracy is not only instrumental, it is constitutive of individual freedom. Positive liberalism also must recognize this noninstrumental value of democracy. In this realm, positive liberals and deliberative democrats converge because the value of personal freedom depends on the control it allows people to exercise over their own lives. Without the institutions of deliberative democracy, personal freedom would be unjustifiably limited in those areas where collective decision making is unavoidable.

What about those areas where collective decision making is avoidable, where a society can place personal freedoms effectively beyond popular control, through constitutional and institutional constraints on popular rule? Autonomy also qualifies the value of popular rule, and thereby "liberalizes" democracy. Popular rule is illegitimate if it limits personal freedoms that are essential to the identity of a self-governing, deliberative person. It is legitimate where it defends personal freedoms better than any other form of rule *or* where personal freedoms are not essential to individual autonomy. The latter cases, where autonomy authorizes limitations on negative freedom, are likely to be the most controversial, both in theory and practice. An accountable legislature deliberates, with adequate information, and decides to prohibit the sale of life-endangering, addictive drugs and to require helmets for motorcyclists. The justification for these policies, which certainly limit personal freedom but arguably not autonomy, depends on distinguishing between freedoms that are separable and those that are inseparable from autonomy. Reasonable, fully informed, and well-educated people may disagree over what freedoms are essential to autonomy. As long as all the personal freedoms necessary for free deliberation are safeguarded, deliberative procedures may result in limiting some personal freedoms for the sake of realizing other valuable goods, a result that should be acceptable to democrats and liberals alike who accept the ideal of autonomy.

On this understanding, the marriage of liberalism and democracy is not one merely of convenience. Deliberative democracy is constitutively, as well as instrumentally, related to personal freedom. And personal freedom, on the positive conception of liberalism, is not simply freedom from interference. The greatest freedom a person possesses over a vast range of choices, consistent with the like freedom of other individuals, is the freedom to deliberate and decide political issues consistently with the like freedom of every other adult member of one's society. Liberalism cannot deny the importance of this freedom without undermining its own commitment to respecting the freedom of individuals to live lives they identify as their own.

But does the tension between liberalism and democracy disappear? Perhaps not entirely, at least not in theory. The deliberative processes legitimated by autonomy may result in the subordination of certain personal freedoms, those unnecessary for autonomy, democracy, or deliberation, to other social goods. For example, the freedom to spend one's income as one wishes may be subordinated to a democratic decision to fund the arts. The leading contemporary conception of positive liberalism, John Rawls's *A Theory of Justice*, explicitly denies the justice of such a democratic decision with language that seems also to challenge its legitimacy. Rawls argues with reference to public subsidies for universities, opera, and theater, that "there is no more justification for using the state apparatus to compel some citizens to pay for unwanted benefits that others desire than there is to force them to reimburse others for their private expenses."[34]

In *Democratic Education*, I criticized Rawls's claim, drawing on standards of deliberative democracy.[35] Do liberal standards support the conclusion that public funding of the arts is as unjustified as forcing me to pay for your yacht? Why should Rawlsian liberalism oppose a democratic decision to tax citizens to fund the arts for the sake of supporting human perfection, where the decision is made through appropriately deliberative processes? Taxation restricts personal freedom, and the issue of arts funding need not be put on the political agenda. It can be constitutionally shielded from democratic decision making. But Rawlsian liberalism does not grant priority to all personal freedoms, and certainly not to freedom from taxation. Quite the contrary, Rawls includes political liberties among the freedoms that take priority over fair equality of opportunity and the difference principle. How then can he conclude that a democratic decision to fund the arts is illegitimate or as unjustified as forcing people to pay for other people's private consumption?

Perhaps Rawls does not think that democratically sanctioned subsidies to the arts are illegitimate, or as unjustified as a policy that forced us to subsidize other people's purely private expenses, only that art subsidies are unjustified by his ideal theory. As a citizen, one may decide to oppose such subsidies, but still recognize the legitimacy of a democratically sanctioned policy. This position entails a division of theoretical labor between the tasks of deliberative democracy and Rawlsian or any other conception of positive liberalism. Rawlsian liberalism is a theory of *justification,* rather than one of *legitimacy.* Whereas theories of legitimacy, like deliberative democracy, specify the principled conditions of deliberation that render political decisions *legitimate,* theories of justification, like Rawls's, specify the principles that should guide democratic deliberations and determine public policy, at least under ideal conditions.

This principled division of labor renders Rawlsian liberalism compatible with deliberative democracy, but not coincident with it. Deliberative democrats need not accept Rawlsian principles of justice, but those who do may invoke Rawlsian principles to criticize the justice of the results of democratic deliberations without challenging their legitimacy. There is nothing illegitimate about a publicly debated, well-informed legislative decision to fund the arts for the sake of supporting a society of artistic excellence, where citizens are free to appreciate or not the artistic excellence that characterizes their society. Such a decision is consistent with, indeed may even express, the autonomy of citizens.

The common criticism that some citizens, those in the minority, will be forced against their will to pay taxes to support art they do not appreciate does not constitute a critique, although it reveals a distinctive tension of deliberative democracy. The decision of whether or not you and your children live in a society characterized by artistic excellence cannot be an individual choice; it must be collective. And it is a choice that people who share a society typically and reasonably want to make together, arguing about the relative merits of different social policies. We would be mistaken to claim that they would be freer or more autonomous in a society that made public support for the arts unconstitutional on grounds that public funding violated the freedom or autonomy of individuals. Autonomy requires that citizens have a chance collectively to deliberate and decide whether or not they want to live in a society of artistic excellence, that will be more conducive to artistic appreciation, and more costly for those who would not otherwise pay for the arts, than a society that leaves the support of art to private decisions. The democratic decision to fund art is reasonable, even if it is not justified by Rawlsian principles. I doubt that the decision is un-just, provided that taxation is neither regressive nor effectively depriving anyone of a decent life. But here I want only to es-tablish the compatibility of deliberative democracy and con-ceptions of positive liberalism that recognize the value of self-governance and therefore do not give absolute priority to negative freedom.

The value of self-governance is inclusive. It embraces pro-totypically liberal freedoms of speech, thought, religion, and association, and various forms of privacy that are necessary for shaping one's own life. It also includes distinctively democratic values of collective deliberation and decision making that permit us to be self-governing under conditions of social interdepend-ence, to share intelligently and responsibly in governing our society, and in holding our representatives accountable for the decisions made in our name.

The personal freedoms that permit us to act according to our own judgment may be constrained by the results of the political freedoms that permit us to share in shaping the future (of our society). This is a tension of deliberative democracy that is in-ternal to the ideal of autonomy itself. A democratic society that regulates dangerous drugs constrains the personal freedom of citizens who have good reason to prefer another, more libertar-ian policy. But the tension does not constitute a contradiction or paradox of deliberative democracy, analogous to that of populist democracy. On matters that require a decision at the level of public policy, autonomy demands public deliberation, decision making, and accountability of the decision makers. The results of these decisions may limit personal freedom, but the demands of autonomy are not violated so long as the limitations do not deprive citizens of their share in making decisions that demand deliberation and in holding their authorized decision makers accountable.

Because deliberative democracy understands autonomy to be an inclusive value, it does not succumb to Berlin's critique of autonomy as a species of positive freedom that justifies tyranny in the name of self-mastery.[36] Deliberative democracy seeks to maximize the scope of self-determination for interdependent individuals.[37] It supports those political processes that enlarge the capacity of individuals to make informed decisions about their lives. Autonomy qualifies the value of both personal freedom and popular rule to accommodate one another, the purpose of the accommodation being to enable people to govern their lives deliberatively, not according to any master plan or the judgment of a superior philosophical intellect or political authority. The accommodation is not perfect, however, because well-informed collective decisions are rarely unanimous, and some individuals in the minority may have good grounds for dissenting. Reasonable, conscientious, and well-informed dissent from collective decisions is to be expected in a democracy, at times even encouraged in the name of autonomy. Dissent does not undermine the justification of democratic decision making. This disharmony of deliberative democracy is its testimony to incommensurability and its tribute to autonomy. Because autonomous people cannot be expected to agree on all issues that are legitimately subject to collective decision making, this disharmony is an inescapable feature of any society that deserves to be called free and democratic.

The disharmony more commonly associated with American politics, the gap between established practices and liberal democratic principles, is escapable. Closing this gap is both possible and desirable.[38] Liberal democratic principles, properly understood, are not at odds with the institutional requirements of modern government. To the extent that modern government actually requires, as Samuel Huntington claims, "hierarchy, inequality, arbitrary power, secrecy, deception, and established patterns of superordination and subordination," liberal democratic principles must accommodate those requirements.[39] But there is no evidence that our current levels of economic inequality, political deception, secrecy, hierarchy, superordination, and subordination are necessary to the functioning of modern government, except in its present corrupt and unjust form. Grant that "the imperfections of human nature mean the gap [between principles and practices] can never be eliminated."[40] This need not temper our principled criticism of American, or any other, politics.[41] Political principles are tools of constructive criticism; they help us conceive alternative institutions and practices that would constitute a moral improvement over existing ones, given our understanding of human nature and the requirements of modern government.[42]

To locate the gap between our ideals and institutions, we must first understand our ideals. I have suggested that deliberative democracy is a more comprehensive and coherent political ideal than either populist democracy or negative liberalism. Narrowing the gap between the ideal of deliberative democracy and our political practices would decrease the disharmony of American democracy that fuels our criticism of it. But were the gap closed, a disharmony internal to the ideal of deliberative democracy itself would remain. Even a perfect people with ideal institutions could not eliminate the disharmony of democracy that is rooted in the tension between living your life as you see fit, and recognizing that to live your life as you see fit, you must share political power with many other people and therefore you may not be able to live every part of your life just as you see fit. Some of the most divisive political controversies in the United States today, including the battles over abortion, capital punishment, drugs, and pornography entail fundamental conflicts among goods. Legitimate resolutions of these conflicts critically depend on public deliberation, the absence of which is among the most disturbing features of contemporary American politics.

Even in light of its disharmony, democracy has value for individuals apart from its instrumental satisfaction of interests, although less value to the degree that decisions are undeliberative and decision makers are unaccountable. Being a democratic citizen is part, an important part, although by no means all, of what it means for us, and an increasing number of people throughout the world, to be autonomous, self-governing individuals. Self-governance is demanding, more demanding than either populist democracy or negative liberalism admit. It may also be an agonizing experience, and worth the agony. The alternatives are worse.

NOTES

1. "America's principal contribution to political theory is a conception of democracy according to which the protection of individual rights is a precondition, not a compromise, of that form of government." Ronald Dworkin, "The Reagan Revolution and the Supreme Court," *The New York Review of Books,* July 18, 1991, p. 23.

2. See Samuel Huntington, *American Politics: The Promise of Disharmony* (Cambridge: Harvard University Press, 1981).

3. Ibid., pp. 156–57.

4. Joseph Schumpeter, *Capitalism, Socialism, and Democracy* (London: George Allen & Unwin, 1943), p. 269.

5. As Robert Dahl points out, Schumpeter's understanding "leaves us with no particular reason for wanting to know whether a system is 'democratic' or not. Indeed, if a demos can be a tiny group that exercises a brutal despotism over a vast subject population, then 'democracy' is conceptually, morally, and empirically indistinguishable from autocracy." Robert A. Dahl, *Democracy and Its Critics* (New Haven: Yale University Press, 1989), pp. 121–22.

6. Brian Barry, "Is Democracy Special?," in Peter Laslett and James Fishkin, eds., *Philosophy, Politics, & Society,* 5th Series (New Haven: Yale University Press, 1979), pp. 156–57.

7. Ibid., p. 158.

8. Ibid., pp. 167–72.

9. Dahl, *Democracy and Its Critics,* p. 129. See pp. 126–30 for a defense of this constraint.

10. The same could be said for variations on these constraints. The analysis that follows does not depend on accepting this particular procedural interpretation of democracy.

11. See Richard Wollheim, "A Paradox in the Theory of Democ-

racy," in Peter Laslett and W. G. Runciman, eds., *Philosophy, Politics, and Society*, 2d Series (Oxford: Oxford University Press, 1984), pp. 153–67. For the response establishing the nonexistence of Wollheim's paradox, see Ted Honderich, "A Difficulty with Democracy," *Philosophy & Public Affairs* 3 (Winter 1973), pp. 221–26. See also J. Roland Pennock, "Democracy is Not Paradoxical: Comment," *Political Theory* 2, no. 1 (February 1974), pp. 88–93.

12. Jeremy Waldron, "Rights and Majorities: Rousseau Revisited," in John W. Chapman and Alan Wertheimer, eds., *Majorities and Minorities*, NOMOS XXXII (New York and London: New York University Press, 1990), pp. 44–75. Waldron's chapter offers an excellent analysis of the democratic possibilities of defending individual rights.

13. Ibid., p. 56.

14. Judith N. Shklar, "The Liberalism of Fear," in Nancy L. Rosenblum, ed., *Liberalism and the Moral Life* (Cambridge: Harvard University Press, 1989), p. 21.

15. Ibid.

16. What about the personal freedom to participate in collective decisions? Insofar as liberalism must recognize this freedom as one among the many valued by individuals, it too is internally disharmonious. Its disharmony parallels that of deliberative democracy, which I discuss in Section 3.

17. For the distinction between policy and principle, and an important alternative account of liberalism based on treating people as equals, see Ronald Dworkin, "Liberalism," in his *A Matter of Principle* (Cambridge: Harvard University Press, 1985), pp. 183–204.

18. All personal freedoms may be linked in some way to the formation of political preferences. Democratic theory must distinguish between close and distant links to political preference formation. Otherwise the constraints on outcomes become so demanding as to hijack the value, and practice, of popular government.

19. This example is taken from Cass Sunstein, "Ideas, Yes; Assaults, No," *The American Prospect* no. 6 (Summer 1991), pp. 35–39. See Sunstein in this article for a defense of such a regulation on democratic grounds.

20. Ibid., p. 38.

21. Isaiah Berlin, "Two Concepts of Liberty," *Four Essays on Liberty* (London: Oxford University Press, 1969), pp. 118–72.

22. For a discussion of the distinction between legitimacy and justification in the context of a defense of majoritarianism, see Waldron, "Rights and Majorities," pp. 45–46.

23. Ibid., p. 45.

24. See Dworkin, "The Forum of Principle," in his *A Matter of Principle,* esp. pp. 70–71.

25. For a direct challenge to Dworkin's argument, see Waldron, "Rights and Majorities," pp. 66–71.

26. Shklar, "The Liberalism of Fear," p. 37.

27. Although Michael Walzer does not explicitly invoke the conception of autonomous persons, this conception may help account for his defense of democracy: "The citizens must govern themselves.... What counts is argument among citizens. Democracy puts a premium on speech, persuasion, rhetorical skill. Ideally, the citizen who makes the most persuasive argument—that is, the argument that actually persuades the largest number of citizens—gets his way. But he can't use force, or pull rank, or distribute money; he must talk about the issues at hand. And all the other citizens must talk, too, or at least have a chance to talk. It is not only the inclusiveness, however, that makes for democratic government. Equally important is what we might call the rule of reasons." *Spheres of Justice* (New York: Basic Books, 1983), p. 304.

28. Arthur Kuflik, "The Inalienability of Autonomy," *Philosophy & Public Affairs* 13, no. 4 (Fall 1984), p. 272.

29. Dahl, *Democracy and Its Critics,* p. 91. I use the terms "autonomy" and "moral autonomy" interchangeably, although a distinction can be drawn. Moral autonomy is self-governance in the range of morally relevant choices. Autonomy is self-governance in the entire range of choices affecting one's life. The distinction is not important for our purposes.

30. Several contemporary theorists—including S. L. Hurley, James Fishkin, Robert Dahl, and Joshua Cohen and Joel Rogers—defend versions of deliberative democracy. See, for example, S. L. Hurley, *Natural Reasons: Personality and Polity* (New York: Oxford University Press, 1989), ch. 15; James Fishkin, *Deliberative Democracy* (New Haven: Yale University Press, 1991); Dahl, *Democracy and Its Critics;* and Joshua Cohen and Joel Rogers, *On Democracy: Toward a Transformation of American Society* (New York: Penguin Books, 1983).

31. See John Stuart Mill, *Considerations on Representative Government,* in J. J. Robson, ed., *Collected Works* (Toronto: University of Toronto Press, 1977), Vol. XIX, pp. 371–577; and *On Liberty* in *Collected Works,* Vol. XVIII, pp. 213–310. For a contemporary defense of this assumption, see Hurley, *Natural Reasons,* pp. 348–51.

32. For development of the nature and basis of mutual respect in liberal democratic politics, see Amy Gutmann and Dennis Thompson, "Moral Conflict and Political Consensus," *Ethics* 101 (October 1990), pp. 64–88.

33. Berlin, "Two Concepts of Liberty," p. 165.

34. John Rawls, *A Theory of Justice* (Cambridge: Harvard University Press, 1971), p. 332.

35. *Democratic Education* (Princeton: Princeton University Press, 1987), pp. 256–63.

36. For an instructive response from the perspective of deliberative democracy to Berlin's critique of autonomy, see Hurley, *Natural Reasons,* pp. 351–56.

37. Dahl, *Democracy and Its Critics,* p. 91.

38. Huntington, *American Politics.*

39. Ibid., p. 39.

40. Ibid., p. 261.

41. The way that Americans define themselves as a nation by their political creed or values may still make the United States unique. As Huntington reminds us: "If it were not for the American Creed, what would Americans have in common?" (Huntington, *American Politics,* pp. 24–25). Our uniqueness in this respect may make the disharmonies of American democracy, the conflict between our ideals and institutions and the tension among our ideals, more keenly felt than in other societies, by virtue of being less tempered by non-ideational forces of social unity. I cannot assess this claim here. See Huntington, *American Politics,* ch. 2.

42. Many theories of justice depend on the critical force created by the gap between a society's ideal and its institutions. Both Rawls's *Theory of Justice* and Michael Walzer's *Spheres of Justice* draw their critical force from the existence of such a gap, although their theoretical understandings of the gap differ. Walzer's illustrations of the way the gap as experienced by different societies in different historical periods has served as the source of social criticism qualifies Huntington's claim of American exceptionalism. See also Walzer's *Interpretation and Social Criticism* (Cambridge: Harvard University Press, 1987). Inegalitarian ideals do not guarantee, or even favor, social harmony. Depending on their content, hierarchical ideals can, and have, come into conflict with existing institutions, also generating a gap between social principles and practices.

PART III

DEMOCRATIC COMMUNITY AND THE CONSTITUTION

7

BETWEEN DEMOCRACY AND COMMUNITY: THE LEGAL CONSTITUTION OF SOCIAL FORM

ROBERT C. POST

I discuss the concept of "democratic community" from the specific perspective of the American legal system. This perspective, in Ronald Dworkin's elegant and accurate formulation, entails the continual effort interpretatively to grasp the internal point of social institutions.[1] The enterprise is neither purely descriptive nor entirely normative. It instead involves a hermeneutic apprehension of social practices, which are understood as existing independently of the observer and yet as subsisting in purposive structures whose requirements are perennially subject to debate and determination. The American legal system, through the medium of doctrine, aspires to uncover the meaning of social practices and to translate them into governing principles of conduct.

In brief, I argue that for the past sixty years American constitutional law has regarded democratic community as a complex dialectic between two distinct and antagonistic but reciprocally interdependent forms of social organization, which I call "responsive democracy" and "community." I define these forms of social organization in terms of the hermeneutic project of the law. When the law attempts to organize social life based on the principle that persons are socially embedded and dependent, it instantiates the social form of community. When it attempts to organize social life based on the contrary principle that persons are autonomous and independent, it instantiates the social form of responsive democracy. My thesis is that the tension between responsive democracy and community has a characteristic shape. Although the principles of responsive democracy and community often conflict in the outcomes they require for specific cases, American constitutional law has nevertheless recognized that the systemic maintenance of a healthy and viable democracy necessarily entails the maintenance of a healthy and viable community.[2] The concept of "democratic community," therefore, although unstable and contestable, has an essential and respected place in the history of our constitutional jurisprudence.

This chapter has a simple structure. Part I considers legal perspectives on the form of social organization I call community. Part II addresses our constitutional understandings of responsive democracy. Part III explores the distinct and controversial domain of democratic community.

I. COMMUNITY

Although the concept of "community" is "the most fundamental and far-reaching of sociology's unit-ideas,"[3] it has proven exceedingly "difficult to define."[4] The temptation is to think of community as exemplified by a particular culture, having a specific content, and actually situated in time and space. This is certainly what Tonnies had in mind when he charted the development from "Gemeinschaft" to "Gesellschaft."[5] In the 1960s modernization theory displayed similar assumptions using the more sophisticated (but essentially analogous) dimensions of Talcott Parsons's pattern variables.[6]

The enterprise of attempting empirically to locate historical "community," however, has collapsed into a hopeless muddle. In his amusing study of American historiography, for example, Thomas Bender documents how historians have found "community" to be always and continuously dissolving. Respectable monographs, when "placed in serial order, . . . offer a picture of community breakdown repeating itself in the 1650s, 1690s, 1740s, 1780s, 1820s, 1850s, 1880s, and 1920s."[7]

Whenever we look, apparently, we can be certain to find "community" slipping away. Bender suggests, therefore, that we abandon the concept of community as occupying "a specific space," and instead think of it as "a fundamental and enduring form of social interaction."[8] The methodological inquiry would thus shift away from the question of whether a particular culture represents "community," and toward the question of how communal forms of social interaction are instantiated and how they intersect with other kinds of social organization. The shift, in essence, would require us to abandon a concept of community that has determinate content, and to substitute instead a concept of community that entails a substantively empty but formally specific structure of social ordering.

Following Bender's suggestion, and building on the work of Michael Sandel, I define "community" as a form of social organization that provides for its members "not just what they *have* as fellow citizens but also what they *are*, not a relationship they choose (as in a voluntary association) but an attachment they discover, not merely an attribute but a constituent of identity."[9] Within community, therefore, social order is maintained through the inculcation among members of deep and parallel forms of personal identities. This formulation permits us to ground "community" in the empirical processes of primary socialization. George Herbert Mead, for example, has persuasively demonstrated how these processes establish common structures of identity in individual personalities:

> What goes to make up the organized self is the organization of the attitudes which are common to the group. A person is a personality because he belongs to a community, because he takes over the institutions of that community into his own conduct. He takes its language as the medium by which he gets his personality, and then through a process of taking the different roles that all the others furnish he comes to get the attitude of the members of the community. Such, in a certain sense, is the structure of a man's personality. . . . The structure, then, on which the self is built is this response which is common to all, for one has to be a member of a community to be a self.[10]

The work of Erving Goffman illustrates that the creation and maintenance of these common structures of identity does not occur only during early and primary socialization, but instead continues throughout the lifetime of community members through forms of everyday social interaction.[11] For Goffman such interaction is governed by rules of "deference and demeanor."[12] Rules of deference define conduct by which a person conveys appreciation "*to* a recipient *of* this recipient, or of something of which this recipient is taken as a symbol, extension, or agent."[13] Rules of demeanor define conduct by which a person expresses "to those in his immediate presence that he is a person of certain desirable or undesirable qualities."[14] Rules of deference and demeanor constitute "rules of conduct which bind the actor and the recipient together" and "are the bindings of society."[15] By following these rules, individuals both confirm the social order in which they live and constitute "ritual" and "sacred" aspects of their own identity.[16] The price of this process, however, is that each "individual must rely on others to complete the picture of him of which he himself is allowed to paint only certain parts."

> Each individual is responsible for the demeanor image of himself and the deference image of others, so that for a complete man to be expressed, individuals must hold hands in a chain of ceremony, each giving deferentially with proper demeanor to the one on the right what will be received deferentially from the one on the left. While it may be true that the individual has a unique self all his own, evidence of this possession is thoroughly a product of joint ceremonial labor, the part expressed through the individual's demeanor being no more significant than the part conveyed by others through their deferential behavior toward him.[17]

In the forms of social interaction that Goffman classifies as "ceremonial," persons create shared identities by reference to common social expectations or norms. Because a community subsists in the "special claims which members [of a community] have on each other, as distinct from others,"[18] these norms, when taken together, also define for a community "its distinctive shape, its unique identity."[19] That is why Richard Rorty can define immoral action as "the sort of thing which, if done at all, is done only by animals, or by people of other families, tribes, cultures, or historical epochs. If done by one of us, or if done repeatedly by one of us, that person ceases to be one of us. She becomes an outcast."[20]

We can define community, therefore, as a form of social organization that strives to establish an essential reciprocity between individual and social identity. Both are instantiated in social norms that are initially transmitted through processes of primary socialization and are thereafter continually reaffirmed through the transactions of everyday life. It is for this reason that Sandel can speak of community as inhering in attachments that are discovered and not merely chosen. In the social particularity and historical contingency of that discovery lies the "mystic foundation" of which Pascal so movingly speaks:

> Custom is the whole of equity, for the sole reason that it is accepted; that is the mystic foundation of its authority. Anyone who tries to trace it back to its first principles will destroy it.[21]

The truth of Pascal's observation is reflected in the shape of contemporary ethical theory, which, in its most sensitive applications, does not seek closed deductive systems, but rather reflective equilibria that are ultimately anchored in the contingent particularity of our given perspectives.

I do not mean to imply, however, that persons in communities are robots, automatons programed inevitably to follow fixed social norms. If we conceptualize the operation of social norms from the perspective of individual actors, we might perhaps imagine a subtle and inescapable language that can communicate various messages.[22] For example, I can convey respect by maintaining a discrete distance and obeying applicable norms of privacy. Or, in the identical situation, I can instead indicate contempt by violating these same norms and inappropriately intruding into a partner's personal space. Although the choice is mine, the choice is made meaningful only because of the existence of commonly shared norms. The message conveyed by my choice, in turn, reflects on the identity of its intended audience. In Charles Taylor's words, "Our 'dignity' . . . is our sense of ourselves as commanding (attitudinal) respect."[23] The point is powerfully supported by sociological work demonstrating the extent to which reiterated infractions of social norms, conveying indignities large and small, can profoundly unhinge identity.[24]

I also do not mean to imply that communities are static and unchanging. Social norms are typically contestable, subject to interpretation and reinterpretation.[25] What is at stake in such contests is the shape of our dignity, our common identity, our community. Although it is implausible to contend that we can redefine ourselves altogether, it is clear that to some unspecifiable extent we can reimagine some of the norms that comprise us. We can, by degrees, alter what we are and so affect the corresponding nature of our community. This reimagination can occur slowly, invisibly, and by accretion. Or it can occur in jumps, as for example when distinct groups separate from and divide a community. In such circumstances a communal form of social organization can continue to exist only if there are authoritative cultural institutions, like state educational systems, which work to articulate the norms that reciprocally define individual and social identity and inculcate these norms in a manner that spans social divisions. That is why, if social divisions are sharp enough, groups will typically struggle to capture (or retain control of) authoritative cultural institutions.

The formal universality of the law, exemplified by its assertion of control over all cultural groups within the jurisdictional boundaries of the state, makes the law a particularly significant prize in these struggles. That the law functions to enunciate minimum acceptable standards to which all citizens of the state, regardless of cultural affiliation, must conform, is commonly recognized. It is less obvious that for centuries the common law in England and America has also functioned authoritatively to define and enforce norms that are part of a communal form of social organization, norms that simultaneously instantiate both personal and community identity. Of course the common law has not enforced all such norms, just those deemed by those who control the law to be exceedingly important, which I call "civility rules." The extent to which the law has performed this task is of course subject to historical investigation. But to briefly summarize the conclusions of work I have developed elsewhere, it is clear that the doctrinal structure of the common law "dignitary" torts of defamation,[26] invasion of privacy,[27] and intentional infliction of emotional distress[28] can best be explained in terms of the legal definition and enforcement of civility rules.

Each of these torts penalizes uncivil communication on the assumption that the self of the addressee of such speech is intrinsically damaged, either through the loss of essential dignity and respect, or through the infliction of emotional distress and injury. Communication is understood to cause such injury because common law doctrine conceptualizes the self as dependent on the observance of civility rules for the maintenance of its integrity. In this way the law conceives civility rules as the measure of a common identity. By enforcing these rules the law also determines which speech is "utterly intolerable in a civilized community,"[29] and thereby defines the boundaries and meaning of community life. Under conditions of cultural heterogeneity, therefore, the common law can and has functioned as a powerful hegemonic force for the articulation of authoritative visions of community life.[30]

II. DEMOCRACY

American constitutional law is rich in its characterizations of democracy. Democracy has clearly implied what Frank Michelman calls "self-rule," the belief "that the American people are politically free insomuch as they are governed by themselves collectively."[31] This commitment to self-rule is sometimes equated with majoritarianism.[32] Even so powerful a constitutional theorist as Frederick Schauer can argue that "any distinct restraint on majority power, such as a principle of freedom of speech, is by its nature anti-democratic, anti-majoritarian."[33] But the essence of constitutional law lies in its normative principles, and if majoritarianism is understood as such a principle, rather than as a mere rule of procedure, its foundation most naturally rests on some form of utilitarian preference maximization. There is rather strong evidence that American constitutional law has decisively rejected that ideal.[34]

A far more persuasive account of the project of American constitutional law is one that begins with "the distinction between autonomy and heteronomy: Democratic forms of government are those in which the laws are made by the same people to whom they apply (and for that reason they are autonomous norms), while in autocratic forms of government the law-makers are different from those to whom the laws are addressed (and are therefore heteronomous norms)."[35] Simple majoritarianism fits awkwardly with the value of autonomy, because it contemplates the heteronomous imposition of majority will on the minority.[36] The solution to this difficulty, clearly envisioned by Rousseau, lies in the postulation of social processes anterior to majoritarian decision making that somehow connect the democratic system as a whole to the autonomous will of the entire citizenry.

A wide range of modern theorists have understood democracy in exactly this way. Hans Kelsen, for example, defines democracy as an "ideal type" of government instantiating the value of autonomy and resting on "the principle of self-determination."[37] In explaining exactly how a collectivity can serve to realize the autonomy of its individual members, Kelsen initially reflects Rousseau's formulation in *The Social Contract,* but then quickly gives that formulation a distinctively modern spin:

> A subject is politically free insofar as his individual will is in harmony with the "collective" (or "general") will expressed in the social order. Such harmony of the "collective" and the individual will is guaranteed only if the social order is created by the individuals whose behavior it regulates. Social order means determination of the will of the individual. Political freedom, that is, freedom under social order, is self-determination of the individual by participating in the creation of the social order.[38]

Because it is unconvincing to imagine that the individual will can be "in harmony" with the general will in all matters of political moment, Kelsen ultimately locates the value of self-determination in the ability of persons to participate in the process by which the social order is created. The social order is thus conceived as anterior to particular acts of majoritarian decision making. The creation of the social order is itself open to the participation of all because it pre-eminently occurs through processes of communication:

> The will of the community, in a democracy, is always created through a running discussion between majority and minority,

through free consideration of arguments for and against a certain regulation of a subject matter. This discussion takes place not only in parliament, but also, and foremost, at political meetings, in newspapers, books, and other vehicles of public opinion. A democracy without public opinion is a contradiction in terms.[39]

For Kelsen, then, democracy serves the principle of self-determination because it subjects the political and social order to public opinion, which is the product of a dialogic communicative exchange open to all. The normative essence of democracy is thus located in the communicative processes necessary to instill a sense of self-determination, and in the subordination of political decision making to these processes. This logic is widely shared. It leads Benjamin Barber, for example, to conclude that "there can be no strong democratic legitimacy without ongoing talk."[40] It leads John Dewey to remark that "democracy begins in conversation."[41] It leads Durkheim to observe that the "more that deliberation and reflection and a critical spirit play a considerable part in the course of public affairs, the more democratic the nation."[42] It leads Claude Lefort to claim that "modern democracy invites us to replace the notion of a regime governed by laws, of a legitimate power, by the notion of a regime founded upon *the legitimacy of a debate as to what is legitimate and what is illegitimate*—a debate which is necessarily without any guarantor and without any end."[43]

In fact the notion that democratic self-determination turns on the maintenance of a structure of communication open to all commands an extraordinarily wide consensus. Jürgen Habermas characterizes that structure as shaped by the effort to attain "a common will, communicatively shaped and discursively clarified in the political public sphere."[44] John Rawls views it as a process of "reconciliation through public reason."[45] Frank Michelman regards it as the practice of "jurisgenerative politics" through the "dialogic 'modulation' of participants' pre-political understandings."[46] For all three thinkers the goal of the structure is to facilitate the attainment of "agreement" that is "uncoerced, and reached by citizens in ways consistent with their being viewed as free and equal persons."[47]

Coercion is precluded from public debate because the very purpose of that debate is the practice of self-determination. The

goal is "agreement" (or the attainment of "a common will") because in such circumstances the individual will is by hypothesis
completely reconciled with the general will. It is important to
understand, however, that this goal is purely aspirational, what
Kant might call a "regulative idea."[48] In fact it is precisely because
absolute agreement can never actually be reached that the debate
that constitutes democracy is necessarily "without any end," and
hence must be independently maintained as an ongoing structure of communication. Adopting the term used by the U.S.
Supreme Court, I call this structure of communication "public
discourse."[49]

Without public discourse, the simple kind of majoritarian rule
Schauer equates with democracy loses its grounding in the principle of self-determination, and merely represents the heteronomous submission of a minority to the forceful command of
a majority. This would be true even if majority and minority
positions were determined accurately by sensitive voting procedures.[50] With a structure of public discourse in place, on the
other hand, both majority and minority can each be understood
to have had the opportunity freely to participate in a "system"[51]
of communication on which the legitimacy of all political arrangements depends. Whether that opportunity will actually establish the value of autonomous self-determination for both
majority and minority is a complex and contingent question,
dependent on specific historical circumstances. But, in the absence of that opportunity, realization of the value of autonomous
self-determination will be precluded under conditions characteristic of the modern state.[52]

It should by this point be obvious that the concept of democracy that I am sketching, which I call "responsive democracy," has little to do with the usual paraphernalia of descriptive
social science. It does not specifically address systems of representation, voting mechanisms, interest groups, and the like. Its
essence lies instead in its hermeneutic apprehension of the meaning of our democratic institutions. I claim that American constitutional law has for the past sixty years employed the ideal of
responsive democracy to shape the nation's political landscape.

This is most obvious in the Court's First Amendment jurisprudence, which most directly concerns the articulation of dem-

ocratic aspirations. If Schauer were correct in his equation of democracy with majoritarianism, First Amendment restrictions on majoritarian lawmaking would indeed be "anti-democratic." But from the very beginning of the First Amendment era[53] the Court has instead consistently viewed the First Amendment "as the guardian of our democracy,"[54] and it has characterized freedom of expression as "vital to the maintenance of democratic institutions."[55] It has thematized the democratic values protected by the First Amendment in terms that explicitly evoke the principle of self-determination:

> The maintenance of the opportunity for free political discussion to the end that government may be responsive to the will of the people and that changes may be obtained by lawful means, an opportunity essential to the security of the Republic, is a fundamental principle of our constitutional system.[56]

A brief overview of four significant implications of the concept of responsive democracy illustrates both its central importance to the structure of American constitutional law and its complex relation to the concept of community.

First, the function of responsive democracy is to reconcile, to the extent possible, the will of individuals with the general will. Responsive democracy is therefore ultimately grounded on a respect for individuals seen as "free and equal persons."[57] In the words of Jean Piaget:

> The essence of democracy resides in its attitude towards law as a product of collective will, and not as something emanating from a transcendent will or from the authority established by divine right. It is therefore the essence of democracy to replace the unilateral respect of authority by the mutual respect of autonomous wills.[58]

The fundamental project of responsive democracy thus points sharply toward the individualism that pervades American constitutional law.[59] Hence the project necessarily presupposes a very different image of the person than does community. Responsive democracy begins with the premise of independent citizens who desire to fashion their social order in a manner that reflects their values and commitments. Community, on the other hand, begins with the opposite premise of the citizen whose very identity requires the maintenance of particular forms of social order. Responsive democracy posits persons with autonomous selves; community posits persons with socially embedded selves. Responsive democracy strives to open up the field of social choice, community to restrict it.

These differences are most obvious in the contrasting regulation of public discourse within community and responsive democracy. Community conceives public discourse as the medium through which the values of a particular life are displayed and enacted. The common law thus freely regulates public speech that violates civility rules.[60] Responsive democracy, on the other hand, conceives public discourse as the communicative medium through which individuals select the forms of their communal life. It therefore resists the closure of that medium through the enforcement of civility rules that reflect pre-existing social commitments. It requires that "in public debate our own citizens must tolerate insulting, and even outrageous, speech."[61] The point, as the Court stated in the landmark case of *Cantwell v. Connecticut,* is that the First Amendment mandates a social order in which "many types of life, character, opinion and belief can develop unmolested and unobstructed."[62] This conception of social life as labile and evolving flows directly from the individualist premises of responsive democracy, and it has led the Court to interpret the First Amendment sharply to restrict the enforcement in public discourse of community-reinforcing torts like defamation, invasion of privacy, and intentional infliction of emotional distress.[63]

Second, the individualist premises of responsive democracy necessarily imply some form of public/private distinction. This is because the state undermines the raison d'être of its own enterprise to the extent that it coercively forms the "autonomous wills" that responsive democracy seeks to reconcile into public opinion. The importance of this public/private distinction is most paradigmatically visible in the protection for individual conscience provided by the Religion Clauses of the First Amendment, which safeguard "the right of each individual voluntarily to determine what to believe (and what not to believe) free of any coercive pressures from the State."[64] "In the domain of conscience there is a moral power higher than the State."[65] The

public/private distinction can also be seen in the branch of substantive due process doctrine that establishes the so-called constitutional "right to privacy," which protects the capacity " 'to
define one's identity that is central to any concept of liberty.' "[66]

The public/private distinction must, of course, be understood
as inherently unstable and problematic, for all government regulation influences, to one degree or another, the formation of
individual identity.[67] For this reason the distinction must, from
the perspective of responsive democracy, be regarded as a pragmatic instrument for identifying those aspects of the self considered indispensable for the exercise of political and moral
autonomy and hence as beyond the coercive formation of the
state.[68] In creating this sheltered haven, American constitutional
law not only limits the reach of responsive democracy, but also
curtails the ability of communities to use the force of law to
require individuals to conform to community norms.

Third, responsive democracy is inherently incomplete. This
is because the "autonomous wills" postulated by democratic theory do not and cannot appear *ex nihilo*. The only reason that a
person posseses a personality capable of autonomous choice is
because the person has internalized "the institutions of [the]
community into his own conduct."[69] This process of socialization,
which is prerequisite for personal identity, is not itself a matter
of independent election, but is rather attributable to accidents
of birth and acculturation. It most typically occurs through institutions like the family and the elementary school. In these
settings a child's identity is created in the first instance through
decidedly undemocratic means; it "comes to be by way of the
internalization of sanctions that are de facto threatened and
carried out."[70] Responsive democracy thus necessarily presupposes important (not to say foundational) aspects of the social
world organized along non-democratic lines.

The incompleteness of responsive democracy implies that its
very stability depends on the maintenance of appropriate forms
of community life.[71] Responsive democracy presupposes an
overarching commitment to the value of self-determination.[72]
Although responsive democracy must conceptualize that commitment as grounded in a collective act of autonomous consent,
it is clear that such consent is chiefly mythical.[73] We must there-

fore understand the commitment to derive instead from principles instilled in persons as part of their socialization into community values.[74] This creates an obvious tension with the public/private distinction, a tension that is most manifest in the institution of coercive public education. The tension is pragmatically (if not entirely satisfactorily) reconciled in the conceptual distinction between the child who must learn and the adult who can choose.[75]

A good example of how American constitutional law recognizes the paradoxical dependence of responsive democracy on community forms of life may be found in the branch of substantive due process doctrine that insulates from majoritarian decision making fundamental institutions "deeply rooted in this Nation's history and tradition."[76] Unlike the constitutional right to privacy, which subordinates community norms to individual rights, this strand of substantive due process doctrine enables deeply important community arrangements to circumscribe the competence of responsive democracy.[77] It is particularly forceful in its protection of the family, as the locus of primary socialization, from "statist" interference.[78]

Fourth, responsive democracy, like all forms of government, must ultimately be capable of accomplishing the tasks of governance. As Alexander Meiklejohn notes, "Self-government is nonsense unless the 'self' which governs is able and determined to make its will effective."[79] Democratic governments must therefore have the power to regulate behavior. But because public discourse is understood as the communicative medium through which the democratic "self" is itself constituted, public discourse must in important respects remain exempt from democratic regulation. We use the speech/action distinction to mark the boundaries of this exemption. All "words are deeds,"[80] so this distinction is purely pragmatic. We designate the communicative processes necessary to sustain the principle of collective self-determination "speech" and thus insulate it from majoritarian interference.

This insulation, together with the public/private distinction and the dependence of responsive democracy upon the survival of essential community institutions, illustrates the extent to which constitutional limitations are a necessary implication of responsive democracy. Whether or not these limitations are enshrined in a written document or enforced by an independent judiciary, they must exist as operative restraints on majoritarian decision making if responsive democracy is to remain faithful to its own normative premises. It is therefore vastly oversimplified to brand judicial review as antidemocratic because of the notorious "counter-majoritarian difficulty."[81] Although generations of constitutional lawyers have adopted this perspective, the American tradition of judicial review is better interpreted as itself evidence of a commitment to the principles of responsive democracy.

III. Democratic Community

On one level it is relatively easy to imagine an unproblematic account of the concept of "democratic community." If democracy is defined in terms of majoritarian decision-making procedures, we can envision a government in which such procedures are used to enact community values into law. We could call such a government a democratic community, and we could accurately ascribe this status to most contemporary democracies. Even our own government would qualify, for in America laws enacted through majoritarian procedures commonly function to place the force of the state behind the norms of the national community. A good example would be the many antidiscrimination laws that resulted from the civil rights movement, which serve graphically to express our communal commitment to egalitarian ideals.

But this account of "democratic community" is unsatisfactory if what we mean by democracy is not the external mechanics of a decision-making procedure, but rather the hermeneutic project of responsive democracy. For this project appears in important respects to contradict the purposes of community. Thus if we put ourselves in the position of a lawmaker who must fashion law to create forms of social order, we will face a constant choice whether to design legal doctrine to sustain the common, socially embedded identities of citizens, or instead to design them so as to protect the space for autonomous citizens independently to create their own social arrangements. To put the matter concretely, we must, if we are judges, decide whether constitutionally to permit or to prohibit the prosecution of flag burners.[82] To opt for the former is to enable law to be used to maintain popular identification with a particular conception of our community; to opt for the latter is instead to clear a public space in which hurtful and offensive (and therefore profoundly different) conceptions of our community can be displayed with impunity. Or, to offer another example, we must decide whether to allow persons to sue for compensation for emotional harms caused by unconscionably outrageous speech in public discourse.[83] If the function of law is to uphold norms that reciprocally define personal and communal identity, such suits ought to be permitted. They ought to be prohibited, however, if the function of law is instead to enable independent persons to advocate and exemplify new forms of life.

Such examples can be multiplied indefinitely; they are the stuff of everyday constitutional adjudication. They suggest a vision of responsive democracy and community as deeply antagonistic forms of social order. That vision, it is fair to say, is uniquely characteristic of the legal order of the United States,[84] due no doubt to the reciprocally reinforcing influences of our immense cultural diversity and the centrality of individualism to what Samuel Huntington has aptly termed our "American Creed."[85] The sharp polarity of that vision runs like a rift throughout our constitutional tradition, dividing in contemporary times "liberal" from "conservative" justices.[86]

But this polarity is misleading, for whereas it signifies the real tension between community and responsive democracy at the level of particular cases, it obscures the fact that at a more general systemic level, responsive democracy actually requires the maintenance of healthy and vigorous forms of community life. This is true for at least three reasons. First, as I have discussed previously,[87] responsive democracy is predicated on a commitment to the value of self-determination, which presupposes community institutions designed to inculcate this value. Hence the importance to democracy of establishing, as a matter of sheer "conscious social reproduction," a "nonneutral" educational system aimed at "cultivating the kind of character conducive to democratic sovereignty."[88]

Second, responsive democracy attempts to reconcile individuals with the general will by establishing processes of deliberation that will instantiate a sense of self-determination.[89] The formal opportunity to speak and to hear constitutes a necessary but not sufficient condition for the creation of this sense of self-determination.[90] Necessary also is the feeling of participation that at root must rest on an identification with the aspirations of a culture that attempts to reconcile differences through deliberative interaction. This identification is essential for the functioning, as well as for the reproduction, of responsive democracy, and it too must ultimately depend on the inculcation of particular forms of identity through community institutions.

Third, responsive democracy aspires to conditions of deliberation, to some form of "reconciliation through public reason." Such deliberation, in turn, presupposes civility and respect, for speech lacking these qualities is likely to be experienced as coercive and irrational, as an instrument "of aggression and personal assault."[91] The exercise of public reason is thus always inseparable from and made possible by historically particular community norms that give content to the values of respect and civility. In this sense also, responsive democracy requires the continued maintenance of healthy forms of community life.

The concept of democratic community, therefore, cuts a complex figure in our constitutional tradition. At the level of specific cases, responsive democracy and community appear oppositional, dictating conflicting perspectives and conclusions. But at the systemic level they appear reconcilable, perhaps even interdependent. This strange disjunction renders the concept of democratic community intrinsically unstable and contestable. In any particular circumstance it can always be argued either that legal enforcement of community norms is necessary for the survival of community, and hence for the ultimate health of responsive democracy, or that such enforcement is not necessary for the maintenance of community and therefore merely a betrayal of the principles of self-determination required by responsive democracy. The first form of argumentation was stressed during the McCarthy era, whereas the Warren Court subsequently recast vast stretches of American constitutional law according to the individualist premises of responsive democracy. More recently, courts have once again retrenched, enabling, for example, legal restrictions on public speech where necessary to inculcate "the habits and manners of civility . . . indispensable to the practice of self government."[92]

The tension in American law between community and responsive democracy closely resembles the contemporary debate among American political philosophers between proponents of communitarianism and advocates of liberalism. The manner in which our law has accommodated this tension contains a useful lesson for the philosophical debate, for it starkly illustrates the extent to which the problem resists resolution *tout court,* and requires instead situational and pragmatic adjustment. This can be illustrated by what I have elsewhere termed the "paradox of public discourse."[93] The specific purpose of public discourse is the achievement of some form of "reconciliation through public reason," yet because the identity of democratic citizens will have been formed by reference to community norms, speech in violation of civility rules will characteristically be perceived as both irrational and coercive. Thus the First Amendment, in the name of responsive democracy, suspends legal enforcement of the very civility rules that make rational deliberation possible.

The upshot of this paradox is that the separation of public discourse from community depends in some measure on the spontaneous persistence of civility.[94] In the absence of such persistence, even a Court imbued with the principles of responsive democracy may be required on purely pragmatic grounds to permit the enforcement of civility rules. Exemplary is the Court's decision in *Chaplinsky v. New Hampshire,* in which "fighting words"—words "which by their very utterance inflict injury"—were held to be unprotected by the First Amendment because they "are no essential part of any exposition of ideas, and are of such slight social value as a step to truth that any benefit that may be derived from them is clearly outweighed by the social interest in order and morality."[95]

The practical accomodation between responsive democracy and community characteristic of American constitutional law is also visible in its delineation of the distinct domain of public discourse.[96] Responsive democracy requires that public discourse be broadly conceived as a process of "collective self-definition"[97] that will necessarily precede and inform government decision making. Although the Court has sometimes attempted to define public discourse by distinguishing speech about "matters of public concern" from speech about "matters of purely private concern,"[98] it is evident that this definition is conceptually incoherent. This is because democratic self-governance posits that the people control the agenda of government. They have the power to determine the content of public issues simply by the direction of their interests. This means that every issue that can potentially agitate the public is also potentially relevant to democratic self-governance, and hence potentially of public concern. The distinction between matters of "public concern" and matters of "purely private concern," insofar as it is used to exclude speech from public discourse, is therefore incompatible with the very democratic self-governance it seeks to facilitate.

It does not follow, however, that all communication ought therefore to be classified as public discourse, for any such conclusion would pre-empt virtually all community control of speech and hence endanger the survival of the very community on which responsive democracy itself depends. For this reason the Court has been forced to define public discourse by evaluating the totality of circumstances surrounding particular speech acts, by reviewing a communication's "content, form, and context...as revealed by the whole record."[99] This inquiry, however, is neither more nor less than a determination of whether, in the circumstances presented, the values of self-determination embodied in public discourse ought to prevail over the values of the socially embedded self protected by community controls on speech. Thus the law will protect outrageous speech when disseminated in the pages of a nationally distributed magazine,[100] because the reading public ought with good reason to be regarded as autonomous self-governing citizens. But it will permit the regulation of such speech within the workplace, because the managerial control and social interdependence of the employment setting would render a similar attribution of autonomy patently out of place.[101] The distinction between responsive democracy and community is thus pragmatically and situationally justified.

This messy solution can be theoretically illuminated by George Herbert Mead's distinction between the "I" and the "me." Mead identified the socialized structure of the individual personality with what he called the "me." He was quite aware, however, that there could be no such thing as a completely "institutionalized individual."[102] Persons always retain the inherent and irreducible capacity to modify or transcend socially given aspects of themselves. Mead identified this capacity as the "I":

> The "I" is the response of the organism to the attitudes of the others; the "me" is the organized set of attitudes of others which one himself assumes. The attitudes of the others constitute the organized "me," and then one reacts toward that as an "I."[103]

The "I" is spontaneous, unpredictable, and formless; the "me" is structured and relatively static. Mead viewed each as a fundamental and indispensable aspect of the self. He associated the "me" with "social control," and the "I" with "self-expression."[104] "Taken together, they constitute a personality as it appears in social experience. The self is essentially a social process going on with these two distinguishable phases."[105]

The sharp contrast between community and responsive democracy can be understood as flowing from the distinction between these two phases of the self. Law in the service of community upholds the values associated with the "me," which is to say the community norms and attitudes that form the structure of personality. Law in the service of responsive democracy safeguards the values associated with the "I," which is to say the potential for individual modification and transcendence of that structure. But just as the "me" and the "I" are necessarily complementary and interdependent, so also are the social forms of community and responsive democracy. The tension between the two is irreducible and constant; the law merely provides the vehicle for its social embodiment. It throws the weight of the state behind one or another phase of the self, as circumstances require.

IV. Conclusion

We are thus led to an image of democratic community as a complex dialectic between two equally necessary but opposing phases of the self and their corresponding social formations. The law is the instrument of this dialectic, tacking to and fro as directed between contradictory values. The result is a hodgepodge of conflicting legal judgments, certain to frustrate purists of either camp, but nevertheless explicable as an ongoing process of dynamic, contextual, and practical accommodation. In this regard, the ultimate revelation of the law is merely the shape and contours of our own deepest commitments.

NOTES

1. Ronald Dworkin, *Law's Empire* (Cambridge: Harvard University Press, 1986), pp. 49–65.

2. I do not discuss legal treatment of the converse question, whether the maintenance of a healthy and viable community necessarily entails the maintenance of democracy. In our constitutional tradition democracy has always functioned as an essential first premise.

3. Robert A. Nisbet, *The Sociological Tradition* (New York: Basic Books, 1966), p. 47.

4. Thomas Bender, *Community and Social Change in America* (New Brunswick: Rutgers University Press, 1978), p. 5.

5. See Ferdinand Tonnies, *Community and Society* (Charles P. Loomis, trans.) (New York: Harper & Row, 1963).

6. Bender, supra note 4, at 21–23. See Talcott Parsons, *The Social System* (Glencoe: Free Press, 1951), pp. 58–77.

7. Bender, supra note 4, at 45–53.

8. Id. at 43.

9. Michael J. Sandel, *Liberalism and the Limits of Justice* (Cambridge: Cambridge University Press, 1982), p. 150.

10. George Herbert Mead, *Mind, Self, and Society* (Charles W. Morris, ed.) (Chicago: University of Chicago Press, 1962), p. 162. See also Sandel, supra note 9, at 152–64.

11. Erving Goffman, *Interaction Ritual: Essays on Face-to-Face Behavior* (New York: Pantheon Books, 1967), pp. 84–85.

12. Id. at 47.

13. Id. at 56.

14. Id. at 77.

15. Id. at 90.

16. Id. at 91.

17. Id. at 84–85.

18. Joseph Gusfield, *Community: A Critical Response* (Oxford: B. Blackwell, 1975), p. 29.

19. Kai Erikson, *Wayward Puritans: A Study in the Sociology of Deviance* (New York: Wiley, 1966), p. 11.

20. Richard Rorty, *Contingency, Irony, and Solidarity* (Cambridge: Cambridge University Press, 1989), p. 59.

21. *Pascal's Pensées* (Martin Turnell, trans.) New York: Harper & Row, 1962), p. 72.

22. For a fuller discussion, see Robert Post, "The Social Foundations of Privacy: Community and Self in the Common Law Tort," *California Law Review,* 77 (1989), 972–74.

23. Charles Taylor, *Sources of the Self: The Making of Modern Identity* (Cambridge: Harvard University Press, 1989), p. 15.

24. Erving Goffman, *Asylums: Essays on the Social Situation of Mental Patients and Other Inmates* (Garden City: Anchor Books, 1961).

25. See, for example, Ronald Dworkin's parable of the interpretation of the norms of courtesy. Ronald Dworkin, supra note 1, at 46–49.

26. See Robert Post, "The Social Foundations of Defamation Law: Reputation and the Constitution," *California Law Review,* 74 (1986), 691.

27. See Post, supra note 22.

28. See Robert Post, "The Constitutional Concept of Public Discourse: Outrageous Opinion, Democratic Deliberation, and *Hustler Magazine v. Falwell,*" *Harvard Law Review,* 103 (1990), 601.

29. Restatement (Second) of Torts Sec. 46 comment d (1977).

30. See, e.g., Post, supra note 22, at 959–78; Post supra note 26, at 713–15.

31. Frank Michelman, "Law's Republic," *Yale Law Journal,* 97 (1988), 1500–1501. Michelman notes that "no earnest, non-disruptive participant in American constitutional debate is quite free to reject" this "belief." Id. at 1500.

32. Robert Alan Dahl, *A Preface to Democratic Theory* (Chicago: University of Chicago Press, 1956), p. 67.

33. Frederick Schauer, *Free Speech: A Philosophical Enquiry* (Cambridge: Cambridge University Press, 1982), p. 40. Schauer writes:

> The more we accept the premise of the argument from democracy, the less can we impinge on the right of self-government by restricting the power of the majority. If the argument from democracy would allow to be said things that the "people" do not want to hear, it is not so much an argument based on popular will as it is an argument against it.

Id. at 41.

34. See, e.g., Cass Sunstein, "Naked Preferences and the Constitution," *Columbia Law Review,* 84 (1984), 1689.

35. Norberto Bobbio, *Democracy and Dictatorship* (Peter Kennealy, trans.) (Minneapolis: University of Minnesota Press, 1989), p. 137.

36. For an earnest if unsuccessful effort to meet this problem, see Carol C. Gould, *Rethinking Democracy: Freedom and Social Cooperation in*

Politics, Economy, and Society (Cambridge: Cambridge University Press, 1988), pp. 236–38.

37. Hans Kelsen, *General Theory of Law and State* (Anders Wedberg, trans.) (New York: Russell & Russell, 1961), pp. 284–86.

38. Id. at 285. What makes Kelsen's perspective distinctively modern, of course, is its shift from substance to process. Rousseau had presupposed a substantive correspondence between the content of the general will and the will of individuals. In contrast Kelsen postulates only an identification of individual wills with the process by which the general will is formed.

39. Id. at 287–88.

40. Benjamin R. Barber, *Strong Democracy: Participatory Politics for a New Age* (Berkeley: University of California Press, 1984), p. 136. See Hanna Fenichel Pitkin and Sara M. Shumer, "On Participation," *Democracy* (Fall 1982), 43–54.

41. *Dialogue on John Dewey* (Corliss Lamont, ed.) (New York: Horizon Press, 1959), p. 58.

42. Emile Durkheim, *Professional Ethics and Civic Morals* (Cornelia Brookfield, trans.) (Glencoe: Free Press, 1958), p. 89.

43. Claude Lefort, *Democracy and Political Theory* (David Macey, trans.) (Minneapolis: University of Minnesota Press, 1988), p. 39.

44. Jürgen Habermas, *The Theory of Communicative Action* (Thomas McCarthy, trans.) (Boston: Beacon Press, 1987), p. 81.

45. John Rawls, "Justice as Fairness: Political Not Metaphysical," *Philosophy & Public Affairs,* 14 (1985), 230.

46. Michelman, supra note 31, at 1527.

47. Rawls, supra note 45, at 229–30; Michelman, supra note 31, at 1526–27; Jurgen Habermas, *The Theory of Communicative Action* (Thomas McCarthy, trans.) (Boston: Beacon Press, 1984), pp. 25–26.

48. See J. N. Findlay, *Kant and the Transcendental Object: A Hermeneutic Study* (Oxford: Clarendon Press, 1981), p. 241.

49. *Hustler Magazine v. Falwell,* 485 U.S. 46, 55 (1988).

50. See Barber, supra note 40, at 136–37.

51. Owen Fiss, "Foreword: The Forms of Justice," *Harvard Law Review,* 93 (1979), 38.

52. I do not mean to foreclose the possibility that, under special conditions of charismatic leadership or identification with traditional authority, the value of self-determination can be achieved in the absence of a communicative structure of public discourse. I mean only to imply that such conditions will not ordinarily obtain in the modern rational and bureaucratic state.

53. For practical purposes, the effective use of First Amendment

doctrine to protect free speech dates back only to the case of *Stromberg v. California*, 283 U.S. 359 (1931).

54. *Brown v. Hartlage*, 456 U.S. 45, 60 (1982). See *Buckley v. Valeo*, 424 U.S. 1, 93 n.127 (1976); *Richmond Newspapers, Inc. v. Virginia*, 448 U.S. 555, 587–88 (1980) (Brennan, J. concurring); *Saxbe v. Washington Post Co.*, 417 U.S. 843, 862–63 (1974) (Powell, J., dissenting).

55. *Schneider v. State*, 308 U.S. 147, 161 (1939). See *Virginia Pharmacy Bd. v. Virginia Consumer Council*, 425 U.S. 748, 765 n.19 (1976); *Thomas v. Collins*, 323 U.S. 516, 530 (1945).

56. *Stromberg v. California*, 283 U.S. 359, 369 (1931). The principle of self-determination manifestly underlies the crucial repudiation of seditious libel in *New York Times Co. v. Sullivan*, 376 U.S. 254 (1964). The decision turned on Madison's differentiation of American and English forms of government: In England "the Crown was sovereign and the people were subjects," whereas in America the " 'people, not the government, possess absolute sovereignty.' " Id. at 274. Thus in America " 'the censorial power is in the people over the Government, and not in the Government over the people.' " Id. at 275.

57. Rawls, supra note 45, at 230. For a general account of the value of "autonomy" as "a constitutive normative ingredient of American democratic constitutionalism," see D. A. J. Richards, "Autonomy in Law," in *The Inner Citadel: Essays on Individual Autonomy* (John Christman, ed.) (New York: Oxford University Press, 1989), pp. 246–58.

58. Jean Piaget, *The Moral Judgment of the Child* (Marjorie Gabain, trans.) (Glencoe: Free Press, 1948), p. 366.

59. For a study of the individualism of First Amendment doctrine, see Robert Post, "Cultural Heterogeneity and Law: Pornography, Blasphemy, and the First Amendment," *California Law Review*, 76 (1988), 314–24. For salient examples of the influence of individualism in other areas of constitutional law, see, e.g., *City of Richmond v. J.A. Croson Co.*, 488 U.S. 469 (1989); *Zablocki v. Redhail*, 434 U.S. 374 (1978); *Weber v. Aetna Casualty & Surety Co.*, 406 U.S. 164 (1972); *Reynolds v. Sims*, 377 U.S. 533 (1964).

60. See, e.g., Post, supra note 28, at 627–33; Robert Post, "Defaming Public Officials: On Doctrine and Legal History," *American Bar Foundation Research Journal*, 1987, 539, 552–54; *Dominguez v. Stone*, 97 N.M. 211, 638 P.2d 423 (1981).

61. *Boos v. Barry*, 485 U.S. 312, 322 (1988).

62. 310 U.S. 296, 310 (1940).

63. See, e.g., *New York Times Co. v. Sullivan*, 376 U.S. 254 (1964); *Philadelphia Newspapers, Inc. v. Hepps*, 475 U.S. 767 (1986); *The Florida Star v. B.J.F.*, 491 U.S. 524 (1989); *Cox Broadcasting Corp. v. Cohn*, 420

U.S. 469 (1975); *Hustler Magazine v. Falwell*, 485 U.S. 46 (1988). For a classic statement of the First Amendment position, see *Cohen v. California*, 403 U.S. 15 (1971). For a general discussion, see Post, supra note 28, at 626–49.

64. *Grand Rapids School. Dist. v. Ball*, 473 U.S. 373, 385 (1985). See *Lyng v. Autonombile Workers*, 485 U.S. 360, 369 (1988); *Wallace v. Jaffree*, 472 U.S. 38, 50–53 (1985); *Abood v. Detroit Bd. of Educ.*, 431 U.S. 209, 235 (1977); *Cantwell v. Connecticut*, 310 U.S. 296, 303 (1940).

65. *Girouard v. United States*, 328 U.S. 61, 68 (1946). For a general discussion, see D. A. J. Richards, *Toleration and the Constitution* (New York: Oxford University Press, 1986), pp. 67–164.

66. *Roberts v. United States Jaycees*, 468 U.S. 609, 619 (1984). An early and influential decision recognizing the right is *Meyer v. Nebraska*, 262 U.S. 390 (1923), in which the Court struck down a Nebraska statute that prohibited the teaching of foreign languages to young students. Justice McReynolds wrote:

> In order to submerge the individual and develop ideal citizens, Sparta assembled the males at seven into barracks and intrusted their subsequent education and training to official guardians. Although such measures have been deliberately approved by men of great genius, their ideas touching the relation between individual and state were wholly different from those upon which our institutions rest; and it hardly will be affirmed that any legislature could impose such restrictions upon the people of a state without doing violence to both letter and spirit of the Constitution.

Id. at 402.

67. See, e.g. Cass Sunstein, "Legal Interference with Private Preferences," *University of Chicago Law Review*, 53 (1986), 1138–39.

68. Quite apart from the ultimate merits of *Roe v. Wade*, this line of analysis has rather significant implications for John Ely's influential criticism of the right to privacy in *Roe* as wholly lacking in "connection with any value the Constitution marks as special." John Hart Ely, "The Wages of Crying Wolf: A Comment on *Roe v. Wade*," *Yale Law Journal*, 82 (1973), 949.

69. Mead, supra note 10, at 162.

70. Habermas, supra note 44, at 38.

71. For a theoretical statement of this position, see Charles Taylor, *Philosophy and the Human Sciences: Philosophical Papers* (Cambridge: Cambridge University Press, 1985), pp. 205–9.

72. Joseph Raz, "Liberalism, Skepticism, and Democracy," *Iowa Law Review*, 74 (1989), 779–84.

73. David Hume, *A Treatise of Human Nature* (2d ed.; L. A. Selby-Bigge, ed.) (Oxford: Clarendon Press, 1978), pp. 534–53. Even if the ratification of the Constitution could be convincingly analogized to an

188 Robert C. Post

explicit act of collective consent, it still would not follow that *we,* who are two centuries removed from the ratifiers, have also consented. See Robert Post, "Theories of Constitutional Interpretation," in *Law and the Order of Culture* (Robert Post, ed.) (Berkeley: University of California Press, 1991), p. 23.

74. To the extent that America is a culturally heterogeneous nation, a common commitment to the value of responsive democracy must derive from something like the "idea of an overlapping consensus" that has been developed by John Rawls. John Rawls, "The Idea of an Overlapping Consensus," *Oxford Journal of Legal Studies,* 7 (1987), 1. See Dahl, supra note 32, at 76–81. On the role of education in achieving that consensus, see Amy Gutmann, *Democratic Education* (Princeton: Princeton University Press, 1987).

75. For a stimulating analysis of the more general tension entailed by the dependence of the autonomous democratic citizen upon ongoing forms of disciplinary socialization, see Peter Fitzpatrick, " 'The Desperate Vacuum': Imperialism and Law in the Experience of Enlightenment," in *Post-Modern Law: Enlightenment, Revolution and the Death of Man* (Anthony Carty, ed.) (Edinburgh: Edinburgh University Press, 1990), pp. 90–106.

76. *Moore v. East Cleveland,* 431 U.S. 494, 503 (1977) (plurality opinion). See *Bowers v. Hardwick,* 478 U.S. 186, 192 (1986).

77. For a discussion of the differences between these two strands of substantive due process doctrine, see Robert Post, "Tradition, the Self, and Substantive Due Process: A Comment on Michael Sandel," *California Law Review,* 77 (1989), 553.

78. *Parham v. J.R.,* 442 U.S. 584, 603 (1979). Thus *Pierce v. Society of Sisters,* 268 U.S. 510, 535 (1925):

> The fundamental theory of liberty upon which all governments in this Union repose excludes any general power of the state to standardize its children by forcing them to accept instruction from public teachers only. The child is not the mere creature of the state; those who nurture him and direct his destiny have the right, coupled with the high duty, to recognize and prepare him for additional obligations.

See also, e.g., *Hodgson v. Minnesota,* 110 S.Ct. 2926, 2942–44 (1990) (Opinion of Stevens, J.); *Moore v. East Cleveland,* 431 U.S. 494 (1977); *Planned Parenthood of Central Missouri v. Danforth,* 428 U.S. 52 (1976); *Stanley v. Illinois,* 405 U.S. 645 (1972); *Griswold v. Connecticut,* 381 U.S. 479 (1965); *Poe v. Ullman,* 367 U.S. 497, 551–52 (1961) (Harlan, J., dissenting).

79. Alexander Meiklejohn, *Political Freedom: The Constitutional Powers of the People* (New York: Oxford University Press, 1948), p. 14.

80. Ludwig Wittgenstein, *Culture and Value* (G. H. von Wright, ed.; Peter Winch, trans.) (Chicago: University of Chicago Press, 1980), p. 46e.

81. Alexander Bickel, *The Least Dangerous Branch: The Supreme Court at the Bar of Politics* (New Haven: Yale University Press, 1962), pp. 16–17.

82. See, e.g., *United States v. Eichman*, 110 S. Ct. 2404 (1990); *Texas v. Johnson*, 491 U.S. 397 (1989).

83. See, e.g., *Hustler Magazine v. Falwell*, 485 U.S. 46 (1988).

84. On American exceptionalism, see Post, supra note 28, at 626–38; Post, supra note 59, at 305–24.

85. Samuel P. Huntington, *American Politics: The Promise of Disharmony* (Cambridge: Belknap Press, 1981), p. 14.

86. See Robert Post, "Justice William J. Brennan and the Warren Court," *Constitutional Commentary*, 8 (1991), 11–19.

87. See supra text at notes 71–75.

88. See Gutmann, supra note 74, at 41–47.

89. See supra, text at notes 49–52.

90. Recent proposals for the regulation of racist speech, for example, might most profitably be conceptualized as setting forth the claim that formal opportunities for communication have not translated for victimized minorities into the experience of participation necessary for responsive democracy, and that such regulation is necessary, as a matter of contingent historical circumstances, to realize the value of self-determination. See Robert Post, "Racist Speech, Democracy, and the First Amendment," *William & Mary Law Review*, 32 (1991), 302–17.

91. *Time, Inc. v. Hill*, 385 U.S. 374, 412 (1967) (Fortas, J., dissenting). Alexander Bickel once remarked that deeply uncivil communication "amounts to almost physical aggression." Alexander Bickel, *The Morality of Consent* (New Haven: Yale University Press, 1975), p. 72. See *Cohen v. California*, 403 U.S. 15, 27 (1971) (Blackmun, J., dissenting). Thus "fighting words" are understood to be those which "by their very utterance inflict injury." *Chaplinsky v. New Hampshire*, 315 U.S. 568, 572 (1942). Outrageous words intentionally inflicting emotional distress are "nothing more than a surrogate" for a "punch or kick." R. George Wright, "*Hustler Magazine v. Falwell* and the Role of the First Amendment," *Cumberland Law Review*, 19 (1988), 23. "Ridicule" is experienced as a form of "intimidation." John Dewey, "Creative Democracy—The Task Before Us," in *Classic American Philosophers* (Max Harold Fisch, ed.) (New York: Appleton-Century-Crofts, 1951), p. 393. Pornography is received not as "expression depicting the subordination of women, but [as] the *practice of subordination* itself." Paul Brest and Ann Vandenberg, "Politics, Feminism, and the Constitution: The Anti-Pornography Movement in Minneapolis," *Stanford Law Review*, 39 (1987), 659 (emphasis in the original).

Blasphemous communications are nothing more than a form of "brawls." Francis Ludlow Holt, *The Law of Libel* (London: J. Butterworth, 1816), pp. 70–71. And racist speech is simply "a form of assault, [of] conduct." Kenneth Lasson, "Group Libel Versus Free Speech: When Big Brother *Should* Butt In," *Duquesne Law Review,* 23 (1984), 123.

92. *Bethel School Dist. No. 403 v. Fraser,* 478 U.S. 675, 681 (1986) (quoting Charles Beard and Mary Beard, *New Basic History of the United States* 228 [1968]. See *FCC v. Pacifica Foundation,* 438 U.S. 726 (1978); Post, supra note 28, at 681–83.

93. See Post, supra note 28 at 626–46.

94. Hence Justice Brandeis's observation that democracy "substitutes self-restraint for external restraint." Letter from Justice Louis Brandeis to Robert Walter Bruere (Feb. 25, 1922), *Letters of Louis D. Brandeis* (Melvin I. Urofsky & David W. Levy, eds.) (Albany: State University of New York Press, 1978), p. 46.

95. 315 U.S. 568, 572 (1942).

96. The argument contained in the following two paragraphs is developed at length in Post, supra note 28, at 667–84.

97. Hanna Pitkin, "Justice: On Relating Private and Public," *Political Theory,* 9 (1981), 346.

98. *Dun & Bradstreet, Inc. v. Greenmoss Builders, Inc.* 472 U.S. 749, 758–59 (1985) (plurality opinion); see *Philadelphia Newspapers, Inc. v. Hepps,* 475 U.S. 767, 775 (1986).

99. *Dun & Bradstreet, Inc. v. Greenmoss Builders, Inc.,* 472 U.S. 749, 761 (1985) (plurality opinion) (quoting *Connick v. Myers,* 461 U.S. 138, 147–48 [1983]).

100. *Hustler Magazine v. Falwell,* 485 U.S. 46 (1988).

101. See, e.g., *Rogers v. EEOC,* 454 F. 2d 234, 237–38 (5th Cir. 1971); *EEOC v. Murphy Motor Freight,* 488 F. Supp. 381, 385 (D. Minn. 1980); *Alcorn v. Anbro Engineering, Inc.,* 2 Cal. 3d 493, 468 P. 2d 216, 86 Cal. Rptr. 88 (1970); *Contreras v. Crown Zellerbach Corp.,* 88 Wash. 2d 735, 565 P. 2d 1173 (1977); cf. *Meritor Savings Bank v. Vinson,* 477 U.S. 57, 65–66 (1986).

102. George Herbert Mead, *On Social Psychology* (Anselm Strauss, ed.) (Chicago: University of Chicago Press, 1964), p. 239.

103. Id. at 230.

104. Id. at 238, 240.

105. Id. at 238.

8

LIBERAL DEMOCRATIC COMMUNITY

RICHARD J. ARNESON

Communitarians criticize liberal political philosophy on the ground that it is inhospitable to the value of community.[1] No doubt several lines of thought converge at the point of this criticism, but I concentrate on a single objection that impresses me as sound. This communitarian objection holds that contemporary philosophical liberalism relies on the shaky claim that the state should strive to be neutral on the question of the good life. I briefly review some responses to this objection and find them inadequate. I then show how adding a utilitarian account of the good to a liberal political doctrine improves its capacity to withstand the objection. From the perspective of a liberalism influenced by this component of utilitarianism, neutrality on the good can be abandoned without giving up the core case for broad toleration that had been phrased in the language of neutrality. Finally, I use the view of liberalism and communitarianism developed here to criticize Robert Post's interpretation of American constitutional law regarding freedom of expression in terms of tension between the values of "responsive democracy" and "community." Post believes that this tension resists definitive resolution and sees in this fact a lesson for the debate in political philosophy between liberals and communitarians: Like the legal issue, the philosophical problem resists any tidy solution and "instead requires situational and pragmatic adjustment."[2] In my

191

view, this summary judgment vastly overstates the damage inflicted on philosophical liberalism by its communitarian critics.

LIBERAL NEUTRALITY

According to Ronald Dworkin, liberalism is committed to a theory of equality that "supposes that political decisions must be,
so far as is possible, independent of any particular conception
of the good life, or of what gives value to life."[3] John Rawls
writes that when democratic civil liberties are respected, "a diversity of conflicting and irreconcilable comprehensive doctrines
will emerge" and persist. So for Rawls the ideal of a political
society united in a community affirming a single comprehensive
doctrine could be sustained only by "the oppressive use of state
power."[4] Expounding the idea that liberalism significantly involves the requirement that citizens refrain from appealing to
some of their beliefs—for example, religious beliefs—to justify
the adoption of a governmental policy, Thomas Nagel writes,
"We accept a kind of epistemological division between the private
and the public domains: in certain contexts I am constrained to
consider my beliefs merely as beliefs rather than as truths, however convinced I may be that they are true, and that I know it."[5]
Charles Larmore offers a succinct formula: "The fundamental
liberal principle is that the state should remain neutral toward
disputed and controversial ideals of the good life."[6]

Ignoring important differences among these formulations, I
note that all involve a distinction between a presumptive common
ground of moral beliefs to be affirmed by all citizens and used
by them in reasoning about justice and a zone of presumptively
intractable disagreement. The philosophers quoted earlier associate this distinction with an aspect of the distinction between
the public realm and private life: As citizens we are to agree to
appeal only to a subset of our moral beliefs when we advance
proposals and arguments concerning public policy. The position
that I call "pure philosophical liberalism" links this understanding of private-versus-public to the epistemic priority of the right
over the good.[7] Knowledge of the right is presumed to be in
theory attainable by all citizens, and to be the legitimate and
enforceable basis of their social unity. Conceptions of the good

are presumed to be divisive. About these matters, so important for each of our individual lives, we must agree to disagree and must resolve maturely to give up utopian aspirations to society-wide consensus or to the coercive imposition of our favored opinion.

At one level, the question arises whether pure philosophical liberalism accurately interprets the core liberal political values: Is it really a hallmark of liberalism that the state ought to be strictly neutral as between, for instance, the ideal of the life of the long-term heroin addict and the ideal of a life free of heavy use of hard drugs? At another level, questions arise as to whether the radical asymmetry in the availability for the theory of justice of conceptions of the good and conceptions of the right can be sustained. If we cannot know anything useful about the nature of the good life in a sufficiently robust way that we can apply these truths to questions about how society should be organized and how we should treat each other, why suppose that we can know anything useful about the nature of the right and about social justice? In a review of *A Theory of Justice*, Thomas Nagel observes that for Rawls "the principles of justice are objective and interpersonally recognizable in a way that conceptions of the good are not."[8] But why not? To some extent it's a matter of definitions. Philosophical liberals use "the right" as a name for principles that tell us how we ought to deal with one another when people's interests conflict and "the good" as a name for principles of prudence that tell how it is rational to behave insofar as one should be guided by self-interest. If one denies that reasonable agreement on the right is impossible to obtain, one will probably not write treatises on social justice. Still, one wonders how in the absence of any shared understanding of what is good for individuals it can be decided how it is fair for individuals to deal with each other in conflict situations.

If it is assumed that people will persist in deep disagreement about the meaning, value, and purpose of life and about the kind of life that is good for the individual who lives it, it is hard to see how one can simultaneously assume that people can reach full agreement about principles of right and justice. It would be more natural to suppose that disagreements about the good will spill over into disagreements about what is right. Someone who believes that what matters in life is whether or not we gain everlasting happiness in heaven is unlikely to agree about principles of right conduct with someone who believes that life must be taken on its own terms and leads to nothing beyond the grave.

Rawls explains why original position arguments for principles of justice should be insulated from influence by conceptions of the good: "That we have one conception of the good rather than another is not relevant from a moral standpoint. In acquiring it we are influenced by the same sort of contingencies that lead us to rule out a knowledge of our sex and class."[9] But our convictions about social justice are also influenced by morally arbitrary contingencies such as our social class and sex and what the opinions of our parents happen to have been. If probable influence by morally arbitrary factors is a good reason to prevent our convictions about the good from entering into arguments for principles of social justice, this is equally a good reason to prevent our convictions about social justice from entering into arguments for principles of social justice. The entire project of searching for rational foundations for principles of justice would otherwise go up in smoke. If on the other hand we respond to this problem of contamination by resolving as best we can to liberate ourselves in thought from our contingent origins and to reason impartially, then this problem no longer appears to generate a good reason for bracketing all convictions about the good from arguments over justice.

This association of philosophical liberalism with skepticism about the good, at least so far as the theory of justice is concerned, is a major stimulant to communitarian criticism. Liberalism so construed strikes some as abstract and lifeless and the austere theory of justice that abstracts from controversies about human good seems to advance principles that ignore what really matters to most of us. Justice in this vision guarantees you certain rights and immunities and perhaps an entitlement to resources of some kind, but none of these provisions necessarily fosters a good life nor guarantees you access to a good life.

The norm of neutrality on the good in philosophical liberalism (i.e., government should not carry out policies justifiable only by appeal to the presumed superiority of some controversial way of life or conception of the good) is meant to embody a strong version of toleration, but it has some odd consequences.[10] Liberal principles of justice that satisfy neutrality will not treat people differently depending on the quality of the lives they lead as assessed by a theory of the good life. The idea is that how well or badly an individual's life goes is that individual's responsibility, not the responsibility of society, provided the individual is treated justly. But how can we know that individuals have been treated justly without assessing the opportunities for a good life that society's treatment affords them? A society that fully satisfies principles of neutral justice could be a desolate shopping mall bereft of satisfying communal attachments. Perhaps individuals who suffer from shopping mall culture are morally responsible for their own suffering, but perhaps not. To decide the point we would need to know whether our collective responsibility to provide individuals adequate opportunities for a good life has been satisfied. A theory of justice that is not informed by a substantive theory of human good will be incapable of distinguishing when this obligation is or is not fulfilled.

The complaint that liberalism is insensitive to the significance of community is an instance of this objection. The defining characteristics of the idea of community that figures in this complaint are "shared final ends and common activities valued for themselves."[11] A shared final end is a goal that all members of a given group can share because the good is collective relative to the group—the good is such that consumption of it by one group member leaves none the less for others to enjoy—and moreover the goal is shared in the further sense that each member wants all the members to gain the goal. A set of persons is a community to the extent that they share final ends and common activities valued for themselves. If one supposes that human beings need community and cannot attain good lives without it, and the proper business of society is to foster human good, then one has a criticism of philosophical liberalism insofar as the theory ignores this dimension of political justice and a criticism of liberalism as a political practice if liberal institutions fail adequately to foster community.

THE RIGHT AND THE GOOD: LIBERAL REVISIONS

Perhaps in response to criticisms like those already discussed, recent philosophical liberal writings strike out in new directions.

In recent writings Rawls has argued for his principles of justice by attempting to show that they would be chosen in a fair original position by persons motivated by three Kantian moral interests. The two top priority interests are (1) a sense of justice, the desire to cooperate with others on terms reasonably believed to be fair, and (2) rational autonomy, the desire to choose a conception of the good after rational deliberation and to revise that conception if further deliberation and argument urge revision. A lesser priority interest is (3) satisfaction, the desire to fulfill whatever conception of the good one happens now to embrace.[12]

However, the stipulated interests in rational autonomy and the sense of justice as a first priority do not plausibly support either Rawlsian principles of justice or the ordinary civil liberties that these principles are intended to rationalize. Persons who give strict priority to these Kantian interests and who are choosing principles of justice will note that in actual societies people often fail to accord priority to these interests in their conduct either through settled conviction, weakness of will, ignorance, or confused reasoning. Hence Kantian persons will be moved to choose principles that secure conformity to Kantian interests from persons who would backslide if given the chance. This line of thought supports paternalistic coercion of citizens in the name of the Kantian interests that are imputed to them. The paternalistic rules generated by this argument will not mesh with current conceptions of civil liberties. For example, the right of free speech as ordinarily understood is the right of willing speakers to engage willing audiences. Free speech permits citizens to refrain from listening to others if they choose. But eschewing rational discussion sometimes violates rational autonomy. Hence the Kantian version of the original position will generate principles that endorse forcing citizens by law to participate in rational dialogue to the extent that such forcing can be expected to enhance people's rational autonomy over the course of their lives. This is not freedom of speech as we know and value it. In a similar vein, giving strict priority to the aim of rationally choosing a life plan over the aim of fulfilling one's present plans turns out to have counterintuitive implications for policy.[13]

The ideal of rational autonomy is a perfectionist ideal of the good, so a commitment to advance it will not dovetail with liberal neutrality. Retreat from strict neutrality might be well-advised, but the proper extent of the retreat needs further analysis. But the main difficulty with Rawls's Kantian gambit is that the perfectionist ideal of Kantian rational autonomy does not provide convincing reasons to support liberal principles and liberal freedoms.

Ronald Dworkin follows a strategy of argument that is somewhat similar to Rawls's.[14] The idea is to seek a relatively uncontroversial and widely shared abstract account of the good and to demonstrate that this liberal account of the good and a liberal account of justice are mutually reinforcing. So anyone who accepts the liberal account of the good will thereby have some reason, though perhaps not a conclusive one, for endorsing the liberal account of justice. The aim is to characterize a reasonable reflective equilibrium between views of the good and views of justice that citizens of modern democratic society will find attractive and plausible after considered reflection.

In pursuing this project Dworkin's master distinction is between what he calls "impact" and "challenge" models of the good. According to the former view, the goodness of an individual life consists in the objective value that it adds to the world both for the individual and for others. Whether or not I lead a good life depends on the impact of my life on the world. In contrast, the "challenge account finds ethical value in the performance of living rather than in the independent value of some product a life leaves behind." On this view the value of a life "consists in the skillful, in most cases intuitively skillful, managing of a challenge."[15] The idea seems to be that life presents individuals with a challenge, which they must interpret and solve in their own way, leading their life so that it enacts the solution. A good life is a skillful performance in response to the challenge posed by (some of) the given circumstances of that life.

One who accepts the challenge view is an ethical liberal. Dworkin elaborates it in an attempt to demonstrate that the ethical liberal committed to it is ipso facto provided strong reasons to endorse the political morality of liberalism, the liberal theory of the right.

For the purposes of this chapter the crucial link between the liberal view of the good and the liberal view of justice is the claim that according to the challenge view one cannot improve individuals' lives by coercing or manipulating them to lead their lives according to a conception of the good that one regards as superior to the conception that would inform their life if such coercion and manipulation were eschewed. Paternalism of this sort cannot succeed. This is supposed to be so not because it is somehow guaranteed that the person tempted to coercion for the good of another cannot be right in thinking the person she or he wants to help is pursuing an inferior conception of the good. She or he may indeed be right! But this thought, according to Dworkin, cannot justify paternalism because one cannot improve another's life by coercing or manipulating that person to live according to a conception that person does not accept, or would not accept but for this coercion or manipulation. For example, even if Roman Catholicism is superior as a religion to Methodism, one's life taken as a performance does not improve in value if one is forced to follow Roman Catholic ritual against one's Methodist beliefs.

Dworkin concedes that short-term paternalism against present convictions might be justifiable if the individuals will predictably come to endorse the values in whose name they have been coerced, provided the coercion itself does not render their later endorsement irrational or bogus. He seems to regard the practical political significance of this concession as slight. According to Dworkin, if we accept the challenge model of value in human life we must then "insist on the priority of ethical *integrity* in any judgment we make about how good someone's life is. Ethical integrity is the condition someone achieves who is able to live out of the conviction that his life, in its central features, is an appropriate life for him, that no other life he might live would be a plainly better response to the parameters of his ethical situation rightly judged."[16] The priority of ethical integrity means that a life that fails to achieve integrity cannot be superior to a life that has it.[17]

The priority of integrity asserted by Dworkin is an extraordinary doctrine and, many will suspect, a radically implausible one. Consider its implications: Imagine that Smith has sensible values generally but adheres to two silly ideas: (1) It is of overwhelming ethical importance to commit suicide in response to any unsuccessful romantic episode and (2) one absolutely ought never to disobey the law for any reason. Smith experiences severe romantic disappointment in the course of a teen-age crush and concludes that his life would go best if he committed suicide. But because he lives in a society whose laws prohibit suicide, he never acts on this conviction, which he never abandons, that his life would go best if ended immediately by his own hand in response to this past romantic trauma. Smith goes on to lead a fulfilling life, according to standards that would withstand rational scrutiny, except that he retains his idiosyncratically extreme beliefs in romantic heroism and fidelity to law. The priority of integrity applied to this case requires us to hold that however good and long Smith's life is, it would have been better for him if the laws had permitted suicide so that he might have taken his life foolishly at age fifteen. I suspect that once its implications are understood, the priority of integrity will attract few adherents.

In Dworkin's argument, the priority of integrity is bound up with the challenge view. Now taken by itself, the challenge view as sketched is implausible. The thought that the value of a human life is its value as a performance or response to challenge, no matter how broadly interpreted, runs against the commonsense idea that how well one's life goes depends on good fortune as well as on one's skill at responding to life's challenges. A poor peasant might devote her life to sustaining her family and friends through hard times, and show consummate skill, intelligence, and persistence in working toward this goal, but to no avail. Famine, drought, and disease might bring about the premature death of her family despite her best efforts. Virtue is no guarantee against misery and tragedy. No philosophical dogma should force us to say that the virtuous peasant's tragically miserable life must be a success because we cannot fault any of her life activities regarded as performance.

Even if this criticism is set aside, a more important objection looms. From the assumption that the value of a person's life is its value as a performance it does not follow, nor is it an independently plausible claim, that the individual performer is the final judge of the value of the performance. Dworkin claims that on "any plausible interpretation" of the challenge model, "the connection between conviction and value is constitutive: my life cannot go better for me in virtue of some feature or component I think has no value.... For intention is part of performance: we do not give credit to a performer for some feature of his performance he was struggling to avoid."[18] I would suppose there can be happy unintended accidents of performance that improve the performance, but in any event whether one intends an element of one's performance and how one values the element are separate and distinct matters.

Imagine that Smith's dominant aim in life is to write a great novel, and he succeeds spectacularly in fulfilling that ambition, but being diffident, he goes to his grave believing his novel worthless. Insofar as his dominant desire was to succeed and not merely to believe in his success, his life should be judged a success. In this scenario Smith's life goes better in virtue of a component that he mistakenly thinks has no value.

The challenge model and the priority of integrity together do not suffice to condemn paternalism of the sort that plainly violates the neutrality ideal and that Dworkin plainly wishes to show to be unjustifiable. To illustrate this point, suppose that Smith is disposed to experiment with hard drugs and adopt the lifestyle of a junkie. But he lives in a society that prohibits hard drug usage from concern for the predictably low quality of the life of a junkie. Consequently, he does not act on this disposition, becomes a stockbroker instead, and acquires values that rank stockbrokering above drug addiction and that are held on grounds just as reasonable as the grounds that would have led him to endorse hard drug usage if it had been legal. If we endorse the view that hard drug usage is inimical to the good life, we may endorse a paternalistic ban on hard drug usage for the sake of Smith and others like him. So far as I can see, the challenge model and the priority of integrity are compatible with these endorsements, so challenge does not support neutrality as Dworkin supposes.

Dworkin resists this conclusion for reasons I do not understand. He replies that the line of thought sketched here "misunderstands the challenge model profoundly," because it "assumes that we have some standard of what a good life is that *transcends* the question of what circumstances are appropriate for people deciding how to live, and so can be used in answering that question, by stipulating that the best circumstances are those most likely to produce the really correct answer."[19] But if the challenge model as Dworkin conceives it is correct, a good life for a person is a skillful performance in response to the challenge she or he encounters in facing her or his life. What counts as a skillful performance cannot on this view be determined independently of knowing, or interpreting, the specific challenge that this person faces. As Dworkin puts it, the challenge model presupposes a distinction between parameters and circumstances. Some of the circumstances of one's life are *parameters:* they constitute the challenge a successful response to which constitutes living well. (To some extent individuals have some choice about which features of their situation are to be counted as parameters.) According to Dworkin, prior to a determination of parameters, the question of what would be a good life has no determinate content.

Accepting Dworkin's terminology, though with some misgivings, I find implausible the implicit claim that we cannot judge some parameters as superior to others that might constitute the defining life challenge for a person. With paternalistic restrictions in place, Smith will face one set of parameters (or a range of possible sets). Without paternalism, he will face a different set (or a different range). Unless one gives up the idea that we can sometimes know some ways of life to be superior to others, then we can sometimes know such propositions as that lives that avoid disease, addiction, mindless violence, and lovelessness are worse lives, other things equal, than lives that include these afflictions. But judgments of this sort are the basis of nonneutral paternalism. Dworkin does not succeed in showing that challenge and integrity commit one to the rejection of neutrality-violating paternalism without relying on skepticism about knowledge of the good that, consistently followed through, would erode his own position.

Even if Dworkin were right that paternalistic coercion forcing individuals to lead their lives according to values they do not endorse could never improve the value of those lives, that rejection of paternalism does not come close to supporting state neutrality on the good. Let us say that a *neutral* state is one whose policies do not aim to support any ways of life or conceptions of the good espoused by some citizens over those espoused by other citizens. Consider a simple example. For the sake of the argument assume that coerced conformity to the externals of Catholic doctrine is valueless. But this does not even rule out state establishment of a religion. If Catholicism is the true religion and lives dedicated to Catholicism are, other things equal, superior in value to lives dedicated to other religions or to nonreligious values, then many actions are available to the state that would efficiently increase the numbers of people who reflectively endorse Catholicism and lead lives dedicated to it. The state could require all citizens to send their children to state-sponsored parochial schools in which Roman Catholic doctrine is taught as the authoritative truth, for example.[20]

Neither the abstract Kantian view of the good embraced by Rawls nor Dworkin's challenge view successfully answers the communitarian challenge by showing how an attractive and plausible doctrine of the good can be integrated into a liberal theory of justice that upholds satisfactory principles with respect to paternalism, toleration, and neutrality.

A Fresh Start: Taking a Leaf from the Utilitarian Book

Up to this point my task has been purely destructive. None of the recent attempts by philosophical liberals to defend policies of liberal tolerance and liberal neutrality succeeds. To this extent the communitarian distrust of the treatment of the good in philosophical liberalism is well-founded. However, a more robust defense of policies of tolerance and of a norm close to liberal neutrality is ready to hand. Attempting to rehabilitate the role of the good (understood in a communitarian way) in political philosophy, Michael Sandel argues that "utilitarianism gave the good a bad name, and in adopting it uncritically, [philosophical liberalism] wins for deontology a false victory."[21] But Sandel's dismissal of the utilitarian understanding of the good as a resource for liberal theory is too glib. Sandel identifies the utilitarian conception of the good with desire satisfaction, which he plausibly asserts to be patently inadequate. But to find the elements of a better conception we need not go beyond utilitarianism. Assembling points urged by John Stuart Mill in *Utilitarianism* and in *On Liberty,* I show that there is a way to construe the good as utility that renders it a building block in liberal arguments for tolerance and wide individual liberty.[22]

That the satisfaction of desire is an inadequate conception of human flourishing is evident from the fact that the desires that are satisfied might be ill-considered, confused, based on faulty reasoning or false belief. Suppose that Smith successfully organizes his life around his dominant ambition to complete a novel. If Smith would not have adopted this desire were it not for the fact that he falsely believes that he possesses extraordinary writing talent, satisfaction of this dominant aim does not constitute attainment of a good life.

This line of thought suggests the alternative idea that the good life is constituted by cognitively refined or rational desire satisfaction. The greater the extent to which an individual's basic preferences (a) would be affirmed by that individual after ideally well-informed rational deliberation and (b) are fulfilled, the better the individual's life. "Preference" here may be a slightly misleading word choice. We are most confident in ascribing a preference to individuals when their felt desires, personal value judgments, and choice behavior are all congruent, so that when they prefer *a* over *b* for its own sake (1) they feel that they want *a* more than *b* when the issue is on their mind, other things equal, (2) they judge that *a* would be better for them than *b*, and (3) they are disposed to choose *a* over *b,* all else being equal, when presented with a choice between them. But when these elements of preference split apart as they often do, personal value judgments take priority in determining what individuals' preferences are for the purpose of determining how well their lives are going.

Some further clarifications will help convey what I mean by the "rational preference satisfaction" conception of the good.

First, the more important a preference is to individuals, the more its satisfaction augments the goodness of their lives.

Second, not all preferences are self-interested, but only self-interested preferences count in determining the goodness of a person's life. I assume that persons sometimes have preferences, at least in the felt desire and choice behavior sense, that are grounded in their sense of what is morally required or in their notions of what is good for others or nonmorally good from an impersonal standpoint. That is, persons in their own experience can distinguish self-interested from non-self-interested preferences. All things considered, I may prefer to give the money I was saving for a holiday trip to a fund for famine relief, while being clear in my mind that this donation will improve the lives of distant others but will make my life go worse on balance. The slight glow of self-righteous virtue that giving to charity affords me does not compare with the expected self-interested benefit of the holiday. And sometimes it is clear to persons that their self-interest encompasses the interest of another person with whom they are associated, so that "sacrifices" for their child's welfare on balance increase the extent to which their own lives go well. In other cases, of course, it may be radically unclear to individuals just where the boundary of their self-interest lies. "Self-interested" is not equivalent to "selfish."

Third, sometimes when a person's preferences change, the new preference is cognitively superior to the one it supplants—it would better withstand informed rational scrutiny. To the extent that this is so, the cognitively superior preference supersedes the inferior competing preference. When preferences change but the change does not reflect cognitive improvement, or deterioration, I would hold that all preferences count equally, weighted by the length of time in one's life that one has held them. So failure to undergo a deathbed conversion that one wanted at death's door improves the quality of one's life on balance, if one strongly and unconditionally[23] preferred not to undergo a deathbed conversion for most of one's life.

Rational preference satisfaction is a construal of what is sometimes called the idea of the nonmorally good. A person who is charitable, just, kind, fairminded, and virtuous in other ways is morally good. Nonmoral good in contrast is the object of just one virtue, prudence. The prudent person is someone who acts efficiently to make his or her own life go as well as possible, at least when the good of others is not at stake. Rational preference satisfaction is a candidate construal of what it is that the prudent person qua prudent seeks.

Notice that nothing said so far about rational preference satisfaction creates any presumption regarding the merits of liberal policies of tolerance, antipaternalism, and neutrality. For all that has been said so far, it might be that some sound argument definitively establishes that there is one true religion and fostering adherence to this religion by all citizens is the best available strategy for helping all citizens lead good lives, lives with the best overall prospects for rational preference satisfaction.

A political doctrine that begins with the idea that the good consists in rational preference satisfaction only begins to assume a recognizably liberal shape when further claims about individuality are added:

1. Individuals are different, and what is good for an individual depends on her or his particular nature. In this regard it is unnecessary to adopt a Romantic individualist position, acording to which the good for each is unique to that individual. It suffices to hold that there is a large variety of types of individuals and that what is good for an individual varies depending on her or his type.

2. Individual natures are nontransparent. Learning enough about an individual's nature to enable one to judge authoritatively what is good for her or him is difficult. Our natures are not merely nontransparent to other people but to ourselves as well. If there are a finite number of types of individual, there is usually great uncertainty as to which type any given individual belongs, and this uncertainty is often intractable. But because our natures are not completely opaque, and we are not completely unlike one another, learning about other persons and about societies and cultures conveys useful information in deciding what is good for oneself. So experimentation, wide observation, "liberal" education, and individual reflection are needed if one is to have a good chance of discovering one's nature sufficiently well to identify one's own good. This last claim particularly holds true for modern industrialized societies in

which the division of labor is extensive, many ways of life are options, individual freedom de facto to choose among many ways of life or cobble together one's own mixed life is extensive, technological and cultural change is rapid and pervasive, and as an early commentator on modernity put it, "all that is solid melts into air" and "all new-formed [relations] become antiquated before they can ossify."[24]

3. Rational preference satisfaction provides a subjective criterion of a person's well-being (i.e., the goodness of her life) according to a distinction between subjective and objective articulated by Thomas Scanlon: "By an *objective criterion* I mean a criterion that provides a basis for appraisal of a person's level of well-being which is independent of that person's tastes and interests, thus allowing for the possibility that such an appraisal could be correct even though it conflicted with the preferences of the individual in question, not only as he believes they are but even as they would be if rendered consistent, corrected for factual errors, etc."[25] The idea is that according to a subjective criterion of individual good one cannot determine what is good for a person except by consulting that very person's (corrected) point-of-view on his or her situation. The perspective for determining the good is provided for each person by his or her own tastes and values, and refined for each person by inquiring how these might change under rational scrutiny. So one can say that rational preference satisfaction is an empty basket. Its content is determined for each person from that person's own standpoint. We can say formally what is good for a person without consulting and engaging his or her own subjective point-of-view, but to determine substantively what is good for a person, what fills the basket, consultation and engagement are necessary.

Formality, not neutrality, is crucial for the justification of toleration. A state that bases its policies on a rational preference satisfaction conception of the good is clearly nonneutral. Its policies evince commitment to a single conception of human good. But this conception is formal, and the substance of what is good for a person is determined from that very person's standpoint. The state should then be neutral among the many and diverse ways of life and substantive conceptions of the good that could be reasonably affirmed by citizens. The state should neither enact policies justified by appeal to the superiority of some of these reasonable conceptions over others, nor should the state aim to promote some of these reasonable conceptions over others.

4. People can and do make mistakes about where their good lies, from the trivial to the tragic and sublime. They make mistakes not only about how to get what they want but about what is worth having. Sometimes Jones knows what is good for Smith better than Smith knows. Hence a state that seeks rational preference satisfaction for its citizens does not in principle renounce all paternalism, not even strong paternalism that involves coercion of persons for their own good on behalf of values that they do not currently accept.[26] But the liberal state should be guided by a powerful presumption against paternalism because individuals usually know their own interests better than state officials, need to find their own path and learn from their mistakes, and are so diverse in their needs that any paternalistic coercion is almost bound to hurt some persons and may help none. Also, in many cases the information gathering that officials would have to undertake to develop a warranted paternalistic policy in some domain would violate norms of privacy that the state ought to respect for the good of citizens generally.

UTILITY, FREE EXPRESSION, AND TOLERATION

From a rational preference satisfaction standpoint, the argument for freedom of expression is instrumental. In principle nothing rules out the possibility that preferences affirmed in ignorance and in the absence of reasoned deliberation might turn out to be rational preferences—preferences that *would* withstand informed rational scrutiny if such scrutiny were undertaken. The admiration felt by many persons for the ways of life of primitive hunter-gatherer tribes underscores this point. Similarly, in principle it is possible that the preferences people would be manipulated or coerced into embracing under the paternalistic guidance of a benevolent monarch or dictatorial party might turn out to be more rational by the counterfactual test than the preferences they would come to have under a regime that respects civil liberties and offers wide freedom. So other things equal, people in this case could be expected to lead better lives under dictatorship than under liberal freedom. The premise of a liberalism that incorporates a utilitarian understanding of the good is that these logical possibilities are not empirical likelihoods. In the modern world, individuals are far more likely to affirm rational preferences if they freely engage in informed deliberation than if they persist in uncritical acceptance of their given preferences or are denied the opportunity for informed deliberation. With the exception of the feebleminded and the seriously emotionally ill, individuals who try to develop informed rational preferences in a culture that is supportive of this endeavor are more likely to succeed in developing such preferences than those who do not try or whose attempts are hampered by an unsupportive culture.

These considerations support a division of labor between society and individuals in which the individuals are assigned major responsibility for the way of life and conception of the good that they embrace. The responsibility of society is to secure optimal conditions for rational preference formation and an institutional structure that generates resources for individuals that enable them to satisfy a fair proportion of their preferences. The liberal understanding of optimal conditions for preference formation is that they include broad discretion for competent parents to introduce their children to their own way of life provided that each child receives an education that prepares him or her broadly for a wide range of careers and life choices and that includes training in critical analytical and deliberative skills.[27] For adults, optimal conditions of preference formation on the liberal view include freedom of thought and expression, encouragement of citizens to adapt their empirical beliefs toward current scientific knowledge, provision of the stimulus to experimentation of a wide array of goods and services through economic markets, and wide freedom to live out whatever way of life and conception of the good one embraces at the present. In short, wide individual liberty is needed to facilitate the formation of rational preferences as well as to enable individuals to satisfy them.

Similar claims for individual liberty were advanced in uncompromising form by J. S. Mill. Rawls comments that "even Mill's contentions, as cogent as they are, will not, it seems, justify an equal liberty for all." The problem according to Rawls is that "whenever a society sets out to maximize the sum of intrinsic value or the net balance of the satisfaction of interests, it is liable to find that the denial of liberty for some is justified in the name of this single end."[28] Rawls's comments identify the essential weakness in Mill's arguments not in their teleological structure—that rights are justified by their contribution to some further goal—but rather in the specifically utilitarian character of the teleology to which Mill appeals. Utilitarianism holds that what is right is the maximization of the good, which is construed as utility. Maximization can recommend policies that intuitively strike us as unfair, such as policies that impose very severe losses on already worse-off persons to secure slight gains for a great many already better-off citizens. But the rejection of straight maximization of aggregate utility leaves open the possibility that justice is properly concerned with achieving the good, construed as utility, for citizens in ways that are fair. The simplest proposal for what counts as "fairness-constrained maximizing" is that society ought (1) to strive impartially to advance the good of all but (2) in doing so to give priority to achieving gains and avoiding losses for the worse off.

Fairness-constrained maximizing is still maximizing of a sort, and might recommend the imposition of great burdens on some citizens to secure gains for others, which might be thought problematic. Consider, for example, the propriety of a military draft in time of war, or of redistributive taxation policies that significantly curb the economic liberty of better-off citizens. But it is doubtful that basic liberties of equal citizenship such as the right to freedom of expression would fail to receive support from fairness-constrained maximizing. This is so owing to the connection between free expression and rational preference formation. Engagement in public discourse contributes to the common stock of practical wisdom and so benefits everyone who draws on that stock in preference and value formation. In the short run, free expression gives rise to conflict, when speech offends some or otherwise threatens their interests, but in the long run all citizens have a stake in the maintenance of an open society for goal formation.

So the evident unfairness of straight utilitarian maximizing does not settle the issue whether achievement of the good for individuals, understood as utility, should have a central place in a liberal theory of justice. Any justification of civil liberties starting from this premise would rest on contingencies, but the contingencies that underpin a utility-based case for civil liberties are robust. And surely our convictions regarding civil liberties are founded on contingent beliefs. For example, if it turned out that free speech made everyone worse off, we would stop supporting it.

Post on Community versus Responsive Democracy

Within the portions of the law that regulate speech and expression, Post identifies the civil law dignitary torts of defamation, invasion of privacy, and intentional infliction of emotional distress with "community" and the constitutional law tradition of protections of freedom of expression with "responsive democracy." The dignitary torts restricting speech protect a certain communal way of life, whereas the strong constitutional guarantees of freedom of expression protect the liberty of individuals freely to choose their own way of life and to participate in free dialogue about how we together should live that in the ideal case might reconcile majority rule and individual self-determination.

Post discerns two conflicting tendencies in the law regulating speech and expression. On the one hand, it is natural that like-minded persons forming a community would wish to use civil and criminal law sanctions to uphold and enforce their shared values, if they can capture the power of the state by majority vote. From this perspective regulation of speech can be instrumental in sustaining community in the same way as the regulation of any other activity. On the other side, the idea of responsive democracy is the aspiration to a society ruled by laws that are affirmed by a unanimous rational consensus after ideal deliberation among all citizens. Ideal deliberation is unconstrained deliberation in the sense that no legal barriers as to topic of discourse or content of utterance limit free discussion among willing speakers and hearers.

In any given case, the courts must choose to favor either community or responsive democracy when they come in conflict, as they often do. Post uses the example that the courts must either affirm the constitutionality of laws that ban flag-burning or deny that flag-burning statutes are constitutional. To affirm is to favor community, to deny is to favor responsive democracy. On the surface, we have values in conflict. Post thinks that under the surface the issues are more complex and messy than this formulation acknowledges. Practices of responsive democracy can sustain themselves only if individuals are socialized successfully to believe in them. Responsive democracy practices must be supported by responsive democracy communal values and these have to be reproduced as do any communal values.

Post is surely right in claiming that one cannot in all circumstances simultaneously maximize the extent to which society (1) protects each individual's right to listen to whatever any willing speaker wishes to say or to speak whatever she or he has a mind to any willing listener and (2) secures the fulfillment of citizens' communal, and other, values. When (1) and (2) conflict, some rule specifying acceptable tradeoffs between them would seem to be called for. Post seems to assume, and to be led by communitarian philosophy to think himself right to assume, that no principled adjudication of these values is possible so that the courts and citizens generally must tack back and forth between them making "pragmatic" adjustments. But it would be premature to conclude that conflicts between (1) and (2) must force us into a philosophical impasse prior to investigating strategies of reconciliation.

From a rational preference satisfaction standpoint, possibly both the protection of free expression and the enforcement of communal values are means to the further and ethically more fundamental goal of helping citizens fairly to lead good lives. In Ronald Dworkin's succinct formulation, the goal is to create a "society that is most conducive to human beings' making intelligent decisions about what the best lives for them to lead are, and then flourishing in those lives."[29]

On this view, preserving free speech and sustaining community are both means to a further goal. The maximization of this goal provides a principled standard for determining how to balance freedom of expression and community against each other when they conflict.[30] Moreover, from a rational preference satisfaction perspective, citizens can be confident that preserving community ties that they value really will enhance their lives only if freedom of expression and other institutions fostering rational preference formation are operating successfully. Communal ties passionately embraced can be ugly and destructive as easily as they can be life-enhancing. A political doctrine that gives pride of place to the values of community must have the resources to distinguish desirable and undesirable communal forms. Deliberation on community addresses two concerns: whether the particular form of community under consideration is good for its members and whether sustaining this particular community is unfairly costly to the interests of other affected individuals.

Maintaining guarantees of freedom of expression does not guarantee that citizens will engage successfully in reasoned deliberation so that their communal attachments are rational and fulfillment of them makes their lives go better. But in the absence of political guarantees of freedom of expression and a political culture that encourages reasoned deliberation, citizens cannot be as confident of the reasonableness of their communal, and other, values as they could be if freedom of expression were thriving. Participation in the discourse about values and ways of life that freedom of expression exists to protect enables individuals to come to know when fulfillment of their communal identities advances their good in ways that are fair to others. Moreover, even those who do not participate in discourse about values in a society that protects free expression will typically benefit from free expression by free-riding on those who do participate. If I unreflectively follow ways of life that are popular, or popular among classes of persons I respect, in a society with vigorous discourse protected by free expression my value selection is likely to be better than it would be in a society that lacks legally guaranteed opportunities for free expression.

Post paints a picture of fundamental conflict of values here by identifying responsive democracy with autonomous choice and community with nonchosen values constitutive of embedded selves. According to Post, when law makers act on the assumption that individuals are "socially-embedded and dependent," the law promotes community, and when law makers act on the assumption that individuals are "autonomous and independent," the law promotes responsive democracy. Following Michael Sandel, Post postulates as a matter of definition that *community* provides for its members "not just what they *have* as fellow citizens but also what they *are*, not a relationship they choose (as in a voluntary association), but an attachment they discover, not merely an attribute but a constituent of identity."[31] But this dichotomy of choice and discovery obscures important continuities. One may choose whether or not to engage in deliberation, but one does not in that sense choose one's convictions that are the outcome of deliberation: One reflects and reasons, and as a result one's beliefs may change. Through deliberation one discovers which beliefs one provisionally accepts. This is as true of beliefs about values as beliefs about facts. And on the side of community, the question must always be faced whether the nonchosen values into which one has been socialized are reasonable, can stand up to critical scrutiny. Achievement of autonomy comes from being responsive to reasons, not from willfully choosing values and preferences. After all, the communal identity that one discovers to be a constituent of identity can reveal itself under examination to be pretty rotten. Such revelations can and should induce change in the constituents of one's identity. Discovery and rediscovery of one's identity (those aspects of oneself that one regards as important and is stably inclined to endorse) are part and parcel of the achievement of autonomy, not a process antithetical to it.[32]

Some social thinkers think of community ties as of great value yet highly fragile and easily destroyed by skeptical rational thought. In this vision reason and community are enemies. Post seems to flirt with this perspective. On the nature of community he quotes Pascal approvingly as follows: "Custom is the whole of equity, for the sole reason that it is accepted; that is the mystic foundation of its authority. Anyone who tries to trace it back to its first principles will destroy it." But of course acceptance is the mystic foundation of good and bad custom, of slavery, pogroms, gay-bashing, and the feminization of poverty as well as of nice democratic community. If one eschews rational scrutiny of custom for fear of destroying it one foregoes the opportunity to figure out what sorts of communities one is identified with and what the moral costs of that identification are. Of course one might doubt whether reason is ever competent to make these discriminations. If it is not, Pascal is correct that the foundation of its authority must reduce to mere acceptance. But if this is Post's considered view, one wonders what value he sees in the processes of ostensibly rational deliberation that rights of freedom of expression and the other practices he identifies with responsive democracy aim to foster. It is hard to discern a consistent point of view from which both community and responsive democracy as Post characterizes them can be simultaneously affirmed. Nor is the reader's confusion eased when Post goes on to claim that Pascal's view about the "mystic foundation" of custom is accepted by current philosophers who embrace reflective equilibrium methods in ethical theory. The wide reflective equilibrium affirmed by Rawls as the ideal outcome of an agent's ethical deliberation is the state of belief one would reach after canvassing and analyzing all possible relevant arguments with full information and with full deliberative rationality. Acceptance of principles in wide reflective equilibrium is supposed to be more than mere acceptance.[33]

This criticism of Post might appear misguided in that he is interpreting American law regulating speech, not proposing a normative theory of free expression in his own voice. But if the best interpretation of the law optimally balances the tasks of explaining and so far as is possible justifying the settled law and precedents, then Post's interpretation is defective in prematurely giving up the possibility of showing the contemporary free speech doctrine of the courts to be coherent and justifiable.[34] Instead of searching for coherence Post leaps to embrace paradox.[35]

THE PARADOX OF PUBLIC DISCOURSE

Post's writings on the First Amendment express a vividly imagined Hegelian sense of pure liberal negativity feeding on itself self-destructively. The lesson is that freedom conceived in purely negative terms has to be bounded at some point by common sense community norms.

Post draws a further lesson for the practice of philosophy. He observes that the tension he sees in American law between community and responsive democracy is similar to the conflict between communitarians and liberals among contemporary American political philosophers. His further comments imply that just as the law cannot go whole hog for either responsive democracy or community but must reach pragmatic compromise, so too the philosphical debate will be resistant to any sweeping resolution. I take it that Post supposes that the debate between liberals and communitarians is primarily a debate between advocates of individualist and communitarian values. Otherwise I cannot see why he thinks the legal situation as he characterizes it resembles the philosophical debate. If this construal of Post's position is correct, then it does not adequately comprehend the philosophical debate. Liberal and communitarian theorists tend to affirm much the same values and much the same institutional arrangements. The two camps disagree about what is the most illuminating approach to theoretical understanding of the values and institutional arrangements that they both, for the most part, endorse.

According to Post, the paradox of public discourse is the idea that in trying to extend freedom of speech at some point one inevitably begins to destroy one of the preconditions of that rational dialogue that freedom of speech is supposed to foster. In his words, "Thus the First Amendment, in the name of responsive democracy, suspends legal enforcement of the very civility rules that make rational deliberation possible."[36]

I find it hard to construe this argument, so I quote Post's statement at some length:

> The two requirements of public discourse thus stand in contradiction. The aspiration to be free from the constraint of existing community norms (and to attain a consequent condition of pure communication) is in tension with the aspiration to the social project of reasoned and noncoercive deliberation. The first aspiration is sustained by the values of neutrality, diversity, and individualism; the second by the deliberative enterprise of democratic self-governance. Although the success of public deliberation depends on both requirements, the primary commitment of modern first amendment jurisprudence has unquestionably

been to the radical negativity that characterizes critical interaction, which defines the initial, distinguishing moment of public discourse. As a consequence the constitutional structure that regulates the domain of public discourse denies enforcement to the very norms upon which the success of the political enterprise of public discourse depends.[37]

Post thought that outrageously uncivil and impolite communication will be experienced by its targeted audience as invasive, irrational, even as "violent and coercive." Outrageously uncivil speech is deemed to fail to contribute to rational dialogue and to inhibit those who experience it from presenting reasoned views. Rational dialogue cannot persist in the absence of civility. Hence extension of First Amendment protection to uncivil speech undermines rational dialogue.

In response, first we should put little weight on a priori speculation about the overall effects of uncivil speech. Consider the crude satire that was the subject of litigation in *Hustler Magazine v. Falwell* or the slogan "Fuck the Draft" displayed on a jacket that provoked the disorderly conduct conviction that was reviewed by the Supreme Court in *Cohen v. California*.[38] Let us assume that the Reverend Falwell, the target of the satire, experienced it as invasive and coercive. But many other readers may have responded differently; some may have been provoked into thought. No doubt the satire in question was crude in the extreme, but Flynt might have known his audience. Perhaps satire that was subtler would have gone over their heads. Satire does not lower the level of rational debate unless its audience would have thought better about the issues and been more disposed to contribute in a useful way to public discussion if it had never been printed. And similarly for Cohen's profane display, which probably elicited a range of responses in those who saw it ranging from disgust to smiles to solidarity to a sense of anarchic liberation to puzzlement regarding the alienation of 1960s youth. To gauge the overall effects of speech one would also have to measure long-term as well as short-term effects on the audience. We should not be confident in generalizing about the on balance effects of uncivil communications on public discourse. Diffidence on this point lends support to the unwillingness of the Supreme Court to enforce civility in these cases.[39]

Even if uncivil communication unquestionably lowers the reasoned quality of a dialogue, it might motivate hitherto silent voices to participate, so the value of inclusiveness would have to be set against the lowered rational tone. Imagine that at a public forum sponsored by a City Council on a currently controversial issue someone approaches the microphone and angrily curses at Council members.[40] Subsequent debate is passionate, unfocussed, confused, and unruly. But perhaps the initial uncivil speaker triggers participation by a stratum of the audience that would otherwise remain silent. In the ensuing discussion more representative voices are heard, though less that is articulate is said. All things considered, one may judge that the quality of public debate is improved and not ruined by the uncivil curses. It is not true by definition that the violation of civility rules of speech causes public dialogue to deteriorate.

So far I have urged that the relation between the incivility and rationality of dialogue is more complex than Post allows. What is more odd about Post's formulation can be brought out by noting that American courts following First Amendment principles do not just fail uniformly to enforce civility norms on the domain of public discourse. The courts equally decline to enforce laws of logic, principles of sound reasoning, or even minimal standards of intelligibility in discourse. Have we then discovered further disturbing paradoxes of public discourse? Hardly. The norm of freedom of expression aiming at rational society-wide consensus is based on the assumption that the public and organized subgroups like the scientific community in it will in the long run do better at screening good from bad arguments than a government that attempted to improve matters by censorship. A similar assumption inhibits a liberal government committed to freedom of expression from enforcing norms of politeness and civility in public discourse. The hope is that democratic citizens, not just as individuals but in part by means of the screening of institutions and associations, will gravitate toward appropriate modes of discourse that will facilitate reasoned choice by individuals and by the public. This assumption is obviously controversial and might in the end prove right or wrong, but I do not see that acting on it automatically generates anything that deserves to be termed a paradox or a contradiction, as appears to be the case in Post's analysis.

This point can be put another way. In applying the ideal of responsive democracy to issues of First Amendment constitutional interpretation, the theorist needs to distinguish norms that should be promoted as moral virtues and upheld by the public culture of democracy from norms that should be enforced by law. It is easy to make the case for norms of politeness, moderation, mutual respect, and civility in matters of public discourse, from the standpoint of the ideal of responsive democracy, if one is arguing for their inclusion in public morals. For instance, we might well argue that we should teach these norms to our children in the public schools. It is quite another and much trickier matter to decide whether some aspects of these norms should be backed by criminal law sanctions.[41]

I do not mean to say that civility or politeness should never be made legally binding. In contemporary societies, given the salience and divisiveness of racial and ethnic conflict, perhaps there ought to be laws forbidding speech that incites racial hatred, or laws that explicitly forbid face-to-face harassment by racial or ethnic slurs and epithets.[42] For my purposes these questions can be left entirely open. My point is merely that in discussing Supreme Court decisions such as *Cohen v. California* or *Hustler Magazine v. Falwell,* one must mark the distinction between the moral rules that reasonable citizens abstracting from their communal and personal commitments will want taught to their children as authoritatively binding and the rules that these citizens will want to see enacted as legally binding.

Once this distinction is made, I do not see why even the most generous constitutional insulation of public debate about public figures from the constraints of the torts of invasion of privacy, defamation, or intentional infliction of emotional distress must pull the rug out from under citizens' adherence to norms of civility and politeness in debate. *The National Inquirer* and *Hustler Magazine* are not the nation. Nor are they arbiters of moral standards for most of us, including most of their readers, one suspects. So even if a few sleazy publications would be inhibited by none except legal sanctions in deciding what stories to commission and print, many citizens might retain moral inhibitions in these matters.

Compare Post:

> Surely, we tell ourselves, Larry Flynt's parody cannot be the stuff of rational deliberation; yet the constitutional protection afforded the parody undercuts our assurance. In the absence of legal support, our condemnation of the parody, and the values underlying that condemnation, become somehow relativized and drained of authority ... in this sense a decision like *Falwell* endangers our hold on the very concept of rational deliberation.[43]

Why so? I do not see that the *Falwell* decision weakens most people's conviction that Flynt's parody was crude and vile any more than the extension of legal tolerance to creation science arguments and New Age arguments for reincarnation weakens informed citizens' judgment that such arguments are hokum. Norms not backed by legal coercion need not fade out of existence. They may or may not. In any given case, empirical evidence is needed to lend credibility to hunches that the sky will fall if the laws permit it.

My guess is that what underlies this aspect of Post's jurisprudence is skepticism about the capacity of any standards to survive in a modern culture unless they are hammered into us by primary socialization and bolstered by pervasive adult socialization and supported by legal coercion.

Post's proclaimed paradox of public discourse appears nonparadoxical for another reason. The ideal of responsive democracy as Post describes it, the ideal of society-wide consensus attained through ideal deliberation among ideally rational and moral citizens, has no direct implications for constitutional interpretation or for policy. That is, if one accepts the ideal as a goal to be pursued, it is not immediately clear what are the best means to the goal in circumstances where the ideal conditions do not obtain. If all citizens were perfectly rational and moral agents, many problems that free speech jurisprudence for the real world must confront would not arise. Less than fully rational and moral agents are prone to confusion and subject to manipulation in ways that the ideal deliberation ideal ignores. In particular, it cannot be assumed that maximizing citizens' freedom from any legal constraints on what they might wish to speak, and thus enabling them to attain a state of "pure communication," is the best way to achieve the closest possible approximation to ideal deliberation about public matters in the nonideal world. Some constraints that would be irrelevant or unnecessary for talking angels may be needed for men and women even if we put aside all nonspeech values that constraints might serve and consider only how to come as close as possible to achieving the goal of ideal deliberation among citizens. So the two requirements of public deliberation—the requirement that speech be unconstrained as to content and the requirement that speech conform to norms of rationality—that Post sees contradicting each other are better viewed as subsumed under a broader goal of ideal deliberation. In pursuit of the broader goal in a world of less than fully rational citizens, some constraints and some departures from ideal rationality may be conducive to the best deliberation we can get.

Two examples will serve to illustrate the point.

Consider the issue of group defamation. Suppose it is held that false reputation-damaging statements about groups should not be allowed to trigger civil liability for defamation on the ground that the the inference from broad polemical generalizations about groups (e.g., "Niggers are lazy") to any specific claim about an individual member of the group is bound to be improbable, so that reasonable persons on hearing the group libel would not be led to form invidious beliefs about any individual. Hence, the argument continues, any harms to individuals generated by group libel are bound to be slight and diffuse, so these harms are outweighed by the chilling effect that group libel laws would have on polemical public debate. This argument is not dispositive. Being less then fully rational, the intended audience for group libel statements might be disposed to make just such shaky inferences from negative claims about a group to negative claims about an individual member that are held to be irrational and hence unlikely. A successful argument against group libel laws must balance expected harms and benefits using realistic assumptions about the likely reactions of speakers and audiences.

Consider also the issue whether or not public officials and candidates for public office, who are indisputably public figures, should be deemed to retain some rights of privacy over details of their personal, particularly sexual, lives. This is a nonissue at the level of ideal theory, for fully rational agents would never make unwarranted inferences from revelations about candidates' sex lives to judgments about their fitness for public office. At least, if we put aside the harm to public officials from loss of privacy as inconsequential in comparison to the expected public benefit from wider debate, this result holds. But even if our only concern were to foster ideal public discourse, a genuine issue arises for democracies with less than fully rational citizens, who might predictably reason better about political matters if denied access to volatile intimate facts about the sex lives of public officials. Think of a declared homosexual candidate for U.S. President hounded by the press. I myself think that on balance the current constitutional understanding of the implied waiver of privacy rights by pubic figures is probably correct, but the issue is delicate. The constitutional ideal of open, robust, and uninhibited debate is not an aspiration to a state of pure communication, whatever that might mean.

Conclusion

Post has written important essays using sociological theory and communitarian moral philosophy to illuminate common law and constitutional law interpretations of freedom of speech. His work is informed by a sophisticated appropriation of the communitarian framework of ideas. Post finds a pervasive tension in American law between the claims of autonomy and community, individualism and collective identity, democratic self-determination and the protection of community mores that are thought to constitute the selves of these supposedly self-determining citizens. I find Post's work on this theme fascinating but flawed by the communitarian framework in which his insights are embedded. Perhaps Post's analysis can serve as a test case for the utility of communitarian philosophy. If even so careful a cultural theorist as Post is led astray trying to distill his thought in communitarian categories, as I have tried to show, that is evidence that these categories themselves are blunt tools of limited use for theory construction. I have also tried to indicate that the philosophical liberalism that communitarians criticize is not so vulnerable to their objections as some, like Post, have supposed.

NOTES

1. By "communitarians" I refer to Michael J. Sandel, *Liberalism and the Limits of Justice* (Cambridge: Cambridge University Press, 1982); Charles Taylor, *Philosophy and the Human Sciences: Philosophical Papers*, vol. 2 (Cambridge: Cambridge University Press, 1985), see esp. "Atomism" and "What's Wrong with Negative Liberty?"; Alasdair MacIntyre, *After Virtue: A Study in Moral Theory* (London: Duckworth, 1981); and Richard Rorty, *Contingency, Irony, and Solidarity* (Cambridge: Cambridge University Press, 1987). Michael Walzer is a fellow traveler. See Walzer, *Spheres of Justice* (New York: Basic Books, 1983).

2. Robert Post, "Between Democracy and Community: The Legal Constitution of Social Form," chap. 7 in this volume. See also Post, "The Constitutional Concept of Public Discourse: Outrageous Opinion, Democratic Deliberation, and *Hustler Magazine v. Falwell*," *Harvard Law Review* 103 (January 1990): 601–686.

3. Ronald Dworkin, "Liberalism," reprinted in his collection *A Matter of Principle* (Cambridge: Harvard University Press, 1985), 191.

4. John Rawls, "The Domain of the Political and Overlapping Consensus," *New York University Law Review* 64 (May 1989): 233–255; see 235.

5. Thomas Nagel, "Moral Conflict and Political Legitimacy," *Philosophy and Public Affairs* 16 (Summer 1987): 215–240; see 230.

6. Charles Larmore, *Patterns of Moral Complexity* (Cambridge: Cambridge University Press, 1987), xx.

7. Of the philosophers quoted in the previous paragraph, Dworkin, Larmore, and perhaps Rawls would qualify as pure philosophical liberals. Nagel is an outlier.

8. Thomas Nagel, "Rawls on Justice," *Philosophical Review* 82 (1973): 220–234; see 228.

9. John Rawls, "Fairness to Goodness," *Philosophical Review* 83 (1973): 536–554; see 537.

10. For clarification of different senses of *neutrality*, see Larmore, *Patterns of Moral Complexity*, 42–48; Joseph Raz, *The Morality of Freedom* (Oxford: Oxford University Press, 1986), 111–124; also Arneson, "Neu-

trality and Utility," *Canadian Journal of Philosophy* 20 (June 1990): 215–240.

11. John Rawls, *A Theory of Justice* (Cambridge: (Harvard University Press, 1971), 525.

12. John Rawls, "Kantian Constructivism in Moral Theory: The Dewey Lectures 1980," *Journal of Philosophy* 77 (September 1980): 515–572.

13. For further development of the line of thought in this paragraph, see my "Primary Goods Reconsidered," *Nous* 24 (June 1990): 429–454; see 438–441.

14. Ronald Dworkin, "Foundations of Liberal Equality," in Grethe B. Peterson, ed., *The Tanner Lectures on Human Values,* vol. 11 (Salt Lake City: University of Utah Press, 1990), 1–119; also Ronald Dworkin, "Liberal Equality," *California Law Review* 77 (May 1989): 479–504.

15. Dworkin, "Foundations of Liberal Equality." This quotation and the one in the previous sentence of the text are from p. 8.

16. Dworkin, "Foundations of Liberal Equality," 80.

17. Dworkin acknowledges that a lack of ethical integrity can stem from causes other than subjection to paternalism. When any of these causes prevents a person from attaining ethical integrity, the priority of integrity offers no bar to paternalistic restriction of liberty. If I doubt that the life I have chosen is any better than many other courses I might have chosen, paternalistic coercion that pushes me to one of these other courses does not lessen my slight ethical integrity. If I value reading Shakespeare but tend to act on the nonvalued desire to read pulp detective fiction, again the priority of ethical integrity offers no bar to paternalistic restriction that prompts me to switch from detective fiction to Shakespeare.

18. Dworkin, "Foundations of Liberal Equality," 77.

19. Dworkin, "Foundations of Liberal Equality," 84.

20. For a similar argument to which I am indebted, see Brian Barry, "How Not to Defend Liberal Institutions," *British Journal of Political Science* 20 (January 1990): 1–14.

21. Sandel, *Liberalism and the Limits of Justice,* 174.

22. John Stuart Mill, *Utilitarianism,* chap. 2, in *Collected Works,* ed. J. M. Robson vol. 10 (Toronto and Buffalo: University of Toronto Press, 1969): Mill, *On Liberty,* chap. 3, in *Collected Works,* ed. J. M. Robson vol. 18 (Toronto and Buffalo: University of Toronto Press, 1977).

23. The qualifier "unconditionally" is necessary because some preferences are conditional in structure, as when one wants a birthday cake

on one's sixtieth birthday provided that this desire persists to that time, or epistemically conditional, as when one wants to build a monument to someone's great virtue provided that person really was exceptionally virtuous. Conditional preferences with false antecedent clauses are null in the sense that their satisfaction does not increase the goodness of one's life.

24. Karl Marx and Friedrich Engels, "Manifesto of the Communist Party," in Robert Tucker, ed., *The Marx-Engels Reader,* (New York: W. W. Norton and Co., 1978): 476.

25. Thomas Scanlon, "Preference and Urgency," *Journal of Philosophy* 72 (1975): 655–669; see 658.

26. Some may object that the mixture of utilitarianism and liberalism asserted in the text fails to register the core ideal of liberal toleration. Imagine that a person harms no one and violates no one's rights but persists in seeking to fulfill a conception of the good for herself or others that differs from rational preference satisfaction. She seeks to live a life of spontaneity or a life of dedication to anything opposed to a life of maximal satisfaction. The mixed liberal might favor paternalistic imposition when that would reliably increase her rational preference satisfaction score, but the true liberal should reject restriction of liberty on these grounds. In reply: If the individual is not relying on confused reasoning or factual mistakes or other failures of reflection in forming judgments regarding her goals in life, then satisfying those goals just *is,* by definition, satisfying her rational preferences. The rational preference satisfaction standard is purely formal and does not dictate the content of the individual's goals. Whether or not the individual from her own standpoint would identify these goals with what she takes to be her rational preferences is immaterial. But if the person's judgments that define her life goals are cognitively defective, then paternalism in principle cannot be ruled out, on the mixed conception. Whether such principled tolerance of paternalism deserves the name "true liberalism" I leave for the reader to decide.

27. Cf. *Wisconsin v. Yoder,* 406 U.S. 205 (1972). In that case the Supreme Court held that the state's requirement that youths must attend school until age 16, applied to the Old Order Amish, who object to high school education for their children on the ground that it fosters worldly concerns, violates the Free Exercise clause of the Constitution. Although the issue would require a thorough discussion, a rational preference satisfaction approach suggests either that this case was wrongly decided or that the First Amendment correctly interpreted is an unfair political principle. All children have a right to an education that prepares them for a wide range of careers and ways of life any of

which they might choose as adults. This right trumps the religious preferences of their parents, just as it would trump a parent's insistent desire that a child should forego school in order to devote herself full-time to sports or dance.

28. Rawls, *A Theory of Justice*, 210–211.

29. Ronald Dworkin, "Do We Have a Right to Pornography?", in his *A Matter of Principle*, 338. It should be noted that Dworkin does not endorse the position that he is characterizing in this quotation.

30. But it must be acknowledged that pending further discussion of what "fairness-constrained maximization" would amount to, allusions to "this goal" are premature. For purposes of this chapter I am assuming that this programmatic sketch can be completed in a satisfactory way. For further discussion, which urges that a liberal principle of distributive justice should be concerned with the opportunities available to individuals, not the final outcomes they happen to reach, see Arneson, "Equality and Equal Opportunity for Welfare," *Philosophical Studies* 56 (May 1989): 77–93; Arneson, "Liberalism, Distributive Subjectivism, and Equal Opportunity for Welfare," *Philosophy and Public Affairs* 19 (Spring 1990): 158–194; Arneson, "Property Rights in Persons," *Social Philosophy and Policy* 9 (Winter 1992): 201–230; and Arneson, "Equality," in Robert Goodin and Philip Pettit, eds., *A Companion to Political Philosophy* (Oxford: Basil Blackwell, forthcoming).

31. Sandel, *Liberalism and the Limits of Justice*, 150, cited after Post, "Between Democracy and Community."

32. For the points in this paragraph, see Will Kymlicka, "Liberalism and Communitarianism," *Canadian Journal of Philosophy* 18 (June 1988): 181–204; also Allen E. Buchanan, "Assessing the Communitarian Critique of Liberalism," *Ethics* 99 (July 1989): 852–882; also Joel Feinberg, *The Moral Limits of the Criminal Law*, vol. 4, *Harmless Wrongdoing* (Oxford: Oxford University Press, 1988), chap. 29A.

33. See Rawls, *A Theory of Justice*, 46–53; also Norman Daniels, "Wide Reflective Equilibrium and Theory Acceptance in Ethics," *Journal of Philosophy* 76 (May 1979): 256–282.

34. This notion of what an interpretation of the law should aim to accomplish is drawn from Ronald Dworkin, "Hard Cases," chap. 4 of his *Taking Rights Seriously* (Cambridge: Harvard University Press, 1978).

35. Post's skepticism about reason hinders his interpretation of the constitutional law of free speech at other points. See, for example, his reading of the distinction between "fact" and "opinion" in the constitutional law that sets First Amendment limits on civil liability for def-

amation and intentional infliction of emotional distress. The courts have distinguished statements of fact, which are held regulable by civil law in accordance with their truth or falsity, from statements of opinion, which are held not so regulable. To date the courts have not been very forthcoming in elucidating this distinction. Post interprets it as a distinction between statements that make claims that purport to be valid only for those who accept the standards of a given community (these are claims of opinion) and statements that make claims that purport to be valid for all, regardless of community affiliation (these are claims of fact). But this way of drawing lines would require the courts to treat as "fact" and therefore regulable all controversial claims about justice and the theory of human good that are asserted as valid for all persons whatever their community membership. But the intent of the courts is surely to include such claims at the core of protected speech under the First Amendment, not because it is denied that no such claims could be valid for all, but because free expression is deemed to be the best medium for establishing their validity. See Post, "The Constitutional Concept of Public Discourse," 649–661.

36. Post, "Between Democracy and Community," p. 167, chap. 7 in this volume.

37. Post, "The Constitutional Concept of Public Discourse," 642.

38. *Hustler Magazine v. Falwell,* 108 U.S. 876 (1988); *Cohen v. California,* 403 U.S. 15 (1971).

39. See also Mill's arguments against the position that free expression of all opinions should be limited by the condition that the manner of expression must be "temperate" and must not "pass the bounds of fair discussion," in *On Liberty,* 258–259.

40. Compare the somewhat similar circumstances of *Rosenfeld v. New Jersey,* 408 U.S. 901 (1972).

41. Another aspect of Post's association of civility norms with community and First Amendment protection of free expression with responsive democracy is puzzling. No doubt laws establishing civil or criminal liability for defamation, invasion of privacy, and intentional infliction of emotional distress implicitly define a community of citizens anxious to avoid such harms, but the possibility needs to be considered that any citizen considered ex ante in abstraction from his or her specific communal attachments has an interest in the maintenance of effective rules that protect against such harms. It might be the case, but surely need not be the case, that existing civility laws regulating speech are framed in ways that favor some particular community attachments and ways of life over others—Christians over Jews, Hindus, and atheists,

for example, or whites and Asian-Americans over Afro-Americans and Hispanics.

42. See the discussion of these issues in Kent Greenawalt, *Speech, Crime, and the Uses of Language* (Oxford: Oxford University Press, 1989), 292–301.

43. Post, "The Constitutional Concept of Public Discourse," 643.

9

THE REAL WORLD OF
DEMOCRATIC COMMUNITY

GERALD N. ROSENBERG

INTRODUCTION

Robert Post examines democratic community through the perspective of the American legal system, focusing on the Supreme Court and constitutional law. He understands democratic community as "a complex dialectic between . . . two phases of the self and their corresponding social formations."[1] Believing that Court decisions both shape and uncover social practices, he examines constitutional jurisprudence, arguing that the dialectic of democratic community is contestable and that the Court strives to find a balance in ever-changing circumstances. "The ultimate revelation of the law," Post concludes rather mystically, "is merely the shape and contours of our own deepest commitments."[2]

In this chapter, I suggest that Post mischaracterizes democratic community because he constructs artificial views of both democracy and community, and focuses his analysis too narrowly on the Court. He does not ground democracy, community, the Court, or constitutional law in the political, social, and economic environment in which they exist. Also, because he does not give determinate meaning to the terms "community" and "autonomy," his description of constitutional law as mediating the tension between them is vague. To understand them one must identify the values that autonomy comprises and the interests that form community. In doing so, one finds that the role of the Court has been to support majority preferences and the interests of those controlling power, wealth, and status. Legal victories for individuals occur most often when there is no tension between their interests and the interests of those controlling power, wealth, and status, or when the matter is trivial. Further, the implicit assumption that constitutional law can be understood as a conflict between two notions of the self idealizes the role of constitutional law and removes the Court from the real world in which it operates. Finally, relying on judicial decisions to understand the larger society creates two important problems. First, it overstates the importance of the Court by assuming that Court opinions matter in a uniform and consistent way. Second, focusing solely on cases cannot distinguish between those that are trivial for the larger society and those that reflect important trends. Whether studying constitutional law or democratic community, claims about importance and meaning need grounding in the real world.

To proceed, I summarize Post's argument, examine the Court's relation to governmental, commercial, and majority interests, and explore how a grounded investigation of community and autonomy sheds greater light on the nature of democratic community.

Post's Argument

Post's argument is based on his understanding of community and democracy. For Post, the social form of community is what gives individuals identity; it constitutes what they are. It is not something they choose, as in joining an association, but an attachment they discover. This approach to community views people as socially embedded and dependent. In contrast, democracy is based on the principle that people are autonomous and independent. Identity is self-determined, not socially embedded. Whereas community strives to restrict the field of social choice, autonomy strives to open it. For Post, democracy as autonomy, and community, are "deeply antagonistic forms of social behavior."[3]

A democratic government requires both community and democracy, in which the laws are made by the same people to whom they apply.[4] For this to occur, for there to be democratic self-determination, there must be an open structure of communication. "Coercion is precluded from public debate"[5] by this notion, and both the majority and minority must have the opportunity to participate fully and freely. Indeed, the "legitimacy" of democracy depends on maintaining a system of communication that preserves this openness. Without such public discourse, government is reduced to majority tyranny. Post calls this understanding of democracy "responsive democracy."

The nature of democratic community, then, is the clash between community and responsive democracy. The role of the Court is to struggle to balance the two. Examining that struggle, Post finds a tradition that gives "central importance" to the concept of responsive democracy.[6] Several important aspects of democratic community follow from this.

First, the Court relies on "the ideal of responsive democracy to shape the nation's political landscape."[7] Post finds this "most obvious" in the Court's First Amendment jurisprudence.[8] Second, responsive democracy, with its emphasis on autonomy, highlights the individualism pervasive in American constitutional law. This includes a public/private distinction and a right to privacy that has created a "sheltered haven,"[9] particularly for the family. Third, responsive democracy is paradoxically dependent on community forms of life for the formation of autonomous individuals. Fourth, because responsive democracy must be able to govern, some sort of constitutional limitations are required. Majority decision making must be restrained from interfering with the communicative process. In this sense, judicial review, rather than being antidemocratic, is "better interpreted as itself evidence of a commitment to the principles of responsive democracy."[10]

COURTS, LAW, AND SOCIETY

An important part of Post's argument is that the Supreme Court, in mediating between community and responsive democracy, has given central importance to the core concepts of autonomy. To ground this claim, it is important to examine the relation between the Court and the broader society. There is a considerable social science literature that examines Court practice within the political, social, and economic environment in which it operates.[11] And this literature suggests that the Court, far from supporting individual autonomy, is generally deferential to government preferences, business interests, and majority opinion. In other words, constitutional practice suggests the central importance of the interests of those controlling power, wealth, and status, not responsive democracy. Analytically and empirically, the Court is particularly responsive to interests that are not captured by the tension highlighted by Post.

LAW AND GOVERNMENT

A good deal of evidence suggests that the Court, rather than defending individuals, is supportive of the federal government. To begin with, the appointive process limits judicial independence. Judges do not select themselves. Rather, they are chosen by politicians, the president, and the Senate at the federal level. Presidents, although not clairvoyant, tend to nominate judges who they think will promote their judicial philosophies. Clearly, changing court personnel can bring court decisions into line with prevailing political opinion. The role of the Court, then, is to further the views of the ruling coalition, not to mediate the tension between abstract categories.

In at least two important ways Congress may constrain court actions, and limit judicial defense of responsive democracy. First, in the statutory area, Congress can override decisions, telling the courts they misinterpreted the intent of the law. That is, Congress may rewrite a provision to meet court objections or simply state more clearly what it meant so that the courts' reading of the law is repudiated.[12] Second, although Congress cannot directly reverse decisions based on constitutional interpretations, presumably untouchable by the democratic process, it may be able to constrain them by threatening certain changes in the legal structure. A large part of the reason is the appointive process. But even without the power of appointment, the Court may be susceptible to credible threats. Historical review of the relations of the Court to the other branches of the federal government suggests that the Court cannot for long stand alone against such pressure. From the "court-packing" plan of Franklin Delano Roosevelt to more recent bills proposing to remove federal court jurisdiction over certain issues, court-curbing proposals may allow Congress to constrain courts.[13]

American courts are particularly deferential to the views of the federal government. At the Supreme Court, the solicitor general is accorded a special role. The office has unusual access to the Court and is often asked by the Court to intervene in cases and present the government's position. When the solicitor general petitions the Court to enter a case, the Court almost invariably grants the request, regardless of the preferences of the parties.[14] The government is also unusually successful in convincing the Court to hear cases it appeals and not to hear those it opposes.[15] The solicitor general's access to the Court carries over to the winning of cases. Historically, the solicitor general (or the side the government is supporting when it enters a case as *amicus*) wins about 70 percent of the time.[16] It appears that the federal government has both extraordinary access to and persuasive influence on the Court. That does not comport with notions of a judicial system able to defy political majorities to defend individual autonomy.

THE COURT, COMMERCIAL INTERESTS, AND MAJORITY PREFERENCES

In assessing the role of the Court in furthering responsive democracy, it makes sense to examine the relation of the law to the institutions and interests that comprise the body politic. It may well be that Court decisions mediate between individuals and minority interests that do not necessarily reflect community values. Further, Court decisions may support minority interests of wealth, status, and power, *and* suppress other minority interests that challenge the existing distribution of those resources. Rather than looking to community or individuals, one might more profitably examine judicial support of the government, business interests, and majority preferences.

Business interests, historically, have been successful in Court. During the late 19th and first part of the 20th century an important function of judge-made law was to allow unfettered economic exploitation of human resources.[17] By means of the judicially created doctrine of substantive due process, legislative attempts to protect workers were struck down. It makes little sense to interpret the Court as mediating between autonomy and community here. But perhaps Post means to limit his inquiry to only those areas where autonomy is directly challenged. However, as I argue shortly, even in this limited area his argument fails, both substantively and analytically. The Court has consistently reflected majority preferences and the interests of the wealthy and powerful. Far from being protective of autonomy, it is generally responsive to the larger political system.

Enhancing responsive democracy requires that court decisions not invariably reflect public opinion. However, Supreme Court decisions, historically, have seldom strayed far from what was politically acceptable.[18] Rather than suggesting autonomy, this judicial unwillingness often to blaze its own trail perhaps suggests, in the words of Finley Peter Dunne's Mr. Dooley, that "th' supreme coort follows th' iliction returns."[19]

Judicial Review

Another example of insufficient groundedness and indeterminate meaning is Post's attempt to defend the practice of judicial review against the charge that because it invalidates the acts of democratically elected officials, it is antidemocratic. Post defends judicial review on the ground that by defending autonomy and the communicative process, it preserves and promotes democracy. This invites an empirical inquiry as to whether the Court has done so. In general, this inquiry informs us that the Court has traditionally supported property over individual rights, large concentrations of capital over the health, safety, and livelihood of citizens, and claims of national security over their democratic rights.[20] To make his case, Post carefully selects a *small* number of *recent* Supreme Court cases. From child labor to working conditions to race and gender discrimination to environmental degradation, the full sweep of American judicial history calls into question Post's assertions.

Post also argues that constitutional limitations are a necessary implication of responsive democracy, but they need not be enshrined in a written document or enforced by an independent judiciary. What, then, are they? How do they differ from custom or tradition? Nations like Britain and France protect autonomy and an open communicative process without the benefit of judicial review or, in the case of Britain, a written constitution. The practice of judicial review may play a special role in the American democratic community, but that role must be carefully delineated.

American history and practice suggest that the judiciary lacks the necessary independence from public opinion, the preferences of the federal government, and business interests that giving autonomy central importance requires. The nature of democratic community, and the Court's contribution to it, cannot be understood in a vacuum.

The Indeterminate Meaning of Community

A large part of the difficulty with Post's analysis derives from his not giving content to the meaning of American community. What are the values that comprise it? How are they formed? How are they to be discovered? Unless and until these questions are answered, examining Court cases to determine how the tension between community and autonomy is resolved won't be informative. All legal decisions involving individuals and the state involve claims of autonomy. But to view this as the result of courts mediating between community and autonomy is to mistake the form of cases for their substance. By relying on indeterminate, abstract terms, and neglecting to ground them in practice, Post's analytic framework does not deepen understanding. Without knowing the determinate meaning of community one cannot meaningfully examine how judicial decisions resolve conflicts between community and individual interests.

Post has a narrow conception of the relation between community and autonomy. He seems to exclude the possibility that they may not always, or necessarily, be in conflict. First, the community may act not only to restrict the field of social choice as Post describes it, but also to open up choice and increase autonomy by removing barriers to individual action. Government action prohibiting discrimination, for example, helps individuals to participate more freely in the larger community and the democratic process. Second, it may be that protecting the autonomy of some limits the autonomy of others. Increasing autonomy in some spheres may lessen it in others. Thus, tension may exist not between community and autonomy but rather between different understandings of autonomy. Third, defense of autonomy for some individuals may support community values. Conceptions of community, in other words, may reinforce some notions of autonomy, not threaten them. Depending on the meaning of the American community, the tension between community and autonomy varies.

Although Post does not explicitly define community, his use of it suggests certain meanings. Community might mean the interests of the government. Much of Post's legal analysis involves government attempts to limit autonomy by stopping individuals from acting in certain ways. Or perhaps it means public opinion, or shared beliefs. His emphasis on the First Amendment as a protector of autonomy supports this possibility. Mediating between community and autonomy would then mean that the Court protects and defends individuals against constraining governmental regulations, public opinion, and the tyranny of widely shared beliefs. But these definitions do not succeed either as a description of Court action or as a sensitive understanding of the meaning of the American community. They do not succeed because neither government action nor public opinion invariably represent the larger community. Governmental decisions may not be community values because of the influence of powerful interests on government. Public opinion may not reflect community values because their meaning, intensity, and importance is notoriously difficult to measure. Further, the Court has historically supported the interests of government, powerful interests, and majority views against individuals. The Court has seldom given responsive democracy "central importance."

How might one proceed to understand democratic community in a more useful way? One would look to the forces that structure Americans' lives, the institutions through and in which they live their lives, and to their beliefs. This approach would place the Court and the law in the midst of the social, political, and economic environment in which they operate.

Post defines community as the constituent elements of identity but provides no substantive content. To do so, one would look to the constituents of identity that mold how Americans live, think, and act. Entirely missing from Post's analysis are race, ethnicity, religion, gender, and class, which are powerful forces that are the constituent elements of American identity. Where Americans live, where they work and what they do, how they relax, who their friends are, and how they participate in politics are deeply structured by these forces. One cannot understand the nature of American democratic community without focusing on them. They must be the starting point of any analysis, and they must inform it every step. And this is no less the case because the way in which they interact changes over time. All this means that the nature of the American democratic community changes as well.

Perhaps the paradigmatic example of this structuring is the role of race in American society. For centuries, African-Americans have been denied even the most basic rights of community membership. The Court, rather than furthering responsive democracy, first denied that African-Americans were citizens[21] and then, when the Civil War and the ratification of the Fourteenth Amendment overturned that decision, provided constitutional protection for segregation.[22] Denying autonomy to African-Americans, far from being in tension with community values, supported them. Today, with the present effects of past discrimination fusing with current discrimination, African-Americans have fewer options and opportunities than other

Americans. This widely accepted fact of American life must be part of any meaningful definition of community.

Gender provides another example. From the home to school to the workplace to the political process, gender structures and constrains choice. Women have fewer opportunities, less control over decisions, and receive fewer rewards than men in all these realms. Whether the issue is responsibility for child care and household chores, access to education, job opportunity, workplace advancement and pay, or political representation, women are less well-off than men. Socially constructed gender differences are an important part of the modern American community. To further responsive democracy one must give women the tools to overcome these barriers. As I argue here, it is not at all clear that enlarging spheres of autonomy will do this.

Consider, also, the issue of the political system and Americans' participation in politics. People participate at appreciably different rates from one another, and those differences are most persuasively explained by differences in socioeconomic status.[23] Income, education, and wealth must be part of any sensitive understanding of the meaning of community. Further, Post premises responsive democracy on open communication, the removal of coercion. Yet protecting individuals can serve to reinforce the unequal power relations that structure community. Open communication, on its own, may not help those who lack the education, self-confidence, and access to wealth to effectively participate.[24]

Finally, one can examine the belief structure of the American citizenry. Public opinion data capture what they tell pollsters it means to be American.[25] Among these views are beliefs in private property, individualism and antistatism, and religion, and little tolerance for those who challenge them.[26] Such beliefs must play an important role in understanding the meaning of democratic community.

To understand the formation of community identity, the meaning of autonomy, and the role of the Court and law, one must look explicitly at how Americans live their lives. With this in mind, I turn to two issue areas that Post highlights, privacy and speech, and show how a grounded approach, one that understands American community as largely structured by race, gender, and class, offers a more compelling understanding of both the role of the Court and the nature of democratic community.

PRIVACY

In examining the importance of privacy in democratic community, the problems of indeterminate meaning and lack of grounding in practice become apparent. To understand the content of privacy, one must know *who is protected from what in taking what actions*. What is the content of the "sheltered haven" of the family that is protected from state intervention and community coercion? Can a family do anything it wants? How has the substantive due process right upon which Post understands privacy to be based developed? Fortunately, these questions can be answered. In practice, privacy is a mixed bag, protecting autonomy in some cases and impairing it in others. Because class and gender structure American society, autonomy interacts with community in ways that sometimes impede responsive democracy.

There is difficulty with Post's analysis in part because in failing to ground his abstract category "individualism" in practice, he equates all individualism with the autonomy necessary for responsive democracy. But historically this has not been the case. Individualism, and privacy, have been tools to defeat responsive democracy and destroy autonomy. In the early 20th century the Court's substantive due process decisions aided employers in contracting with workers by invalidating legislation guaranteeing minimum wages and maximum hours. The avoidance of state interference with an individual's choice to contract to work certainly carved out an area of autonomous choice free from state intervention. Workers were treated as individuals and were "free" to make any bargain, exploitative though it might be. In carving out a realm of privacy and individualism for employment arrangements the Court was supporting autonomy, but in a way that limited open communication and responsive democracy. In effect, the Court supported commercial interests at the expense of the majority. Expanding areas of privacy and individual choice does not necessarily further the goals of responsive democracy.

The danger of privacy to autonomy, communication, and responsive democracy is clearly illustrated by the treatment of women, particularly in the "sheltered haven" of the family. By carving out a large realm of privacy for the family and sexual relations, American law has exposed women to unconstrained male violence. Women suffer from violence at the hands of men at frightening levels, violence that is condoned if not protected by judicial behavior. At the most deadly end of the violence continuum, the U.S. Department of Justice reports that 30 percent of all female murder victims in 1990 were murdered by husbands or boyfriends.[27] Over 102,000 forcible rapes were reported in 1990,[28] nearly triple the amount reported in 1970.[29] In the family, there is also the issue of the so-called marital-rape exemption that makes it legally impossible for a husband to rape his wife. The exemption is included in the Model Penal Code and, as of the late 1980s, most states retained some form of it. Although about half the states have moved to permit prosecution in some instances, as where the couple has formally separated, over a quarter have *expanded* the exemption to cover cohabitants.[30] As a male California state senator put it in 1979, "If you can't rape your wife, who can you rape?"[31]

Other kinds of violence against women in the family are even more prevalent. A special report from the U.S. Justice Department in 1986 estimated that 2.1 million women were victims of domestic violence at least once in the previous 12 months.[32] Other estimates vary from 3 to 4 million women a year,[33] to 34 percent of married women.[34] And a study reported in the *Journal of the American Medical Association* found that "battering appears to be the single most common cause of injury to women—more common than automobile accidents, muggings, and rapes combined."[35] What these figures suggest is "a tacit acceptance of woman-battering."[36] Indeed, as Murray A. Strauss puts it, "Our society actually has rules and values which make the marriage license also a hitting license."[37] The stark reality is that male violence against women remains prevalent. Privacy for American women is a mixed blessing. And although a married woman can be raped in the "sheltered haven" of the home, protected from state interference, the Supreme

Court has held that two consenting adults of the same gender cannot express their love for each other sexually, even in private.[38] The point is simple: One cannot understand the meaning of privacy, democratic community, or the role of the Court in a democratic community without grounding that meaning in practice. And that practice does not support the case that the Court consistently defends individualism in ways that preserve autonomy.

OPEN COMMUNICATION AND THE FIRST AMENDMENT

Key to responsive democracy is communication free from coercion and open to all. Post argues that the Court uses the First Amendment to shape the political landscape and provide this. Indeed, as he points out, the Court, over the last half century, has labeled the First Amendment the "guardian of our democracy" and freedom of expression "vital to the maintenance of democratic institutions." But these statements cannot be the end of the inquiry. To understand the nature of democratic community one must know whether the United States has in fact an open system and what role the Court has played in creating and maintaining it. For here, too, it may be that the role of the Court is to support majority preferences against unpopular views.

Post limits his analysis to the post–1931 years. Nearly 150 years of American history are swept away. What does this imply about the nature of democratic community? Responsive democracy? Have neither existed for most of American history? The problem exists because the First Amendment and the Court did little to maintain open communication in the pre–1931 days. At best Post's analysis applies only to the modern democratic community. But the modern American democratic community did not spring from thin air. It has a history in which institutions have been built and behavior molded. A grounded analysis would start with the ratification of the Constitution and the Bill of Rights and examine threats to open communication. And the record, even in Post's modern era, is not so good. The First Amendment and the Court have failed to protect consistently non-coercive communication and the open discussion necessary for responsive democracy. Rather than shaping the political landscape the Court defers to the status quo, defending open communication mainly in trivial areas,[39] or where those attacking it have done so in opposition to national goals and beliefs.[40]

To appraise Post's argument one can sensibly look at the treatment of political dissidents. Existence of dissent allows one to examine the extent of open communication when the status quo is threatened. At times of little or no dissent, one has no way of knowing how well communication is protected. Only when there is substantive political dissent can one measure the extent to which the Court has protected open debate.

Post's argument is strongest in the record of the United States in press censorship. Since 1931 writings challenging the status quo have seldom been suppressed. However, a few examples exist of successful suppression.

In 1971 the U.S. government made a major attempt to censor the press, bringing cases in New York and Washington, D.C. federal district courts to prevent the *New York Times* and the *Washington Post* from publishing the so-called "Pentagon Papers." The government won a temporary restraining order against the *Times* and publication was delayed for several weeks.[41] Another case where a government attempt at prior restraint was initially successful (for about six months) but eventually abandoned involved the politically left *Progressive*. In this 1979 case, the government won a restraining order from a federal district court prohibiting publication of an article on the scientific principles underlying the making of a hydrogen bomb.[42] Although the information for the article was gathered solely from material in the public domain, the *Progressive* was prohibited from publishing. However, shortly before oral argument on appeal, several newspapers published comparable information and the government, after a brief attempt at another restraining order, dropped the case.

Turning to the less established press, the record is not nearly as good. This is particularly true of the 1960s and early 1970s where the anti-war and counterculture movements spawned an "underground" press comprised, at its height, of approximately 450 papers with a circulation of about 5 million.[43] Irreverent, and often virulently anti-government, these publications were often treated with hostility by local authorities. Instances of harassment of underground papers are documented in many cities including, but not limited to Washington, D.C., Los Angeles, San Diego, Dallas, Jackson, Mississippi, New Orleans, and Buffalo.[44] In Washington, D.C. alone, the Hoyts found that in the late 1960s and early 1970s two underground papers were "subject to some 300 incidents of harassment by the District of Columbia police."[45] And army surveillance of anti-war activists during the Nixon era that came to light in *Laird v. Tatum* included at least 58 underground papers in 1969 and 1970.[46] Incidents such as these led the Twentieth Century Fund, in a 1971 study, to conclude that "there has been a double standard of treatment, one for the underground and one for the established press—a double standard that is inconsistent with the First Amendment's guarantee of freedom for all the press."[47]

Post's analysis is more problematic as to political speech and beliefs. In general, in the post-World War II United States, those who wish to challenge the status quo have been able to do so without fear. However, at certain times in the postwar years *all* levels of *all* branches of government have acted to suppress speech. The most obvious example is the treatment of African-Americans in the South who were denied the most basic democratic rights. However, because African-Americans have historically been denied rights, they were in effect excluded from the political community. Unlike with dissidents, there were no times of non-repression. The race issue clouds the focus on rights in the abstract. However, there is another obvious choice, left-leaning political dissidents, particularly members of the American Communist Party (CPUSA). Their treatment provides a good test of Post's position. And because he rests so much of his argument on the open communication aspect of responsive democracy, and the Court's protection of it, the treatment of political dissidents deserves attention.

In 1940 Congress passed the Alien Registration Act, also known as the Smith Act. Although general in language, and aimed in part at Nazi and fascist groups, the act was soon turned against the CPUSA. Passed overwhelmingly, with only four negative votes cast in the House, it punished whoever knowingly or willfully advocates, abets, advises, or teaches the duty, necessity, desirability, or propriety of overthrowing or destroying the government of the United States or the government of any State...by force or violence...or...organizes or helps or attempts to organize any society, group or assembly of persons who teach, advocate, or encourage the overthrow or destruction of any such government by force or violence; or becomes or is a member of, or affiliates with any such society, group, or assembly of persons, knowing the purposes thereof.[48]

In July 1948, the national leadership of the CPUSA was indicted under the Act. Despite the Act's open assault on communication, the courts had little trouble convicting the defendants. Their convictions for conspiracy to organize and advocate in violation of the Act were upheld by the U.S. Supreme Court in 1951 in the *Dennis* case, with only two dissenting votes.[49]

After *Dennis,* the government went after secondary CPUSA leaders, indicting nearly 150 of them. By 1957, more than 100 had been convicted.[50] After a brief interlude of some judicial protection,[51] Party leaders who served their terms and were released from prison were rearrested and charged with violation of the "membership" clause of the Act. The Court, given another opportunity to defend open communication, and after the worst of the anti-Communist hysteria had passed, declined to do so. It upheld the use of this clause in 1961 in *Scales v. United States.*[52]

A second piece of legislation enacted to stifle dissent was the Internal Security Act of 1950.[53] Enacted over President Truman's veto, it required "Communist-action" and "Communist front" organizations to register with the U.S. Attorney General, report names of officers, sources of funds, and, in the case of Communist-action organizations, membership lists.[54] A Subversive Activities Control Board (SACB) was created with power to hold hearings and order registration. The Attorney General moved quickly and on November 22, 1950, petitioned the SACB to order the CPUSA to register as a Communist-action organization. A frontal attack on open communication, the Act was upheld by the Court, after nearly a decade of litigation.[55]

A final piece of major legislation[56] denied the protection of the National Labor Relations Act to any union unless the union's officers, and the officers of any national or international labor organization to which it belonged, filed non-Communist affidavits. Section 9(h) of the Taft–Hartley Act of 1947[57] required every union officer to swear that "he is not a member of the Communist Party or affiliated with such party, and that he does not believe in, and is not a member of or supports any organization that believes in or teaches, the overthrow of the United States Government by force or by any illegal or unconstitutional methods." The Act was effective in removing dissidents from union leadership positions and the National Labor Relations Board estimated that in the years 1947–1957, there were "at least 1,500,000 individual affidavits filed."[58] Rather than striking down this legislative attempt to limit open communication, the Supreme Court upheld the legislation in 1950.[59]

This attack on political dissent, and the lack of protection for open communication, also can be seen in a host of other bills limiting the provision of government benefits to non-dissidents. For example, the National Science Foundation Act of 1950[60] required applicants to take an oath as to their political beliefs and memberships, and applicants for student loans under the National Defense Education Act of 1958[61] faced the same requirement. A 1962 amendment made it a criminal offense for any member of an organization under a final order to register with the SACB even to apply for student aid under the act. Title VII of the 1964 Civil Rights Act, which banned employment discrimination on the grounds or race, color, religion, sex, or national origin, specifically excluded from the prohibition any member of the CPUSA or of any organization required to register with the SACB (Section 703 (f)).[62] And this is just a partial list.

There were also, of course, the famous legislative investigations of the House Un-American Activities Committee and state committees patterned on them. Relying on the spotlight of exposure, and supported by the contempt powers of the Congress, the Committee probed into the political beliefs of Americans. After initially raising questions about these practices, the Supreme Court upheld them against constitutional challenge.[63] Its successor, the House Internal Security Committee, was not abolished until 1975.

Efforts were also made at all levels of government to purge political dissidents from employment and to prevent their hiring. Starting in 1947, federal, state, and local governments, as well as some private employers such as universities, began requiring current and potential employees to swear loyalty oaths. Executive order 9835 (1947), for example, required an investigation into the loyalty of every person seeking or holding employment with the United States. Congress provided a general legislative basis for the security program in 1950 by empowering heads of "sensitive" agencies to suspend employees "in the interests of national security."[64] The suspended employee could be dismissed with few procedural safeguards. For example, the right to see all the charges against one or to be informed of, or cross-examine, witnesses, was not guaranteed. Executive Order 10450 (1953) implemented the act and extended it to all departments and agencies of the government. And much action was taken on the state level.

The federal loyalty programs touched millions of Americans. By 1955, for example, at least 9 million were covered by federal programs and about half the states required oaths for their employees, including teachers.[65] Over the period 1947 through "slightly past" 1951, Westin reports that the political beliefs of 4 million federal employees were investigated. After Eisenhower's first year in office, 2,611 employees were dismissed for security reasons and 4,315 resigned before a determination could be made.[66] By the end of 1956, Brown reports that approximately 11,500 Americans had lost their jobs under loyalty-security programs.[67]

The states also entered the act, sometimes following and sometimes leading the federal government. Whereas their pre-World War II record was particularly poor, the post-war record contained many actions to squelch dissent. For example, eleven states, including California, Michigan, and Texas, adopted registration laws similar to the Internal Security Act of 1950 and eight states, including Massachusetts and Pennsylvania, adopted laws similar to the Communist Control Act of 1954 outlawing the Communist Party or making membership in it a crime. Other state action prevented dissidents from "becoming lawyers, jurors, or accountants and (in Indiana) from obtaining licenses as professional boxers."[68]

Many states also banned dissidents from running for political office. In 1947 Chafee found that "at least five states have lately excluded certain radical parties from a place on the ballot."[69] By 1958, thirty-five states had enacted statutes prohibiting a party or person advocating violent overthrow of the government from running for office. Eighteen of these states also banned the Communist Party from electoral competition by name.[70] Such exclusions were upheld by the New Jersey Supreme Court in 1954[71] and by the Connecticut Attorney General in 1964.[72] As late as 1968 Minnesota denied the Communist Party a place on the ballot[73] and Indiana's exclusion of the Communist Party from the ballot remained good law until 1974.[74] And, whereas there has not been much practice of excluding elected political dissidents from the legislatures since the first part of the 20th century,[75] in the 1960s Georgia did bar civil rights and anti-war activist Julian Bond from taking his seat in the Georgia House of Representatives.[76]

An area that received much attention, and created a good deal of litigation, involved the exclusion of lawyers from the Bar on the basis of their political beliefs. Led by the American Bar Association whose House of Delegates voted in 1951 that all state and local Bar associations expel from their ranks any member of the Communist Party or anyone who "advocates Marxism-Leninism,"[77] many states inquired into lawyers' and bar candidates' political beliefs and disbarred or denied bar admission to those thought subversive. Given Post's assertion that the Court's protection of responsive democracy can best be seen in its defense of open communication, these cases should have been easy. However, on the whole, the Supreme Court upheld such exclusions.[78] And on the federal level, the Attorney General attempted for five years to have the National Lawyers Guild listed as a subversive organization.

In the 1960s and 1970s, government at all levels took steps to harass civil rights and anti-war activists. It is now well-known, for example, that the FBI had Dr. Martin Luther King, Jr., under surveillance.[79] The Black Panthers were also watched and harassed, with numerous arrests, although few convictions. The anti-war movement, too, suffered the same governmental attacks on fundamental freedoms. For example, in early 1968 a group of anti-war leaders including Dr. Benjamin Spock and Rev. William Sloane Coffin, Jr., were indicted for conspiracy to counsel, aid, and abet draft resistance. Convicted at trial, it took a lengthy and expensive appeal to preserve their right to criticize government actions.[80] The federal government also engaged in massive surveillance of the lawful political actions of countless Americans, surveillance that was upheld by the Supreme Court in 1972 in *Laird v. Tatum*.[81] U.S. Senator Goodell, a Republican critic of the war, discovered that his phone was tapped.[82] And, the FBI kept a "confidential file on the United States Supreme Court from 1932 until at least 1985," wiretapped or monitored conversations involving Justices Earl Warren, William O. Douglas, Abe Fortas, and Potter Stewart, and used select Court employees to report information heard in the Court building and to keep tabs on who came and went.[83]

As a final note, many have wondered if the excesses of these actions carry over against dissent of all types, further chilling fundamental democratic rights. Richardson reminds us that "the threat of punishment breeds fear, and fear self-censorship."[84] Writing of those people who thoughtfully criticize governmental policies, Chafee suggests that "when you put the hotheads in jail these cooler people do not get arrested—they just keep quiet."[85] Stouffer, in a massive nation-wide 1954 survey of both citizens and community leaders, found that 13 percent of both samples felt less free to speak out than they used to.[86] And Nunn and his colleagues, in their 1973 surveys re-examining Stouffer's findings, reported that 20 percent of their sample felt less free than before to speak.[87] As Oakes suggests, it might be "wrong to underestimate the lasting effects of such an atmosphere on government, on the professions, and on the public and private life in general."[88] The effect of Court decisions limiting communication may run deep.

To summarize, although most Americans retained the right to participate in debate in the post-World War II years, that right was protected only so long as they communicated acceptable ideas. When they did not, the First Amendment and the Court did not protect the open communication key to responsive democracy. As Mark Twain put it: "It is by the goodness of God that in our country we have those three unspeakably precious things: freedom of speech, freedom of conscience, and the prudence never to practice either of them."[89] Indeed, the U.S. record in the post-World War II years has stood out among Western democratic nations, characterized by Dahl as a "deviant case"[90] and, more bluntly by Shapiro, as "pathological."[91] By ignoring this recent history, and more fundamentally by not placing the Court and the community in the context of unequal wealth, status, and power, Post's analysis remains detached from the American democratic community. There may be a Court and a democratic community that fit Post's description, but they are not to be found in modern America.

Conclusion

To understand the American democratic community, and the role of the Court and law, one must focus on them in practice. To divorce them from their political, social, economic, and institutional settings, as Post does, reifies concepts and weakens them as explanatory tools. This does not mean that we should reject abstract approaches to understanding the world, or not attempt to understand "the shape and contours of our own deepest commitments." It does emphatically mean that such abstractions must be carefully tested and refined in the light of practice. Failing to do so runs the danger of creating artificial views of our world. Only when such a careful, grounded, approach is combined with the insights that Post offers can one hope to understand the nature of the American democratic community.

NOTES

1. Robert Post, "Between Democracy and Community: The Legal Constitution of Social Form," Chap. 7 in this volume, p. 182.
    2. Id. at 183.

3. Id. at 103–64..

4. Post, in his next sentence, changes the meaning of democracy by arguing that "simple majoritarianism fits awkwardly with the value of autonomy, because it contemplates the heteronomous imposition of majority will upon the minority." But this confuses democracy with consensus. Contested votes do not affect the claim that those who make the laws are bound by them. This confusion may stem from Post's focus on autonomy rather than institutions and procedures of representation as the essence of democracy.

5. Id. at 171.

6. Id. at 173.

7. Id. at 172.

8. Id.

9. Id. at 173.

10. Id. at 177.

11. In general, see any introductory textbook on the courts and social science. Two representative samples include John B. Gates and Charles A. Johnson, *The American Courts: A Critical Assessment* (Washington, D.C.: Congressional Quarterly, 1991); and Stephen L. Wasby, *The Supreme Court in the Federal Judicial System*, 3rd ed. (Chicago: Nelson-Hall, 1988).

12. The Civil Rights Restoration Act of 1991, for example, overturned several Supreme Court decisions.

13. Stuart S. Nagel, "Court-Curbing Proposals in American History," *Vanderbilt Law Review*, 18 (1965), 925; Gerald N. Rosenberg, "Judicial Independence and the Reality of Political Power," Paper Presented at the Annual Meeting of the American Political Science Association, New Orleans, Aug. 29–Sept. 1, 1985.

14. In the years 1969–1983, the solicitor general petitioned to enter 130 cases without the consent of the parties. The Court granted access in 126 of those cases (97 percent) (S. Sidney Ulmer and David Willison, "The Solicitor General of the United States as *Amicus Curiae* in the United States Supreme Court, 1969–1983 Terms," Paper Presented at the Annual Meeting of the American Political Science Association, New Orleans, Aug. 29–Sept. 1, 1985).

15. Whereas the Court agrees to hear, on average, about 7 or 8 percent of cases appealed to it (13 or 14 percent not including petitions from prisoners), the solicitor general's petitions are accepted almost three-quarters of the time. When the solicitor general opposes an appeal, the Court rarely accepts the case, doing so, for example, in only 4 percent of the cases during the 1969–83 period (Ulmer and Willison, supra note 14).

16. Robert Scigliano, *The Supreme Court and the Presidency* (New York: Free Press, 1971); Ulmer and Willison, supra note 14.

17. See, for example, *Allgeyer v. Louisiana*, 165 U.S. 578 (1897); *Lochner v. New York*, 198 U.S. 45 (1905); *Adair v. U.S.*, 208 U.S. 161 (1908); *Coppage v. Kansas*, 236 U.S. 1 (1915); *Hammer v. Dagenhart*, 247 U.S. 251 (1918); *Drexel v. Bailey Furniture*, 259 U.S. 20 (1922); *Adkins v. Children's Hospital*, 261 U.S. 525 (1923).

18. Robert G. McCloskey, *The American Supreme Court* (Chicago: University of Chicago Press, 1960), pp. 223–24. More specifically, comparing the Court's opinions with those of the public on issues in 146 decisions over the years 1935–86, Marshall found consistency nearly two-thirds of the time (Thomas R. Marshall, *Public Opinion and the Supreme Court* [Boston: Unwin Hyman, 1989], chap. 4).

19. Finley Peter Dunne, "The Supreme Court's Decisions," in *Mr. Dooley's Opinions* (New York: R. H. Russell, 1901), p. 26.

20. See, for example, Arnold M. Paul, *Conservative Crisis and the Rule of Law* (Ithaca: Cornell University Press, 1960); Arthur S. Miller, *The Supreme Court and American Capitalism* (New York: Free Press, 1968); McCloskey, supra note 18.

21. *Dred Scott v. Sanford*, 19 How. (60 U.S.) 393 (1857).

22. *Plessy v. Ferguson*, 163 U.S. 537 (1896).

23. Sidney Verba and Norman H. Nie, *Participation in America: Political Democracy and Social Equality* (Chicago: University of Chicago Press, 1972).

24. Lynn M. Sanders, "Against Deliberation," *Political Theory* (forthcoming).

25. See, for example, Herbert McClosky and John Zaller, *The American Ethos: Public Attitudes Toward Capitalism and Democracy* (Cambridge: Harvard University Press, 1984); Herbert McClosky and Alida Brill, *Dimensions of Tolerance* (New York: Russell Sage, 1983).

26. Samuel A. Stouffer, *Communism, Conformity, and Civil Liberties: A Cross-Section of the Nation Speaks Its Mind* (Gloucester: Peter Smith, 1963), p. 33; McClosky and Zaller, supra note 25 at 134, 140, 120, 84, 25.

27. Only 4 percent of all male murder victims were murdered by wives or girlfriends. U.S. Department of Justice, Federal Bureau of Investigation, *Uniform Crime Reports for the United States—Crime in the United States 1990* (Washington, D.C.: Government Printing Office, 1991), p. 13.

28. Id. at 15.

29. U.S. Bureau of the Census, *Statistical Abstract of the United States: 1990*, 110th ed. (Washington, D.C.: Government Printing Office, 1990),

p. 173. These figures need to be seen in light of police estimates that only 53.2 percent of rapes were reported in 1987, the most recent year for which data are available (*Abstract*, p. 168).

30. Deborah L. Rhode, *Justice and Gender: Sex Discrimination and the Law* (Cambridge: Harvard University Press, 1989), p. 251.

31. Michael D. A. Freeman, "'But if You Can't Rape Your Wife, Who[m] Can You Rape?': The Marital Rape Exception Re-examined," *Family Law Quarterly*, 15 (1981), 1.

32. Patrick A. Langan and Christopher A. Innes, *Preventing Domestic Violence Against Women* (Washington, D.C.: U.S. Department of Justice, Bureau of Justice Statistics Special Report, August 1986), p. 3.

33. Cynthia Diehm and Margo Ross, "Battered Women," in *The American Woman 1988–1989: A Status Report,* ed. Sara E. Rix (New York: Norton, 1988), pp. 292–302.

34. Angela Browne, *When Battered Women Kill* (New York: Free Press, 1987), pp. 4–5. The latter figure was for Pittsburgh. For a collection of other survey data, see Donald Dutton, *The Domestic Assault of Women* (Boston: Allyn and Bacon, 1988), particularly chap. 1.

35. "Domestic Violence Intervention Calls for More Than Treating Injuries," *Journal of the American Medical Association,* 264.8 (1990), 939.

36. Del Martin, "Foreword," in *Woman-Battering,* Mildred Daley Pagelow (Beverly Hills: Sage, 1981), p. 7.

37. Quoted in Dutton, supra note 34, at 16.

38. *Bowers v. Hardwick,* 478 U.S. 186 (1986).

39. The flag-burning controversy of the late 1980s that Post cites is a good case in point. Although perhaps a difficult constitutional issue, its effect on the behavior of the overwhelming majority of Americans was trivial.

40. Supporting national goals in the face of local opposition is the most persuasive way of understanding *New York Times Co. v. Sullivan,* 376 U.S. 254 (1964), where the Court rewrote the law of seditious libel to defeat a Southern attempt to put the civil rights movement out of business. Contrary to Post, neither individualism nor the principle of self-determination explain the outcome. If they were crucial, such a decision would have been issued years earlier.

41. The U.S. Supreme Court removed the injunction in *New York Times v. United States,* 403 U.S. 713 (1971) (*per curiam*). Chief Justice Burger and Justices Harlan and Blackmun dissented.

42. *United States v. Progressive,* 467 F. Supp. 990 (W.D. Wis. 1979).

43. Robert Justin Goldstein, *Political Repression in Modern America from 1870 to the Present* (Cambridge: Shenkman, 1978), p. 430.

44. *Press Freedom Under Pressure: A Twentieth Century Fund Task Force Report on the Government and the Press* (New York: The Twentieth Century Fund, 1971), pp. 22–23; Goldstein, supra note 43, at 518; Olga G. and Edwin P. Hoyt, *Freedom of the News Media* (New York: Seabury, 1970), pp. 79–84.

45. Hoyt, supra note 44, at 79.

46. Goldstein, supra note 43, at 480.

47. *Press Freedom Under Pressure,* supra note 44, at 23.

48. 54 Stat. 670 (1940).

49. *Dennis v. United States,* 341 U.S. 494 (1951). Only Justices Black and Douglas dissented.

50. For a chronology and listing of those indicted, see Robert Mollan, "Smith Act Prosecutions: The Effect of the *Dennis* and *Yates* Decisions," *University of Pittsburgh Law Review,* 26 (1965), 705, 708–10.

51. In 1957 the Supreme Court reversed the convictions of 5 defendants (and remanded 9 for new trials) in *Yates v. United States,* 354 U.S. 298 (1957).

52. 367 U.S. 203 (1961). On the same day, a conviction under the membership clause was reversed for lack of sufficient evidence in *Noto v. United States,* 367 U.S. 290 (1961).

53. 64 Stat. 987 (1950).

54. The Act also made it a criminal offense for a member of the Communist Party or of a Communist organization required to register to apply for a passport. Denying citizens the right to travel because of their political beliefs restricts communication. However, that provision remained good law until 1964 when the Supreme Court invalidated it in *Aptheker v. Secretary of State,* 378 U.S. 500 (1964).

55. *Communist Party v. Subversive Activities Control Board,* 367 U.S. 1 (1961). However, the CPUSA then launched a 5th Amendment self-incrimination challenge which was upheld in 1964 in *Communist Party v. United States,* 331 F.2d 807 (D.C.Cir. 1963), *cert.* denied 377 U.S. 968 (1964). The government then attempted to require registration by relying on another section of the Act, and several members of the Party were ordered to register. That order was upheld by the circuit court in *Albertson v. SACB,* 332 F.2d 317 (D.C.Cir. 1964), but reversed by the Supreme Court, 382 U.S. 70 (1965). In February 1965, the government obtained a second indictment of the Party for failure to register. Successful in the lower court, the Party's conviction was overturned on self-incrimination grounds in *Communist Party v. United States,* 384 F.2d 957 (D.C.Cir 1967). The government's efforts gradually petered out and

the Subversive Activities Control Board ceased to function on June 30, 1973.

56. A third piece of major legislation was the Communist Control Act of 1954. Concluding in Section 2 that "the Communist Party should be outlawed," the act denied the CPUSA or it successors "any of the rights, privileges, and immunities attendant upon legal bodies" (Section 3). It also subjected any knowing and willful member of the CPUSA, or of any organization "having for one of its purposes or objectives the establishment, control, conduct, seizure, or overthrow of the Government of the United States, or the government of any State...by the use of force or violence" to the provisions and penalties of the Internal Security Act of 1950 (Section 4). It appears, however, that the government made little use of the Act. See Kathleen Barber, "The Legal Status of the American Communist Party: 1965," *Journal of Public Law,* 15 (1966), 94.

57. 61 Stat. 136 (1947).

58. Cited in Norman Dorsen, Paul Bender, and Burt Neuborne, *Emerson, Haber, and Dorsen's Political and Civil Rights in the United States,* 4th law school ed., vol. 1 (Boston: Little, Brown, 1976), p. 110.

59. *American Communications Association v. Douds,* 339 U.S. 382 (1950).

60. 64 Stat. 156 (1950).

61. 72 Stat. 1602 (1958).

62. 78 Stat. 241 (1964).

63. Questions were raised in *Watkins v. U.S.,* 354 U.S. 178 (1957), and *Sweezy v. New Hampshire,* 354 U.S. 234 (1957). However, two years later, after congressional uproar, the Court found no constitutional problems with the practice in *Uphaus v. Wyman,* 360 U.S. 72 (1959), and *Barenblatt v. U.S.,* 360 U.S. 109 (1959).

64. Pub. Law 733, 64 Stat. 476 (1952).

65. Herbert H. Hyman, "England and America: Climates of Tolerance and Intolerance," in *The Radical Right,* ed. Daniel Bell (Garden City: Anchor, 1964), pp. 289; 290, n. 35.

66. Alan F. Westin, "Constitutional Liberty and Loyalty Programs," in *Foundations of Freedom in the American Constitution,* ed. Alfred H. Kelly (New York: Harpers, 1954, 1958), pp. 208, 211. For other, complementary numbers, see *Report of the Special Committee on the Federal Loyalty-Security Program of the Association of the Bar of the City of New York* (New York: Dodd, Mead, 1956), Appendix A, pp. 219–26.

67. Ralph S. Brown, Jr., *Loyalty and Security: Employment Tests in the United States* (New Haven: Yale University Press, 1958), Appendix A, pp. 487–88. For detailed breakdowns of the application of different laws, see Appendix B, 489–97.

68. Daniel C. Kramer, *Comparative Civil Rights and Liberties* (Lanham: University Press of America, 1982), p. 49.

69. Zechariah Chafee, Jr. *Government and Mass Communications: A Report from the Commission on Freedom of the Press*, 2 vols. (Chicago: University of Chicago Press, 1947), p. 9. Goldstein, supra note 43, at 554 reports that in the 1940 elections the Communist Party was barred from the ballot in 15 states.

70. Barber, supra note 56, at 103, n. 92.

71. *Salwen v. Rees*, 16 N.J. 216, 108 A. 2d 265 (1954).

72. Dorsen et al., supra note 58, at 89.

73. Id.

74. *Communist Party of Indiana v. Whitcomb*, 414 U.S. 441 (1974).

75. In 1919 the New York Legislature expelled 5 socialist members. The same year, the U.S. House of Representatives refused to seat Socialist Congressman-elect Victor Berger of Milwaukee.

76. The U.S. Supreme Court eventually decided in Bond's favor in *Bond v. Floyd*, 385 U.S. 116 (1966).

77. *American Bar Association Journal*, 37 (1951), 312–13.

78. The leading cases upholding exclusions for refusing to answer questions about political beliefs were *Konigsberg v. California*, 366 U.S. 36 (1961), and *In re Anastaplo*, 366 U.S. 82 (1961). In *Law Students Civil Rights Research Council v. Wadmond*, 401 U.S. 154 (1971), the Supreme Court held constitutional questions about political beliefs asked by the New York bar.

79. David J. Garrow, *The FBI and Martin Luther King, Jr.* (New York: Penguin, 1981).

80. *United States v. Spock*, 416 F.2d 165 (1st Cir. 1969).

81. 408 U.S. 1 (1972). On the extent of government surveillance, see Note, "The National Security Interest and Civil Liberties, *Harvard Law Review*, 85 (1972), 1130.

82. Charles Goodell, *Political Prisoners in America* (New York: Random House, 1973), p. 261.

83. "F.B.I. Kept Secret Files on the Supreme Court," *New York Times*, national ed., August 21, 1988, sec. 1: 13.

84. Elliott L. Richardson, "Freedom of Expression and the Function of Courts," *Harvard Law Review*, 65 (1951), 1, 6.

85. Zechariah Chafee, Jr., *Free Speech in the United States* (Cambridge: Harvard University Press, 1942), p. 561.

86. Stouffer, supra note 26 at 80.

87. Clyde Z. Nunn, Harry J. Crockett, Jr., and J. Allen Williams, Jr., *Tolerance for Nonconformity* (San Francisco: Jossey-Bass, 1978), p. 33.

88. John B. Oakes, "Introduction," in Kelly, supra note 66, at xi.

89. Cited in Lee C. Bollinger, *The Tolerant Society* (New York: Oxford University Press, 1986), p. 7.

90. Robert A. Dahl, "Epilogue," in *Political Oppositions in Western Democracies,* ed. Robert A. Dahl (New Haven: Yale University Press, 1966), p. 391.

91. Martin Shapiro, *Freedom of Speech: The Supreme Court and Judicial Review* (Englewood Cliffs: Prentice-Hall, 1966), p. 109.

PART IV

SOME EMPIRICAL
CONSIDERATIONS

10

WHY ALL DEMOCRATIC COUNTRIES
HAVE MIXED ECONOMIES

ROBERT A. DAHL

I am going to argue here that democracy is incompatible with certain types of economic order. Although the most obvious contradiction is between democracy and a socialist command economy, the main thrust of my argument purports that democracy is also incompatible with a strictly free market economy. Historically, all democratic countries have developed mixed economies in which markets, though highly important, are significantly modified by government intervention.

The contention that democracy is inimical to strictly free markets is not novel. This argument, or something close to it, was advanced almost half a century ago by Karl Polanyi in *The Great Transformation*.[1] Many others have touched at least indirectly on a similar theme. But the recent collapse of communism and with it the promise that socialist command economies might provide a desirable alternative to competitive markets has greatly enhanced the appeal both of democracy and the market. Indeed, it seems often to be assumed that democracy and free markets mutually reinforce one another. My aim here is to show that

Reprinted by permission of *Journal of Philosophy*, vol. 3, no. 3 (July 1992).

both historical experience and theoretical considerations contradict this assumption.

1. PRELIMINARIES

In explaining why democracy is incompatible with a particular
kind of economic order, we might assert that certain features of
the economic order would be fatally harmful to democracy; alternatively, however, we might contend that certain features of
democracy would fatally harm that particular kind of economic
order. The causal arrow, so to speak, might go either way: from
the economic to the political or from the political to the economic. In the first case, the argument would be that the economic
order causes the destruction of democracy; in the second, that
democracy causes destruction of the economic order. I argue
here that some economic orders would indeed be likely to destroy
democracy; but the reverse is also true: democracy would almost
certainly lead to the destruction of certain economic orders.
These include not only a socialist command economy and a capitalist command economy but also a strictly free market economy.

Broadly speaking, historical experience provides at least four
major alternatives to a strictly free market economy. These are
a socialist command economy, a capitalist command economy, a
socialist market economy, and a mixed economy in which markets are limited, controlled, regulated, or modified by government intervention. There are good reasons for believing that
the first two are incompatible with democracy. Although we cannot be entirely certain about the third, only the last has coexisted
with democracy.

Let me indicate briefly what I mean by these terms because
the distinctions are crucial to the argument. By democracy I
mean modern representative democracy, and more specifically
the set of political institutions that distinguish modern representative democracy not only from its historical antecedents—
earlier democracies and republics—but also from other contemporary regimes. By a command economy I mean one in which
resources are mainly allocated and prices are fixed by the government of the state (though illegal markets, i.e., black markets,
may exist). In a socialist command economy, enterprises are

mainly owned by "society" or the state; in a capitalist command economy, by "private" parties. In a socialist market economy, enterprises are owned by "society" or the state but prices and allocations are left mainly to markets. By a strictly free market economy I mean a system in which, with minor exceptions, factors of production are purchased and commodities are produced and sold by privately owned firms freely competing in unregulated markets. In short, I mean an economy that largely satisfies the requirements and assumptions of the neoclassical model of a fully competitive economy. Fixing the boundary between a strictly free market economy and a mixed economy is somewhat arbitrary because markets and private ownership predominate and governments intervene in both. But the strictly competitive market sector is significantly smaller and government intervention to modify market outcomes is significantly greater in mixed economies.[2]

Needless to say, the world is far more complex than these categories might suggest.[3] But they will do, I think, for the task at hand.

2. Democracy and Socialist Command Economies

It has often been observed that no democratic country has ever had a socialist command economy, and no country with a socialist command economy has had a democratic political system. How can we account for this striking fact? There are, I believe, two reasons: in one, the causal arrow runs from the political to the economic; in the other it is reversed.

In the first case, socialist command economies have only been introduced by leaders who have adhered to an ideology hostile to democratic institutions, that is, Leninism. In practice, the fundamental tenets of Leninism were, if adhered to by the rulers of a state, sufficient to prevent democratic institutions from developing, and sufficient to justify and encourage their destruction wherever they existed within reach of the Leninist rulers. These antidemocratic tenets include the Leninist conception of the vanguard party with its privileged access to knowledge of the laws of history; the belief that under the guidance of the vanguard party not only the proletariat but all of humankind would be liberated; the consequent denial of legitimacy to and the suppression of all oppositions; the contempt for "bourgeois democracy" as a mere mask for bourgeois domination; and the dynamics of one party rule. Armed with their faith in these beliefs and practices, Leninist rulers did not require a command economy in order to destroy democratic institutions or to prevent them from developing: Their control of the state and its potential for coercion and repression would have been sufficient, as dictatorial regimes have amply demonstrated in noncommunist countries that have retained (or as in Chile under Pinochet even strengthened) market economies.

The Soviet experience provides an illuminating if not wholly conclusive piece of evidence. The New Economic Program (NEP) inaugurated under Lenin and prosecuted for several years after his death encouraged the re-emergence of a market economy. But there was no relaxation in the dictatorship, no growth of democratic institutions. As we shall see in a moment, Jugoslavia provides still another test.

To be sure, in the long run a successful market economy creates conditions—structures, processes, social strata, beliefs, and expectations—that weaken the capacities of dictatorial rulers and enhance the prospects for democracy. My point here, however, is that because socialist command economies have been introduced only by Leninist rulers, and because Leninist rule is incompatible with democracy, we could account for the absence of democracy in a country with a socialist command economy, the Soviet Union, say, simply by taking note of the impact of Leninism.

Yet even if Leninism were not the reigning ideology, a country with a socialist command economy would be unlikely to cultivate and sustain democratic institutions over the long run. In any centralized system the resources of the economy are available to leaders who wish to employ them as rewards and punishments. This is particularly the case in a socialist command economy. To take one simple example: Leaders can deny paper and printing facilities to their political opponents. Or worse, they can curtail food supplies to an obdurate region or group, as in the mass starvation of peasants in the collectivization drive under Stalin in 1932–33. To be sure, actions like these might run counter to the objectives of "rational planning." But would that slender barrier be sufficient to prevent central political leaders from undertaking them? If the leaders also happen to be Leninists, their justification for fully exploiting their potential power would be even more lethal to democratic institutions.

Suppose we now engage in a mental experiment and reverse the causal arrow. What would happen if a central command economy were introduced in a country with democratic institutions so well established that leaders were compelled to adhere to democratic norms and practices? The predictable outcome, I believe, would be that in a short time, political pressures exerted through normal democratic political channels would seriously impair the control of the central planners. The "rational" goals, allocations, and prices of the central planners would immediately become highly politicized. To maintain their decisions intact would require a degree of centralized power, coercion, and independence from democratic controls inconsistent with our assumption. Without it, the attempt to control economic decisions by central command would become a shambles.

3. Democratic Experience with Economic Mobilization

One might object to what I have just written by citing the success of centralized economic mobilization in democratic countries in war-time, particularly the experience of Great Britain and the United States during the Second World War. In both countries for several years all major economic decisions were made by officials of the central government: They fixed prices, allocated (in effect rationed) raw materials, machine tools, and other resources needed for production, established production targets, determined how much would be left over for civilian consumption after essential military needs were met, set ration quotas for consumer goods, and attempted, not always successfully, to freeze wage levels, prevent strikes, and shift labor from civilian to military production. In a surprisingly short time, leaders created organizations that proved amazingly successful in mobilizing economic resources for military purposes and maintaining adequate levels of civilian consumption. In essence, they created a command economy within a capitalist framework.

In view of the extraordinary achievement of these wartime command economies, it was sometimes suggested during and immediately following the war that they should be retained and redirected to the tasks at which the capitalist economies of both Britain and the United States had failed so dismally during the thirties: full and steady employment, eliminating the downswings in the business cycle, achieving a more socially desirable allocation of resources, and so on. In both countries, however, following the end of the conflict the wartime structures for economic mobilization were speedily dismantled.

To describe and account for that enormous and rapid return to the pre-war market-oriented system is a task we need not undertake here. Let me instead offer two observations. First, despite its unquestioned success in war-time, in neither country did the command economy enjoy enough political support to insure its continuation. Second, as even the relatively brief transitional period revealed, no sooner had the threat to national survival been removed than ordinary peacetime political goals and activity, once again permissible, quickly threatened to make a mish-mash of what remained of any efforts to maintain a coherent, coordinated, and comprehensive set of economic controls.

In both countries, then, the wartime command economy was so quickly discarded that we cannot be certain about its long run consequences for democracy. Yet it takes little imagination and less skepticism to imagine how some post-war presidents in the United States might have found quite irresistible the opportunities such a system would have offered for persuasion, inducement, coercion, and corruption. We can be considerably more confident about the arrow of causation that runs in the other direction. Even if a command economy were somehow created in a democratic country, the normal operation of democratic politics is enough to insure that that the command system will be greatly impaired and then largely if not completely destroyed.

4. Dictatorship and Market Economies, Socialist and Capitalist

No one can seriously contest the observation that a market economy is not a sufficient condition for democracy, simply because capitalist market economies have existed in many countries ruled by dictatorships. Indeed, in some—South Korea, Taiwan, and Chile, for example—the economy has been so successful by world standards that reformers in China and the Soviet Union have sometimes considered that "soft authoritarianism" might offer an appropriate model for emulation during the transition from a command to a market economy. As I already suggested, Jugoslavia provides us with an instance in which an economically decentralized socialist market system coexisted for a third of a century with one party rule under Leninist leadership.

Of course, the experience of these countries may also be taken as evidence that a country with a moderately successful market economy will in the long run tend to generate a society that contains many elements supportive of liberalization and democratization.

What are we to say, however, about the possible coexistence of democracy with a decentralized socialist market economy? As to whether a socialist market economy is necessarily injurious to democracy, the experience of Jugoslavia leaves us with an inconclusive answer because of Leninist domination. The best we can do is to try a mental experiment by assuming that a country with well-established democratic institutions, beliefs, and culture adopts a decentralized market economy in which firms are owned not by the state but, say, by the people who work in them. I find it hard to see why such a system would be harmful to democracy. Whether the shift in ownership would oblige us to call the system "socialist," or whether it might be capitalism in a new and different form, is, of course, another issue. The point is, however, that a decentralized market economy with any one of several different forms of ownership of firms does not seem to pose any threat to democratic institutions. Although it may pose problems of efficiency and fairness, it does not appear to be incompatible with democracy.

But would democracy be injurious to an unregulated market

economy based on "social" rather than private ownership? If capitalist democratic countries have rejected unregulated market economies, there is all the more reason to suppose that a democratic country with a socialist ideology would, though committed generally to a market economy, insist on government intervention to allay the hardships caused by unregulated markets. Even Jugoslavia's soft authoritarianism allowed many relatively autonomous political forces to develop and express themselves. The upshot was often a "distortion" of the unfettered operation of markets by way of subsidies, low, zero, or negative real interest rates, prevention of bankruptcy of firms unable to compete effectively, and so on. There is every reason to suppose, then, that if a democratic country were ever to transform privately owned firms into some form of "social" ownership the factors that have brought about extensive government intervention in markets in capitalist countries would also prevail in a socialist country with democratic institutions.

5. Democracy and Unregulated Capitalist Market Economies

Having eliminated two of the five options and clouded the third with some uncertainty, historical experience leaves us only with the option of an economy that is essentially "privately" owned and predominantly oriented toward the institutions of competition and the market.

But capitalist market economies come in many different flavors, which for our immediate purposes I have simplified into two categories: strictly free market economies, and mixed economies in which markets are regulated and modified by government intervention. I scarcely need to point out that the simplification is drastic; in the second category we find many different varieties. My main focus here, however, is on the strictly free market variety.

This is what Karl Polanyi, in the work I mentioned earlier, referred to as "the self-regulating market."[4] Polanyi contended that because human beings are bound to resist the operation of markets, in any political system that allowed them to express and protect their interests, they would attempt to regulate the market and given sufficient political strength they would succeed. Drawing on the experience of Britain, he argued that "for a century the dynamics of modern society was governed by a double movement: the market expanded continuously but this movement was met by a countermovement checking the expansion in definite directions" (Polanyi, *Great Transformation*, 130). Having reached its peak with Poor Law Reform in 1834, the self-regulating market was increasingly subject to modification by government intervention so that by 1884 Herbert Spencer, a free market advocate, was able to compile a long list of examples of "restrictive legislation," much of it supported by liberals who in his view had deserted their principles. These horrendous legislative attacks on the sanctity of the free market seem hardly shocking today. They included laws "making it penal to employ [in mines] boys under twelve attending schools and unable to read or write," giving power "to poor law guardians to enforce vaccination," making illegal "a coal mine with a single shaft," extending vaccination to Scotland and Ireland, appointing inspectors for the "wholesomeness or unwholesomeness of food" regulating chimney sweeping to prevent hurt and death to children ordered to sweep too narrow slots (Polanyi, *Great Transformation*, 146).

As Polanyi and many others have said or implied, in thinking about free markets we must begin with two fundamental axioms: First, the operation of unregulated markets inevitably inflicts harm on some persons, by making them worse off in some way or by reducing their potential gains or advantages: businesspersons, workers, farmers, consumers, lenders, borrowers, school-age children, hospital patients, and so on. Second, if people who are harmed by the market have the freedom, power, and opportunity to do so they will attempt to regulate the market so as to eliminate, or at least limit, the damage they perceive. Whether their actions are "perfectly rational" is, of course, another question.

6. Why Rational Persuasion Fails to Prevent Government Intervention

Efforts people make to control the market in their own favor will of course fail if they can either be persuaded or compelled to accept the harm they believe is done to them. Consider persuasion. To accept the harm they perceive, the injured persons must be persuaded that either (1) in the long run the benefits will so fully and definitely outweigh the short run harm that their own self-interest will be served if they accept the present harm, or (2) whereas their own interests may indeed be injured in the short or long run, others whose interests they prefer to their own will be better off. The first argument appeals to their willingness to trade short run harm for riskier long run benefits. The second appeals to their moral sense of obligation to act so as to aid in achieving a broader good—"the public good," "the greatest good of the greatest number," the will or benefit of "the majority," the general welfare, the social optimum, or some other formulation of the good of a larger collectivity.

Yet if these appeals are reasoned or rational, and not merely emotive or sloganeering, then they must necessarily be cast in a fairly abstract form. Indeed, to be rationally convinced, one might well have to understand and accept an abstract theoretical argument of no little complexity and difficulty, at the level, say, of a textbook in economics. Experience shows, I believe, that abstract appeals ordinarily do not overcome uncertainties about long run possibilities. Nor do they overcome a very human unwillingness to subject one's own good, or the interests of one's own family, group, neighborhood, or any other collective entity to which a person may be attached, to a presumed and probably uncertain larger benefit to others to whom one's attachments are weak or nonexistent.

Attempts at persuasion would stand a greater chance of success in a country where the ideology of free markets is strongly entrenched among both elites and the populace in general, particularly if the ideology is well supported among elites because of the powerful rational appeal of economic doctrine. As Polanyi pointed out, this description roughly fits the situation in England in the 1830s; and it may be an even better description of the United States throughout the nineteenth century. As everyone knows, however, in these two countries as in all other democratic countries, the doctrine of free markets never lacked intellectual and political opposition, nor was it sufficiently persuasive to prevent the development of extensively regulated market economies. Advocates of a free market economy might take this history as evidence of a deplorable incompetence and economic illiteracy among intellectuals, political elites, and ordinary citizens in democratic countries. Yet although general ignorance of economic theory no doubt played a part, the explanation also turns on some crucial defects in the doctrine itself.

A central principle in the doctrine of unregulated markets is the assertion that an economic order in which economic activity is carried on by self-interested individuals and privately owned firms competing freely in unregulated markets will produce better results than any alternative system.

In broad versions of this doctrine, the superior results attributed to capitalism and free markets are many: greater individual freedom, a liberal constitutional and political system, more self-reliant human beings, greater opportunities for personal advancement, greater economic and social progress, and others. To what extent these desirable results are produced by capitalism and free markets has been a subject of unremitting controversy. Consequently, although attempts have been regularly made to fend off government intervention by predicting disastrous consequences for values that nearly everyone holds, an argument along these lines is not likely to be very persuasive to people who suffer or expect to suffer immediate and palpable harm from unregulated markets. On the contrary, people who believe themselves to be injured by the results of competitive markets are likely to dismiss such arguments as propaganda advanced to serve the purposes of their opponents. They are all the more likely to do so because on these questions and so many others there is no firm consensus among political and policy elites, intellectuals, academic experts, and other opinion leaders.

A far more powerful argument, intellectually speaking—though one too abstruse to be highly effective among mass publics—is the claim that a demonstrable outcome of, and a rationally compelling justification for, competitive markets is efficiency.

In its general meaning, efficiency refers to the ratio of inputs to outputs. In its narrowest sense, we might call it engineering efficiency, only resources measured in physical units are counted.[5] An automobile engine might be said to be more fuel efficient if it consumes less fuel per mile. Ordinarily, however, we find it perfectly reasonable to include in our calculations of efficiency the relative *values* we assign to inputs and outputs. Even in appraising the efficiency of automobiles, we can reasonably insist that the relative values of inputs and outputs be taken into account: speed, safety, weight, output of pollutants, and so on.

In any case, it would be foolish to make political and economic decisions solely on considerations of physical efficiency. What about economic costs? For example, what do we have to pay to achieve another significant gain in fuel efficiency? Suppose then that the inputs and outputs we agree to count include only resources whose values are measured by prices established in market transactions. We might call this economic efficiency. One argument for market economies is that they are notably more efficient in allocating resources at given prices than any alternative—at any rate alternatives with which we have experience. This argument has recently gained ground because the collapse of communist authoritarian regimes provides the outside world with an endless supply of evidence about the dismal performance of their economies.

That command economies have proved to be highly inefficient economically does not speak, however, to the relative desirability of mixed economies and strictly free market economies, nor does it help to explain the clear preference in democratic countries for mixed economies. On this issue, advocates of the doctrine of free markets can advance a much stronger argument in behalf of the efficiency of markets, using the term in a quite special sense. Suppose we define an optimal outcome as one that maximizes the welfare of the participants according to a roughly utilitarian standard of one kind or another. We agree, then, that an optimum outcome of economic activity must be one that yields maximum utility, felicity, pleasure, well-being; or, because these are rather ineffable, one that (with a given distribution of income) maximizes people's satisfaction of their preferences with respect to the allocation of scarce resources. Since the publication of Pareto's *Manual of Political Economy* in 1906, among economists an optimal or efficient outcome has of course generally come to mean a Pareto optimum: that is, a situation in which it is impossible for anyone to move to a more preferred position (and in this sense be "better off") without some one else moving to a less preferred position (i.e., becoming worse off). Perhaps we can usefully distinguish this meaning of efficiency, which is virtually unknown to most ordinary citizens but part of the standard vocabulary of professional economists, as economic efficiency (P). This sense of efficiency is directly relevant to our question of democracy and free markets because of the considerable intellectual authority of the view that perfect competition for land, labor, and capital in essentially unregulated markets will lead to economic efficiency (P).

Fortunately we need not attempt to pursue here the vast discussion about efficiency and Pareto optimality, which has moved beyond the bounds of economics to moral philosophy, political theory, and elsewhere. But the question arises: If a competitive market economy produces socially optimal outcomes, why have all democratic countries adopted seemingly more inefficient alternatives that necessarily produce suboptimal outcomes? Does the universal adoption of mixed market economies by democratic countries indicate not merely that the advocates of a strictly free market have failed to persuade their fellow citizens of the validity of their views, but also that the citizens and political leaders in these countries have exhibited an egregious incapacity for making rational judgments on economic matters?

Before turning to these questions, however, we need to emphasize again that whether one arrangement is more efficient than another depends on what one wants to count as valued inputs and outputs, and their relative magnitudes. If maintaining and improving the democratic process is counted as a value of exceptional importance, then the argument up to this point could be construed as saying that centralized command economies are in this respect (as, it appears, in most others!) notably less efficient than market economies; but whether unregulated market economies are more efficient in the broad sense than regulated market economies is an entirely different matter. Other relevant values that might be taken into account include justice or fairness, political acceptability in a democratic system, and so on. I come back to these in a moment. Meanwhile, however, it is easy to see that just as with the more general justifications for a free market economy mentioned earlier, admitting values like these into the appraisal of relative efficiency greatly impairs any argument against government intervention that is justified exclusively on grounds of economic efficiency and may well prove lethal to a justification based only on the Pareto criterion. Indeed, by appealing to one or more broader values, advocates of government intervention have often been able to justify government intervention as superior to unregulated markets.

It would be downright silly to argue that every instance of government intervention to regulate or modify markets in every democratic country has been reasonably designed to achieve justifiable goals. Yet it has has been shown again and again by economists and others that markets have many defects. It is hardly unreasonable to attempt to correct these defects. We cannot conclude, then, that in rejecting the doctrine of free markets and opting for government intervention and mixed economies, the citizens and elected leaders in democratic countries have shown themselves to be irrational or even unreasonable.

Fortunately the defects of unregulated markets have been so extensively examined before and since Polanyi's critique that we do not need to elaborate on them here.[6] However, in explaining why democracy has been historically incompatible with unregulated markets it is helpful to distinguish between several different kinds of problems. First, in order for markets to achieve socially optimal outcomes (economic efficiency [P]) a number of assumptions must be satisfied and certain conditions must be met, and to bring about these conditions and satisfy the assumptions is neither an easy or obvious matter. Some of the conditions are too technical for discussion here. (They are specified by Blaug, *Economic Theory in Retrospect,* 627ff.) Yet once a country has taken a significant step toward modifying one of these conditions, by legalizing trade unions, for example, then we no longer have reason to believe that market outcomes are optimal.

Yet even if all the necessary conditions somehow exist, all economic resources are allocated with maximum efficiency, and thus the economy has attained Pareto optimality, one could still not reasonably conclude that this is the most desirable state of affairs. To arrive at that judgment, one would also have to assume that the initial distribution of incomes (and other resources and endowments) was also fair, or at least that no other feasible distribution would be more just. Surely an assumption of such breathtaking boldness and unrealism would itself require justification. I return to this problem shortly.

Second, even if the necessary conditions for Pareto optimality were met, in some cases unregulated markets would not necessarily produce desirable outcomes; and therefore rational self-interest might reasonably lead to a demand for intervention. Undesirable outcomes include those that are inefficient or suboptimal in Pareto's sense, and outcomes that may be efficient but are ethically unjustifiable. As economists have long pointed out, when social costs are taken into account markets are not always "efficient."[7] Actions taken in unregulated markets can create severe costs to others, as with environmental damage, or they can fail to produce "public goods" that are necessarily consumed jointly and equally and, if supplied, will make everyone better off. Such goods will not be generated by strictly self-interested actions in a competitive market. Examples are national defense, many public health measures like universal vaccination against smallpox or infantile paralysis, and universal schooling.

To be sure, in some instances of market failure, a combination of market and nonmarket arrangements can in principle lead to efficient outcomes; but the arrangements ordinarily require government intervention in some form.

In addition, however, efficient outcomes, whether through the market or nonmarket means, are not necessarily justifiable; and some justifiable outcomes may be inefficient. There are many reasons for which an efficient outcome might reasonably be judged to be unjustifiable, but let us content ourselves with two very broad grounds: justice or fairness, and democracy. As to justice or fairness, one crucial example may suffice. As I pointed out earlier, we would be justified in accepting an efficient outcome as just or fair only on the heroic assumption, which is often stated and thereafter ignored, that the initial distribution of income and bargaining power was also just. An allocation of resources that is maximally efficient (Pareto optimal) is perfectly consistent with an indefinite number of income distributions, ranging from perfect equality to the most extreme inequality.

Thus the statement that unregulated competitive markets are a necessary means to "efficiency" and "socially optimal" outcomes, *and therefore desirable,* is morally trivial unless it is further grounded in an argument about the justice and feasibility of alternative distributions of income and other crucial resources.[8]

No small part of the effort to regulate markets has been stimulated by the attempt to alter the distribution of income, often selfishly no doubt. This is not to say that the results of these efforts have produced a fairer distribution of income (though if fairness requires less unequal incomes then some countries have brought about a more just distribution of income). Nor does it mean that the methods that have been chosen are necessarily the most efficient means available; on the contrary, they may often be highly inefficient, ineffective, and even perverse.[9] It is only to say that if one believes that the existing distribution of income is unjustified, then it is reasonable to attempt to obtain a more justifiable distribution by government intervention. Notice, too, that such an action would be reasonable no matter whether one acts from altruism, public virtue, or rational self-interest.

It is not unreasonable to conclude that the outcome of a system of competitive markets may be excessively harmful to the process and institutions of democratic government. Indeed, it is essential that these processes and institutions be insulated from the market: by making it illegal to sell one's vote, for example, whether as citizen or legislator, or to sell one's services as a government official.

A third major set of problems arises because, as I suggested ealier, for persons who believe themselves injured by the market to accept economically efficient (P) outcomes as desirable would sometimes require that they act not from rational self-interest but rather from a commitment to the general good rather than their own. In older language, they would need to be moved by a strong sense of public virtue. Moving toward Pareto optimality does not guarantee that no one will be injured in the process. It merely specifies that having been achieved, a change would make some people worse off. Likewise, no other relevant criterion of the general good prescribes that no one will ever be harmed for the greater good of society, or whatever. However, if persons injured by market outcomes are confronted with the argument that the greater good of society requires a competitive market even if they themselves are injured in the process, the injured persons are likely to say: so what?

Ironically, the assumption that society will benefit if everyone acts from motives of rational self-interest, in their economic transactions at any rate, stands in sharp contradiction to the requirement that for the optimal state of affairs to be reached the victims must somehow be prevented from acting selfishly to bring about a presumably less socially desirable outcome. But if in order that the general welfare be maximized the victims must not act in their own self-interest, then either they must be deluded about their own interests or they must be willing to sacrifice their own self-interest for the good of some larger entity.[10] Yet in a market society, as indeed perhaps in any large and heterogeneous society, the norms and practices supported by the prevailing culture are unlikely to encourage strong dedication to public virtue.

Finally, in some cases government intervention is likely to come about because the argument for nonintervention is necessarily too abstract and recondite to be persuasive to the general public, not least to the victims. For intellectual and policy elites convinced of the desirability of strictly competitive markets, the costs of persuading those who disagree may be so staggering as to make it virtually impossible. Historical experience seems to indicate that this is indeed the case. And in a democratic country the political elites, though perhaps better informed, may not be sufficiently independent from public opinion to carry out a policy, even though they believe it to be rationally justified, against the preferences of a substantial minority, let alone of a majority.

7. ALTERNATIVES TO PERSUASION

If people who believe themselves to be injured by free markets cannot be persuaded by rational argument to accept their lot, they might be compelled to do so. Even in a democratic country people are compelled to obey laws with which they disagree. After all, policies requiring government intervention to *alter* market relations, processes, and outcomes are not self-enforcing;

ordinarily they are upheld by the threat, and often the enforcement, of coercion in the form of severe penalties for violating
the laws and administrative rulings intended to carry out the
interventionist policies. It is sometimes forgotten, however, that
government policies intended to *inaugurate, protect,* or *maintain*
strictly free markets will, as we have just seen, ordinarily also
require coercion.

If a democratic country were pretty much governed according
to the principle of majority rule, a majority of citizens might
come to believe in the theoretical or practical arguments advanced on behalf of the benefits of unfettered markets. Enough
citizens to form a steady majority might conclude that their own
interests are best served by strictly free markets for all economic
resources; or a majority of citizens might be genuinely committed
to serving the general good and believe that strictly free markets
are necessary to it. Whatever the basis of their belief, we can
imagine that they might be willing to support policies, and to
insist that the government adopt and enforce policies, intended
to avoid or prevent interference with the operation of strictly
free markets. We can also imagine that they might be willing to
bear the costs—moral, personal, social, political, economic—of
enforcing these policies against the resistance of people who
believe themselves harmed.

We can imagine still another possibility. In the real world of
modern democracy, or what I prefer to call polyarchy, political
elites often enjoy a considerable degree of autonomy. We might
imagine, then, that leaders of a persistent majority coalition are
strongly convinced of the importance of maintaining a system
of strictly free markets, and able to bring about the adoption of
the appropriate policies without losing the support of a majority
of voters, many of whom might not be convinced advocates of
the policies of their political leaders.

But in the real world, compulsion is costly. People who are
harmed by policies enforced against their will therefore have
incentives for finding, inventing, and adopting actions, individual and collective, that will prevent or undermine effective
enforcement. Indeed, in liberal democratic systems, for governments to enforce laws effectively against the resistance of a minority is often impossible, or simply too costly for the effort to

be seen as worthwhile. The question of when and how ruthlessly to enforce a law and when and how to yield to its opponents turns into a problem requiring political judgments. It is no longer a matter of abstract principle but of practical and pragmatic decision, a weighing of relative costs and gains in a very broad sense.

We know that government intervention is costly, and it is sometimes contended that the costs of government intervention in market decisions outweigh the benefits. Arriving at a defensible judgment is obviously enormously difficult.[11] Important values must sometimes either be omitted entirely or assigned a highly arbitrary figure. It is relevant, however, that intervention to create or protect markets is also costly; resistance and defiance can generate intolerably high costs. One has only to recall the attempts of governments, sometimes accompanied by violence, to prevent workers from forming trade unions and engaging in strikes and other collective actions.

Even more important than the costs of coercion required to maintain strictly free markets are the familiar dynamics of politics in democratic countries. The rules of the democratic game provide adult citizens with at least one resource, a vote, that in the aggregate possesses great value for elected leaders. The rules of the game also insure that many people enjoy access to the political arena in other ways. Political competition provides elected leaders with incentives for responding to the views and votes of any organized or unorganized aggregate of people numbering more than a handful of potential voters. If one set of competing leaders cannot fashion a response without expecting to lose more support than it gains, another set may find it more profitable to take up their cause.

Majority coalitions are rarely if ever truly homogeneous; they are really coalitions of minorities, collections of people with converging or complementary but not perfectly identical concerns. The coalitions are far from stable in the long run. Hence people whose claims are ignored by the existing government coalition often stand a chance of having their claims taken more seriously by a future government coalition. Moreover, although the extent to which a group outside the incumbent governing coalition can influence government policies varies greatly among democratic countries, governments often accommodate themselves even to groups of voters who currently tend to give their support to the opposition.

One way or another, then, over time the victims of free markets are likely to influence the government—or *some* government, whether local, state, provincial, or regional—to adopt interventionist policies intended to mitigate the harm.

Given the evident impossibility of creating and maintaining a strictly free market, some of its supporters might conclude that the fault is not in the policies themselves but in the democratic processes that allow the unenlightened to prevail over the enlightened. They might even conclude that if the enlightened are to prevail over the unenlightened on economic matters, and perhaps on others as well, then democratic processes and institutions should be replaced by guardianship or elite rule, or to put it more bluntly, by an authoritarian dictatorship. This is not the place to discuss the moral and political folly of such a view.[12] Perhaps the only point worth emphasizing here is that if a free market economy can only be maintained by a nondemocratic political system, then the vision of nineteenth-century liberalism lies in utter ruins.

CONCLUSION

The upshot is, then, that every democratic country has rejected the practice, if not always the ideology, of unregulated competitive markets. Although it is true that a market economy exists in all democratic countries, it is also true that what exists in every democratic country is a market economy modified by government intervention. These mixed economies take many different forms, from the corporatist systems of the Scandinavian countries, Germany, Austria, and the Netherlands to the more fragmented systems of Britain and the United States.[13] Moreover, the extent and forms of intervention vary not only from country to country but also over time.

As we have seen, neither historical experience nor theoretical considerations provide grounds for believing that in countries with market economies and democratic political systems the complex patterns of government intervention and markets will ever be perfectly stable or substantially similar in all such countries. There is no convincing evidence that points to the existence of a Platonic ideal equilibrium toward which these various patterns converge. On the contrary, we have strong reasons for concluding that (1) different countries will continue to display different patterns and (2) within any particular country the pattern will continue to change together with changes in the society, the economy, the political forces, and the ideas, beliefs, perceptions, and values of its people.[14]

Fortunately no part of my task here is to appraise the virtues and vices of the various systems of government intervention that have developed in different democratic countries, much less to take on the daunting and probably impossible task of arriving at a reasoned judgment as to whether one system is clearly superior to the others. My aim is far more modest: to explain why all democratic countries have not only rejected a centralized command economy as an alternative to a market economy, but have also rejected a strictly free market economy as an alternative to a mixed economy in which market outcomes are substantially modified by government intervention.

NOTES

1. New York: Farrar & Rinehart, 1944. Even in 1944, of course, the theme of increasing "collectivism" acting to limit extreme "individualism" was hardly novel. For example, in his influential *Law and Opinion in England in the Nineteenth Century,* Second Edition (London: Macmillan, 1914), A. V. Dicey had described the rise of "collectivism" in (as the title indicates) both public opinion and legislation in England in the nineteenth century.

2. One might define the boundary operationally by specifying that a strictly free market economy would be one that satisfied the implicit or explicit prescriptions of Friedrich A. Hayek in *The Road to Serfdom* (Chicago: University of Chicago Press, 1944); Milton Friedman, in *Capitalism and Freedom* (Chicago: University of Chicago Press, 1962); Robert Nozick, *Anarchy, State and Utopia* (New York: Basic Books, 1974); and/ or James M. Buchanan, *The Limits of Liberty* (Chicago: University of Chicago Press, 1975).

3. For more nuanced views, see Charles E. Lindblom, *Politics and*

Markets (New York: Basic Books, 1977); Gosta Esping-Andersen, *Politics Against Markets* (Princeton: Princeton University Press, 1985); and John R. Freeman, *Democracy and Markets, The Politics of Mixed Economies* (Ithaca: Cornell University Press, 1989). Freeman's discussion illustrates some of the difficulties of rigorously classifying the important variations in the predominantly privately owned, market-oriented economic systems of democratic countries. He offers four criteria, each of which is dichotomous, but reduces the sixteen theoretically possible types to four (82–84 and 97ff). Where I have used the term "mixed economy" here to mean market economies with a significant admixture of state intervention, by "mixed economy" he means one with a significant state-owned sector, in contrast to "private enterprise economies."

4. Polanyi, *Great Transformation*. He describes its assumptions on pages 68–69.

5. A Pareto-like conception of efficiency in the narrowest sense would be to say that a system is inefficient if by moving a physical input from producing output A to producing output B, the output of B would be increased with no decrease in A. A system would be fully efficient, then, if no such move were possible. I am indebted to James Tobin for clarification on this point.

6. See the works cited in note 2, and Marc Blaug, *Economic Theory in Retrospect,* Third Edition (New York: Cambridge University Press, 1978).

7. See, for example, Blaug, *Economic Theory in Retrospect,* 632ff. and citations at 644.

8. The attempt at the turn of the century by the American economist J. B. Clark to demonstrate that the distribution of income resulting from competitive markets is also normatively just was quickly rejected as fallacious and abandoned by other economists, who have adopted the view that the distribution of income is a given from which the validity of their analysis begins. See Blaug, *Economic Theory in Retrospect,* 450ff. For a critique from the standpoint of political theory, see Ian Shapiro, "Three Fallacies Concerning Majorities, Minorities, and Democratic Politics," in *Majorities and Minorities,* Ed. John W. Chapman and Alan Werthermer, Nomos 32 (New York: New York University Press, 1990).

9. For a discussion of some desirable and undesirable solutions to inequalities in incomes and other crucial resources, see James Tobin, "On Limiting the Domain of Inequality," *The Journal of Law and Economics* XIII (2) (October, 1970): 263–277.

10. One might ask, what larger entity? Humankind? If not humankind, why any smaller aggregation? Although the problem of what

aggregate of people is to be taken as relevant in determining an optimal outcome seems to me to pose a neglected question of central importance, I am going to follow the usual (if lamentable) practice of ignoring it here.

11. The most recent effort to estimate the costs and gains in the United States is by Robert W. Hahn and John A. Hird, "The Costs and Benefits of Regulation: Review and Synthesis," *Yale Journal on Regulation* 8 (1991): 233–278. Their estimates of the annual costs for 1988 in regulating international trade, telecommunications, agricultural price supports, airlines, railroads, postal rates, milk marketing, natural gas, barges, and a half dozen other activities amounded to $45.3–$46.5 billion in efficiency costs and $172.1–$209.5 billion in transfer payments (Table 1, p. 251). They estimate the 1988 costs of social regulation of the environment, highway safety, occupational safety and health, nuclear power, drugs, equal employment opportunities, and consumer product safety in the range of $78–$107 billion, and the benefits $42–$182 billion (Table 2, p. 256). "Unlike economic regulation," they note, "where the benefits are thought to be negligible in most cases, social regulation has the potential to confer significant benefits. Because social regulation can address specific 'market failures,' it may provide net benefits to society" (253).

12. I have done so in *Democracy and Its Critics* (New Haven: Yale University Press, 1989).

13. See, for example, Freeman, *Democracy and Markets*. Even the Scandinavian countries followed markedly different paths in economic policy-making. For example, the "three Nordic countries have developed very different mechanisms for political control of the business cycle. The Norwegian social democrats have primarily emphasized planning with credit control and, lately, government purchase of industrial stock. The Swedes have relied primarily on labor market control but after the 1960s they also began to promote a more active role in investment. Finally, the Danish social democrats have failed to institute public direction and control of finance, labor market, or investment behavior. In all three countries, but especially in Norway and Denmark, government intervention in income determination assumed major proportions during the 1970s" (Esping-Andersen, *Politics Against Markets*, 236–237).

14. The famous "Swedish model" provides an illuminating example. After having developed gradually during a half century of predominantly social democratic governments, its major elements were often seen in Sweden and elsewhere as virtually unalterable components in a fundamental social compact. However, voter dissatisfaction in the

1980s led to a scaling down of income tax rates (to a maximum of 50 percent), and in September 1991 produced the worst defeat for the Social Democratic Party since the 1920s. As a consequence, the non-socialist parties formed a government and are likely to introduce further, if gradual, changes in some key policies.

11

LEARNING PLURALISM: DEMOCRACY AND DIVERSITY IN FEMINIST ORGANIZATIONS

CARMEN SIRIANNI

With the beginning of its second wave, and especially its more radical variants since the late 1960s, feminism has been concerned with redefining democratic community on more participatory grounds. To this end organizational processes, deliberative styles, and communicative ethics have been refashioned. Initially, little was distinctively feminist in this, as young women's movement leaders drew on the model of the "beloved community" they had been practicing in Student Nonviolent Coordinating Committee (SNCC), or on the "participatory democracy" of Students for a Democratic Society (SDS), the major black and white student movement organizations respectively. To be sure, there was a feminist subtext from the beginning.

Ella Baker, middle-aged grandaughter of a rebellious slave minister and chief staffer who had organized Southern Christian Leadership Conference's (SCLC) central offices before being displaced by yet another male minister, had articulated an approach

The following people provided welcome suggestions and critical insight: Karen Hansen, Jenny Mansbridge, Peter Conrad, Shula Reinharz, Claire Reinelt, Andrea Walsh, Robin Leidner, and Ian Shapiro.

to facilitative group leadership that was an alternative to both the bureaucratic movement organizational form of the NAACP and the charismatic form dominated by the male preachers of SCLC. Baker argued that "you must let the oppressed themselves define their own freedom," and nurtured in SNCC an organizing style that recognized leadership inchoate in every community and in every individual. Through her influence on SNCC activists, and both directly and indirectly on SDS leaders, Baker can be said to have been the midwife of participatory democracy in the student movements of the 1960s. When Mary King and Casey Hayden confronted both student organizations with their own strictures on female leadership, and began to form a separate movement in the process, they turned to the teachings of Ella Baker, as well as to the experience they had gained in facilitative leadership among hundreds of indigenous "mamas" turned community activists across the South.[1]

However, despite this clear inspiration from an African-American woman with years of activist experience and an explicit critique of male leadership, only with the development of a separate women's liberation movement in the late 1960s did participatory democratic community begin to acquire explicitly feminist emphases. A feminist ideal soon emerged that stressed egalitarian participation, democratization of all leadership roles, elimination of all competitiveness in organizational life, careful listening, respect for the experiences of all women, self-transformation, and autonomy through intimate sharing and small group support. In short, what later came to be called a distinctively, though not exclusively, female "ethic of care" in feminist theory was grafted onto a radically egalitarian version of participatory democracy and community.

Ironically, at this very time participatory democracy in SDS was unravelling through the pull of its own ambiguities and contradictions, not the least between its civic republican and existential variants, and beloved community in SNCC had given way to authoritarian and dogmatic sectarianism as its redemptive ethos proved incapable of accomodating a plurality of activist styles or democratic leadership transitions.[2] This would not have been a surprise to competitive elite theorists of democracy, who warned of the totalitarian potential of too much participation.[3]

But some in the student movements were themselves beginning to develop a coherent critique of the excesses and ambiguities of participatory democracy. And by the end of the 1960s, a number of political theorists had begun to articulate a pluralist version of participatory democracy that valued participation and self-management in expanding democracy, and yet recognized limits and decried excesses, arguing instead for fundamentally plural democratic forms, decision criteria, styles of citizenship, and degrees of commitment. Robert Dahl and Michael Walzer, in particular, affirmed important elements of what I would call participatory pluralism, simultaneously broadening pluralist theory to accomodate the participatory revolution of the era, yet critiquing any pretense to singular democratic forms or ideals of citizenship.[4]

This rethinking of participatory democracy as the ideal and singular form of democratic community had no discernible impact on the radical women's movement's organizational development at the time. Few prominent women's movement leaders seem to have been aware of it, and those that may have been did not cite this literature, either because they saw it as alien or feared that others in the movement would view it as such.[5] It is hardly a surprise that the movement, far from transcending the problems of participatory community that had plagued the student movements, recapitulated many of them, and some in even more extreme forms precisely because of the movement's distinctive feminist emphases.

Yet, if one of the central justifications for participation in political theory has been its educative impact on participants,[6] the feminist movement might be said quickly to have generated internal learning processes enabling it to refine the meanings and forms of participatory community. After presenting the ideal of democratic community and feminist process that emerged in radical women's organizations, I argue that this learning has pointed predominantly, though not entirely or consistently, in the direction of participatory pluralism. As a result of having to confront issues of democratic representativeness, informal tyranny, imposed sisterly virtue, distorted communication, forced consensus, democratic accountability, and strategic efficacy, the movement was compelled to rediscover and relearn many of the lessons of pluralist theory. Not only did its own internal resources prove quite substantial for this task, but distinctively feminist emphases on care and difference more recently have enabled feminism to expand the range of issues that a participatory pluralism must confront, even if some of the movement's own innovations remain quite problematic and theoretical issues are yet unresolved.

FEMINIST PROCESS: THE EMERGENCE OF AN ORGANIZATIONAL IDEAL

Neither SNCC nor SDS was able to respond effectively to the feminist critique that emerged in 1964–1965. SNCC was rent by black–white sexual tensions on staff, and by fierce conflict between the so-called "freedom high" and "structure" factions. SDS's not inconsiderable capacities for organizational learning and political debate about the meanings and forms of democracy were overwhelmed by the massive influx of new recruits with the escalation of the Vietnam war, and the competitive male intellectual styles that alienated many women in early SDS gave way to even more offensive macho styles of the newly arrived anarchist "prairie dog" leaders. Women's leadership styles, which had begun to come into their own in community organizing projects, were further marginalized by the antiwar emphasis on large mobilizations and rallies, and draft resistance accorded the male experiences of vulnerability and heroism a privileged role in movement culture and personal politics. Campus SDS chapters, which might have served better for sustaining and feminizing the ideals of participatory democracy, were often dominated by male cliques. As Sara Evans notes, "Stardom was increasingly defined by glamour and rhetorical verbal skills, and the talents that could prove effective in small groups or in community organizing had little place in the broader movement."[7]

As a consequence, many women moved outside, and began to redefine participatory group dynamics with distinctly feminist emphases. Consciousness raising (CR) groups, and small collectives that combined CR with political projects, were the primary forms for this in the late sixties and early seventies, although city-wide women's liberation unions often established a broader framework for feminist participation on the bases of small groups. CR philosophy and techniques were drawn from a variety of sources: the "speak bitterness" campaigns of the Chinese revolution popularized by such books as *Fanshen*, SDS "Guatemala Guerrilla" organizing, SNCC and ERAP personal discussion styles, and experiential learning in the Mississippi freedom schools. Kathie Sarachild, who is widely credited with developing specifically feminist CR techniques and who had herself been a Freedom Summer volunteer in 1964, urged women to scrap the old theories and build feminist theory and politics on the basis of personal experience: "In our groups, let's share our feelings and pool them. Let's let ourselves go and see where our feelings lead us. Our feelings will lead us to ideas and then to actions."[8]

Sharing would help define common problems and dispel self-blame. Personal revelation was especially appropriate when the oppressed were in intimate relations with their oppressors.[9] The authority of personal experience recognized that all women had something to say about oppression, and so had the right in women's groups to attentive listening and moral support. These would not only yield insight, but transform the passive into self-confident activists, even leaders. These early CR experiences were the practical loci for feminist theorists' later insight that autonomous selves are formed not in isolation but in supportive relations, which is in contrast to liberal theory's view of individuals and their rights.[10] Indeed, if every woman were seen as a potential leader, as Ella Baker and Mary King would have it, then leadership roles should be widely dispersed, skills shared, power diffused. Mutually supportive participation at the small group level could have educative and transformative effects, and prefigure a society based on non-hierarchical relationships.

Hundreds of thousands of women took part in these small groups in the late sixties and early seventies, and many testify to the educative and empowering effects they had on their lives. As Evans has noted,

> They provided a place, a "free space," in which women could examine the nature of their own oppression and share the growing knowledge that they were not alone. The qualities of intimacy, support and virtual structurelessness made the small group a brilliant tool for spreading the movement. Anyone could form a

group anywhere: an SDS women's caucus, a secretarial pool, a friendship circle, a college dorm, a coffee klatch.

Their spontaneous and contagious formation was later given an added boost when the National Organization for Women (NOW), the major arm of the mainstream women's movement, began officially propagating them, indeed becoming their primary proponent, after initially feeling that they would divert women's energies away from political action. Many chapters institutionalized CR courses with specific topics, and the Los Angeles NOW Consciousness Raising Committee distributed a 60-page CR Handbook.[11]

Small participatory groups, often set up as collectives, have been particularly suited to a variety of women's self-help, service, and cultural projects. Women's health collectives have aimed to disperse knowledge and skills widely, and thus demystify medical expertise for both staff and patients, to enable women to gain greater control over their own bodies. In this they have spearheaded a broader critique of professional ideologies and practices that disempower those they are supposed to serve. Perhaps the most famous of these is the Boston Women's Health Book Collective, which published *Our Bodies, Ourselves* in 1973 (and a subsequent 1984 edition), a book that has had a profoundly democratizing impact on the constitution of medical knowledge and the delivery of services in traditional as well as alternative settings. The shelter movement for battered women has also frequently used the democratic collective, and other participatory forms, because in the process of establishing active engagement and equal respect among staff and residents, the latter are provided with a living alternative to the domination they have experienced and the passivity of mere victim status.

In one shelter studied by Noelie Maria Rodriguez, all members of the staff had at one time been victims of battering or incest, and most had themselves been residents of the shelter. Although some board members have professional credentials, none are required for regular staff. Current and past residents are active in all aspects of decision making, from hiring and administration to program details, and communication among staff and residents is continuous and open. Staff serve as role models of those who have been able to redefine their lives without violence and victimization, and residents support and empower each other through peer counseling. Participation is meant to be empowering and therapeutic at the same time, and to serve as an alternative to the professional social service model.[12]

INTERNAL CRITIQUE OF STRUCTURELESS DEMOCRACY AND SISTERLY VIRTUE

The feminist movement's acute attention to group process, however, quickly began to generate a trenchant critique of small, relatively structureless groups. Jo Freeman's 1972 essay, "The Tyranny of Structurelessness," which had been circulating before its publication in several places, was the most important document in triggering a process of critical reflection that has been going on ever since.[13] Diffuse participatory methods, according to Freeman, often do little really to democratize power, and can, in fact, make those who wield the most influence in an organization even less responsible and less accountable to members. The refusal to name leaders often means that the membership is also unable to name the elites that emerge informally, and in many cases constitute oligarchic enclaves.

Informal dominance is based on networks not all that different than old boys networks in how they operate, a great irony for a movement that historically has sought to democratize power by formalizing methods of selection and decision making. Entry into informal networks is often based on friendship, marriage to New Left men with valued resources (mailing lists, presses), or on appropriate class, race, and educational backgrounds and personally attractive styles. Some become de facto leaders simply by their ability and willingness to invest the most time, thereby creating the problem of representativeness that had deeply concerned both Dahl and Walzer. As Ann Popkin noted in her study of the Bread and Roses collective in Boston, this presented a real problem for women with full-time jobs, who often felt marginalized from the inner circle of "heavies" (the word members chose to describe the reality of power they felt proscribed from naming directly), or for those who had multiple political commitments. Formally democratic mechanisms were not available to control the power cliques, and the informal norms of steep time investment made it difficult for women with multiple commitments to achieve recognition as serious feminists with a role to play in formulating program and political direction.[14]

Communicative and decision-making processes could also be distorted by certain egalitarian procedures and personalized styles. Redstockings of New York, for instance, devised a system of equalizing opportunities to speak by distributing 12 disks to each member, one of which was forfeited each time a person spoke. As Jane Mansbridge has pointed out, this helped make women conscious of inequalities among themselves and alerted the more aggressive to the limits on their speech. But it did not reduce inequalities of influence, because the more powerful still were able to mobilize support networks and command through rhetoric when members' interests came into conflict. When interests tended to converge, it actually obstructed careful debate on the most optimal solution by discouraging short helpful comments by those with most to contribute. And it tended to orient people to the frequency rather than the quality of speech.[15] Expressive personal styles, such as prefacing comments with "I feel" or "it freaks me out that," often sowed confusion or concealed political direction in the guise of openness. At mass meetings of women's unions, such styles made it difficult to pursue orderly discussion or get people to respond sequentially to another's arguments. Decisions were often not carried out, because of free-flowing discussion or the absence of minutes, which were seen as distinctly bureaucratic.

Lack of formal structure made some feel even more inadequate and disempowered, because it appeared that all could speak and be listened to equally, and hence fear of speaking or lack of persuasiveness was more easily perceived as one's own personal failing. In many cases, egalitarian styles bred conformity and stifled dissent by branding it "unsisterly" to challenge another woman's ideas or to claim individual authorship of an article. In denying a proper place for political and personal competition, which were viewed as peculiarly male, suppressed anger and hostility often came in through the back door in ways that were destructive of democratic process and personally hurtful. The result, as Karen Hansen has argued, was "an environment where only the brave, the politically correct, or the thick-skinned would speak. Many women described the mass meetings as almost unbearable."[16]

Personal politics in the small groups could become particularly oppressive, even totalitarian, according to Freeman and others, on issues of sexual preference. As many lesbians stepped out of the closet, lesbianism came to be interpreted not only as a right of sexual preference, but as a political choice and as a criterion of feminist trustworthiness. Those who chose not to become a "woman-identified woman" and to explore full sexual love and commitment were often seen as compromised or, worse yet, as traitors to other women. This sisterly version of Rousseauian virtue was often enforced through small group process with particular vehemence, causing much personal trauma, even nervous breakdowns, and leaving the feminist identities of many committed activists shattered. Even where sexual preference was not at issue, politicizing the personal often meant escalating the emotional risks one was expected to take and exposing one's personal life to the continual scrutiny of the group. Just as existential daring infused the student movement's interpretations of participatory democracy, so did intense emotional risk taking become a standard for participatory openness and sisterly virtue in the radical women's movement. Many women recognized this to be a "perversion of the 'personal is political' argument," and resisted the creeping notion that "a woman's life is the political property of the women's movement," but not before many women's groups were destroyed in the process of learning how to draw the boundaries.[17]

The radically participatory and egalitarian ethos entailed profound ambivalence about leadership, and those who took initiative often received confused and contradictory messages about their efforts. On the one hand, they felt that the movement expected them to speak at local gatherings and national conferences, because moral pressure to be available and preach the gospel whenever needed was great. They were expected to provide theoretical analysis and strategic guidance, and their essays and books were enthusiastically welcomed and debated. On the other hand, they were accused of being elitist when they did take initiative or enter the limelight, of being manipulative when they did formulate plans and develop strategies, of being on a "male trip" of rational analysis when they did generate and debate theories.[18]

Ambivalence about leadership was so deep, and egalitarian impulses so strong, that many groups could not sustain a rational debate about what democratic leaders should be like or how the movement might produce them. If leadership potential was present in all women, many groups reasoned, then any woman should be able to run a mass meeting, every woman should be interested in theory, and no woman need be trained to manage an organization. One faction among the Feminists from New York tried to prescribe at the Second Congress to Unite Women in early 1970 that "*everyone* in the movement must be in groups which operate COLLECTIVELY (i.e. use the LOT SYSTEM)," and no woman could speak before the media unless chosen by lot or could earn a living from writing or speaking about women's liberation.

The results of these attitudes were often quite debilitating. Organizational structurelessness bred a peculiarly destructive psychodynamics of leadership trashing. Competitive impulses could not be recognized and legitimated, nor could they be easily contained and channeled. Those who felt guilty and self-hating for asserting themselves, fearful of being accused of elitism, envious of others who achieved recognition, or inadequate for being unable to live up to the ideal of all women as leaders or theorists, could project their unwanted feelings onto the "heavies" by caricaturing and trashing them, disempowering them even as they expected to be empowered by them. The result was a dampening of initiative among many—as Linda Gordon has noted of Bread and Roses—or complete, though usually temporary, withdrawal from the women's movement, thus creating leadership vacuums and depriving the movement of much needed talent.

The first generation of leaders, in particular, suffered so greatly from what they called the "trashing" and "witchhunts" that they were almost completely decimated. Naomi Weisstein, for instance, who had felt profoundly empowered by her experience in supportive small groups in the late 1960s, and who had successfully overcome her terror of speaking before large audiences to become a brilliant orator, felt that by being trashed as an elitist star the women's movement had "given her a voice and then taken it away again." And as in SDS and SNCC, the inability of the movement to name leaders who could be held accountable made it all that much easier for the media to choose its own stars to put on the cover of *Time* magazine or the CBS evening news, creating even more resentment toward them and reinforcing their sense that they were "feminist refugees" who should try to reach other women through the media and not the movement. As Freeman has argued, "The movement's greatest fear became a self-fulfilling prophecy. The ideology of 'structurelessness' created the 'star system' and the backlash to it encouraged the very kind of individualistic nonresponsibility that it most condemned."[19]

Structurelessness also left the larger feminist organizations vulnerable to control by disciplined sectarian groups. With membership open and criteria loose, leadership chosen according to who was willing to put in the most time, and meetings run haphazardly without previously circulated agendas or recorded attendance and minutes, cadre organizations could assert disproportionate influence by packing the mass meetings with women not previously active in chapters, volunteering a great deal of time in the office, and propounding their own line as if it were that of the feminist group as a whole. In some cases, not only were the dominant sentiments of the group not well represented, but views contrary to feminism itself were propagated. These unwelcome results of loose inclusiveness confronted feminists with severe challenges to their innocent notions of sisterly solidarity and open participation, and forced them to pose the question explicitly, "What demos?" "Whose voice?" By what criteria is membership established and the right to speak in the name of others bestowed? Is having one's name on a list enough to qualify for membership, or does one have to be active in a chapter, pay dues, or subscribe to a particular program or ideology? And how does one demonstrate commitment and belief? Practically, these questions presented women's groups with the option of purging members of political sects, which was an agonizing decision that many saw as inherently anti-feminist, and that paralyzed various groups and exhausted their leaders. Not a few dissolved shortly after such membership crises.[20]

The tension between prefigurative and strategic orientations, which Wini Breines sees as having been the key unresolved tension in the student movement, thus manifested itself in the participatory politics of the women's movement as well.[21] Structureless groups aiming to prefigure a utopia of radical equality in their internal process had a difficult time setting priorities or following through on decisions. Many socialist-feminist unions paralyzed themselves in the elusive search for the ideal project. Internal crises produced continual fragmentation. And the groups that resisted formalizing structures for organizational maintenance were the very ones that spent the most time and effort on revising their structures and trying to maintain their organizations, time that was drained from actual or planned projects and effective political work.[22]

The tensions, however, were not just between the prefigurative and the strategic, but *within* those very processes imagined to prefigure the ideal. As Naomi Weisstein and Heather Booth noted in 1975, "Our organizations and our alternate institutions die from internal bleeding long before they succumb to external pressure."[23] Informal dominance, expressive manipulation, leadership trashing, false consensus, enforced sisterly virtue were all problems that, to a considerable degree, were generated by the very attempts to prefigure an ideal of participatory openness and egalitarian process. And many were eventually contained only by elevating strategic considerations to a *higher* level of priority in women's organizations. The fault line between the prefigurative and the strategic cannot serve metanarratively to map the fundamental dilemmas of democratic participation, feminist or otherwise, because faults crisscross each of these in many directions and generate multiple tensions within and between them. And although the prefigurative ideal continues to reappear in feminist theory and feminist organizations, often in strikingly unitary form, the critique generated within the movement itself has created an increasingly profound capacity to manage, and imagine, a multiplicity of tensions and a plurality of forms.

FORMALIZING STRUCTURES: DILEMMAS OF EMPOWERMENT

Concerns with personal self-development and calculations of political efficacy, which have served as important justifications in
political theory for increased participation,[24] further anchored
the emerging critique of structureless democracy in the women's
movement. Since the radical women's movement of the late sixties and early seventies was largely a youth movement, it is not
surprising that many activists, like those in SNCC and SDS, eventually began to formulate plans for lifetime commitment and to
distance themselves from forms of organization that colonized
so much time, excluded familial and career obligations, or exposed them to premature burnout. The attrition rate in small
collectives was always quite high, reflecting de facto strategies
for self-development and efficacy via exit. But choices were increasingly made in good conscience once the time and wage costs
of egalitarian work were framed within the broader critique of
the feminine volunteer syndrome that would deny women independent careers. And such concerns were often shared by
poor, working class and Third World women activists, who
found the egalitarian rejection of formalized authority and
professional status to serve neither their own developmental
needs nor the practical delivery of services to their communities.
In fact, the structureless democratic ideal has often proven
rather exclusivist for those who do not have white, middle-class
privileges to fall back on, and making room for increased race
and class diversity in the women's movement has meant revising
what had appeared to be unambiguously egalitarian and
prefigurative.[25]

As careers, political and otherwise, have opened up for
women generally, feminist activism imagines itself less singularly
within an egalitarian form of participatory democracy. Myra
Marx Ferree's comparative study of the women's movements in
the United States and the Federal Republic of Germany shows
the more autonomist and collectivist women's movement in the
latter to be revising its structures and outlook as careers and
political opportunities begin to open up for women. And many
of the more radical feminist proponents of egalitarian collectives

in the United States have never been that interested in maintaining the organizations they set up; often they quickly move on to new projects as part of their own "careers" in innovation, albeit not without excoriating those who compromise the ideal in order to stabilize their achievements.[26]

The movements against domestic violence and rape are cases in point. In the early 1970s, shelters for battered women and rape crisis centers were frequently structured as democratic collectives heavily dependent on volunteer efforts and with little formalization of authority or division of labor. They developed critiques of male violence and practical methods of empowerment that eschewed the passivity of social service client models. But as demand increased, many were forced to close or cut back services. Staff were burning out and moving on, and volunteers had always been a relatively uncertain resource. Those committed to stabilizing and even expanding services, and to utilizing the cumulative experience developed by the movement to empower women against violence, increasingly opted to formalize structures. Staff were paid, and increasingly well, as a way of securing long-term commitment and upgrading services, and more women of color and working-class women were recruited and retained as a consequence. Board structures were formalized to provide broader skills and political influence, and fundraising activities were given new emphasis. Funding from state agencies came to be seen not just as a cooptative trap, but as an opportunity to expand services and transform the way various agencies defined battering and rape.

As Nancy Matthews has shown, state funding, as well as the support of more hierarchical organizations such as SCLC and the YWCA, were crucial in some instances to broadening the anti-rape movement to minority communities and to overcoming the exclusivist practices of collectives staffed by radical white feminists. The anti-rape movement in Los Angeles has become multiracial and multicultural with resources provided by the state and other organizations, yet it has creatively modified bureaucratic requirements to resist tendencies to parcellize and clientelize victim needs. Barbara Levy Simon shows how staff rebelled against the structureless democracy and the radical feminist director of a local rape crisis center, in order to check the informal tyrannies and exclusivist practices based on friendship cliques, racial identity, and sexual preference; to stabilize and upgrade services; and to transform police practices and media coverage.

Institutionalization did not lead to modifying goals in a conservative direction, as Weber and Michels might have predicted, but to expanding goals and enhancing internal democracy, while maintaining a sense of community that allowed the center to resist cooptation. One broad survey of rape crisis centers finds much structural diversity, although the original collective model had become "virtually extinct" by the 1980s, without, however, leading to a decline in political activity and education concerning rape. The shelter movement has also increasingly moved away from the democratic collectivist form to create "modified collectives" and "modified hierarchies" that can reap the benefits of more formalized structure while still sharing information and decision making broadly, and remaining committed to the feminist goals of empowering battered women.[27]

Choices to formalize and expand activities reflect the dilemma "empower whom?" Implicitly, if not always explicitly, shelter and anti-rape activists, have decided that empowering women who had been victims of violence was not served well by imagining that they could simultaneously empower all staff and volunteers equally in the running of the shelters and crisis centers. The two goals of empowering women were in tension, rather than in sisterly harmony, and the participatory ethos has come to be modified. Formalizing authority and tasks, stabilizing staff and services, modifying the collective form, and developing a politics for state funding and educating bureaucrats have come to be seen as more effective ways of empowering the great number of victims of male violence.

Such tendencies in the women's movement, which became more prominent already by the mid–1970s, have not left it less democratic or more subject to oligarchical tendencies. In fact, formalized organizations have often resulted in greater internal democracy. Formal elections, priorities agreed on and clearly delimited by vote, committee structures to ensure follow-up, and other routine practices have counteracted tendencies of informal leaders and nonelected activists to determine the agenda. As

Staggenborg's comparison of the more formalized Chicago NOW chapter and the more radically egalitarian Chicago Women's Liberation Union, as well as her comparison of pro-choice organizations, have shown, institutionalization has not inevitably meant less radical goals, although it often entails narrowing to an organizationally manageable number of them.[28] Formalized structures have also made possible the participation of a wider variety of women, including those who cannot afford the high time costs of engagement, hence pluralizing feminist citizenship styles in ways that have been of central concern to Dahl and Walzer.

Although in 1968 NOW resisted radical attempts to have its officers chosen by lot and to rotate all positions frequently, the vast influx of younger members in the early 1970s and the rapid proliferation of chapters led it to incorporate much of the ethic of participatory democracy. Local chapters have a great deal of autonomy, engage in grassroots activism, and conduct much of their internal affairs according to informal and egalitarian norms. Consciousness raising became an important part of NOW activity in the 1970s, and shaped the communicative ethics of political work in chapters. Nonauthoritarian and supportive styles of empowerment and self-development, consensus seeking and mutual understanding, helpful and noncompetitive ways of expressing criticisms and of listening to others have characterized chapter work to greater and lesser degrees. The National Consciousness Raising Committee advises the board at the national level, as well as national officers and the general membership, and currently conducts annual meetings to confront issues such as racism and homophobia within the organization. Much opportunity exists for lateral communication among chapters and committees, and information is widely disseminated rather than monopolized by the central offices. Albeit a large national organization, with over 250,000 members and 700 chapters, NOW functions in a manner that is quite decentralized, open, mobilized at the grassroots, and attentive to internal democratic and feminist process.[29]

Movement organizations with formalized structures have significantly greater capacities to sustain coalitions, because they can maintain more effective contact with delegated representatives from a variety of groups. Even simple things like being able to meet downtown at a convenient time in the middle of the day give paid staff a significant advantage over grassroots volunteers in coalition work. If alliances among diverse groups of women with multiple interests and identities are central to postmodern feminist politics, as Nancy Fraser and Linda Nicolson have argued, then we must pay increasing attention to those organizational features that facilitate and sustain coalitions. In this sense, formally democratic and representative structures seem to be as key to a postmodern feminism as to a democratic pluralism.[30]

CARE, COMMONALITY, AND DIFFERENCE: DILEMMAS OF A FEMINIST POSTMODERN PLURALISM

The National Women's Studies Association is another organization that has developed national representative structures while continuing to innovate in ways that are responsive to feminist concerns with difference among women and to the practical meaning of an ethic of care in organizational life. It provides a nice case study of more recent attempts to recognize rights of differentiated citizenship based on distinctive group identities in feminist organizations.[31] Since its founding in 1976, NWSA has progressively formalized its structure and delineated its hierarchy, which consists of an annual Delegate Assembly of 150, a Coordinating Council of 24 that meets semi-annually and can now initiate legislation, a Steering Committee of five that convenes between these semi-annual meetings, and a National Coordinator.[32] Greater hierarchy was a response to some of the usual problems of an effective executive and daily administration, as well as to the relatively chaotic yearly meetings of the Delegate Assembly that were vulnerable to disruption by small vocal minorities whose demands were perceived as coercive. But while creating greater formal hierarchy, the meetings at the various levels have tried to achieve consensus, wherever possible, and one-person-one-vote representation has been modified by a weighted voting system based on caucuses, such as women of color, lesbians, and others.

Although NWSA is premised on a *commonality* among all

women, it also recognizes basic *differences* in experiences and types of oppression, and special mechanisms necessary to achieve inclusiveness. Members of caucuses, and especially the women of color caucus, are overrepresented in the Delegate Assembly and the Coordinating Council, and this is justified in various ways: to ensure that all views are represented adequately, to lower the costs and increase the benefits of joining for previously underrepresented groups, and to provide the special access to insight that particularly oppressed groups possess.

As Robin Leidner points out, following Mansbridge's analysis in *Beyond Adversary Democracy*, these reasons draw on both unitary and adversary democratic arguments: unitary, to the extent that airing all relevant perspectives and having access to special insight can serve the common interests of all women; and adversary, insofar as the aim is to represent all possible constituents, rather than just current members, by altering the cost/benefit structure of joining. But unitary processes, especially in face-to-face settings, also represent what Carol Gilligan calls an ethic of care. NWSA caucus processes are concerned not just with an ethic of justice or rights to formal equality and fairness, but with whether some individuals and groups feel hurt by decisions and ignored as distinctive constituencies. This ethic of care recognizes that all are diminished by the oppression of others, that all are responsible for one another and have a positive duty to give voice to those who are especially oppressed.[33]

This system of representation addresses the dual problem of commonality and difference among women in a creative way, and yet it is an unstable accomplishment, marked by continual conflict and revision. There remain multiple sources of tension, as Leidner's analysis so nicely demonstrates. First, no unambiguously clear criteria of special oppression exist, and in an organization where all members feel oppressed as women, caucuses have begun to proliferate as a way of giving voice to all those who feel the need for distinctive representation. Thus women's studies program administrators and Jewish women have formed caucuses, although others felt these groups were already well represented. Caucuses have also formed for Poor and Working Class Women, Community College, Pre-K–12 Educators, and others, with options for multiple caucus membership and hence multiple weighting of votes. Here the adversary logic of self-identified corporatist group representation competes with that of distinctive types and degrees of oppression whose special insight aims to produce unitary outcomes. And to the extent that some, such as program administrators, do not feel that the politicized criteria for representation have served the interests of academic programs, they have recently begun to hold separate conferences, and could conceivably shift the emphasis of their activity outside the perhaps functionally too inclusive NWSA structure.

Second, the unitary caring model can stifle dissent, because those who disagree are often made to feel morally inferior, especially if disagreement is with those designated as having distinctive oppression and special insight. Guilt serves as a powerful weapon, above and beyond the weighted voting, but it also has generated considerable resentment among those who do not have the same access to it, and who often see the views of the majority overridden by smaller groups who wield it at will. Furthermore, I would add, those who resist guilt and appeal to an ethic of rights and fairness of representation in NWSA may feel themselves to be just as motivated by care for the constituencies of women they serve and the important yet still fragile programs they nurture. Resentment over the asymmetrical uses of guilt causes some to exit, or to reduce their participation, thus adding yet another potential source of concern about democratic representativeness.

Third, the meanings of equality that are invoked are varied and shifting, and in the heat of conflict often confused. Sometimes arguments are made for equal power of all individuals, and sometimes for all groups. At other times the emphasis shifts away from equal power to equal satisfaction or equal outcomes, which would entail much more radical concessions by majority to minority views about what constitutes feminist activity or what programs should receive priority. Equal satisfaction, as Leidner argues, is a radical expectation that strains to the limit a heterogeneous organization, and one premised on equality among individual women. The NWSA has yet to clarify when it believes that such expectations might and might not be legitimate.

This case illustrates several general challenges of a feminist politics of participation. First, there are new, even postmodern, twists to the old problem of defining "what demos?" An organization that aspires to be inclusive in the face of obdurate exclusionary practices in the broader society must engage in various kinds of imaginary indexing of the missing voices. Who is missing and who should speak for them? Weighted group voting becomes one way of doing this. But the gap between the present and the absent provides a permanent source of tension, because imagining the missing citizens is at once a source of uncertainty and a claim to disproportionate power. Furthermore, if we admit the logic of difference into systems of representation, can we legitimately limit it to certain groups agreed to be especially disadvantaged, or must we open it up to all who *define themselves* as groups in need of distinctive voices? And by what criteria can we limit it, especially if, as in feminist movement organizations, virtually all members feel oppressed and work in various other institutional settings where they experience disadvantages of voice?

Feminists can draw on certain resources to limit the logic of proliferating demands for group representation, for example, distinctive critiques of racism and homophobia. But their own common identity as women who are oppressed, together with the very multiplicity of settings in which they work, point in the direction of unrestricted self-definitions of legitimate group voice. The latter might also occur as a method of regaining the relative weight of voice lost by some due to the initial modifications of one-person-one-vote principles, and so be driven by the logic of power balancing as much as identity, thereby introducing further ambiguity and tension into the logic of repreation.

Furthermore, the various rationales for weighted group voice can have different implications for the norms of democratic discourse. Adversarial justifications for numerically privileging a group to lower the costs and increase the benefits of participation for current and future members of that group do not, of themselves, tend to privilege individual speakers. They are relatively compatible with universalist premises of democratic discourse, which guarantee no special insight to a particular individual's speech outside of a dialogue with others, and view truth as a function of the content of speech rather than the specific identity, racial or otherwise, of the speaker. But unitary justifications that appeal to special access to insight in the interests of all, and buttress this with the weapon of guilt, are more likely in practice to conflate the privilege accorded the group with the privileged utterances of an individual who speaks in its name, generating a much more profound source of tension with the norms of open dialogue and fallible speech. And this is further exacerbated if the individual speaks in the name of a united and disciplined caucus. This tension can be profoundly educative, to the extent that majority groups feel compelled to recognize insights of minority ones, and to accept them as being in the common interest, and to the extent that minority groups learn to admit fallibility without increasing their vunerability. But it can also be diseducative to the extent that some come to feel that controversial issues are determined by appeal to insight that is above challenge, thereby corrupting a key premise of democratic dialogue.

Recent controversy over the firing of a paid black staff member in the national office of NWSA reveals the precariousness of some of these representational strategies.[34] The Women of Color Caucus at the national convention in 1990, privileging the account of this staff person and arguing her right to fully self-determine her own conditions of work, escalated its demands for representation to 50 percent of positions on all bodies as the only way to overcome the racism alleged to dominate the entire organization, and others proposed to further remove any pretense to one-person-one-vote by adding to this self-designated majority the weighted votes of other oppressed groups. Not all women of color agreed with this position, and some argued forcefully that limits on speech in personnel matters should be respected rather than dissolved in an open convention discussion. But such dissenters themselves felt silenced by the caucus, which made appeals to a fundamentalist analysis of racism as all-pervasive, thereby dismissing previous anti-racist work of NWSA and denigrating those women of color who had been elected to serve on its governing bodies as having been hand-picked and coopted by white women, who were in turn holding hands with white male power in the universities. The complex organizational structure, which had evolved partly as a response to the demands for distinctive group voice, was now condemned as having been designed to mystify women of color and impose hierarchy on grassroots activists. When substantial voting margins rejected the non-negotiable demands to reinstate the fired staffer, dismiss the entire leadership and ban them from future positions for five years, the Women of Color Caucus resigned, though attempts are now under way to put some of the organizational pieces back together again.

Although some, such as Iris Young, have made an important theoretical argument for differentiated citizenship and group representation, in contrast to traditional universalist conceptions that ignore or suppress difference, the dynamics in NWSA and other organizations attempting to accommodate muticultural claims alert us to the hazards of emphasizing difference, privileging particular voices, and modifying universalist principles of speech and representation, especially when attached to strong claims for weighted voting, veto power, and the like. In fact, some of the lessons of participatory democratic pluralism learned in earlier years have now come into profound tension with the issues being raised by multicultural pluralism and differentiated citizenship, and no easy theoretical or practical resolution is yet apparent.

Learning Feminist Pluralism

Over the past quarter of a century, the women's movement has been engaged in complex learning processes about the meanings and forms of participation. This has involved rediscovering and relearning many of the lessons of pluralist theory, while at the same time expanding its limits and providing the basis for a distinctively feminist participatory pluralism. Striking is how quickly the feminist movement began to articulate issues at the heart of pluralist theory, and yet how little guidance it sought in the writings of Dahl, Walzer, or Kaufman, whose critical appreciations of participatory democracy appeared just at the point when the radical women's groups were beginning to wrestle with their own internal dynamics.

Although Jo Freeman's "The Tyranny of Structurelessness"

first appeared in late 1972, many of its themes were actively discussed at conferences and in women's groups at least as early as the spring of 1970. Undoubtedly some of the soul searching within the remnants of SDS, as represented in Richard Rothstein's compelling critique of participatory democracy that had emerged from Chicago activist circles overlapping Freeman's, had some influence here, and vice versa. But it was largely on the basis of their own experiences that radical women's groups discovered the problems of informal tyranny and cadre control in the absence of formal representation and accountability. They came to recognize the legitimacy of plural citizenship styles among women with varied commitments, rather than excluding as less committed those who could not make similarly intensive time investments. They questioned whether unstructured expressiveness was more confusing than clarifying for democratic discourse. They resisted the enforcement of new forms of sisterly civic virtue and false consensus. They learned how to nurture leadership among distinctive individuals rather than trashing it in the name of the diffuse leadership of all. As they grew older and began to confront the possibilities of feminist commitment over the life course, they began to appreciate the tensions between egalitarian democracy and their own self-development and political efficacy.

These learning processes in the younger and more radical wing of the women's movement drew on resources in feminist group dynamics built up over several years. They were facilitated by the existence of organizations like NOW that were staffed by women with more established careers and experience in a variety of democratic political organizations, and that simultaneously resisted the extreme anti-organizational tendencies in the radical branch and yet rather quickly made room for participatory styles, consciousness raising, and feminist process. Some activists were members of NOW and various radical groups simultaneously. The organizational conditions for intergenerational learning about democratic participation were considerably more favorable than they were for SNCC or SDS. In addition, by the early 1980s, theoretical contributions, such as Mansbridge's *Beyond Adversary Democracy* and her subsequent essay, "Feminism and the Forms of Freedom," although recognizing the strengths of unitary democracy, offered feminism, and other movements for face-to-face democracy, a bridge to political theory that was deeply pluralist in spirit.[35]

Of course, in a movement as diverse and innovative as the women's movement, we see no single learning trajectory, no set of common lessons that all have recognized equally or common problems that all have resolved fully. By the early 1970s, as Freeman has argued, both NOW and many in the radical groups were beginning to recognize that different styles, perspectives, and forms of organization were not weaknesses but strengths that allowed the movement to reach different constituencies and serve different functions. Staggenborg's recent analyses show that successful social movements are likely to include a variety of types of organizational structures, each making different kinds of contributions. Formalized and centralized movement organizations, like the Chicago NOW chapter, are more likely to maintain themselves and the movement over a number of years and to bring about specific policy changes in institutional arenas. Decentralized and non-bureaucratic organizations, like the Chicago Women's Liberation Union, on the other hand, are more likely to develop innovative tactics and alternative institutions that in turn provide cultural resources for future mobilizations.[36]

The latter have also provided the most vibrant settings for learning to participate, even when some of the lessons women learned resulted from painfully negative experiences, and when they subsequently left to work in more established organizations or to form new ones with more formalized structures. Difficult to imagine are the distinctive emphases on listening, empathy, empowerment, and attentiveness to difference, even in these formal settings, had it not been for the early and, in some sectors of the movement, repeated attempts to prefigure egalitarian participation. Prefigurative democracy is perhaps educative for the very reason that it *is* a double-edged sword, with the energy and vision of utopianism, as well as its pitfalls and illusions. In a democratic culture, which has broadly framed the historical context of participatory learning and has provided multiple options for engagement and few restrictions on exit, the repressive aspects of participatory utopianism that have so worried some competitive elite theorists appear relatively minor.

But feminist theory and organizational practice have not simply rediscovered and recast problems central to pluralism, they have enriched and expanded our understanding of them considerably. Feminists have increasingly come to question forms of organization, such as the small democratic collective, if these can only be reproduced through processes of homogeneous recruitment, and thus exclude those of different cultural and sexual orientations, or disadvantaged racial and economic backgrounds. What initially was, in many parts of the movement, the unitary and hegemonic ideal, has been dislodged in favor of a multiplicity of forms aimed at ensuring inclusiveness and not presuming resources that might make that ideal work.

Furthermore, a politics of diversity can no longer be presumed to result simply from the free flowering of democratically decentralized units, but must concern itself with how to form and maintain coalitions among women with different identities, perspectives, and interests. In this, formalized and sometimes centralized, albeit democratically representative, organizations generally prove superior. Feminists have increasingly attempted to incorporate a recognition of difference into the heart of the communicative process itself, avoiding a lazy, even relativist accomodation of adversarial interests and striving to make this recognition serve common interests in women's, and human, liberation. Group representation, weighted voting, and strong claims to special insight, and hence special obligation to listen and question majority perspectives, have become important ways of pluralizing democracy, challenging privilege, and compelling genuine deliberation. A distinctively feminist argument for multivocality has emerged, and this now needs to be linked to organizational analyses that recognize the multiplicity of structural forms and participatory arenas necessary for articulating different voices.

And "a different voice" of care has also enriched a pluralist conception of process by theorizing the submerged practices and discourses of nurturance, relatedness, and empathy often associated with women. But where these are linked in a privileged fashion with the unitary ideal of the democratic collective, the pluralist impulses of feminism are themselves in danger of becoming submerged and flattened. Kathy Ferguson's global critique of bureaucracy in favor of anarcho-feminist collectives that embrace the whole person, embody unambiguous caring and trust, and emphasize process over outcome, is the most striking example of this tendency to translate Gilligan into narrow organizational terms. As Patricia Yancey Martin has argued, we need much more nuanced and dimensional concepts of bureaucracy, as well as of feminist organizations, than Ferguson provides, including a renewed emphasis on feminist outcomes rather than such exclusive focus on internal structures.[37]

An ethic of care can at best provide ambiguous and often contradictory guidance for organizational process and structure. Those rape crisis centers and battered women's shelters that choose to formalize authority and limit unstructured participation do so in the name of providing effective care. Those in NWSA who resist overpoliticizing decision-making processes and modes of representation do so in order to be able to nurture often fragile women's studies programs that serve the needs of many. Care, in short, is subject to multiple and conflicting interpretations, and provides no unambiguous guidance for democratic process or organizational goals. And we cannot imagine equity and autonomy in complex societies without utilizing universalistic ethics of justice and rights. As Mansbridge notes, "It is too easy in some feminist visions to mistake the corrective for the whole story, or to mistake the stress on nurturance or empathy for the conclusion that all human relations can be encompassed in nurturance."[38] Metanarratives elaborated from Gilligan's important distinctions, and grafted onto those of anarchist or radical democratic theory, do not help further the project of providing effective capacities for plural voice, but threaten to constrict them and to truncate the educative processes that have been going on for several decades.

A feminist theory of participation is confronted with its own set of perhaps irreducible paradoxes and permanent tensions. Illusions of the singular ideal of fully egalitarian, diffuse, nurturant, and transparent relations are unable to sustain themselves, even as they often prove educative and provide resources for further democratization. Managing commonality and difference is an unstable achievement open to pragmatic solutions that themselves generate new conflicts and problems. Key questions admit no unambiguous answers: What (missing) demos? Empower whom? Care how? Weight voice how much? Delimit difference where? The innovativeness of feminist practice is to pose these and other questions in ways that pluralize more profoundly the ways in which we imagine citizens in a participatory democracy.

NOTES

1. Ella Baker, "Developing Community Leadership: An Interview," in Gerda Lerner, ed., *Black Women in White America: A Documentary History* (New York: Vintage, 1973), 345–352; Mary King, *Freedom Song* (New York: Morrow, 1987), chaps. 12–13.

2. James Miller, *"Democracy Is in the Streets"* (New York: Simon and Schuster, 1987); Emily Stoper, *The Student Nonviolent Coordinating Committee* (New York: Carlson, 1989).

3. Carole Pateman, *Participation and Democratic Theory* (Cambridge: Cambridge Univ. Press, 1970), chap. 1.

4. Robert Dahl, *After the Revolution?* (New Haven: Yale Univ. Press, 1970); Michael Walzer, "A Day in the Life of a Socialist Citizen," in *Radical Principles* (New York: Basic Books, 1980), 128–138; see also Arnold Kaufman, "Participatory Democracy: Ten Years Later," in William Connolly, ed., *The Bias of Pluralism* (New York: Atherton, 1969), 201–212; and Carmen Sirianni, *Participation and Society* (Cambridge: Cambridge Univ. Press, forthcoming).

5. Jo Freeman is the most likely feminist leader to have been influenced, directly or indirectly, by Dahl, Walzer, and others, as will become apparent later, but even she fails to cite their work.

6. Pateman, *Participation and Democratic Theory.*

7. Sara Evans, *Personal Politics* (New York: Vintage, 1979), 176, passim.

8. Quoted in Evans, *Personal Politics*, 214.

9. Jane Mansbridge, "Feminism and the Forms of Freedom," in Frank Fischer and Carmen Sirianni, eds., *Critical Studies in Organization and Bureaucracy* (Philadelphia: Temple Univ. Press, 1984), 474.

10. Jennifer Nedelsky, "Reconceiving Autonomy: Sources, Thoughts and Possibilities," *Yale Journal of Law and Feminism* 1 (1989),

7–36; and Jane Mansbridge, "Feminism and Democratic Community," chap. 13 in this volume.

11. Evans, *Personal Politics*, 215; Jo Freeman, *The Politics of Women's Liberation* (New York: McKay, 1975), 86; and Anita Shreve, *Women Together, Women Alone* (New York: Viking, 1989).

12. Noelie Maria Rodriguez, "Transcending Bureaucracy: Feminist Politics at a Shelter for Battered Women," *Gender and Society* 2: 2 (1988), 214–227.

13. Freeman, *The Politics of Women's Liberation*, chap. 4. This is an expansion of "The Tyranny of Structurelessness," which appeared in *Ms., The Berkeley Journal of Sociology*, and at least one collection on radical feminism in the early 1970s.

14. Ann Popkin, "Bread and Roses," unpublished Ph.D. diss., Brandeis University, 1978, chaps. 4–5; "The Social Experience of Bread and Roses: Building a Community and Creating a Culture," in Karen Hansen and Ilene Philipson, eds., *Women, Class and the Feminist Imagination* (Philadelphia: Temple Univ. Press, 1990), 182–212.

15. Mansbridge, "Feminism and the Forms of Freedom," 478–479.

16. Karen Hansen, "Women's Unions and the Search for Political Identity," in Hansen and Philipson, eds., 227; Popkin, "Bread and Roses."

17. Anne Koedt, quoted in Freeman, *The Politics of Women's Liberation*, 134ff; Miller, *"Democracy Is in the Streets."*

18. Hansen, "Women's Unions," 223; Todd Gitlin, *The Whole World is Watching* (Berkeley: Univ. of California Press, 1980), 156.

19. Freeman, *The Politics of Women's Liberation*, 121; Naomi Weisstein, cited in Evans, *Personal Politics*, 223; Linda Gordon, untitled history of Bread and Roses, quoted in Popkin, "Bread and Roses," 156; Maren Lockwood Carden, *The New Feminist Movement* (New York: Russell Sage, 1974), 87ff; Alice Echols, *Daring to Be BAD* (Minneapolis: Univ. of Minnesota Press, 1989), 204–210.

20. Suzanne Staggenborg, "Stability and Innovation in the Women's Movement: A Comparison of Two Movement Organizations," *Social Problems* 36:1 (February 1989), 75–92; and Freeman, *The Politics of Women's Liberation*, 129ff.

21. Wini Breines, *Community and Organization in the New Left*, second edition (New Brunswick: Rutgers Univ. Press, 1988).

22. Staggenborg, "Stability and Innovation"; Hansen, "Women's Unions," 219ff.

23. Naomi Weisstein and Heather Booth, "Will the Women's Movement Survive?" *Sister* 4 (1975), 1–6.

24. Pateman, *Participation and Democratic Theory;* Carol Gould, *Rethinking Democracy* (Cambridge: Cambridge Univ. Press, 1988).

25. See Susan Schechter, *Women and Male Violence* (Boston: South End Press, 1982), 108, 249; Stephanie Riger, "Vehicles for Empowerment: The Case of Feminist Movement Organizations," in Julian Rappaport, Carolyn Swift, and Robert Hess, eds., *Studies in Empowerment* (New York: Hayworth, 1984), 99–117.

26. Myra Marx Ferree, "Equality and Autonomy: Feminist Politics in the United States and West Germany," in Mary Fainsod Katzenstein and Carol McClurg Mueller, eds., *The Women's Movement in the United States and Western Europe* (Philadelphia: Temple Univ. Press, 1987), 172–195.

27. Nancy Matthews, "Surmounting a Legacy: The Expansion of Racial Diversity in a Local Anti-Rape Movement," *Gender and Society* 3:4 (December 1989), 518–532; Elizabethann O'Sullivan, "What Has Happened to Rape Crisis Centers? A Look at Their Structures, Members and Funding," *Victimology* 3:1–2 (1978), 45–62; Barbara Levy Simon, "In Defense of Institutionalization: A Rape Crisis Center as a Case Study," *Journal of Sociology and Social Welfare* 9 (1982), 485–502; Janet Gornick, Martha Burt, and Karen Pittman, "Structure and Activities of Rape Crisis Centers in the Early 1980s," *Crime and Delinquincy* 31 (1985), 247–268; Susan Schechter, *Women and Male Violence,* 98ff; and Claire Reinelt, "Moving onto the Terrain of the State: The Battered Women's Movement and the Politics of Contradictory Locations," forthcoming in *Signs,* for a particularly interesting analysis of a statewide movement to transform official practices while maintaining significant shelter autonomy at the local level.

28. Staggenborg, "Stability and Innovation"; and "The Consequences of Professionalization and Formalization in the Pro-Choice Movement," *American Sociological Review* 53 (August 1988), 585–606.

29. Maren Lockwood Carden, *The New Feminist Movement* (New York: Russell Sage, 1974), chap. 9; Freeman, *The Politics of Women's Liberation,* chap. 3.

30. Nancy Fraser and Linda Nicolson, "Social Criticism Without Philosophy: An Encounter Between Feminism and Postmodernism," in Linda Nicolson, ed., *Feminism/Postmodernism* (New York: Routledge, 1990), 35.

31. For a general argument along these lines, though one with somewhat different organizational requirements than those of NWSA, see Iris Young, "Polity and Group Difference: A Critique of the Ideal of Universal Citizenship," *Ethics* 99:2 (January 1989), 250–274; an explicitly postmodern reading is more apparent in her "The Ideal of

Community and the Politics of Difference," *Social Theory and Practice* 12:1 (Spring 1986), 1–26, reprinted in Nicolson, ed., *Feminism/Postmodernism,* 300–323.

32. Robin Leidner, "Stretching the Boundaries of Liberalism: Democratic Innovation in a Feminist Organization," *Signs* 16:2 (1991), 263–289. Leidner does not consider the most recent changes, but the logic of her argument is equally relevant here.

33. Jane Mansbridge, *Beyond Adversary Democracy* (New York: Basic Books, 1980); Carol Gilligan, *In a Different Voice* (Cambridge: Harvard Univ. Press, 1982).

34. See the accounts in *Sojourner: The Women's Forum,* August 1990, 8–9; October 1990, 9–12; and *off our backs,* August–September 1990, 1, 10–25.

35. Mansbridge, *Beyond Adversary Democracy;* "Feminism and the Forms of Freedom," in Fischer and Sirianni, eds.

36. Freeman, *The Politics of Women's Liberation,* 83; Staggenborg, "Stability and Innovation," 90.

37. Kathy Ferguson, *The Feminist Case Against Bureaucracy* (Philadelphia: Temple Univ. Press, 1984); Patricia Yancey Martin, "A Commentary on *The Feminist Case Against Bureaucracy* by Kathy Ferguson," *Women's Studies International Forum* 10:5, 543–548; and "Rethinking Feminist Organizations," *Gender and Society* 4 (1990), 182–206.

38. Jane Mansbridge, "Feminism and Democracy," *The American Prospect* 1 (Spring 1990), 132.

12

CAN AN ISLAMIC GROUP AID DEMOCRATIZATION?

BRUCE K. RUTHERFORD

When one thinks of opposition in a democracy, organizations such as the British Labor Party, the French Conservative Party, and the German Social Democratic Party come to mind. These share several characteristics: regular elections of leaders, annual conferences where party policy is debated, and some institutional mechanisms for rendering the organization responsive to the wishes of its members. They usually express unwavering commitment to democratic government, pursue power only through electoral means, and cooperate with the regime on many aspects of day-to-day governing. They constitute a "loyal opposition" that facilitates the daily business of democratic government and channels dissent into politically manageable forms.

A less typical kind of opposition also contributes to democratic politics: associations that are undemocratic in internal organization and/or goals. For example, the Catholic church has served as a democratizing opposition in many settings. From Poland to

The field research for this article was funded by the Program on Southwest Asia and Islamic Civilization, the Fletcher School of Law and Diplomacy, Tufts University. I am very grateful to the program's director, Andrew Hess, for his support and advice. I also received many valuable suggestions from Ian Shapiro and John Chapman. Any errors are, of course, mine alone.

Spain to the Philippines, it has opposed dictatorships vigorously, as well as aided the construction of democratic political institutions.[1] Yet, it is clearly not a democratic organization. Few institutions in Western societies are more hierarchical or show greater indifference to the views of their members.

An even more striking example can be found in the communist parties of Western Europe during the 1960s and 1970s. Particularly in France and Italy, Eurocommunist parties were not only internally undemocratic, but they pursued the objective of ending "bourgeois democracy." Yet, the tactics employed by these parties included participation in democratic institutions such as elections, parliaments, and even governments. As a result, these institutions were strengthened. Furthermore, participation in democratic politics seems to have gradually transformed Eurocommunism's objectives to the point where they became reformist rather than revolutionary. By the early 1980s, Eurocommunists were advocating incremental changes that would leave Europe's political systems intact.[2]

The contribution of undemocratic social movements to democracy has received serious attention from political theorists. Tocqueville argued that a stable democracy needed undemocratic religious groups in its civil society.[3] He believed that a "principle of authority" in religion was necessary to delineate a set of core values that could provide the foundation for a functioning society, as well as offset the negative influences of individualism and materialism. For these reasons, dogmatic religion helps citizens to realize their "self-interest properly understood."[4] He predicted that Roman Catholicism, the most autocratic major religion of his day, would assume a central role in American democracy. Its "discipline and great unity" would render it far more attractive to the fledgling democrats than any variant of Protestantism.[5]

The premise that undemocratic groups can contribute to democracy is developed further in the literature on interest group pluralism. Bentley's classic statement excludes any reference to a group's ideology or objectives. He attends exclusively to how the group behaves: the interest it represents; its relative power; its intensity; and, its technique.[6] Its internal characteristics and objectives are irrelevant, as long as it participates in politics according to the rules of democratic procedure. V. O. Key agrees, arguing that democracy is not the adoption of a pervasive set of "democratic beliefs," but rather the competition of interests mediated by a government that protects the public's interest.[7] Schumpeter reiterated this emphasis on process and procedure in his definition of democracy as "that institutional arrangement for arriving at political decisions in which individuals [representatives] acquire the power to decide by means of a competitive struggle for the people's vote."[8]

In the political development literature, Rustow explores this concept of democracy at some length, holding that democracies often emerge from competition among organizations pursuing goals unrelated to democratization.[9] Democratic institutions develop as a functional response to conflict in society. In this perspective, democracy is an unintentional byproduct of competition.

Despite this theoretical and empirical literature on the democratizing potential of some undemocratic groups, scholars have not applied its explanatory power to the Islamic world. Islamic groups are generally regarded as uniquely dogmatic and rigid, and therefore incapable of any constructive contribution to democratization.[10] This assumption was reinforced by the revolution in Iran. The stringency of Khomeini's regime—particularly its extreme acts of intolerance, such as the holding of American hostages in Teheran and Beirut, executions of political opponents, and the death sentence imposed on Salman Rushdie—skewed Western perceptions of Islam. The fact that Iran's revolutionary regime espouses a minority form of Islam, *shi'ism*, that came to power in a highly unusual combination of historical and political circumstances receives little attention. Political scientists are generally content to assume that politicized Islam will always take the form of theocracy.

I attempt to correct this impression by examining the democratizing influence of an undemocratic Islamic group in Egypt, the Muslim Brotherhood. I hope to demonstrate that this organization facilitates democratization by strengthening the institutions and practices of democratic politics, while also gradually modifying its ideology in a democratic direction.

My case study has two components: a brief analysis of the Brotherhood's ideology, goals, and internal organization; and, an analysis of its impact on democratization in Egypt since 1971.

THE BROTHERHOOD'S IDEOLOGY, GOALS, AND INTERNAL ORGANIZATION

Establishment of an authentic Islamic society has been the Brotherhood's goal ever since its founding in 1928. Its early literature focused on achieving this by implementing Islamic law (*shari'a*) and building the public's commitment to Islamic values. This literature contains few references to the specific political and social institutions that an Islamic society might contain. The movement's vision is indicated only by analogy, in the group's frequent references to the Golden Age of Islam (610–661 A.D.) as the single historical example of a genuinely Islamic society. This Golden Age was grounded in the Koran, the actions and sayings of the Prophet (the *Sunnah*), and the actions of the first four successors to Mohammed (the Rightly Guided Caliphs).[11] Its blueprint is autocratic. It includes:

- Leadership by a single individual who exercised direct political, military, judicial, and fiscal control over the community. Although the leader was required to consult with other senior members of the community, in practice he faced no significant constraints on his power.
- Regulation of the community according to Islamic sacred law, the *shari'a*, derived entirely from scholars' interpretations of the Koran and the *Sunnah*. Man-made law was based entirely on the *shari'a* and played only a minor role in society.
- A highly stratified social order with little mobility. Arab Muslims were at the top, non-Arab Muslims were next, followed by "people of the book" (Jews and Christians), and then slaves.

Though the Brotherhood spoke of updating this model to fit contemporary conditions, it considered these basic features of the Golden Age the standard for creating an Islamic society.

In 1945, the Brotherhood further codified its objectives in a set of by-laws. The document reiterates the call for an Islamic order in which every aspect of private and public life would be

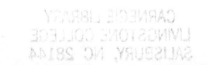

regulated by strict interpretation of the *shari'a*.[12] The founder, Hassan Al-Banna, added in later writings that the Brotherhood would establish a state in which political parties would be prohibited, administrative posts would be held only by those with religious education, and the government would maintain strict control over private morality and education.[13] To establish this Islamic society, al-Banna called for aggressive action:

> We seek the taking-over of the executive power from those hands which do not apply the upright Islamic laws. The Muslim Brothers do not ask power for themselves ... [but if no alternative group emerges] the Brothers will make every effort to seize power from the hands of any government which does not carry out the orders of God.[14]

According to al-Banna, the struggle against un-Islamic forces would proceed in two phases. The first would involve "peaceful propagation" aimed at gaining the widest possible support. Once sufficient support was achieved, armed conflict would begin.[15]

Throughout the 1930s and 1940s, the Brotherhood undertook widespread propaganda activities, built a small network of schools and hospitals, and expanded its military operations against the British. It also took action against the corrupt Farouk monarchy. The organization's "secret apparatus" was held responsible for the assassination of a judge and a prime minister, the bombing of several government buildings, and several plots to overthrow the government. Although Al-Banna denied Brotherhood involvement in these acts, he was assassinated in 1949 by members of the secret police seeking revenge for the murder of the Prime Minister.

In the wake of al-Banna's demise, the Brotherhood split into two factions: the "secret apparatus," which favored military confrontation with the regime; and, a less belligerent faction, led by Hassan al-Hudeibi, which favored greater emphasis on propaganda and education. Hudeibi, a former judge and legal scholar, believed that once the people were convinced of the rightness of Islam, they would peacefully persuade their government to implement the *shari'a*.

Both factions of the Brotherhood held the same objective: creation of an authentic Islamic society. Both also claimed to be the rightful successors to al-Banna's legacy. But they disagreed over which "phase" of al-Banna's tactics was appropriate, whether to rely on force or persuasion.

With Gamal Abdal Nasser's rise to power in 1952, the Brotherhood faced severe repression. Its emphasis on Islam collided with Nasser's secular vision for Egypt. But, more fundamentally, the Brotherhood constituted a well-organized and popular opposition to the regime. Nasser recognized this formidable threat and forced the organization underground from 1954 through 1970.

The Brotherhood reemerged as a result of Anwar as-Sadat's calculations for political survival. When Sadat assumed power in 1970, he faced a serious challenge from the more doctrinaire Nasserites on the Left. He revived the Brotherhood, hoping to undercut the Left's strength on university campuses. He thought the Brotherhood would mobilize the urban middle and lower middle classes into the political competition at universities, thereby offsetting the radical students and workers organized by the Left.[16] The tactic was effective. Sadat soon won his confrontation with the Left in the "Corrective Revolution" of 1972. The Brotherhood was permitted to broaden its organization gradually throughout the 1970s and 1980s, though it was never granted legal status as a religious association or a political party.

The repression of the Nasser era purged the Brotherhood of its most violent members. The leadership that emerged in the 1970s was committed to the peaceful pursuit of an Islamic society. Yet, the organization's ideology retained its original, undemocratic character. Its literature in the 1970s contained two themes that were especially undemocratic:

1. A call for unification of religious and political authority. The state should become a religious institution subject only to Islamic law (*shari'a*). In this Islamic order, any non-Islamic opposition would be blasphemous. Organizations who attempted to constrain the regime could be punished for interfering with divinely sanctioned power.
2. Systematic discrimination against women. In accordance with the Koran, the Brotherhood claimed that women should hold second-class status in public life.

The Brotherhood's internal organization also remained undemocratic, the top leadership being determined exclusively by seniority. Appointments to middle-level posts were only from above. Decision making was hierarchical and the decisions of the Supreme Guide were not subject to review or appeal.[17]

THE BROTHERHOOD'S DEMOCRATIZING IMPACT ON POLITICS

Despite this undemocratic ideology and structure, the Brotherhood's political actions have facilitated Egypt's progress toward democracy. To explain this paradox, I consider the Brotherhood's policies in five areas: tactical principles; participation in electoral politics; engagement with the regime; assuaging of the concerns of groups threatened by a more Islamic society; and strengthening civil society.

Tactical Principles

The Brotherhood's leaders claim that their goal of an Islamic society will be achieved through participation in a multi-party democracy. The Supreme Guide, Hamid Abu al-Nasr, has reiterated this in several interviews, stating that he supports democracy because it "opens the door for all thoughts and minds."[18] He added in 1987, "we have no objection to everyone having the right to form political parties. All views in this respect should be discussed, after which the decision would be up to the people."[19]

Yet, the Brotherhood has not described how its multi-party democracy will work. Abu al-Nasr says that democracy should exist "within the framework of not deviating from the principles of *shari'a,* on which there is a [social] consensus with no room for individual interpretation."[20] Abu al-Nasr frequently repeats this notion of accepting free political debate but only within loosely defined Islamic boundaries. A statement from a 1987 interview summarizes this outlook: "Islam welcomes differences of opinion so long as right prevails in the end."[21] "Right" is left undefined.

It would, however, be misleading to portray Abu al-Nasr's view as a semantic disguise for an autocratic style of politics.

Rather, it draws on a well-established precedent in Islamic law of defining truth through a process of consultation and debate (*shura* and *ijma*). Although the Koran and the *Sunnah* are still regarded as the repositories of Islamic law, the interpretation of these sources is left open to a process of dialogue among Muslims. Brotherhood thinkers stressed this aspect of Islamic law since the mid-1950s.[22] This process of dialogue is compatible with some conceptions of multi-party democracy. The Brotherhood evidently has this in mind in its contemporary literature when it interprets the goal of "implementing *shari'a*" as debate and discussion geared ultimately to deepening the society's commitment to Islam.[23]

The goal of broadening the social role of Islam includes a populist component. The Brotherhood's leadership emphasizes that an Islamic society can be achieved only through campaigning and education. In the words of its parliamentary leader, "We do not want the government to legislate *shari'a* on an unwanting public. The goal is to have the public's desire for *shari'a* build until it demands *shari'a* from the government."[24] This strategy involves gradual Islamization of Egyptian society, beginning with family, school, and mosque.[25]

The Brotherhood has shown considerable flexibility during this social transformation. When questioned as to why the Brotherhood had not yet formed a shadow cabinet, the Supreme Guide responded that the time was not ripe because, "the general atmosphere is not conducive to the establishment of an Islamic state. We are like the Muslims of Mecca in the early days, when they did not have the ability to establish an Islamic state."[26] He went on to observe that the Brotherhood's tactics "must change with changing conditions" as the organization accommodates "Egypt's special circumstances of time, place, and human need."[27] As precedent for this incrementalism, he noted that even the Prophet Mohammad "phased-in" the prohibition against alcohol over several years and through three stages.[28]

This gradualist strategy led the Brotherhood to renounce violence. Abu al-Nasr frequently repeats the Koranic injunction to gain recruits only through "wisdom and beautiful preaching," rather than coercion.[29] The Supreme Guide adds that, "we reject violence and attacks on any individual or group, no matter how great their violations against Islamic tenets."[30] Abu al-Nasr's predecessor as Supreme Guide during the 1970s shared this view. He intervened repeatedly on university campuses to dissuade students from using violence in protests against government policy.[31]

These tactical precepts can lead to political action that promotes democratization. Beyond their repudiation of violence, they lend credibility to multi-party politics, build respect for flexibility and compromise, and broaden political participation.

Participation in Electoral Politics

The Brotherhood took part in national elections from 1984 through 1989, and then boycotted the parliamentary elections in December 1990. The primary goal of both participation and boycott was to increase political freedoms, so that the Brotherhood could more easily spread the word of Islam. When campaigning, it called for greater political and civil freedoms, as well as broader powers for the Parliament. When boycotting the 1990 election, it attempted to use its popularity and legitimacy to pressure the regime for political reform.

The Brotherhood's electoral participation began with the parliamentary elections of 1984. Unable to form its own political party, due to an Egyptian law that forbids religious parties, the Brotherhood formed an alliance with the New *Wafd*. This match was odd in light of the New *Wafd*'s reputation as the leading secular opposition party in Egypt. The Brotherhood's leader justified participation in the alliance on the ground that implementation of the *shari'a* was so important that it mandated the organization's immediate entry into parliamentary politics.[32] The Supreme Guide assured his followers that he agreed to the alliance only after the leader of the New *Wafd* had rejected secularism and affirmed his support for *shari'a*.[33] The New *Wafd*–Brotherhood alliance won 58 of the 434 seats in the People's Assembly. The Brotherhood got only 8 of these. Dispute over this low representation and disagreement over the pace for implementing *shari'a* led to serious fissures in the alliance as early as 1985, resulting in its dissolution in 1986.[34]

In 1987, the Brotherhood allied with the Liberal Party and

the Socialist Labor Party. The Liberal Party had a record of secularism extending back to its founding in the mid-1970s. It advocated reduction in the state's involvement in the economy and an expansion of political freedoms. The Socialist Labor Party came from a different ideological tradition. Its roots lay in Nasserism, which called for a secular Egypt with large state involvement in the economy. The Brotherhood persuaded these disparate parties to support implementing *shari'a* and to grant leadership positions in each organization to supporters of the Brotherhood.

The two parties agreed to the alliance for tactical reasons. Egyptian electoral law requires a party to earn 8% of the vote nationwide before it may get representation in Parliament. Neither party had the popularity or the organization necessary for reaching this threshold on its own. The alliance with the Brotherhood provided a chance for representation in Parliament, but at the price of significant ideological compromise.

The Brotherhood–Labor–Liberal alliance officially won 1.1 million votes in the 1987 parliamentary election,[35] out of 5.8 million cast. It received 60 seats in the 434 seat Parliament, with 38 going to the Brotherhood. The alliance's success was attributed primarily to the Brotherhood's grass-roots organization, especially of the urban middle and lower middle classes, which enabled it to register thousands of new voters.[36]

The Brotherhood retained its commitment to the electoral process through 1989. In that year, the elections to the Consultative (*Shura*) Council were boycotted by all opposition groups except the Brotherhood-led alliance. The boycotting groups argued that the government had not provided sufficient guarantees of fairness in the elections. The Brotherhood leadership did not disagree, but it emphasized the importance of participating in elections to "let people know what their rights are, and to draw their attention to their duties"[37] during the campaign.

In 1990, however, the Brotherhood's frustration at the slow pace of political reform led to a change of tactics. Despite six years of lobbying by the Brotherhood, the regime still significantly restricted basic political freedoms, particularly the freedom to form political parties, and undertook widespread rigging of national and local elections. The Brotherhood decided to boycott the December 1990 parliamentary elections on the ground that the electoral law lacked sufficient guarantees of political fairness. In the words of the Brotherhood's parliamentary leader, "It's not a free election and we already know the result [to be a victory by the ruling party, due to rigging]."[38] It is significant that the Brotherhood did not ask its members to reject the Egyptian political system and resort to revolutionary action. Rather, it called on the Parliament to develop a new electoral law, with opposition participation, that would permit all political actors to participate in free and fair elections. In essence, the Brotherhood was using its formidable popularity to pressure the regime for electoral reform. If Mubarak wanted the Brotherhood to lend its legitimacy to the elections and to the regime, he must permit Parliament to provide firm legal guarantees of a fair election.

At the time, this tactic was shrewd. Mubarak had just sent 10,000 Egyptian troops to participate in the American-led campaign to expel Iraqi forces from Kuwait. Mubarak's overt affiliation with the United States against a fellow Arab state weakened his legitimacy at home. He needed a boost in popularity and credibility, which the Brotherhood could provide. Unfortunately, the Brotherhood's tactic has not yet borne fruit. The election proceeded on schedule, with Mubarak's National Democratic Party winning by a wide margin and resuming its dominant position in the Parliament.[39]

Lacking representation in Parliament, the Brotherhood pursues its goals through the judiciary. It has announced plans to challenge the constitutionality of the electoral law as well as the political parties law.[40] In conjunction with other opposition parties, it issued a proposal for improving the fairness of elections by appointing members of the judiciary to supervise the nomination of candidates and the casting of ballots.[41] The Brotherhood's stated objectives are to have a fair electoral law and a Brotherhood party established in time for the 1995 parliamentary elections.[42]

These actions by the Brotherhood facilitate democratization in several respects. Its participation in elections deepened the legitimacy of a flawed electoral system. Its boycott of the December 1990 parliamentary elections creates pressure for reforming and strengthening this system. Its participation in alliances with groups holding significantly different ideologies reinforces the principles of compromise and tolerance in the political process. Its attempts, through the courts, to revise the political parties law and the electoral law bolster the courts as a neutral, fair arbiter. Finally, its activities have mobilized entire blocks of voters into politics for the first time.

Engagement with the Regime

The Brotherhood has further attempted to broaden political freedoms through compromise and bargaining with the regime. It cooperated with Sadat as early as 1971 by joining his battle against the Left. In return, the still-illegal Brotherhood was permitted to publish a journal, *al-Da'wa,* on condition that it exercised self-restraint in criticizing Sadat and the army.[43] The Brotherhood cooperated, and even praised Sadat for his expulsion of Soviet advisors in 1972 and for his victory in the 1973 war.[44] It supported Sadat in the 1976 Presidential elections and, after Sadat's trip to Jerusalem in 1977, refrained from calling for his overthrow. It publicly asked Arab states not to ostracize him over the peace treaty with Israel.[45] The Brotherhood has also supported Sadat's successor, Hosni Mubarak, who is praised as a "very good, intelligent, clear man."[46] The Brotherhood backed his nomination for a second term as president in 1987, on the grounds that "his regime provides relative freedom, which provides an opportunity to broaden Islamic public opinion."[47] In exchange, the Brotherhood was permitted to form alliances with legal political parties, which gave it access to Parliament and to regular publication in party newspapers.

The Brotherhood engaged the regime most importantly through action in Egypt's Parliament, the People's Assembly. Until its decision to boycott the December 1990 election, the Brotherhood attempted to use its parliamentary platform for "constructive criticism...that unites rather than divides."[48] Its work in Parliament was professional. Members served on legislative committees, showing skill in manipulating parliamentary procedure. From within its alliance with the Labor and Liberal parties, the Brotherhood lobbied for several specific policies:

greater parliamentary influence on the development of the national budget; parliamentary approval of any economic agreements reached with the International Monetary Fund (IMF); removal of laws that impeded freedom of the press and freedom of assembly; application of *shari'a*, in accordance with the relevant article of the Constitution; release of political prisoners; closing of factories that produce alcohol; and, an end to the state of emergency that has prevailed since 1982.[49]

The Brotherhood also used Parliament to criticize the government within the legal constraints of the Egyptian system. It abstained from the parliamentary vote on the government's program, budget, and 5-year plan, on the ground that Parliament had not been adequately involved in the drafting of the documents.[50] It also criticized the government's failure to implement *shari'a*, its use of torture,[51] and its rigging elections.[52]

The Brotherhood's style of engaging the regime has aided democratization in several respects. The very fact that it interacts with the regime strengthens the government and political institutions. Its willingness to cooperate with a regime that it considers ideologically misguided highlights the importance of tolerance and pragmatic compromise in Egyptian politics. Its performance in Parliament, in particular, bolstered participatory government. The policies that it advocated further aided democratization by increasing the pressure for broadening Parliament's powers, constraining the executive, and widening political and civil liberties. Its boycott of the December 1990 elections also contributes to liberalization by generating pressure for further reform of the electoral system. If these reforms occur, the Brotherhood's return to the electoral scene in 1995 (or earlier, in local elections) will help legitimize both the regime and the reform process.

Assuaging the Concerns of Groups Threatened by a More Islamic Society: Coptic Christians, Secularists, Businessmen, and Women

Coptic Christians are about 12% of the population. As Islam assumes a more prominent role in society, they fear treatment as second-class citizens. The Brotherhood attempts to allay this concern primarily by rhetoric. A Brotherhood parliamentarian wrote in 1988 that the *shari'a* "gives each individual rights and duties regardless of his religion."[53] Its parliamentary leader presents a similar view, stating that "*shari'a* assures non-Muslims that what applies to Muslims also applies to them."[54] The former Supreme Guide, Umar al-Tilimsani, noted that Christians lived freely and held positions of responsibility throughout Islamic history. This tradition would continue under a more Islamic government.[55] The Brotherhood has also taken some actions designed to calm the fears of the Copts. It accepted them in the alliance's parliamentary delegation and held several meetings with Coptic leaders to assure them that their rights will be respected.[56]

With other groups, it is less accommodating. The Brotherhood appreciates the importance of meeting the fears of secular and business leaders. Secular leaders, drawn primarily from the professions and university faculties, worry that a more Islamic society would discard basic freedoms of speech and organization. Business leaders are concerned that a more Islamic regime would adopt practices hostile to commerce, such as mandatory charitable contributions and banning interest payments. Although the Brotherhood's leadership has met with leaders from each of these groups and offered general assurances,[57] these understandings were not publicized and no firm agreements or formal pacts were reached.

The Brotherhood makes no serious effort to meet the concerns of women. It opposes measures that would give them greater control over their lives. When Sadat decreed an expansion of women's rights in 1979, the Brotherhood reiterated its support for polygamy and the husband's exclusive right to initiate divorce.[58] It continues to advocate separate schools for women that limit their career options to areas relevant to family life, such as nursing and education. It insists that women should not vote, nor should they participate in public life. Any effort to alter the role of women is taken as a threat to the family, which the Brotherhood regards as the fundamental social unit that underlies the society's solidarity and prosperity.[59]

The Brotherhood's attitude toward threatened groups shows some potential for democratization. Its willingness to assuage the concerns of Copts contributes to greater tolerance of religious and cultural diversity. But its resistance to compromise with the interests of secularists, businessmen, and women indicates that its pragmatic ideological flexibility has limits. It would, however, be mistaken to assume that these limits are fixed. Illiberal attitudes toward women, business, and personal freedoms are part of a complex dynamic in which power, sex, wealth, history, and religion are all involved. This dynamic has undergone, and continues to undergo, significant transformation.[60]

The limits on personal freedom espoused by the Brotherhood resemble those found in some democracies at early stages of their development. The United States denied women the vote for 144 years, grudgingly granting them the right only in 1920 after protracted campaigning. Similarly, Switzerland did not grant women the vote in federal elections until 1971, 123 years after the founding of the Swiss federation. We have no a priori reason to assume that an Islamic regime is less capable of gradually broadening freedoms in response to social pressures.[61]

Strengthening Civil Society

The Brotherhood has worked steadily to secure leadership in associations throughout Egyptian society. In 1987, candidates espousing the Brotherhood's views won student leadership posts at 11 colleges and institutes, including Cairo University (with 90% of the vote), Ayn Shams (90%), and Al-Azhar (70%).[62] In addition, Brotherhood members have achieved leadership in professional associations of doctors, journalists, and lawyers.[63]

The Brotherhood's most significant contribution to civil society is its *da'wa* activity. *Da'wa* is a long-standing tradition that requires Muslims to volunteer their time and money to charitable enterprises in an effort to spread the word and deed of Islam. Activities include medical clinics, nurseries, senior citizens homes, libraries, and dispensaries, which are all centered around a local mosque and organized by the Brotherhood.[64]

According to one of its leaders, the Brotherhood has steadily expanded its *da'wa* activity during the past decade due to "a rising sense of Islamic social consciousness and sense of social responsibility among Muslims."[65] This clearly has political repercussions. As Egypt's economic crisis deepens, the government has been progressively less able to meet basic needs.[66] The Brotherhood's willingness to bridge this gap conveys a clear message to the poor that it can deal with some of their needs more effectively than the government.[67] It also provides a viable institutional alternative to the network of government ministries and agencies.

The value of a strong civil society to democracy is well documented. Autonomous groups serve as an important restraint on the state and press for further decentralization of economic and political power. The Brotherhood contributes to this process both through professional and student associations and through its charitable organizations.

In summary, the Brotherhood has facilitated democratization in Egypt in three ways. It has dispersed power by strengthening civil society, by upholding the judiciary, and by using the Parliament to criticize and confine the executive. It has strengthened political participation through involvement in the electoral process, the party system, and the Parliament. And, it has promoted a more democratic political culture through repeated calls for broader political and civil rights, by encouraging the regime toward gradual change, and through demonstrating tolerance and a willingness to compromise.

Its political activity has also led to important ideological modification. The organization now places greater emphasis on tolerance and compromise than originally mandated in its by-laws. It has shown greater respect for gradual change, as opposed to sweeping revolution. Increasingly, it avoids reference to specific legal precepts as its goals. Instead, it conceptualizes the advance of an "Islamic society" as a process of steadily deepening Egypt's Islamic identity.

These modifications may simply be tactical adjustments to Egyptian political reality. The movement may revert to rigid ideology if it achieves power. But this scenario takes insufficient account of the reciprocal relations between ideology and political reality. The Brotherhood seems to have undergone a transformation as a result of the give-and-take of democratic politics. If the organization continues to move toward a more Islamic society through the multi-party system, it may well continue to incorporate democratic procedures and institutions into its ideology. Islamic history contains many examples of leaders who adapted Islamic principles to specific circumstances, while retaining the key elements of their religion.[68] The Brotherhood shows many indications of conforming to this tradition.

Regardless of the ultimate goals of the Brotherhood, its participation in Egyptian politics has facilitated progress toward democracy. In Giovanni Sartori's words, the Brotherhood's actions demonstrate an "empirical understanding" of democracy. This includes a willingness to proceed by trial and error; the acceptance of defeats while remaining within the system; adoption of some flexibility in ideology, including a willingness to compromise; and an "instinctive concern with the way things work out," rather than an obsession with the technical details of how the political system operates.[69]

Looking at the Brotherhood's behavior in the perspective of Dahl's *Polyarchy* suggests a similar conclusion. It expands contestation, through the dispersion of power. It also broadens participation, through attracting citizens sympathetic to Islam into the multi-party political process. The Brotherhood's behavior adds legitimacy to the institutions, practices, and culture of competitive politics.[70]

The Brotherhood also meets Lijphart's conditions for aiding democratization in a religiously diverse, plural society.[71] Its leadership recognizes the dangers inherent in a fragmented system, shows a commitment to system maintenance, demonstrates ability to transcend subcultural cleavages at the elite level, and remains willing to forge appropriate solutions for the demands of subcultures, with the important exception of women's interests or rights.

Is the Brotherhood experience likely to be duplicated elsewhere in the Middle East? The conditions that enabled it to play a constructive role are not rare. In the Egyptian case, a period of intense repression rendered the option of violent systemic change impossible and forced opposition groups to adopt more peaceful tactics. A regime crisis was also pivotal. The weakness of Sadat in the early 1970s prompted him to bring the Brotherhood into politics to moderate its calls for change and to draw oon its popularity. The Mubarak government faces an even more serious crisis of legitimacy arising from its unpopular economic reforms, and so faces a similar need to draw the Brotherhood into the mainstream. This combination of repression and regime crisis is common in the Middle East.

The democratizing characteristics of the Brotherhood are also quite common, the key characteristic being an instrumental conception of its ideology that permits compromise with alliance partners and the regime. The ideology also includes respect for doctrinal adaptation achieved through debate and discussion. The group's size and relatively sophisticated organization were also important for making it a "player" in Egyptian politics that the regime needed to accommodate to retain power. Islamic groups in Algeria and Tunisia have exhibited all of these features.[72]

Similarly, the political avenues used by the Brotherhood are appearing in several Middle Eastern countries. These include opportunities to participate in election campaigns, Parliament, the legal system, and coalitions with other groups. Opportunities to build independent organizations through political and social services are also expanding in the Middle East.[73]

The factors that led the Brotherhood to modify its ideology in a democratic direction are also present in much of the Middle East. In the Egyptian case, pressure from a powerful minority group, Coptic Christians, made it necessary for the Brotherhood to modify its ideology and goals to make any progress toward power. The need for ideological adjustment was made even more imperative by legal obstacles erected by the regime that forced the Brotherhood to form alliances with ideologically diverse parties. Comparably powerful minorities, though not always religious minorities, are present in Algeria, Tunisia, and Morocco as well as the Levant. The region also has no lack of centralized regimes that create obstacles to political organization and, simultaneously, need the legitimacy that a popular Islamic group can bring to politics.

The future of democracy in the Middle East may well include a prominent role for Islamic groups.

NOTES

1. An analysis of the Catholic church's role in a democratic transition can be found in Juan J. Linz, "Church and State in Spain from the Civil War to the Return to Democracy" *Daedalus* 120 (Summer 1991), 159–78.

2. See: David E. Albright (ed.) *Communism and Political Systems in Western Europe* (Boulder: Westview, 1979); Peter Lange and Maurizio Vannicelli (eds.) *The Communist Parties of Italy, France and Spain* (London: George Allen & Unwin, 1981); Robert A. Dahl, "Patterns of Opposition" in Robert A. Dahl (ed.) *Political Oppositions in Western Democracies* (New Haven: Yale University Press, 1966), p. 343.

3. Alexis de Tocqueville, *Democracy in America,* the Henry Reeve text as revised by Francis Brown and further corrected by Phillips Bradley (New York: Random House, 1981), p. 440.

4. Jean-Claude Lamberti, *Tocqueville and the Two Democracies* (Cambridge: Harvard University Press, 1989), p. 179; John Stone and Stephen Mennell (eds.) *Alexis de Tocqueville on Democracy, Revolution, and Society* (Chicago: University of Chicago Press, 1980), pp. 93, 95; Roger Boesche, *The Strange Liberalism of Alexis de Tocqueville* (Ithaca: Cornell University Press, 1987), p. 185.

5. Tocqueville, p. 320; Lamberti, pp. 149–50.

6. Arthur F. Bentley, *The Process of Government* (Cambridge: Belknap Press, 1967), pp. 212–16.

7. V. O. Key, *Politics, Parties, and Pressure Groups,* Fifth Edition (New York: Thomas Y. Crowell, 1964) pp. 149–50.

8. Joseph A. Schumpeter, *Capitalism, Socialism, and Democracy* (New York: Harper, 1950), p. 269.

9. Dankwart A. Rustow, "Transitions to Democracy: Toward a Dynamic Model" *Comparative Politics* 2 (April 1970), 357.

10. See: Samuel P. Huntington, "Will More Countries Become Democratic?" *Political Science Quarterly* 99 (Summer 1984), 208; Larry Diamond, Juan J. Linz, and Seymour Martin Lipset, "Democracy in Developing Countries: Facilitating and Obstructing Factors" in Raymond D. Gastil (ed.) *Freedom in the World: Political Rights and Civil Liberties, 1987–88* (New York: Freedom House, 1988), p. 236. An interesting perspective on the source of these assumptions can be found in Edward Said, *Orientalism* (New York: Pantheon, 1978).

11. See: Charles Wendell (trans.) *Five Tracts of Hasan Al-Banna* (Berkeley: University of California Press, 1978), pp. 16–17, 64, 88–89, 92; Ishak Musa Husaini, *The Moslem Brethren: The Greatest of Modern Islamic Movements* (Westport, CT: Hyperion Press, 1956), pp. 17, 44;

Nadav Safran, *Egypt in Search of Political Community* (Cambridge: Harvard University Press, 1961), pp. 232–37. Mitchell argues that the Brotherhood is more explicit about its political goals. His analysis of early political texts by Brotherhood thinkers suggests that they supported a form of popular sovereignty in which the people would have the authority to dismiss a leader if he failed to implement Islamic law. Richard P. Mitchell, *The Society of the Muslim Brothers* (London: Oxford University Press, 1969), pp. 246–48. However, this theoretical reference to popular sovereignty in the Brotherhood's literature has little bite. The institutions that would assess a leader's fealty to Islamic law consist of scholars and jurists appointed by the leader. Safran further explores the concept of social contract that the Brotherhood writers employed. He notes that the "contract" (*bay'ah*) that Islamic law requires between ruler and ruled reinforces the sovereignty of God in Islamic communities, not the sovereignty of the people. It in no way resembles the social contract of Western political thought. Safran, p. 19.

12. *Qanun al-Nizam al-Asasi li Haiat al-Ikhwan al-Muslimin al-Amma* (Cairo: Dar al-Ansar, 1945). Cited in Mohammad A. Rais, *The Muslim Brotherhood: Its Rise, Demise, and Resurgence* (Unpublished Ph.D. dissertation, University of Chicago, 1981), pp. 83–85.

13. Rais, p. 143.

14. Yusuf Qardawi, *al-Tarbiyah al-Islamiyah: Madrasat Hasan al-Banna* (Cairo: n.p., 1979), pp. 51–58. Cited in Rais, pp. 111–12.

15. Ahmed M. Gomaa, "Islamic Fundamentalism in Egypt During the 1930s and 1970s: Comparative Notes" in Gabriel R. Warburg and Uri M. Kupferschmidt (eds.) *Islam, Nationalism, and Radicalism in Egypt and the Sudan* (New York: Praeger, 1983), p. 152. Husaini makes a similar point, but says the strategy was divided into three phases. Husaini, p. 39.

16. Raymond William Baker, *Sadat and After: Struggles for Egypt's Political Soul* (Cambridge: Harvard University Press, 1990), p. 248.

17. These organizational characteristics were originally put in place by al-Banna. Mitchell, p. 295.

18. The most extensive interview is in the newspaper *Al-Ahrar* June 2, 1986. Also see Barry Rubin, *Islamic Fundamentalism in Egyptian Politics* (New York: St. Martins, 1990), pp. 145–46; and, "Hamid Abu al Nasr" *Middle East Times* September 7–13, 1986.

19. "Hamid Abu al Nasr" *Middle East Times* September 7–13, 1986.

20. "Interview with Hamid Abu al-Nasr" *Al-Anba'* June 13, 1989.

21. "Hamid Abu al-Nasr Interviewed" *Al-Sharq al-Awsat* January 11, 1988.

22. Mitchell, pp. 238–39.

23. "Interview with Hamid Abu al-Nasr" *Al-Anba'* June 13, 1989.

24. Maamoun al-Hudeibi, personal interview, Cairo, August 8, 1987.

25. Baker, p. 261.

26. "Hamid Abu al-Nasr Interviewed" *Al-Sharq al-Awsat* January 11, 1988.

27. ibid.; Also, "Interview with Hamid Abu al-Nasr" *Al-Anba'* June 13, 1989; and, Baker, p. 246.

28. Rubin, p. 133.

29. Cited in, Ibrahim Sa'dah, "A Reply to the General Guide" *Akhbar Al-Yom* January 14, 1989. Also see "Interview with Maamoun al-Hudeibi" *Al-Watan* July 4, 1989.

30. "Interview with Hamid Abu al-Nasr" *Al-Anba'* June 13, 1989.

31. Baker, p. 249. Abu al-Nasr's predecessor was Umar al-Tilimsani.

32. Rubin, p. 131.

33. ibid., p. 31.

34. ibid., p. 129.

35. The Brotherhood claims that government tampering with the results led to a gross distortion of its true popularity. The organization believes that a fair counting of the ballots would have given it 1.65 million votes, 30% of the total. *Al-Majallah* April 22, 1987.

36. Egyptian electoral laws require a person to register in December of each year, five months before the parliamentary election. The Brotherhood was the only organization that undertook an aggressive campaign to get its followers registered. *Middle East Times* April 12–18, 1987. Also, *Middle East Times* April 19–25, 1987.

37. "Interview with Maamoun al-Hudeibi" *Al-Watan* July 4, 1989.

38. Sarah Gauch, "A Flawed Victory" *The Middle East* January 1991, p. 18.

39. The NDP won 348 of 444 seats in Parliament, 79.6% of the total.

40. Rubin, p. 34. Faruk Abdel Salam, "God Is on Our Side, Mr. President" *Liwa al-Islam* April 26, 1990.

41. Majid Atiyah, "Proportional Preferable, Provided It Is Purged of Defects" *al-Musawwar* June 1, 1990.

42. Gauch, p. 18. Also, Gehad Auda, "Egypt's Uneasy Party Politics" *Journal of Democracy* 2 (Spring 1991), 70–78.

43. Rubin, p. 16.

44. *Al Nour* May 6, 1977.

45. Rubin, p. 29.

46. ibid., p. 30.

47. Mohammad Abdel Qaddous, personal interview, Cairo, July 26, 1987.

48. "Abu al-Nasr Interviewed" *Al-Hawadith* February 5, 1988.

49. *Al-Shaab* June 30, 1987. Also, "An Interview with 'Isam al-'Aryan" *Al-Khalij* August 29, 1987.

50. "An Interview with 'Isam al-'Aryan" *Al-Khalij* August 29, 1987.

51. *Al Nour* December 31, 1986.

52. Maamoun al-Hudeibi claims that, during the 1987 parliamentary elections, the government arrested 1300 opponents to prevent them from voting. He adds that government officials manipulated the vote counting so that the Brotherhood did not receive its fair share of parliamentary seats. See the interview with Hudeibi in *Middle East Times* July 5–11, 1987. Also, "Vote Rigging" *Al-Wafd* June 11, 1989.

53. Cited in Rubin, p. 126. Hassan al-Banna offered a comparable view of Islam's tolerance toward Christians. See Wendell, p. 119.

54. "Interview with Maamoun al-Hudeibi" *Al Majallah* March 22–28, 1989.

55. Rubin, p. 145.

56. Hudeibi interview in *Middle East Times* July 5–11, 1987.

57. Maamoun al-Hudeibi, personal interview, Cairo, August 8, 1987.

58. Ali E. Hillal Dessouki, "The Islamic Resurgence: Sources, Dynamics, and Implications" in Ali E. Hillal Dessouki (ed.) *Islamic Resurgence in the Arab World* (New York: Praeger, 1982) pp. 20–21.

59. This rationale for restricting the freedom of women appears often in Mediterranean societies. See Julian Pitt-Rivers, *The Fate of Shechem, or The Politics of Sex: Essays in the Anthropology of the Mediterranean* (Cambridge: Cambridge University Press, 1977).

60. Pitt-Rivers offers an analysis of this dynamic with respect to women's rights. ibid.

61. Mitchell notes that several influential intellectuals of the Brotherhood anticipated granting women political rights after they achieved adequate levels of education and society became genuinely Islamic. Mitchell, pp. 257–58. Baker makes a similar observation, pp. 265–70.

62. "An Interview with 'Isam al-'Aryan" *Al-Khalij* August 29, 1987. "Islamic Groups Win Majority" *Al Wafd* November 27, 1987.

63. Rubin, p. 34.

64. *Al-Nour* July 8, 1987.

65. Maamoun al-Hudeibi, personal interview, Cairo, August 8, 1987.

66. Shortages of electricity, some foods, quality medical care, good education, and reliable employment are common. The government has

also been unable to provide enough preachers to staff all the mosques in the countryside. The Brotherhood has filled the gap. Hassan Amer, "Islamic Extremists Filling Gap Left by Lack of Teachers" *Middle East Times* September 7–13, 1986.

67. Gehad Auda disagrees with this interpretation. He argues that *da'wa* activity occurs only after the organization receives a permit from the government. Therefore, the government receives the credit for this charitable work. Gehad Auda, personal interview, Cairo, July 11, 1987. Also see Baker, pp. 261–62.

68. For an analysis of this tradition, see Alan Taylor, *The Islamic Question in Middle East Politics* (Boulder: Westview, 1988), especially pp. 17–20. Also see: John Esposito, *Islam and Politics* (Syracuse: Syracuse University Press, 1984), pp. 26–28; Albert Hourani, *Arabic Thought in the Liberal Age, 1798–1939* (Cambridge: Cambridge University Press, 1983), p. 20; John Obert Voll, *Islam: Continuity and Change in the Modern World* (Boulder: Westview, 1982), pp. 158–65, 322–30; Mitchell, pp. 238–39.

69. Giovanni Sartori, *Democratic Theory* (New York: Praeger, 1965), p. 245.

70. Dahl, *Polyarchy*, pp. 17–32.

71. According to Lijphart, a plural society has religious divisions reinforced by political parties, interest groups, media, schools, and voluntary organizations. Arendt Lijphart, *Democracy in Plural Societies* (New Haven: Yale University Press, 1977), pp. 3–4, 71. Also, Arendt Lijphart, "Typologies of Democratic Systems" *Comparative Political Studies* 1 (April 1968), 3–44. The most important subculture in Egypt is Coptic Christian.

72. Lisa Anderson, "Obligation and Accountability: Islamic Politics in North Africa" *Daedalus* 120 (Summer 1991), 93–112; Lisa Anderson, "Political Pacts, Liberalism and Democracy: The Tunisian National Pact of 1988" *Government and Opposition* 26 (Spring 1991), 244–60; Daniel Brumberg, "Islam, Elections, and Reform in Algeria" *Journal of Democracy* 2 (Winter 1991), 58–71.

73. See the papers from the symposium, "Democratization in the Middle East: Report of the Middle East Study Group, American Political Science Association" *American-Arab Affairs* (Spring 1991), 1–30. The papers by Michael Hudson, Robert Bianchi, and Clement Henry Moore are particularly relevant.

PART V

FEMINIST PERSPECTIVES

13

FEMINISM AND DEMOCRATIC COMMUNITY

JANE MANSBRIDGE

Advocates of individualism tend to assume a zero-sum game, in which any advance in community entails a retreat in protecting individuality. Advocates of greater community tend to assume no tradeoff between these goods, ignoring the ways community ties undermine individual freedom. This essay proposes advancing selectively on both fronts. Democracies need community to help develop their citizens' faculties, solve collective action problems, and legitimate democratic decisions. But community is in tension with individualism. The challenge for most polities is to find ways of strengthening community ties while developing institutions to protect individuals from community oppression. Women's experiences, traditionally neglected in political philos-

I would like to thank Pauline Bart, Nancy Fraser, Virginia Held, Christopher Jencks, Jennifer Nedelsky, Robert Merton, Susan Okin, Robert Post, my two NOMOS commentators, Carol Gould and David Richards, and Kenneth Winston, who read the manuscript carefully twice, for useful and insightful comments. In particular, I urge that Carol Gould's commentary be read in conjunction with this essay. Some of the ideas in the essay were developed earlier in my "Feminism and Democracy," *The American Prospect* vol. 1, no. 1 (1990). I would also like to thank the Center for Urban Affairs and Policy Research at Northwestern University and the Russell Sage Foundation for support.

ophy, help in both prongs of the challenge, by revealing under-valued components of community and underestimated threats to individual autonomy.

I. First Prologue: Democratic Community

Social critics who write about community usually believe that American society in particular and Western societies in general need to redress the balance between individualism and community in favor of community. Redress, they contend, would be good both for the psychological health of the individuals in the society and for the society as a whole.[1] I argue that communal bonds can improve the competitive status of the group as a whole by providing an efficient way of solving problems of collective action.

In a "collective action problem," or social dilemma, each individual's self-interested action interacts with the self-interested actions of others to produce a lower overall product for the group, and, consequently, for the individuals involved. Faced with these dilemmas, communities often use the sanctions as well as the ties of love and duty at their disposal to induce their members to replace some aspects of their self-interested behavior with cooperation. These sanctions and ties can make the community more materially productive, enhancing its competitive status vis-à-vis other communities.[2]

I define a "community" as a group in which the individual members can trust other members more than they can trust strangers not to "free ride" or "defect" in social dilemmas, not to exploit the members of the group in other ways, and, on occasion, to further the perceived needs of other members of the group rather than their own needs. The trust that so defines community derives from ties of love and duty creating mutual obligation, from mutual vulnerability (including vulnerability to the others' sanctions), from mutual understanding and sympathy. The stronger the community, the stronger are the ties of mutual obligation, vulnerability, understanding, and sympathy.[3]

I define a "democratic" community as one that makes decisions in ways that respect the fundamental equality of each citizen, both as a participant in deliberation and as the bearer of potentially equal power in decisions. The appropriate forms of democracy differ depending on the degree of common interest in the polity. The stronger the community, the less useful are aggregative democratic forms like majority rule, developed to handle fundamentally conflicting interests, and the more useful are deliberative democratic forms developed to promote mutual accommodation and agreement. A democracy that is only minimally a "community," with few ties of mutual obligation, vulnerability, understanding, and sympathy, will experience as common interest little more than the coincidence of material interests. As ties of love and duty lead citizens to make the good of others and the whole their own, the incidence of common interest will increase.[4]

All societies depend for their success partly on the ties of community; democracies do so in their own way. Unlike polities based primarily on traditional or charismatic authority, for example, modern democracies claim part of their legitimacy from an egalitarian, individualistic rationality that assumes underlying conflict. The individualistic formula, "each counts for one and none for more than one," comes into play when the interests of some in the community conflict with the interests of others. Yet accepting this individualistic formula in practice requires motivations fostered by community. The socializing agents of a community must help develop citizen commitment to principles of justice such as the principle that each should count for one.

No democracy, however, can meet the absolute requirements of procedural fairness. No polity can guarantee that every individual will count equally in all decisions. Individual preferences are often ordered such that no one outcome is obviously just.[5] And procedures that are just in one context produce injustice in another. (Societies with many cross-cutting cleavages can support systems of majority rule, because each individual can expect, while losing on one, to win on other issues. But in segmented societies, in which one section of the population will be in a minority on most important issues, democratic justice requires proportional outcomes.) In response to these inevitable imperfections, members of a community develop habits and understandings, ideally subject to critical scrutiny, by which they come to accept certain institutions as sufficiently close approximations to the democratic ideal. Without such understandings, democracy cannot work.[6]

The stronger the community in a democracy, the more likely it is that losers will accept a decision by majority rule not only because it is fair (for it can never be perfectly fair), not only because it is a decision (and they benefit from any decision, compared to civil war), and not only because they believe (in polities with cross-cutting cleavages) that they will find themselves in the majority on other issues, but also because, as in traditional non-democratic communities, mutual ties give community members some interest in the fate of others. Even otherwise zero-sum losses may be perceived as not completely losses if the losers see the winners as part of their community.

Most importantly, many democratic decisions are made not by majority rule or even proportional outcomes but by a process of deliberation that generates mutual accommodation and agreement. This process usually requires a strong leaven of commitment to the common good. The classic writers in the liberal democratic tradition, such as John Locke, James Madison, and J. S. Mill, all assumed that democracy as they understood it could not function without such a commitment, at least on the part of the public's representatives. Communal ties of mutual obligation, vulnerability, understanding, and sympathy help create such commitments, making possible a vast range of democratic decisions based in part on common interest.

II. Second Prologue: Gratuitous Gendering

a) "Women's Experiences"

I use the phrase "women's experiences" to mean not just experiences that only women have had or that all women have had, but also experiences that women are more likely than men to have had and experiences that have been "gender-coded" in our society as primarily female rather than male.

Much gender coding is gratuitous, unrelated either to functional necessity or, in some cases, even to observable differences in men's and women's actual behavior. But what I call "gratuitous gendering" is a fact of intellectual life, past and present. Recognizing the subtle yet pervasive influence of gratuitous gendering helps explain why ways of thinking that Western society codes as female have had less influence on its intellectual evolution than ways the society codes as male. The pervasive past influence of gendering also helps explain why feminists want "female" experiences and ways of knowing to play a larger and more respected role in political and philosophical discourse.

To say that women's experiences can add to our understanding of democratic community does not imply that women's experiences are essentially different from those of men, only that the frequency of certain experiences differs by gender. A fairly small average difference in experience or behavior can create a large difference in self-image and an even larger difference in social image. When the social meaning of belonging to a group is strong, cultures magnify the group's distinctive features. Members of each group tend to cleave to the images that their common culture prescribes for them. If one group is dominant, it will tend to avoid the language and images the culture attributes to less powerful groups. Subordinate groups will be torn between pride in their own language and images and a desire to emulate the language and images of the dominant group.

b) The Magnification of Small Differences

Gender is more salient in some societies than in others. Yet in every society gender is one of the three or four most salient traits that distinguish people from one another. When children are born, their gender is one of the few traits reported about them. Among adults, the possibility of sexual contact makes almost everyone notice the gender of others. Sex is sexy. Finally, gender is heavily implicated in reproduction, without which societies cannot continue. It is thus not surprising that some societies consider gender truly cosmic—an organizing principle that explains the fundamental relations in the universe.[7]

Human beings use the categories society gives them to make sense of the world. We learn new information through classification schemes that sort the information as we take it in. When information does not easily fit into familiar categories, we usually forget it. And when a category describes our identities as individuals, we pay even more attention than when it describes something unconnected with ourselves.

Children learn that they are boys or girls before they know much else about themselves, often even their last names. Once they know they are boys or girls, they try to learn what "boy" or "girl" means in order to be it better. Because healthy people want to be who they are, children usually value being a boy or a girl long before they understand the full social connotations of this identity. As a result, socialization to gender is not merely a passive response to punishment and reward, but an active, engaged building of positive self-image.[8]

Human beings also remember the vivid.[9] In two normal distributions, or bell-shaped curves, in which the means of the two groups differ only slightly, an observer would probably not notice differences between the groups for most of the people in that distribution. In a field like math, in which boys excel by a small amount, if the bell-shaped curve of boys is positioned only slightly farther along the skill dimension than the bell-shaped curve of girls and if the curves have generally the same shape, almost half the girls will do *better* than half the boys. For most of the students in a given school, gender differences will not be noticeable. But at the extremes, the differences will become more vivid. Boys will predominate noticeably in the upper "tail" of the distribution. This big difference at the tail provides an interpretative framework for differences elsewhere in the distribution. A girl who is doing better than half the boys at math but better than sixty percent in reading will think of herself as "not good at math."

When differences between groups are tied to relations of domination and subordination, the dominant group will also have an interest in magnifying the salience of these differences.

Because gender is so salient, and its salience has been for these reasons and others greatly reinforced, it has in many societies become an organizing feature for the whole universe. In such societies, every identifiable feature of the universe can be assimilated into either Yin or Yang, the female or the male principle. Every noun in the language can be given a gender, making a table feminine and a wall masculine.

The cultures of this world have produced a great deal of

gratuitous gendering ascribing gender definitions and taboos to many features of social and physical life. Anthropologists report that among the Aleut of North America, for example, only women are allowed to butcher animals. But among the Ingalik of North America, only men are allowed to butcher animals. Among the Suku of Africa, only the women can plant crops and only the men can make baskets. But among the Kaffa of the Circum-Mediterranean, only the men can plant crops and only the women can make baskets. Among the Hansa of the Circum-Mediterranean, only the men can prepare skins and only the women can milk. But among the Rwala of the Circum-Mediterranean, only the women can prepare skins and only the men milk.[10] In the culture of the United States, I would venture, we have created similar, though less mutually exclusive, patterns. We code empathy, for example, as women's work, so that the more both men and women are aware that empathy is the object of attention, the more they slide into their cultural roles.

If gender-coding followed a pattern of "separate but equal" and if all the actions of every individual perfectly fit the appropriate gender code, the pervasiveness of gender coding might be only a charming idiosyncrasy of the human race. But men's unequal power has made male practices and traits the norm for "mankind." In the United States, to give only a few examples from Catharine MacKinnon's impressive list, "men's physiology defines most sports, their needs define auto and health insurance coverage, their socially-designed biographies define workplace expectations and successful career patterns."[11] In practice, the labor, traits, and even philosophical terms that are coded as male are usually more highly valued.

c) Gendered Meanings in the Concept of Community

In the United States today, the term "community" is not gender-free. Its two components, local geographical rootedness and emotional ties, have female connotations. Local communities are the province of women far more than are state or national affairs. Women organize, run, and staff many activities of local communities, which as a cause and consequence feel close to home, almost domestic. Even in the formal political realm, from which women have been excluded in almost every traditional society, local communities in the United States have allowed women the most access. Considerably before women won the vote nationally, several states and localities allowed women to vote in local school elections; today, the percentage of women in city and town councils and the percentage of women mayors far exceeds the percentage of women in state and national legislatures or executive positions. In the recent past, the gendered division of labor insured that when men earned the family wage, and particularly when they worked away from the community, women became the caretakers of local community life.

An even more salient component of "community" involves the quality of human relations.[12] In the United States today, women have particular responsibility for intimate human relations. Talcott Parsons and Robert Bales codified the reigning gender schema in 1955 when they wrote that in households men generally took the more "instrumental" roles and women the more "expressive" roles, maintaining "integrative" relations among the household members.[13] Mothers and wives still tend disproportionately to take on the family's "emotion work" and "kinwork," fostering the relations of connection.[14] One recent review of psychological research noted that the two orientations it studied "have been labeled *masculine* and *feminine, instrumental* and *expressive,* and *assertive* and *communal.*"[15] In this analysis, "communal" is almost synonymous with "feminine."

As the triad "liberty, equality, fraternity" has evolved into "liberty, equality, community," the third element has experienced a gender evolution from male to female.[16] In this evolution, the term has lost legitimacy in a way that affects the balance between individual and community. As a consequence, those who today urge renewed emphasis in liberal individualism on ties of connection in the social world and on the possibility of common interests in politics have to fight not only the well-founded fears of those who see in any move toward commonality the potential for domination, but also, more insidiously, the subtle association of connection and commonality with womanliness. Pamela Conover suggests, for example, that among political scientists eager to be seen as tough-minded, altruism has come to seem sissified.[17] It seems likely that several components of community—the legitimation of intimate connection, emotional ties, particularity, and common interests—suffer the same disability.

In making the case for ties of love and duty, for mutual vulnerability, and for the possibility of common interest in democratic politics, proponents of democratic community are hampered by the female connotations of love, certain kinds of duty, vulnerability, and even common interest. Some feminist theorists have therefore attempted a radical revaluation, recognizing the gender connotations of these elements of community and insisting on their worth. As the next section demonstrates, these theorists draw heavily from women's experiences of intimate human "connection." A later section explores the ways women's experiences of unequal power reveal the potential oppression, blatant and subtle, inherent in communal ties.

III. CONNECTION

Empathy, the quality of being able to put oneself emotionally in another's place, exemplifies the process through which gender differences take on magnified social significance. In the United States, both men and women see women as intuitive, good at understanding others, and sensitive to personal or emotional appeals. Empirical research on empathy shows, however, that gender differences in empathy vary dramatically according to the measure used. The more the person being measured knows that empathy is being measured, the more a gender difference appears. When psychologists try to take physiological measurements of empathy—such as galvanic skin responses on seeing others receive an electric shock; skin conductance, blood pressure, heart rate, or pulse on seeing or hearing newborn infants cry; or sweating while seeing another take a test—they usually find no significant difference between women and men or between girls and boys. When psychologists tell stories to children of other children experiencing happiness, sadness, fear, and anger, and ask after each story, "How do you *feel?*" "Tell me how you *feel?*" or "How did that story make you *feel?*"—a procedure that might lead the child to think that responsive feelings were being measured—either girls score higher than boys on empathy when the experimenter is female and boys score higher than girls when the experimenter is male, or else the differences are not significant. Yet when either children or adults are asked to fill out a questionnaire asking individuals to describe themselves with statements like "I tend to get emotionally involved with a friend's problems" and "Seeing people cry upsets me," the difference between males and females is consistently significant and in the expected direction. On these measures, females always appear more empathetic. The differences are larger among adults than children, and larger still among those who rate themselves high on other measures of stereotypical "femininity" and "masculinity."[18] The more the person knows what is being measured, the older the person is, and the more attached to gender stereotypes, the stronger the relations between gender and empathy.

Gender differences on other themes involving intimate connection may well follow the same pattern as gender differences in empathy. If research on nurturance, care, and other correlates of intimate connection parallels that on empathy, the largest differences will be obtained from female experimenters, fully socialized adults, stimuli likely to elicit empathetic-nurturance responses from women, and clear cues in the stimuli that empathy, nurturance, and care are the subject of investigation. This pattern would not make the differences less "real." When women define themselves and are defined as more attuned to empathy or intimate connection, specific practices draw from and reinforce that connection. Women allow themselves, for example, to demonstrate their empathy openly. Girls and women look more for emotion and expression in their friendships, centering their conversations with friends more on discussions of relations, whereas men develop more instrumental or goal-oriented friendships, based more on shared activities.[19] These gender-coded practices then have effects on the way both genders view the political and social world.

The gender-coding of intimate connection has had a long history in American feminist political argument. The first wave of feminism evolved the idea that women were likely to act more nurturantly not only in the home but also in political life. Six years before women won the vote, Charlotte Perkins Gilman's classic novel *Herland* envisioned a utopia composed only of women, whose communal form of maternal nurturance produced a politics of loving cooperation.[20] Particularly toward the end of the struggle for women's suffrage, arguments for the vote stressed the virtues women would bring to the polity from their experiences as wives and mothers.[21]

The second wave of the feminist movement almost from the beginning incorporated interest in the ways that "women's culture" could be more caring and less rapacious than men's. A 1970 movement article on women's culture quoted Marlene Dixon's derivation of the special skills of "intuition" and "empathy" from women's relative powerlessness, and three years later Jane Alpert attributed to the experience of motherhood the empathy, intuitiveness, and protective feelings toward others of the developing feminist culture.[22]

Related ideas entered the academy a decade or so later. In 1976, the psychologist Dorothy Dinnerstein argued that it is harder for women than men to separate themselves from their mothers.[23] Her work, and in 1978 Nancy Chodorow's greatly more influential *The Reproduction of Mothering*, set the stage through psychoanalytic speculation for academic feminists to recognize and celebrate women's "connection." Chodorow ascribed what she called "women's relatedness and men's denial of relation" to the male child's need to differentiate himself from his mother and create a separate, oppositional, entity. Although for both boys and girls mothers represent lack of autonomy, for boys dependence on the mother and identification with her also represent the not-masculine; a boy must "reject dependence and deny attachment and identification."[24] "The basic feminine sense of self," Chodorow concluded, "is connected to the world, the basic masculine sense of self is separate."[25]

The theme moved into philosophy when in 1980 Sara Ruddick drew attention to the strengths of "maternal thinking,"[26] and in 1981 Sheila Ruth concluded that male philosophers tended to shun or show contempt for female connection: "Flight from woman is flight from feeling, from experiencing, from the affective; it is flight into distance."[27]

In 1982, Carol Gilligan's *In a Different Voice* adopted much of Chodorow's analysis, arguing that "since masculinity is defined through separation while femininity is defined through attachment, male gender identity is threatened by intimacy while female gender identity is threatened by separation. Thus males tend to have difficulty with relationships, while females tend to have problems with individuation."[28] Gilligan's investigations of women's reactions to moral dilemmas led her to conclude that women define themselves "in a context of human relationship" and judge themselves according to their ability to care.[29] Chodorow and Gilligan inspired an outpouring of theoretical writing, including Nel Noddings's 1984 argument that the approach to ethics through law and principle "is the approach of the detached one, the father," whereas the caring approach, the "approach of the mother," is "rooted in receptivity, relatedness, and responsiveness."[30]

I suggest that feminist analyses of maternal and other forms of intimate connection can generate new insights into democratic community. Yet the relation of these insights to actual differences in experience between American men and women is not clear. Chodorow's psychoanalytic theory, although intellectually suggestive, remains to be tested empirically. Gilligan's finding—that in the United States today women are more likely than men to adopt a morality based on preserving relations rather than one based on individual rights—appears primarily among the highly educated, because it is primarily in this class that men distinctively adopt a "rights" or "justice" orientation to which Gilligan's "care" or "relationships" orientation can be compared.[31] Even within this group, we do not yet know how large are the differences between men and women, and whether they might not, like differences in empathy, appear only or most dramatically when the persons being interviewed have some idea of what is being measured. In the population as a whole, the differences are unlikely to be large, since several studies cannot find any difference.[32]

Research since Gilligan's *In a Different Voice* has made it clear that even when no differences appear between men and women on the dimensions of relationships and rights, when researchers describe two orientations to moral conflict, one based on relationships and one on rights,[33] those men and women distinguish between the two orientations in a way that fits traditional gender stereotypes. Both men and women tend to rate Gilligan's care orientation as more feminine and the rights orientation as more masculine.[34] If the American public in the late twentieth century codes connection as female and separation as male, it would not be surprising if the women and feminist theorists of that society tended to make the value of connection their "own."

I find it most useful to treat this literature not as demonstrating any large difference between the actual behavior or even the normative orientations of most men and women in American society, but as drawing attention to the deeply gender-coded nature in this society of the dichotomy of separation versus connection. It is not simply that some groups of modern American women seem in fact to be somewhat more deeply embedded in intimate relationships than some groups of men. It is also, more importantly, that the cultural reification and exaggeration of these gender differences in behavior has influenced popular and philosophical thinking about the various possibilities in human relations.

Anglo-American democratic theory, for example, often portrays the polity as constructed by free and unencumbered individuals who associate to promote self-interest. Such a theory cannot easily draw inspiration from or use metaphors derived from the typically "female" experiences of empathetic interdependence, compassion, and personal vulnerability.

Drawing from experiences of intimate connection, on the other hand, makes it easier to envision preserving individuality and furthering community at the same time. These experiences help generate a vision of democratic community in which autonomy derives from social nurturance, some obligations are given, communal ties derive from emotional connection as well as from principle, the local and particular has legitimately a special moral weight, and a leaven of common interest makes possible a politics based on persuasion as well as power. I consider each of these ideas briefly, pointing out how they draw on

metaphors and experiences relatively untapped in Western political discourse, and suggesting either problems or directions
for further exploration.

a) Autonomy

In classic liberal theory, Jennifer Nedelsky argues, autonomy is
"achieved by erecting a wall (of rights) between the individual
and those around him." An understanding of autonomy based
on more typically female experiences would make connection a
prerequisite for autonomy:

> If we ask ourselves what actually enables people to be autono-
> mous, the answer is not isolation, but relationships—with parents,
> teachers, friends, loved ones—that provide the support and guid-
> ance necessary for the development and experience of autonomy.
> The most promising model, symbol or metaphor for autonomy
> is not therefore property, but childrearing.[35]

In a parallel vein, Virginia Held writes that if we begin our
theorizing about society with the social tie between mothering
person and child instead of with isolated, rational contractors
"the starting condition is an enveloping tie, and the problem is
individuating oneself." For both parent and child, "the pro-
gression is from society to greater individuality rather than from
self-sufficient individuality to contractual ties."[36]

The easily accessible idea that autonomy requires nurturance
in a web of relationships undermines the "either/or" character
of parts of the individualism/communitarian debate. It does not
require claiming that a source in nurturance exhausts the meanings of autonomy,[37] that the idea is in all respects new,[38] or that
all childrearing produces autonomy.[39] Nor does it require claiming that the ideal of motherhood is impervious to abuse.

Drawing from an idealized version of motherhood to enrich
our vision of the potential relation between individual and community is no less subject to abuse as a cover for unequal power
relations than is drawing from idealized models of property or
freely contracting individuals. As with all idealized models, we
need to ask whether the everyday experience on which the model
is based holds in it material from which to draw a critique of the

model itself, and whether the norms inherent in the ideal lend themselves to misuse less than other ideals.

At least in the United States today, the experience of mothering evokes an active and conscious critique of the potential in that practice for suppressing individuality. Contracting, experienced primarily through participation in the labor force, does not as often put the parties in the kind of sustained and intimate relation that makes the information on which a critique may be based as easily accessible. While the history of any patriarchal society indicates that familial models can powerfully obfuscate individual interests, access to a language of critique stemming from the image of a "bad father" or "bad mother" is easily available to all.

Moreover, in a model of community based on idealized maternity, the members of the group take as one of their primary responsibilities the growth into individuality of each member. The potential vices in motherhood—attempts at total control or total unity—are obvious. But the model itself reflects the simple impossibility of these goals. It is not possible for mother and child to be one. The child always grows up; the child is always different; the child is dynamic, not static, and cannot in adulthood remain easily under the power of the mother. No model of motherhood can escape this fact, and good models embrace it. This feature of the maternal model, with its in-built assurance that each is in the end separate as well as connected, should make this model preferable to others for those who see potential totalitarian dominance or mob rule in the communitarian reaction to liberal individualism.[40] A nuanced understanding of the nurturing ties usually coded as maternal makes it easier to see how the members of a polity require nurturance and mutual support, varying greatly by the context and the individual's current needs and always subject to criticism, from communities constituted by mutual obligation, vulnerability, understanding, and sympathy.

b) Nonvoluntary Obligation

The communities in which citizens must make democratic decisions are in some respects given. Although in our mobile and cosmopolitan era most of us can "shop" for geographical and workplace communities we like, the demands of geography, work, and birth also land us in communities with characteristics not totally of our choosing. Ideally, the democratic process should help citizens work through the obligations embedded in the communities in which they live and work, testing those obligations against the selves that develop in the course of living and participating in the relevant democracies. An understanding of the obligations of community based in an evolving process of public and private decision makes these obligations manifold and complex, partly formally "political" and partly not, and as dynamic as a parent's relation with a child. Such obligations are always a mixture of the given and the voluntary, moving back and forth between these poles over the lifetime of the individual and the community, depending on obligation and context.

Theories of obligation based in liberty, such as that of Thomas Hobbes, see all genuine obligations as in some way voluntarily contracted. Theories based in justice stress the natural duty to act justly. Theories based in the experience of nonvoluntary connections add to these forms of obligation—obligations that are neither voluntary nor just or unjust. A mother may think "I *must* help this baby," at moments when "I want to," "I contracted to," and "It is just to" do not accurately describe the sense of obligation she feels.[41]

Some feminist theorists explicitly link a greater consciousness of involuntary obligation to women's greater embeddedness in intimate relationships. Nancy Hirschmann argues, for example, that voluntarist liberal consent theory, based on independence as separation, rests on the principle that "one has control over one's bonds and connections because one creates those bonds."[42] Her own "feminist model," by contrast, "beginning with connection, tries to determine how to carve out a space for the self without violating care." The freedom that is created by "stepping away from, or out of, obligations" must be achieved, and justified with good reasons; it is not a given.[43]

The traditional philosophical literature on nonvoluntary obligation, which produced the "Good Samaritan" dilemmas[44] and the distinction between duty and obligation,[45] has been revived by recent communitarians.[46] Feminists can add women's experiences in negotiating the meaning and demands of given obligations. Understanding how to incorporate given obligations into a fundamentally voluntarist theory of democracy requires drawing both from typically male experiences, like the wartime demand that one risk one's life, and from typically female experiences, like the occasionally life-consuming obligations to children, parents, and kin.[47]

Nancy Hirschmann argues that "if an obligation is given, it does not really make sense to ask how it can arise."[48] But because of the role of power in creating obligation, both women and men are best served by theories of obligation, to the community or to individuals, that are open to critical scrutiny. Women, and all groups with less than equal power, cannot simply accept all the obligations they are "given" without asking how they arose.

When the communitarians Michael Sandel and Alasdair MacIntyre advance the idea of nonvoluntary obligations, they do not explore in depth the possible sources of obligation beyond justice and promising. Intuitionists get us no further than that what we "know" to be true must be confirmed by critical scrutiny. MacIntyre and Rawls, in addition, suggest that obligations of greater and less importance might be attached to socially defined roles and practices, so that for example, a bricklayer might have some obligation to be a good bricklayer, a mother some larger obligation to be, or try to be, a good mother, and a citizen of a given community some obligation to support that community. The "ought" in these cases would derive from the purpose or function that the incumbent of the role is traditionally expected to perform.[49]

The more one explores the potential sources of obligations, however, the harder it becomes to escape all voluntarism. Most real obligations have many sources, including some form of voluntary act. An obligation attached to a role is certainly more binding if one has freely chosen to become, say, a bricklayer or a mother. For a non-voluntary mother, the obligation to the child may be no more than the obligation from natural duty on anyone who has it in his or her power to harm or help an extremely vulnerable human being. For children, born without their consent into particular families and communities, the obligation to care for parents and other members of the community may consist of no more than a combination of the obligation to reciprocate benefits received and the obligation of those strategically placed to protect the vulnerable.[50]

In the domestic realm, the content of given obligations is at least to some degree negotiable. Obligation in families emerges from a process of mutual soundings, trials that end in partial success or failure, and advance or retreat through nuance as well as overt conflict on several often unspecified and simultaneous fronts. This continuous process of negotiation magnifies and diminishes both feelings of obligation and the obligations themselves, solidifying or moderating the norms of what ought to be expected, even creating or eliminating mutual "given" obligations. This familial process matches the ways most obligations are formed in political communities better than do derivations from contract or abstract justice.[51] Through negotiation, the given becomes to some extent voluntary, even if the quality of voluntarism is at times more akin to handing over one's wallet to a mugger than to choosing between a concert or a movie on Saturday evening.

Moreover, obligations attached to roles, the community's conceptions of one's natural duties, and even consciously chosen obligations are structured by social power relations, which one may later conclude are unjust. To be considered binding against one's own contrary desires or interests, any duty or obligation should be able to withstand critical scrutiny, employing emotions and principles drawn from religion, natural law, hypothetical agreement, utilitarianism, empirical understanding (including an understanding of the relevant power relations), gut conviction, and other sources.[52] To the degree that one's obligations withstand scrutiny, and to the degree that in the process of building an identity one reaches out and makes those obligations one's own, the obligations become less "given" and more voluntary.

When the losers in majority rule feel some obligation to support the winners and when citizens feel some obligation to make the good of the community their own, these obligations have a "given" component, for one often did not choose to be obligated to the specific others in one's political community. If we allow our experience of "domestic" given obligations to inform our understanding of "political" ones, we can begin to understand the processes by which those obligations can be rejected in whole or in part, and how they can become more willed, or more one's own without conscious willing, in the course of each individual's life in several interlocking and separate, perhaps conflicting, communities.

c) The Moral Emotions

The mother's "I must" grows not only out of cognitive conviction but out of moral emotions, psychological feelings, and impulses. So too in democratic community, the bonds of mutual obligation, vulnerability, understanding, and sympathy that lead its members to cooperate with one another grow as much from emotional identification as from rational, principled commitment.

"Emotion" and "reason" are today strongly gender-coded, at least among the college-educated. And although the association of "emotional" qualities with women and "rational" qualities with men is almost world-wide, this association has particular strength in the English-speaking world, especially the United States.[53] The strength of this gender-coding gives feminist theorists a special interest in understanding the role of the emotions in creating democratic community.

In moral theory, feminist theorists have recently urged a revitalization of the sympathy-based theories of David Hume and others of the Scottish Enlightenment, as against the reason-based theories of Immanuel Kant.[54] Kant had maintained, in his 1785 *Foundations of the Metaphysics of Morals*, that only actions done from duty, not sympathy, had "true moral worth." It is true, he conceded, that

> there are many minds so sympathetically constituted that, without any other motive of vanity or self-interest, they find pleasure in spreading joy around them, and can take delight in the satisfaction of others as far as it is their own work. But I maintain that in such a case an action of this kind however proper, however amiable it may be, has nevertheless no true moral worth, but is on a level with other inclinations.

If an inclination, such as a sympathetic inclination, is "happily directed to that which is in fact of public utility and accordant with duty," then it "deserves praise and encouragement, but not esteem."[55] More than twenty years earlier, Kant had revealed the "gender subtext" of this distinction:

> Women will avoid the wicked not because it is unright, but only because it is ugly.... Nothing of duty, nothing of compulsion, nothing of obligation!... They do something only because it pleases them.... I hardly believe that the fair sex is capable of principles.[56]

Today, feminist theorists argue that the person who acts spontaneously and emotionally, on impulse, from a personal identity as someone who wants to make another happy, is as moral and deserves as much moral credit ("esteem" as well as "praise and encouragement") as the person who acts cognitively and thoughtfully, though possibly grudgingly, from duty.[57] Their debate with the Kantians draws attention to the restrictive elision of the dichotomies "reason/emotion" and "male/female." If developing democratic community requires developing the capacity for sympathy, men as well as women and the parents of boys as well as girls must consider developing the sympathetic capacities an important part of civic education. The goal is not to substitute sympathy for justice, but to integrate the two in ways that give more weight to the cultivation of sympathetic understanding.

Susan Moller Okin points out that John Rawls argues toward the end of *A Theory of Justice* that a just society requires the development of empathetic sensitivity in the family. The traditional gendered division of labor, she suggests, may have led him to separate reason from feeling (and focus on reason) in the outline and central exposition of his theory while relying on their integration in the theory's development.[58] Liberal democratic theories that begin with fully grown, independent, rational citizens similarly assume the emotional, characterological prerequisites for community that must develop in part in the family.[59] Theories of democracy based entirely on rational self-interest will not work in practice without a non-self-interested leaven of public spirit that derives not only from rational commitment but also from sympathy.[60] Theories that see democracy as rational deliberation will not work in practice without citizens' emotional capacities to understand their own and others' needs.[61]

Sympathy is by no means always good; nor are the emotions, benevolent or malevolent, sure guides to correct action. But the traditional neglect of emotion as compared to reason or rational calculation in the study of philosophy and political science makes it harder to understand the costs and benefits of community to democracy.

d) Particularity

Although it is possible to think of a community of all humankind, the word "community," with its connotations of greater than usual mutual obligation, suggests a unit smaller than the planet, more narrow than humankind. "Community," in most cases, entails particularity.

To argue, as most democratic theorists do, for decisions by one person/one vote on a scale smaller than all humanity requires justifying the decisional boundaries.[62] Such justifications are impossible without invoking some notion of community, and consequently of particularistic obligations.

If democratic community rests in part on particularistic obligations, these might be justified in at least three ways. First, psychologically we feel more responsibility to those closest to us. Although on an extreme Kantian reading that feeling may be irrelevant to our moral duty, the feminist project of giving moral status to the emotions begins to justify favored treatment of some through the mutual emotions engendered by continuing relationship.[63] If we recognize more than one legitimate source of obligation—justified both through principled commitment and emotional ties—we can then begin to envision a world of interlocking spheres of greater and lesser mutual obligation, in which boundaries, though at times set by law to settle certain questions by administrative fiat, are usually in practice negotiable. If communities are groups in which people can trust one another more than they can trust a stranger, then families, friendships, workplaces, towns, ethnic groups, states, nations, international alliances, and humanity all become communities of mutual trust, obligation, vulnerability, understanding, and sympathy in varying degrees.[64] As members of more than one community, individuals must negotiate their identities and obligations with themselves and the other members of those communities, taking into account emotional ties as well as rational commitments.

Second, our obligations to the members of more proximate communities might be constituted, as Michael Walzer once suggested, by the implicit promises created through interaction.[65]

Third, these proximate obligations might be justified by utilitarian functionality, on the grounds that a system based on heightened obligation to those closest works more efficiently than a system of universal obligation, precisely because it is congruent with desire.[66] These two last arguments provide universalistic justifications for particularity.[67]

As we shall see, aspects of the normative mandate to see and credit particularity inspire not only feminists who promote connection but also those who warn against communal domination. Iris Marion Young, Seyla Benhabib, and Martha Minow contend that the universalistic ideal of impartiality entails treating everyone according to the same rules, thus ignoring difference and seeking to "eliminate otherness."[68] Particularity in their analysis entails fostering, noticing, and respecting difference.

e) Persuasion Based on Common Interests

Finally, some feminists who write from the experience of connection emphasize the possibilities of common interest in politics, making possible decisions based in persuasion rather than power. This approach breaks radically from the dominant contemporary definition of politics as power.

As early as 1818, Hannah Mather Crocker stated in print that persuasion was a particularly female art, which may have been a common perception.[69] By the time of women's suffrage, feminists such as Charlotte Perkins Gilman espoused a vision of women's approach to politics that eschewed power.[70] In the mid-twentieth century, a woman, Mary Parker Follett, invented the concepts of "integration" (what some today call "win/win solutions"), and "power with" rather than "power over."[71] In the second wave of the women's movement, Nancy Hartsock suggested that feminism could lead to the "redefinition of political power itself" as not domination but "energy, strength, and effective interaction."[72] Kathy Ferguson similarly urged women to use the "values that are structured into women's experience—caretaking, nurturance, empathy, connectedness" to create new organizational models not dependent on domination.[73] Although these formulations do not deny that power, defined as getting people to do something by threat of sanction or force,[74] plays a legitimate role in human relations, they stress the generalizability to democratic politics of relations based on persuasion. Legitimate persuasion in turn requires common interests, that derive from the ties of community—mutual obligation, vulnerability, understanding, and sympathy—as well as from the simple coincidence of material interests.

Women's frequent stress on persuasion is probably related to the "consultative" style of leadership that, in the United States today, women are more likely to adopt than men. The researchers who find this difference in study after study speculate that gender socialization, organizational positions of lesser power, bias against female leaders, and the greater social skills of women may all contribute to women's more persuasive, consultative style.[75]

If it is not to be manipulative, however, persuasion requires a common interest between the leaders and the led. Leaders committed to the use of persuasion rather than power may exaggerate the degree of common interest on a given issue, and avoid the necessity of exercising power, that is, threats of sanction or force, on issues involving irreconcilable conflict. Yet democratic politics also requires handling irreconcilable conflicts through fair procedures that often involve forcing some, on any given issue, to conform to a policy not in their interests. As the next section shows, feminist theorists who warn against communal domination are particularly aware of the potential, in a politics that works primarily through persuasion, of more powerful groups assuming a common interest or convincing the less powerful of a common interest that does not in fact exist.

IV. Unequal Power and Democracy

Among women, the experience of unequal power is as universal as the experience of connection. Accordingly, for every positive aspect of community into which the experience of intimate connection can give further insight, the experience of pervasive inequality provides a caution. A social role that prescribes empathy, for example, can at the same time proscribe a legitimate concern for self-interest. A social role that prescribes caring can make the carer asymmetrically vulnerable. A social role that prescribes particularity, deriving from bonds that go beyond justice, can eliminate the protection and the moral direction of justice. A social role that prescribes persuasion can make the bearer unfamiliar with, repulsed by, or blind to power.

Women have experienced a long historical legacy of unequal power, particularly in the public realm. Believed incapable of fully human reasoning, barred from owning property, vigorously excluded from the political arena in almost every human society, and until recently deprived of the vote even in Western democracies, women have long been denied equal power, often on the grounds that their interests were the same as the men who exercised power, specifically their husbands and fathers.

Yet women have had, and still have, a unique relation to the class that has benefitted from this unequal power. Many women, no matter how active as feminists, love or have loved individual men—their fathers, their sons, their male lovers or husbands. Moreover, many men love or have loved women, sometimes, at least in the modern era, with a genuine belief in the underlying equality of the relations and sometimes with a strong conscious commitment to recreating in the existing social and political world the equality they see "underneath." As a consequence, women, more than most groups that struggle to redress inequalities of power, have come to learn the subtle as well as the obvious forms that unequal power can take, and its private as well as public faces. Of the many forms of subtle and private power that feminist scholarship and theory have begun to expose, I give just two examples.

a) Subtle Power

One subtle political inequality that particularly affects democratic community emerges in speech. In the United States today, girls and women speak noticeably less than boys and men in mixed settings, both in private and in public.[76] In New England town meetings, women speak half as often as men. Female state legislators speak less than their male counterparts.[77] When women speak, moreover, they adopt more linguistic usages that connote uncertainty.[78] In public meetings, they tend to give information or ask questions rather than stating opinions or initiating controversy. In private, they submit to male interruptions.[79] Since at least the fifth century B.C., when Sophocles warned that "a modest silence is a woman's crown," women have been disciplined by proverbs that criticize their talking.[80]

Training for listening and supportive speech is disempowering. But because this training is also vital for a politics based on persuasion rather than power,[81] women and feminist theorists face the difficult but urgent task of disentangling the evil from the good. The double edge and the subtlety of many forms of unequal power explains the attraction of some feminist thinkers to certain of the writings of Michel Foucault, particularly his concept of "capillary" power, power that carries the lifeblood of the system into the smallest part of the body.[82]

The problem is that the very obligations, vulnerabilities, understandings, and sympathies that make members of a community engage in acts of social cooperation against their narrow self-interest will in many cases subtly or unsubtly privilege the most powerful. If, for example, a democracy relies on face-to-face or consensual procedures to maintain its ties of community, those procedures will usually discriminate subtly against women and other less powerful groups.

On the level of the small group, democracies can fight these subtle biases against women's speech with institutional innovations like breaking into smaller like-minded groups for discussion, rationing speaking time in some way, or making space for the patterns of non-dominant cultures.[83] On the national level, activists and writers in democratic politics have long realized not only that power over decisions in any existing democratic polity is highly unequal but also that the broader process of democratic deliberation is permeated with large, though often subtle and interstitial, inequalities.[84] The women's movement worldwide fights the subtle inequalities of speech by bringing women together in their own groups to speak, decide, make allies, and strategize, usually without the presence of men. The movement also relies heavily on women coming together in domestic contexts. Outside formal politics women find out from one another how their common and divergent experiences let them shape new preferences, new underlying goals and interests, and ultimately new political identities. Precisely because the formal political arena will not usually advance agendas that appropriately address the concerns of non-dominant groups, members of those groups often deliberate in a way that best serves their political needs in associations formed to address traditionally "private" or "domestic" concerns. Just as Marx predicted factories would bring workers together in ways that fomented revolution, so today health, credit, and cooperative shopping associations bring women together across the world in ways that undermine the political dominance of men.

b) Private Power

Sexual intercourse is an archetypically private act. Yet patterns of sexual interaction encode and maintain patterns of unequal power that reverberate far beyond the private realm. Being raped or battered, typically a woman's experience, is a private act that reflects and reinforces public power.

Catharine MacKinnon and Andrea Dworkin point out that dominance is intertwined with heterosexual activity.[85] Marital rape is still legal in some states, partly because sexual possession, by force if necessary, is still often considered a husband's right. Looking at the power implicitly or explicitly involved in sexuality opens up to political analysis an arena previously off limits. As Catherine MacKinnon puts it, the quintessentially private sphere of sexuality "is to feminism what work is to marxism: that which is most one's own, yet most taken away."[86]

Physical violence expresses this private power. Women and children are the primary victims of private battering.[87] Women's traditional primary responsibility for childrearing produces unequal power in the economic marketplace, which in turn produces unequal power in the family. That unequal power results not only in battering but also, in countries subject to food shortages, in inadequate nutrition and higher mortality for female children.[88]

On a less dramatic level, feminists have also begun to investigate the power imbalances inherent in many small, repeated, private acts—the clothing the two genders use, their hairstyles, makeup, laughter, and their attitudes toward food or their own bodies. For women, a significant part of the struggle of self-construction is trying to parse out which of the gendered elements of private, everyday life they want to make their own, as authentic expressions of their individuality, love of life, and sexual desire, and which ones they must discard as whispering to them, every time they take a step or look in a mirror, a message, often the "community's" message, of fundamental inadequacy and inequality.

In developing this analysis, feminist theorists can ally, however uneasily, with Foucault and with the anthropologists and political scientists who have developed in their study of exploited populations the concept of "resistance."[89] Resistance describes any act, no matter how small or private, by a member of a subordinate class that is intended either to mitigate or deny claims made by superordinate classes or to advance its own claims against those classes.[90] To the degree that any community is constructed from ties of mutual obligation, vulnerability, understanding, and sympathy, the struggle against domination will often be a struggle against the obligations imposed by, vulnerabilities exploited by, understandings created by, and sympathies directed toward the dominant classes. The struggle against those classes in the private and public realms will therefore become a struggle against that community, often by creating communities of resistance among the subordinates. If a dominant community is not to overwhelm its members, its social organization must facilitate the creation of communities of resistance.

c) *The Critique of Community*

Their experiences of the pervasive effects of subtle and private inequalities alert many feminist theorists to the dangers of "community."

On the broadest front, Iris Young writes that the very ideal of community "devalues and denies difference."[91] Although actual communities differ on this dimension, some explicitly valuing diversity, all communities nevertheless generate norms that some of their members cannot meet. Indeed, in a world dominated by men, when communities are precisely the given, involuntary communities in which relations are most like the maternal relation, they are most likely to generate norms that women cannot meet—norms, for example, that it is better to be a man.[92]

Looking at some of the constituent features of community, Susan Okin documents the deep gender inequalities in the traditions on which Alasdair MacIntyre relies in his defense of a tradition-based morality of the virtues. Contemplating the shared understandings on which Michael Walzer relies to conclude that different spheres have different criteria for justice, she points out that oppressors and oppressed often disagree fundamentally, generating out of the linguistic meanings they share two irreconcilable accounts of what is just.[93]

Recent understandings of community focus on language in a way that feminists find telling. Michael Sandel writes that a community "in the constitutive sense" is marked by "a common vocabulary of discourse and a background of implicit practices and understandings."[94] Charles Taylor adds that the least alienated human life is lived in communities "where the norms and ends expressed in the public life of a society are the most important ones by which its members define their identity as human beings,"[95] suggesting that these norms, and the institutions and practices that embody them, function "as a kind of language" that is necessary for human interaction, but "can only grow in and be sustained by a community."[96]

For feminists, the analogy to language conjures up the way Western languages reiterate the message of male as norm and female as other. The "common vocabulary" is not neutral among those who use it. Beyond male and female, feminists point out that any word implies, as words must, the dominant or majority subcategory in the category covered by that word, thereby excluding by implication the less powerful or the minority. The use of "men" to mean "human beings" theoretically includes women, except that the word "men" has connotations and establishes expectations that exclude women. Similarly, the word "women" theoretically includes African-American women, except that because white women comprise in the United States the great majority of women, the word in that context has connotations that exclude experiences characterizing the majority of African-American women. In the same way, the phrase "African-American women" implies "heterosexual African American women," and the phrase "heterosexual African-American women" implies "able-bodied heterosexual African-American women."[97] Each category, conjuring up its dominant or majority referent, implicitly excludes those whose experiences differ from that majority.

Community dominance through language thus cannot be avoided. It requires conscious effort to include in one's thinking those who do not fit the dominant or majority image, particularly when the interests of members of that group conflict with the dominant group's interests. Because we must use words, and cannot maintain in consciousness the potentially infinite regress of the implicitly unincluded, we need to recognize that all communication encodes power, and be sensitive both to the worst abuses and to those who bring that power to the surface for conscious criticism.

The feminist sensitivity to the subtle and private forms of communal exclusion may seem to the more powerful somewhat strained. I have argued here that this sensitivity is based on a serious evaluation of the potentially far-reaching cumulative effects of a constellation of large and small violations of self, acts of domination, and inequalities, often hidden from overt public discourse in the realms of private behavior. Women's experience heightens feminists' sensitivity to the problems of the excluded, a sensitivity further heightened by Black, Asian, Latin American, Near Eastern, and African feminists, who point out in racial and international contexts how easily the language and practices of the dominant group exclude and subordinate the less culturally, socially, and politically powerful.[98]

V. WOMEN'S PERSPECTIVES ON COMMUNITY

a) Drawing from the Personal for the Political

The spheres of formal government and personal life, crossed with the politics of power and the politics of persuasion, produce four cells. The cell that combines formal government and power needs no further explanation. It is the cell of traditional pluralist democracy. The cell that combines personal life and persuasion also needs no further explanation. It is the cell of the traditional idealized family. Feminist theory, however, directs us to the two least examined cells. Combining formal government with persuasion produces a theory of democracy that assumes the possibility of creating on some issues a common good. Combining the personal sphere with power produces a theory of interstitial power that manifests itself, for women, in pervasive sexual subordination.

I have drawn from women's experiences in the familiar sphere of intimate and domestic connection to argue that the formal politics of democratic community must use persuasion as well as power. I have drawn from women's experiences in the less familiar sphere of private power to argue that the formal politics of democratic community will be permeated by subtle and "private" forms of domination. For formal politics, this analysis gets its edge from infusing the formally political with the personal. Crossing the line that divides the personal from the political also frequently means resisting a sharp distinction between moral and political obligation, and between moral and political theory more broadly.

Simply to dissolve the governmental into the domestic, or define as "public" every human group, would deprive language and thought of important meanings and connections. This is not usually the goal of those who develop the feminist insight that "the personal is political."[99] Rather, the aim of feminists who focus on "connection" is to release from the realm of taboo, for incorporation into political discourse, a host of experiences and referents related to intimate personal connection. The aim of feminists who focus on subordination is to point out how closely and subtly linked are private and public forms of power.

No borrowing from one experience to another can be perfect. Childrearing and some forms of sexuality, for example, involve an intimacy that renders moot or mutes many outstanding political questions, that have to do quintessentially with relations among relative strangers.[100] But it would be a mistake to make impermeable and mutually exclusive the categories of household and polis.[101] If we assume that neither conceptual end of a spectrum running from the total assimilation of every individual in every other to the total alienation of each from all can support what we think of as "politics," intimate personal life, by standing relatively close to the end of assimilation, suggests various models of human relations, with their attendant problems, from which any theory of political community should be able to borrow. As medieval and non-Western patriarchies have drawn heavily from family relations in conceiving their nondemocratic polities, contemporary theories should be able to draw from other forms of private relations in conceiving democracy. When nineteenth-century feminists suggested "organized mother love" or "social housekeeping" as ideals of democratic political organization, their borrowing from the experience of family relations was no different in kind from the ancient Greek borrowing of "civic friendship" from the personal relation of friends.

b) Maximalism versus Minimalism

In drawing political insight from various realms of private life, this essay embodies a tension, but not a logical contradiction, between "minimalist" and "maximalist" approaches to gender differences. Pointing out the extent of gratuitous gendering in every society suggests a "minimalist" approach to gender differences. This approach, to which I subscribe, holds that although men and women undoubtedly differ in biological characteristics like the ability to give birth and upper body strength, technological advances in contraception, childrearing, and material production have significantly reduced the social importance of these differences in the last several centuries.

Much of the remaining social stress on gender differences is "gratuitous," resting on differences or magnitudes of difference that are neither innate nor socially efficient.[102]

In this essay, however, I also emphasize gender differences throughout, in a way that may seem to align implicitly with the "maximalist" school of feminist analysis, which emphasizes the differences between men and women.[103] Members of this school sometimes suggest that these differences are large and perhaps impossible to change, although few, if any, conclude that they are innate.[104] Nor is innateness the issue. The great variation in women's experience by class and across individuals even in one culture suggests that whether or not the roots of some differences are innate, the differences are susceptible to social change. Moreover, the psychological differences implicated in intimate connection do not seem large compared to many cultural differences.[105]

To make the points about cultural dominance that I have been making, it is not necessary to argue that women are "essentially connected" to other human beings through their biology in a way that differs from men, or even that they have a more connected relation than men to their mothers. There may be some truth to both points. But if there were no truth to either, simply typing women as connected and men as separate would do the trick. If many women grew up thinking of themselves as relatively connected with others and men grew up thinking of themselves as relatively separate, and if men produced the dominant literature, that literature would tend to emphasize the virtues of separation. Connection, or at least "going on" about connection, would have about it just a touch of the effeminate.

In this situation one obvious intellectual strategy would be simply to point out and try to eliminate the gratuitous gendered implications that accrue to various philosophical positions, make the case on its own grounds for the "feminine" position, and move on from the subject of gender. This is a good strategy, with much to recommend it, including prefiguring its goal in its form of argument. It has, however, several weak points.

Most importantly, it is a better strategy for what I perceive as a distant goal than for the present. In the different cultures of the world, the association of gender with various social ideals will presumably begin to wither away as women and men have more of one another's "typical" experiences and recognize the diversity within their own and the other group. However, because it is unlikely that the salience of gender will ever be eliminated, and because the full androgynization of childrearing and workplace roles is in any existing society almost unimaginably distant, it will be hard in the imaginable future to reach a stage at which, when arguments for one or another ideal imply constellations of linked behaviors, those implications could be teased apart and examined without inferences derived from gender. Moreover, if in the future some gendered division of labor should prove socially efficient and normatively acceptable, some ideals would probably remain gendered. A more proximate goal than the abolition of all gender implications, a goal aimed at a world in which some association of gender with particular social ideals persists, prescribes first, that gendering should be reduced to a realistic minimum, and second, that ideals for which there are equally good independent normative arguments should enjoy an equal normative status.

These two prongs of the proximate goal are in tension. Reducing gendering to a minimum, that is, eliminating "gratuitous" gendering, requires downplaying gender implications when they arise in social and philosophical discourse. But arguing for the equal normative status of "female" ideals requires bringing those ideals to center stage and trumpeting their virtues. Moreover, because "male" virtues will be better in some ways and contexts and worse in others, and "female" virtues will be better in some ways and contexts and worse in others, trying to achieve equality in an already hierarchical world will require stressing the ways in which "female" virtues are better.

This essay tries to accomplish both goals. It is logically possible, and I believe an accurate description of much of today's social reality, to say, first, that much of the human race's carrying on about gender could be eliminated without much loss and with a good deal of gain, and second, that so long as gender is still extremely salient and society is still hierarchically organized in regard to gender, some of the ideals more frequently associated with women should be valued more highly than they are now—indeed, that in some ways and contexts those ideals serve human needs better than some ideals more frequently associated with men. Simply pointing out the gendered component of ideals and passing on is not enough.

Another problem with the idea that an argument should stand "on its own," regardless of the gender-coding of its content or the gender of those who espouse it, is that this proposition, while generally an excellent guide to productive thought, tends to obscure the many ways that arguments themselves are gendered. Normative arguments do not consist solely, or even primarily, of deduction from agreed or self-evident principles. These arguments involve telling stories, making analogies, and asking readers to imagine themselves in situations they have never experienced. They can be persuasive only to the degree that they build on something in a reader's experience that the reader values either positively or negatively. To the degree that experience is heavily gendered, and readers do not share in an experience from which an author draws, it becomes possible for readers of a gender different from that of an author simply not to understand the point the author is making. If gendered differences in experience are unequally valued socially, it becomes even harder for readers with the more valued experience to understand points drawn from the less valued experience. (To succeed in the dominant world, however, those with less valued experiences must be able to understand at least in part the dominant experiences.) An argument "standing on its own" may be surreptitiously an argument that draws heavily on male experience. To make this possibility conscious, women must draw consciously on specifically women's experiences. Before we set out to "translate" our insights to men, as to some extent I try to do here, women must also sometimes write as women to women, working out those insights in a context of greater common experience, particularly in those areas neglected by traditional male discourse.

Finally, the strategy of simply pointing out the gender connotations of existing values and moving on fails to take full account of the role in intellectual life of emotional identification with ideas. People often come to think differently about their ideas and values because others exert effort to persuade them to change. Those who exert effort often do so because they identify themselves emotionally with the ideals they are promoting. "Schools of thought" often advance intellectually through emotional as well as cognitive reinforcement, each member reassuring the others that the ideas on which they are working deserve their efforts. Academics who think of the methodological structuralism they espouse as "French" or the methodological individualism they espouse as "Anglo-American" draw some of their intellectual energy from identification with their nation. Women theorists as a group will put more effort into unfolding certain arguments when they identify as women with those ideas.

Even insight itself sometimes requires commitment. Women are more likely than men to have insights on connection and unequal power not only because women are more likely to have had experiences that generate these insights, but also because they are more likely to feel strongly about their insights. Anger, pride, and other of the more disreputable emotions also fuel the intellectual machine. As a woman, I feel angry, and deserve to feel angry, that "our" values have been denigrated. I also feel proud, and deserve to feel proud, of those values, adopting some version of them after scrutiny even more consciously as my own. When the anger women feel on these issues touches off an opposing anger in men, and our pride an opposing pride, these are often acceptable costs of a process that brings the ideas to the surface for critical examination.

Because anger and pride by and large tend to obscure rather than illuminate, this stage in the intellectual process works best if it is only one stage in an ongoing dialectic. It may well be a recurring stage until greater social equality is achieved, because ultimately, in spite of the best efforts of feminist theorists, "female" values are unlikely to be accorded equal worth until women are perceived as the social, political, and intellectual equals of men. But harnessing now for the process of revaluation the anger and resentment generated by the existing system of gendered ideals is likely to make a useful difference in how future generations, at least of philosophers, think of autonomy, obligation, emotion, particularity, persuasion, power, privacy, and other components of a dual stance of welcome and vigilance toward democratic community.

VI. Deepening Community: Enhancing Individuality

"Ties" tie you down. Increasing the number and strength of communal ties usually decreases personal freedom. But recognizing the frequent tradeoff between ties and choices does not entail accepting the present mix between the two. Just as a child who has mastered the bicycle must learn street safety before venturing forth, so progress from a previous equilibrium often requires a move and a countermove to regain a satisfactory equilibrium farther along. Although American society has established an equilibrium of sorts between the competing claims of individualism and community, thought and experimentation should allow us to create a better equilibrium strengthening the community ties that most advance the ends we desire while at the same time creating and strengthening institutions that guard against community domination.[106]

Individualists and communitarians would both gain from recognizing that any step that strengthens people's ties to a democratic community usually requires heightened, institutionalized vigilance against the illusion that all members of the community have common interests. If we look to long-standing groups for cues to which equilibria work in practice, we see that in the realm of democratic procedure, groups that pursue the quest for democratic community to an extreme, by refusing to make any decisions not perceived by all as in the common good, also institutionalize safeguards against the creation of false consensus. Quaker communities make decisions only by consensus, but also fight the social pressure not to disrupt a consensus by making it a religious duty to hold out against a decision one genuinely thinks is immoral or wrong. The Bruderhof, an even more communal association, institutes similar mechanisms.[107] Other smoothly functioning groups that make many decisions by consensus find ways of investigating verbal or nonverbal signs of dissatisfaction to give the possibly silenced members a hearing, to meet their needs in ways not included in the formal decision, or to reopen the question. In all these cases, a move toward community works in tandem with moves to recognize and protect individual difference.

Individualists and communitarians need to recognize the possibility that a polity can strengthen community ties and respect for the individual at the same time. Contemporary feminist theory helps us think about how to perform these seemingly contradictory tasks simultaneously. If, as I argue, liberal individualism and an adversary system of democracy overemphasize atomistic conflict, the greater self-consciousness of women regarding intimate connection makes available metaphors and experiences in which individuals are not so starkly pitted against one another. If, as I argue, all moves toward assuming commonality need monitoring, feminist insights into pervasive and unequal power provide for all individuals conceptual defenses against the pronouncements of the community on who we are or what our good should be.

The main task of feminist theory must be to clarify and help redress gender inequality. In doing so, however, it contributes to a more general understanding of democratic community in ways not available to a liberalism restricted to individuals sprung into adulthood fully grown and a politics that excludes the private.

NOTES

1. E.g., Robert H. Bellah, Richard Madsen, William M. Sullivan, Ann Swidler, and Steven M. Tipton, *Habits of the Heart: Individualism and Commitment in American Life* (Berkeley: University of California Press, 1985); Alan Wolfe, *Whose Keeper: Social Science and Moral Obligation* (Berkeley: University of California Press, 1989); Elizabeth Fox-Genovese, *Feminism without Illusions: A Critique of Individualism* (Chapel Hill: University of North Carolina Press, 1991).

2. On communal bonds as a way of solving collective action problems, see Jane J. Mansbridge, "On the Relation between Altruism and Self-Interest," in Mansbridge, ed., *Beyond Self-Interest* (Chicago: University of Chicago Press, 1990). Communal bonds can also deter material success, as when the community expectation that members will share accumulated wealth produces disincentives for individuals to exert effort in earning.

3. Roberto Mangabeira Unger characterizes communities as "those areas of social existence where people stand in a relationship of heightened mutual vulnerability and responsibility toward each other" (*The*

Critical Legal Studies Movement [1982] [Cambridge: Harvard University Press, 1986], p. 36), and considers sympathy "the sentiment that animates community" (*Knowledge and Politics* [New York: Free Press, 1975], p. 220). Thomas Bender (*Community and Social Change in America* [New Brunswick: Rutgers University Press, 1978], p. 7) describes communities as "held together by shared understandings and a sense of obligation." Although conflict also creates and maintains mutual ties, it undermines "community" when it lowers the trust between members below that which they would feel with strangers.

    4. In *Beyond Adversary Democracy* [1980] (Chicago: University of Chicago Press, 1983) I elaborate on these distinctions, including the forms of equality democracy requires in contexts of common and conflicting interests, and the use of friendship, based on equality of respect, as a model for democratic community. I assume there and elsewhere that both forms of democracy require the protection of minority rights.

    5. Kenneth Arrow, *Social Choice and Individual Values* [1951] (New York: Wiley, 1963). William H. Riker, *Liberalism against Populism: A Confrontation between the Theory of Democracy and the Theory of Social Choice* [1982] (Prospect Heights, Ill.: Waveland Press, 1988).

    6. Community understandings of what constitutes "good enough" (sufficing rather than maximizing) democracy parallel similar understandings of "good enough" (or "mediated") morality (see Mansbridge, "On the Relation between Altruism and Self-Interest," 1990). Such broad understandings facilitate democracy, while not constituting an "agreement on fundamentals," which Carl Friedrich (*The New Belief in the Common Man* [Boston: Little, Brown, 1942], p. 153ff) argued democracies do not require.

    7. Whereas "gender" has social connotations and "sex" connotations of biology and sexual intercourse, I do not make a sharp distinction between the two. On interchangeable usage, see, from different perspectives, Francine Watman Frank and Paula A. Treichler, *Language, Gender, and Professional Writing* (New York: Modern Language Association, 1989), pp. 10–14; and Catharine A. MacKinnon, *Toward a Feminist Theory of the State* (Cambridge: Harvard University Press, 1989), pp. xiii, 113.

    8. Lawrence Kohlberg, "A Cognitive-Developmental Analysis of Children's Sex-Role Concepts and Attitudes," in Eleanor E. Maccoby, ed., *The Developmental Sex Differences* (Stanford: Stanford University Press, 1966).

    9. See Amos Tversky, Daniel Kahneman, and Paul Slovic, eds., *Judgment under Uncertainty: Heuristics and Biases* (Cambridge: Cambridge University Press, 1982), on the availability heuristic.

10. Analysis derived from data in George P. Murdoch and Caterina Provost, "Factors in the Division of Labor by Sex: A Cross-Cultural Analysis," *Ethnology* 12 (1973): 203–225, Table 8. "Circum-Mediterranean" is Murdoch's own neologism. Data of this kind derive from the reports of anthropologists who often did not check their conclusions with the people they described. Had they done so, they might have found that these practices were contested, changing, or more ambiguous than reported (personal communication from David Cohen, Professor of History and Director of African Studies, Northwestern University).

11. Catharine MacKinnon, "Difference and Dominance," in *Feminism Unmodified* (Cambridge: Harvard University Press, 1967), pp. 32–45, p. 36. See also Mary Austin, *Earth Horizon* (Boston: Houghton Mifflin, 1932), cited by Nancy Cott, "Feminist Theory and Feminist Movements," in Juliet Mitchell and Ann Oakley, eds., *What Is Feminism?* (New York: Pantheon, 1986); and Martha Minow, "Justice Engendered," a feminist "Foreword to the Supreme Court 1986 Term," *Harvard Law Review* 101 (1987): 10–95, pp. 32ff.

12. Although in 1955 George A. Hillary, Jr. concluded after inspecting ninety-four different definitions of community that "social interaction within a geographic area" was part of a "minimum" definition ("Definitions of Community: Areas of Agreement," *Rural Sociology* 20 [1955]: 111–123), subsequent thinkers have downplayed the importance of locality. Raymond Plant reported in 1987 that compared to the dispute over whether locality is a necessary component of the meaning of community, "all are agreed that it is something about the quality of the relationships that makes a social grouping into a community" ("Community," in *The Blackwell Encyclopedia of Political Thought* [Oxford: Basil Blackwell, 1987], p. 90). Reviewing "the meanings of community" in 1978, Thomas Bender concluded that it "is best defined as a network of social relations marked by mutuality and emotional bonds," or, in a formal definition, "a community involves a limited number of people in a somewhat restricted social space or network held together by shared understandings and a sense of obligation" (*Community and Social Change in America* [New Brunswick: Rutgers University Press, 1978], p. 7).

13. Talcott Parsons and Robert F. Bales, *Family, Socialization, and Interaction Process* (New York: Free Press, 1955), p. 47.

14. For "emotion work," see Arlie Russell Hochschild, "The Sociology of Feeling and Emotion: Selected Possibilities," in Marcia Millman and Rosabeth Moss Kanter, eds., *Another Voice: Feminist Perspectives on Social Life and Social Science* (New York: Doubleday/Anchor, 1975), pp. 280–307; for "kinwork," see Micaela di Leonardo, "The Female

World of Cards and Holidays: Women, Families and the Work of Kinship," *Signs* 12 (1987): 440–453.

15. Alice H. Eagly and Blair T. Johnson, "Gender and Leadership Style: A Meta-Analysis," *Psychological Bulletin* 108 (1990): 233–256, p. 236, emphasis in original.

16. For the strong male content of "fraternity," see Wilson Carey McWilliams, *The Idea of Fraternity in America* (Berkeley: University of California Press, 1973), chap. 1; and Carole Pateman, "The Fraternal Social Contract," in *The Disorder of Women* (Stanford: Stanford University Press, 1989), and *The Sexual Contract* (Stanford: Stanford University Press, 1988).

17. Pamela Johnston Conover, "Who Cares? Sympathy and Politics: A Feminist Perspective," paper presented at the annual meeting of the Midwest Political Science Association, 1988.

18. Nancy Eisenberg and Randy Lennon, "Sex Differences in Empathy and Related Capacities," *Psychological Bulletin* 94 (1983): 100–131.

19. Ruth Sharabany, Ruth Gershoni, and John E. Hofman, "Girl Friend, Boy Friend: Age and Sex Differences in Development of Intimate Friendships," *Developmental Psychology* 17 (1981): 800–808; Margery Fox, Margaret Gibbs, and Doris Auerbach, "Age and Gender Dimensions of Friendship," *Psychology of Women Quarterly* 9 (1985): 489–502; E. Douvan and J. Adelson, *The Adolescent Experience* (New York: Wiley, 1966); Matya A. Caldwell and Letitia A. Peplau, "Sex Differences in Same-sex Friendships," *Sex Roles* 8 (1982): 721–732; Lynne R. Davidson and Lucile Duberman, "Friendship: Communication and Interactional Patterns in Same-Sex Dyads," *Sex Roles* 8 (1982): 809–822. For a recent review of the literature, see Hazel Markus and Daphna Oyserman, "Gender and Thought: The Role of Self-Concept," in Mary Crawford and Margaret Gentry, eds., *Gender and Thought: Psychological Perspectives* (New York: Springer-Verlag, 1989). There is no meta-analysis of psychological studies involving connection. Much of the work cited in support of greater connection among women is, in the original research, more ambiguous than the citations suggest.

20. Charlotte Perkins Gilman, *Herland* [1915] (New York: Pantheon, 1979).

21. Aileen Kraditor, *The Ideas of the Woman Suffrage Movement* (Garden City: Doubleday, 1971). Although Kraditor stresses the predominance of arguments from women's special virtues toward the end of the suffrage movement, more recent historians (cited in Cott [1986], pp. 50–51) demonstrate that both kinds of arguments flourished throughout the period from 1792 (Mary Wollstonecraft's *Vindication of*

the Rights of Women) to 1921. Cott (1986) provides an excellent short account of "sameness" versus "difference" strands in the first wave of feminism in the United States.

22. Marlene Dixon in *It Ain't Me Babe,* April 7, 1970, p. 8; Jane Alpert, "Mother Right: A New Feminist Theory," *off our backs* 3 (8 May 1973): 6; *Ms.* 2 (1973): 52–55, 88–94. Alice Echols, *Daring to be Bad: Radical Feminism in America, 1967–1975* (Minneapolis: University of Minnesota Press, 1989), p. 7, dates the term "cultural feminism" to 1972, but indicates correctly that the ideas predated the term. Echols, who wants to associate the "rise of cultural feminism" with a turn "away from opposing male supremacy" (p. 5), attributes to "conceptual confusion" (pp. 6, 7, 10) the interlacing of concern with women's culture through much of the early radical women's movement.

"Women's culture" undoubtedly has its roots in women's powerlessness as well as other sources. But as Dixon suggests, roots in a harmful situation do not automatically invalidate a cognitive or emotional insight. A brush with death can make one more appreciative of life in a way one may want to maintain after reducing the threat of death. Per contra, see MacKinnon (1989), pp. 51–58, 153.

23. Dorothy Dinnerstein, *The Mermaid and the Minotaur: Sexual Arrangements and Human Malaise* [1976] (New York: Harper Colophon, 1977), p. 193. Dinnerstein also concludes that the need to invest major energy in perpetuating the species tended to make women specialists in the exercise of capacities "crucial for empathic care of the very young and for maintenance of the social-emotional arrangements that sustain everyday primary-group life" (p. 20). See also p. 68 on the more permeable boundaries of self among women. Dinnerstein drew from Norman O. Brown's conclusion that male domination is the product of the boy's "revolt against biological dependence on the mother" (p. 182, citing Norman O. Brown, *Life against Death* [Middletown: Wesleyan University Press, 1959], n.p.).

24. Nancy Chodorow, *The Reproduction of Mothering: Psychoanalysis and the Sociology of Gender* (Berkeley: University of California Press, 1978), p. 181. Chodorow linked connection with empathy: "Girls emerge from this [oedipal] period with a basis for 'empathy' built into their primary definition of self in a way that boys do not. Girls emerge with a stronger basis for experiencing another's needs or feelings as one's own (or of thinking that one is so experiencing another's needs or feelings)" (p. 167).

25. Chodorow (1978), p. 169.

26. Sara Ruddick, "Maternal Thinking," *Feminist Studies* 6 (Summer 1980): 353; see also Jean Bethke Elshtain, *Public Man, Private Woman:*

Women in Social and Political Thought (Princeton: Princeton University Press, 1981), p. 336, and "Feminist Discourse and Its Discontents: Language, Power and Meaning," *Signs* 7 (1983): 603–621, p. 621.

27. "Methodocracy, Misogyny and Bad Faith: The Response of Philosophy," in D. Spender, ed., *Men's Studies Modified: The Impact of Feminism on the Academic Disciplines* (New York: Oxford University Press, 1981), p. 47 cited in Jean Grimshaw, *Philosophy and Feminist Thinking* (Minneapolis: University of Minnesota Press, 1986), p. 54. See also Jane Flax, "Political Philosophy and the Patriarchal Unconscious: A Psychoanalytic Perspective on Epistemology and Metaphysics," in S. Harding and M. Hintikka, eds., *Discovering Reality: Feminist Perspectives on Epistemology, Metaphysics, Methodology, and the Philosophy of Science* (London: D. Reidel, 1983), for a critique, based on Chodorow, of the denial of primary relatedness in philosophy.

28. Carol Gilligan, *In a Different Voice* (Cambridge: Harvard University Press 1982), p. 8. Several years later, however, in "Moral Orientation and Moral Development," in Kittay and Meyers, eds. *Women and Moral Theory* (Totowa, N.J.: Rowman and Littlefield, 1987), Gilligan criticized Chodorow for tying self-development to the experience of separation, thus sustaining "a series of oppositions that have been central in Western thought and moral theory, including the opposition between thought and feelings, self and relationship, reason and compassion, justice and love" (p. 29). Although I concentrate here on the empirical question of gender differences in "connection," Gilligan was reacting to a line of research that, for reasons probably linked in part to implicit gender coding, considered a rights, or Kantian, orientation higher than other moral orientations. See below on the moral emotions for the feminist critique of this form of Kantian orientation. See also Joan C. Tronto, "Women and Caring: What Can Feminists Learn about Morality from Caring?" in Alison M. Jaggar and Susan R. Bordo, eds., *Gender/Body/Knowledge* (New Brunswick: Rutgers University Press, 1989); and Owen Flanagan and Kathryn Jackson, "Justice, Care and Gender: The Kohlberg-Gilligan Debate Revisited," *Ethics* 97 (1987): 622–637 for a review and critique of the literature.

29. Gilligan (1982), p. 17. Like Chodorow, Gilligan explicitly linked care with empathy, concluding that women's moral judgments "are tied to feelings of empathy and compassion" (p. 69), and that girls' smaller and more intimate playgroups foster the development of "empathy and sensitivity" (p. 11).

30. Nel Noddings, *Caring: A Feminine Approach to Ethics and Moral Education* (Berkeley: University of California Press, 1984), p. 2.

31. Diana Baumrind, "Sex Differences in Moral Reasoning: Re-

sponse to Walker's (1984) Conclusion that There Are None," *Child Development* 57 (1986): 511–521.

32. Nona Plessner Lyons reports the largest differences of any of Carol Gilligan's students. In her sample of 30 upper-middle-class people, identified through personal contact and recommendation, 63 percent of the 16 women were coded as "predominantly connected" compared to none of the 14 men, and 79 percent of the men as "predominantly separate" compared to 13 percent of the women (Nona Plessner Lyons, "Two Perspectives: On Self, Relationships, and Morality," in Carol Gilligan, J. Victoria Ward, and Jill McLean Taylor, eds., *Mapping the Moral Domain: A Contribution of Women's Thinking to Psychological Theory and Education* [Cambridge: Harvard University Press, 1988]).

Other studies do not find significant gender differences, even in college-educated populations. See Maureen R. Ford and Carol R. Lowery, "Gender Differences in Moral Reasoning: A Comparison of the Use of Justice and Care Orientations," *Journal of Personality and Social Psychology* 50(1986): 777–783 (college students); William J. Friedman, Amy B. Robinson, and Britt L. Friedman, "Sex Differences in Moral Judgments? A Test of Gilligan's Theory," *Psychology of Women Quarterly* 11(1987): 37–46 (college students); Robbin Derry, "Moral Reasoning in Work-related Conflicts," *Research in Corporate Performance and Policy* 9 (1987): 25–49 ("first-level managers"). On Kohlberg's measures, see Laurence J. Walker, "Sex Differences in the Development of Moral Reasoning: A Critical Review," *Child Development* 55 (1984): 677–691.

Such differences may be highly context specific. When no other cues are given, the classic Bem Sex-Role Inventory finds American college students linking the words "understanding," "sensitive to the needs of others," and "compassionate" to the "feminine" role (Sandra L. Bem, "The Measurement of Psychological Androgyny," *Journal of Consulting and Clinical Psychology* 42 [1974]: 155–162; and Hazel Markus, Marie Crane, Stan Bernstein, and Michael Siladi, "Self-Schemas and Gender," *Journal of Personality and Social Psychology* 42 [1982]: 38–50). When no cues are given, students also associate the "communal goals" of "selflessness, concern with others and a desire to be at one with others" with women more than men (women 3.81, men 3.03 on a 5-point scale). Yet the same students also see male *homemakers* as more likely to have communal traits than female *employees* (4.11 vs. 3.31), suggesting that the stereotypes derive at least in part from the work in which the two sexes are thought typically to engage. Alice H. Eagly and Valerie J. Steffen, "Gender Stereotypes Stem from the Distribution of Women and Men into Social Roles," *Journal of Personality and Social Psychology* 46 (1984): 735–754.

The anthropologist Ronald Cohen concludes that "empathy" is "not a proper way to behave" in some African tribal societies, and suggests that the Anglo-European focus on empathy may be the historical result of many generations of small, inwardly focussed nuclear families with a relatively low instance of infant death. "Altruism: Human, Cultural, or What?", *Journal of Social Issues* 28 (1972): 39–57. On the other hand, Sandra Harding, "The Curious Coincidence of Feminine and African Moralities," in Kittay and Meyers, eds. (1987), and Patricia Hill Collins, *Black Feminist Thought* (London: Allen and Unwin, 1990), pp. 206ff., suggest that an ethics of "connection" and "caring" may typify the behavior and norms not only of women in the United States, but also of both men and women in Africa. Empirical research on these issues is in its infancy.

33. That a researcher can construct two distinct operationalizations of these two orientations does not mean that analytically the two are entirely separate. On the overlap, see Susan Moller Okin, "Thinking Like a Woman," in Deborah L. Rhode, ed., *Theoretical Perspectives on Sexual Difference* (New Haven: Yale University Press, 1990); George Sher, "Other Voices, Other Rooms? Women's Psychology and Moral Theory," in Kittay and Meyers, eds. (1987); and Flanagan and Jackson (1987). Nondiscretionary rights can be based on relations, as when the primary caretaker has the right to custody after divorce (Mary Becker, University of Chicago Law School, personal communication). Moreover, although about two-thirds of D. Kay Johnston's ("Adolescents' Solutions to Dilemmas in Fables" in Gilligan et al. [1988]) eighty middle-class students focussed on one orientation rather than another in interpreting a moral fable, all were eventually able to adopt the other orientation (about half spontaneously, after being asked, "Is there another way to think about this problem?" and the rest after prompting).

34. Ford and Lowery (1986).

35. Jennifer Nedelsky, "Reconceiving Autonomy," *Yale Journal of Law and Feminism* 1 (1989): 7–36, p. 12. See also Nancy J. Chodorow, "Gender, Relation, and Difference in Psychoanalytic Perspective" [1979], in *Feminism and Psychoanalytic Theory* (New Haven: Yale University Press, 1989), p. 106.

36. Virginia Held on the "mothering parent" in "Mothering versus Contract," in Mansbridge, ed. (1990), p. 300. For summaries of feminist thought and quandaries regarding autonomy, see Christine Di Stefano, "Rethinking Autonomy," paper delivered at the 1990 Annual Meeting of the American Political Science Association, San Francisco.

37. An autonomous self develops not only through the help and care of others, but also through having the material, legal, and psychological wherewithal to create and maintain some form of independence from others and from the state.

38. Like many philosophical points in recent feminist theory, the realization that community precedes autonomy is as old as Aristotle, without the feminist emphasis on nurturance. However, after Aristotle and most subsequent Western philosophers excluded the domestic sphere from the political (indeed defined the political in contradistinction to the domestic), language, analogies, and stories derived from women's experiences in the domestic sphere could have little place in descriptions of what politics is or ought to be.

39. No feminist theorist using experiences from motherhood to illuminate the potential in democratic community wants to suggest that actual mothers have with actual children only the relations conjured up by the ideal. While arguing that the ideal mothering relation empowers the child, Held (1990), for example, would not ignore mothers' frequent exercise of naked power over children in their own rather than the children's interests. Both negative and positive aspects of the practice of childrearing illuminate the values, human processes, and problems inherent in helping develop democratic citizens (Jennifer Nedelsky, University of Toronto Law School, personal communication).

40. For critiques of the maternal model, see Mary G. Dietz, "Citizenship with a Feminist Face: The Problem with Maternal Thinking," *Political Theory* 13 (1985): 19–37; and "Context Is All: Feminism and Theories of Citizenship," in J. K. Conway, S. C. Bourque, and J. W. Scott, eds., *Learning about Women: Gender, Politics, and Power* (Ann Arbor: University of Michigan Press, 1987).

41. Held, (1990), pp. 297–299.

42. Nancy J. Hirschmann, "Freedom, Recognition, and Obligation: A Feminist Approach to Political Theory," *American Political Science Review* 83 (1989): 1227–1244, p. 1238.

43. Hirschmann (1989), p. 1242.

44. See, e.g., references in Robert E. Goodin, *Protecting the Vulnerable* (Chicago: University of Chicago Press, 1985).

45. In *A Theory of Justice* (Cambridge: Harvard University Press, 1971), pp. 113–116, John Rawls follows H. L. A. Hart, C. H. Whiteley, and R. B. Brandt in distinguishing between "obligations," which must arise through promising or tacit understandings, and natural "duties." See also Lawrence A. Blum, *Friendship, Altruism and Morality* (London: Routledge and Kegan Paul, 1980), p. 142, and Noddings (1984), pp. 81–84. Hirschmann ([1989], p. 1243 n. 1) argues that "duty" has not been

as central to liberal theory as "obligation" precisely because "obligation" has been defined as voluntary. I use the word "obligation" broadly, assuming that both moral and political obligations can have multiple sources, some reinforcing and some undermining the others.

46. Michael Sandel (*Liberalism and the Limits of Justice* [Cambridge: Cambridge University Press, 1982], p. 179) writes that certain allegiances "go beyond the obligations I voluntarily incur and the 'natural duties' I owe to human beings as such. They allow that to some I owe more than justice requires or even permits, not by reason of agreements I have made but instead in virtue of those more or less enduring attachments and commitments which taken together partly define the person I am." These attachments, he specifies, are not chosen but discovered. Alasdair MacIntyre writes that "I inherit from the past of my family, my city, my tribe, my nation, a variety of ... obligations. These constitute the given of my life" (*After Virtue* [1981] [Notre Dame: Notre Dame University Press, 1984], p. 220). Roberto Unger, making room for chosen as well as given communities, nevertheless points out that communities "arise from relationships of interdependence that have been only partly articulated by the will," and concludes that "received ideas about ... the sources of obligation cannot readily inform even the existing varieties of communal experience" (*The Critical Legal Studies Movement* [1983] [Cambridge: Harvard University Press, 1986], p. 37).

47. In the United States and most other countries, when children are born, when they get sick, or when parents grow old and get sick, women are expected to care for them and usually accept that responsibility. Women also accept more responsibility for helping in the crises of kin and friends (Carol Heimer, "On Taking Responsibility," presented at the Seminar on Contemporary Social and Political Theory, University of Chicago, April 6, 1989; Janet Finch and Dulcie Groves, eds., *A Labour of Love: Women, Work, and Caring* [London: Routledge and Kegan Paul, 1983]).

48. Hirschmann (1989), p. 1241.

49. MacIntyre (1981/1984), pp. 58–59, 220. Rawls (1971), on learning "the virtues of a good student" and other roles whose content "is given by the various conceptions of a good wife and husband, a good friend and citizen, and so on ... the morality of association includes a large number of ideals each defined in ways suitable for the respective status or role" (p. 468).

50. Goodin (1985) makes a powerful case for the obligation to protect the vulnerable as the root of many specific obligations that liberal philosophers have derived from some form of voluntarism. His discussion of the family, however, provides a less satisfactory account of

why any particular person has such an obligation to any particular other. He argues first, that certain people are the "obvious" candidates to bear such responsibilities, with obviousness coming to have moral significance "by virtue of the reactions of other people" (p. 82). But this criterion seems to provide no recourse against unjust cultural expectations. He also argues that when emotional rather than material interests are at stake, individuals enmeshed in affective ties have obligations to the specific others whose emotional welfare depends on them. But as he points out, if affection is lacking, this criterion absolves family members of any special obligation beyond the "general duty to help those in need" (pp. 88–89). A slightly more utilitarian approach would argue that those strategically placed to be most useful to others in their vulnerability have an obligation deriving from that placement. The nearest person is obliged to rescue a drowning swimmer at least in part because he is objectively the best placed to do so, not simply because others expect him to, as in Goodin's explanation (p. 82). Obligations created this way are then subject to scrutiny over the justice of the underlying placement.

51. Some "political" obligations, for example, are also obligations to specific people with whom one has developed stronger or weaker relations of mutual trust or expectation. The obligation to obey the law may derive from considerations of the justness of a law or of the institutions that produced it, but the obligation to take community office— a complexly negotiated obligation, partaking both of the voluntary and the given—is often in part an obligation to specific members of the community, who would bear the costs of one's reneging on that obligation. Parallels with the domestic realm multiply as one conceives the obligations of political community to extend beyond the traditional political obligation of obeying the law to the obligation to vote against one's self-interest for the community good, or the obligation to give time to political projects.

52. The critical scrutiny I have in mind has affinities with Rawls's (1971) "reflective equilibrium."

53. When university students from 28 countries were asked to rate a set of 300 adjectives as being "more frequently associated with men rather than women, or more frequently associated with women than men," students in all but 1 country associated the adjective "emotional" with women, and in all but 5 countries associated the adjective "rational" with men. A score of 0 indicates complete agreement that the adjective is associated with women, 100 complete agreement on association with men. For the adjective "emotional," the average score in Pakistan was 51, neutral between 0 and 100; the average score across all countries

was 12 and across English-speaking countries 4. Students in the United States were unique in giving "emotional" a score of zero, indicating complete association with women. With 100 indicating complete association with men, the average score for the adjective "rational" across all countries was 75, across English-speaking countries 76, and in the United States, 90. (Students in Bolivia, Norway, Pakistan, Scotland, and Venezuela gave "rational" the relatively neutral average scores of 60, 57, 49, 61, and 62 respectively.) In only one country, the Netherlands (with an average score of 94), did students type "rational" as more masculine than in the United States. Analysis from data in John E. Williams and Deborah L. Best, *Measuring Sex Stereotypes* (Beverly Hills: Sage, 1982), Appendix A.

54. Annette C. Baier, "Hume, the Woman's Moral Theorist?" in Kittay and Meyers, eds. (1987); Joan C. Tronto, "Political Science and Caring," *Women and Politics* 7 (1987): 85–97.

55. Immanuel Kant, *Fundamental Principles of the Metaphysic of Morals*, trans. Thomas K. Abbott [1785] (Indianapolis: Bobbs-Merrill, 1949), pp. 15–16.

56. *Observations on the Feeling of the Beautiful and the Sublime*, trans. John Goldthwait, [1763] (Berkeley: University of California Press, 1960), p. 81. See Carol C. Gould, "Philosophy of Liberation and Liberation of Philosophy," in Carol C. Gould and Marx W. Wartofsky, eds., *Women and Philosophy* (New York: Capricorn/G. P. Putnam, 1976), p. 18; Laurence A. Blum, "Kant and Hegel's Moral Rationalism: A Feminist Perspective," *Canadian Journal of Philosophy* 12 (1982): 287–302; and Grimshaw (1986), pp. 42–44. See also G. W. F. Hegel in *The Philosophy of Right:* "Women regulate their actions not by the demands of universality but by arbitrary inclinations" (Oxford: Oxford University Press, 1952), p. 263, cited in Genevieve Lloyd, "Reason, Gender and Morality in the History of Philosophy," *Social Research* 50 (1983): 491–513, p. 511.

57. Blum (1980); Blum (1982); and Lawrence A. Blum, "Gilligan and Kohlberg: Implications for Moral Theory," *Ethics* 98 (1988): 472–491, in which he suggests a typology of the ways moral theories based on the will can coexist with moral theories based on emotion. See David A. J. Richards, chap. 15 in this volume; Virginia Held, "Feminism and Moral Theory," in Kittay and Meyers (1987) eds., pp. 119ff; and Sher (1987) especially the comment on Bernard Williams on p. 185, for the point that morality requires generalizable principles, although those principles may derive from, and encode distinctions drawn from, particularistic commitment. See also Grimshaw (1986), pp. 205–211.

Blum ([1988], p. 475) makes the moral goal "achieving knowledge of the good for another," not just making an effort to know. Bernard

Williams objects that there is some problem, even an "ultimate and outrageous absurdity" in the idea that "the achievement of the highest kind of moral worth should depend on natural capacities [including "a capacity for sympathetic understanding"] unequally and fortuitously distributed as they are" (Bernard Williams, "The Idea of Equality," in Peter Laslett and W. G. Runciman, eds., *Philosophy, Politics, and Society* [2nd. ser.] [Oxford: Basil Blackwell, 1969], p. 115). Williams thus praises effort rather than success in the act of sympathy. Each human being, he concludes, is owed an "effort" at identification and understanding (p. 117). In Simone Weil and Iris Murdoch's understanding of "attention," the moral mandate also requires noticing and asking rather than succeeding in putting oneself in another's place (see Ruddick [1980], p. 359). Finally, Martha Minow ([1987], pp. 77, 79) and Alasdair MacIntyre ([1981/1984], p. 149), following David Hume (see Baier [1987], p. 41), both seem to make morality at least partly a matter of effort in cultivating the capacity for sympathy.

58. "Reason and Feeling in Thinking about Justice," *Ethics* 99 (1989): 229–249.

59. Seyla Benhabib, "The Generalized and Concrete Other," pp. 32ff, in Seyla Benhabib and Ducilla Cornell, eds., *Feminism as Critique* [1987] (Minneapolis: University of Minnesota Press, 1988).

60. See Mansbridge, "The Rise and Fall of Self-Interest" and "On the Relation between Altruism and Self-Interest" in Mansbridge, ed. (1990).

61. For the role of emotion in deliberation, see Jane Mansbridge, "A Deliberative Theory of Interest Representation," in Mark Petracca, ed., *The Politics of Interests: Interest Groups Transformed* (Boulder: Westview Press, 1992), p. 35; Charles E. Lindblom, *Inquiry and Change* (New Haven: Yale University Press, 1990), p. 32; and Benjamin Barber, *Strong Democracy: Participatory Politics for a New Age* (Berkeley: University of California Press, 1984), p. 174.

62. Michael Walzer, *Spheres of Justice* (New York: Basic Books, 1983); Robert A. Dahl, *After the Revolution* (New Haven: Yale University Press, 1970). Arguments for justice within one nation require similar justifications. See Rawls (1971) and Charles R. Beitz, *Political Theory and International Relations* (Princeton: Princeton University Press, 1979).

63. Robert E. Goodin, *Protecting the Vulnerable* (Chicago: University of Chicago Press, 1985) makes the best modern case for identifying " 'particularity' as the principal enemy of justice" (p. 1). In doing so, he provides a masterly summary of the conclusions of those philosophers, from Maimonides to Bernard Williams, who have argued the claims of particular relations to particular persons. Goodin does not

argue "that we have *no* responsibilities toward those with who we enjoy 'special relationships.' That would be absurd. Nor for that matter shall I deny our firm intuitions that our responsibilities toward them tend to be particularly strong ones" (pp. 10–11). It is not his task, however, to justify those special relations.

64. Although the limiting case of "humanity" undermines the opposition between a community member and a stranger, even here one could treat as relative strangers animals, extraterrestrial beings, and "enemies of humanity." One might also include some animals in the membership of certain primarily human communities, depending on the existence and strength of mutual relations of obligation, vulnerability, understanding, and sympathy between the animals and human members of those communities.

65. Michael Walzer, *Obligations* (Cambridge: Harvard University Press, 1970).

66. C. D. Broad, "Self and Others" [1953], in David R. Cheney, ed., *Broad's Critical Essays in Moral Philosophy* (London: George Allen and Unwin, 1971). I thank Marx Wartofsky for first drawing this point to my attention.

67. Carol A. Heimer, "Doing Your Job *and* Helping Your Friends: Universalistic Norms about Obligations to Particular Others in Networks," in Nitin Nohria and Robert Eccles, eds., *Networks and Organizations: Theory and Practice* (Cambridge: Harvard Business School, 1992).

68. Iris Marion Young, "Impartiality and the Civic Public," in Seyla Benhabib and Drucilla Cornell, eds., *Feminism as Critique: On the Politics of Gender* (Minneapolis: University of Minnesota Press, 1987), pp. 61–62. Benhabib and Minow retain a greater respect than Young for the norms of universalism or impartiality. Benhabib ([1987], p. 81) would replace "substitutionalist" universalism, which surreptitiously "identifies the experiences of a particular group of human beings as the paradigmatic case of the human as such," with "interactive" universalism, which "acknowledges the plurality of modes of being human, and differences among humans, without endorsing all these pluralities and differences as morally and politically valid." Interactive universalism agrees that "normative disputes can be settled rationally, and that fairness, reciprocity and some procedure of universalizability are . . . necessary conditions of the moral standpoint." Minow ([1987], pp. 75–76) accepts a form of impartiality as a goal when she argues that "only by admitting our partiality can we strive for impartiality." "If I embrace partiality, I risk ignoring . . . your alternate reality. . . . I must acknowledge and struggle against my partiality by making an effort to understand your reality and what it means for my own." See also "Symposium on Im-

partiality and Ethical Theory" in *Ethics* 101 (1991), especially Marilyn Friedman, "The Practice of Partiality," pp. 818–835.

69. "Observations on the Real Rights of Women" [1818], in Aileen Kraditor, ed., *Up from the Pedestal* (Chicago: Quandrangle Books, 1968), p. 40.

70. Gilman (1915/1979).

71. Mary Parker Follett, "Coordination" in *Freedom and Coordination: Lectures in Business Organization* (London: Management Publications Trust, 1949), p. 66; see also "Constructive Conflict," in Henry C. Metcalf, ed., *Dynamic Administration: The Collected Papers of Mary Parker Follett* (New York: Harper, 1942), p. 32. Follett is sometimes misinterpreted on this point. She made it clear "definitely that I do not think integration is possible in all cases" (p. 36), and argued that in trying to "find the real demand as against the demand put forward," the first rule for obtaining integration is to "face the real issue, uncover the conflict, bring the whole thing into the open" (p. 38). For a modern use of both Follett's ideas and her concrete examples, see Roger Fisher and William Ury, *Getting to Yes* [1981] (New York: Penguin Books, 1983), esp. p. 41. Dorothy Emmett revived Follett's distinction between "power over" and "power with" (Mary Parker Follett, "Power," in Metcalf, ed. (1942) pp. 101, 109) in "The Concept of Power," *Proceedings of the Aristotelian Society* 54 (1953–1954), pp. 1–26, her presidential address to that society and argued that the Laswellian definition of politics as a struggle for power to obtain deference did not "represent a view of politics in the round," which would include using power for coping with "problems set by events or social situations" (p. 9). Follett and Emmett were the most distinguished women in their professions; although neither considered herself a feminist, their experiences and socialization as women may well have contributed to their unorthodox alternatives to "power over."

72. Nancy Hartsock, "Political Change: Two Perspectives on Power," *Quest* 1 (1974): 10–25, reprinted in Charlotte Bunch, ed., *Building Feminist Theory: Essays from Quest* (New York: Longman, 1981), pp. 9, 10. See also Berenice Carroll, "Peace Research: The Cult of Power," *Journal of Conflict Resolution* 4 (1972): 585–616. For similar points without a feminist perspective, see William E. Connolly, "Power and Responsibility," in *The Terms of Political Discourse* (Lexington: D. C. Heath, 1974) and less directly C. B. Macpherson, "The Maximization of Democracy," in *Democratic Theory: Essays in Retrieval* (Oxford: Oxford University Press, 1973).

73. Kathy E. Ferguson, *The Feminist Case against Bureaucracy* (Philadelphia: Temple University Press, 1984) pp. 25, 119–203. See also

Carol Gould, "The Woman Question: Philosophy of Liberation and the Liberation of Philosophy," in C. Gould and M. W. Wartofsky, eds., *Women and Philosophy: Toward a Theory of Liberation* (New York: G. P. Putnam's Sons, 1976), pp. 5–44; and Held (1990), p. 300. Bertrand de Jouvenel confirms the gendering of this concept by making politics as power through imposition not only the source of "incomparable pleasure" but also manly: "A man feels more of a man when imposing himself and making others the instrument of his will" (Bertrand de Jouvenel, *Power* [1945], cited in Hannah Arendt, "Reflections on Violence," *Journal of International Affairs* 23 [1969]: 1–35, p. 12). See Carroll (1972), p. 588.

74. Peter Bachrach and Morton Baratz, "Decisions and Non-Decisions," *American Political Science Review* 57 (1963): 632–644.

75. Alice H. Eagly and Blair T. Johnson, "Gender and Leadership Style: A Meta-Analysis," *Psychological Bulletin* 108 (1990): 233–256. Socialization, lesser power, and anticipation of bias may also explain why, in the research of Lynn R. Offerman and Pamela E. Schrier, "Social Influence Strategies: The Impact of Sex, Role, and Attitudes toward Power," *Personality and Social Psychology Bulletin* 11 (1985): 286–300, p. 295, fear of having power was significantly correlated with gender.

76. Literature reviews in Nancy Henley, *Body Politics* (Englewood Cliffs: Prentice-Hall, 1977), p. 74; Adelaide Haas, "Male and Female Spoken Language Differences: Stereotypes and Evidence," *Psychological Bulletin* 86 (1979): 616–626; Virginia P. Brooks, (1982), "Sex Differences in Student Dominance Behavior in Female and Male Professors' Classrooms," *Sex Roles* 8 (1982): 683–690; and Cynthia Fuchs Epstein, *Deceptive Distinctions: Sex, Gender, and the Social Order* (New Haven: Yale University Press and Russell Sage Foundation, 1988), pp. 217ff. Epstein's excellent review points out that speaking patterns vary depending on the situation and the definition of that situation. In one study, "when women were told they would be assessed on their leadership ability in a discussion group, they spoke up as much as the men did" (p. 219). I know of no meta-analysis of this literature.

77. On town meetings, see Frank M. Bryan, "Comparative Town Meetings: A Search for Causative Models of Feminine Involvement in Politics," paper delivered at the annual meeting of the Rural Sociological Society, 1975; and Mansbridge (1980/1983), p. 106 and ns. 19–23. On state legislatures, see Lyn Kathlene, "The Impact of Gender on the Legislative Process," a study of the Colorado state legislature, in Joyce McCarl Nielsen, ed., *Feminist Research Methods* (Boulder: Westview, 1990), pp. 246–247.

78. For women's use of constructions such as "can" or "could," tag

questions such as "didn't I?" and imperative constructions in question form, such as "Will you please close the door?" See Julie R. McMillan, A. Kay Clifton, Diane McGrath, and Wanda S. Gale, "Women's Language: Uncertainty or Interpersonal Sensitivity and Emotionality?" *Sex Roles* 3 (1977): 546–559. For women's use of questions and supportive interjections like "mm," and "yeah," see Pamela M. Fishman, "Interaction: The Work Women Do," *Social Problems* 25 (1978): 397–406. In three hearings before the Colorado state legislature in 1989 (Kathlene [1990], p. 247) women were more likely to use qualifiers in their testimony. See also Robin Lakoff, *Language and Woman's Place* (New York: Harper and Row, 1975). A few studies, however, show no gender differences in some of these areas (see Haas [1979] for literature review).

79. On meetings, see Mansbridge (1980/1983), p. 106; on interruptions, see Donald H. Zimmerman and Candace West, "Sex Roles, Interruptions, and Silence in Conversation," in Barry Thorne and Nancy Henley, eds., *Language and Sex* (Rowley: Newbury House, 1975).

80. On modest silence, see Aristotle, *Politics*, 1260a. On men's negative reactions to women's assertiveness, see review in Brooks (1982). See Haas (1979), citing Otto Jesperson's *Language* (New York: Henry Holt, 1922), for proverbs from France ("Où femme il y a, silence il n'y a" ["Where there's a woman, there's no silence"]), China ("The tongue is the sword of a woman, and she never lets it become rusty"), Jutland ("The North Sea will sooner be found wanting in water than a woman at a loss for a word"), and elsewhere. In Williams and Best's study of twenty-eight countries in the late 1970s, the adjective "talkative" was associated primarily with females in all but the Latin countries (analysis from data in Williams and Best [1982], Appendix A).

81. Barber (1984), p. 175.

82. Michel Foucault, "Prison Talk" [1975], in Colin Gordon, ed., *Power/Knowledge* (New York: Pantheon, 1980), p. 39.

83. See Mansbridge (1980/1983) on devices for spreading the opportunity to speak, and on gender and class differences in hesitations and not speaking until angry. See Thomas Kochman, *Black and White Styles in Conflict* (Chicago: University of Chicago Press, 1981) on cultural differences between American Blacks and whites in the public expression of anger.

84. On reducing deliberative inequalities on the national scale, see my "A Deliberative Inquiry of Interest Representation," in Mark P. Petracca, ed., *The Politics of Interests: Interest Groups Transformed* (Boulder, Colo.: Westview Press, 1992) and theorists cited therein.

85. Catharine A. MacKinnon, *Feminism Unmodified* (Cambridge:

Harvard University Press, 1987), pp. 7, 217–218; and Andrea Dworkin, *Intercourse* (New York: Free Press, 1987), passim.

86. MacKinnon (1989), p. 3.

87. Although women report hitting or slapping their spouse in marital disputes as often as men (Murray A. Straus, Richard J. Gelles, and Suzanne K. Steinmetz, *Behind Closed Doors: Violence in the American Family* [Garden City: Doubleday, 1980]), they are more likely to be injured in those disputes (Lisa D. Brush, "Violent Acts and Injurious Outcomes in Married Couples: Methodological Issues in the National Survey of Families and Households," *Gender & Society* 4 [1990]: 56–67). It is also possible that men initiate the physical part of the dispute more often than women and that men act violently more often outside the context of a delimited dispute. The greatest differences appear at the extremes: records for one year in Scotland show 98.5 percent of all reported domestic assaults to be assaults of a husband on a wife, and only 1.5 percent of wife on husband (R. Emerson Dobash and Russell P. Dobash, "Wives: The 'Appropriate' victims of Marital Violence," *Victimology* 2 [1978]: 426–442). Although some of this difference may be due to proclivity to report, great differences also show up in hospital admissions. In one year, 70 percent of the assault victims in Boston Hospital were women attacked in the home (Center for Women Policy Studies, Fact Sheet, 1977, cited in Elaine Hilberman, "Response," in U.S. Commission on Civil Rights, *Battered Women: Issues of Public Policy* [n.p., n. pub: Jan 30–31, 1978]).

88. Susan Moller Okin, *Justice, Gender, and the Family* (New York: Basic Books, 1989), p. 152; Amartya Sen, "More than 100 Million Women Are Missing," *New York Review of Books*, December 20, 1990, pp. 61–66.

89. Foucault (1975/1980), pp. 142, 163; Louise Lamphere on "informal resistance in an apparel plant," in *From Working Daughters to Working Mothers: Immigrant Women in a New England Industrial Community* (Ithaca: Cornell University Press, 1987), pp. 289–325; Jean Comaroff, *Body of Power, Spirit of Resistance* (Chicago: University of Chicago Press, 1985).

90. This definition is adapted from James C. Scott's in *Weapons of the Weak: Everyday Forms of Peasant Resistance* (New Haven: Yale University Press, 1985), p. 290. Scott makes it clear that such resistance has "political" features even when it is individual, unorganized, has only tiny consequences, and combines self-interest with collective motivation.

91. Iris Marion Young, "The Ideal of Community and the Politics of Difference," *Social Theory and Practice* 12 (1986): 1–26, p. 2. See also

"Polity and Group Difference: A Critique of the Ideal of Universal Citizenship," *Ethics* 99 (1989): 250–274.

92. See the prayer from the Jewish morning service: "Blessed art thou, Oh Lord our God, King of the universe, who hast not made me a woman."

93. Okin (1989), chap. 3, whose title, "Whose Traditions? Which Understandings?" responds to MacIntyre's *Whose Justice? Which Rationality?* (Notre Dame: Notre Dame University Press, 1988). For another trenchant critique, see Marilyn Freidman, "Feminism and Modern Friendship: Dislocating the Community," *Ethics* 99 (1989): 275–290.

94. Sandel (1982), pp. 172–173.

95. Charles Taylor, *Hegel and Modern Society* (Cambridge: Cambridge University Press, 1979), p. 90.

96. Taylor (1979), pp. 87, 89.

97. I take these examples from Katharine T. Bartlett, "Feminist Legal Methods," *Harvard Law Review* 103 (1990): 829–888, p. 848, commenting on Elizabeth Spelman's *Inessential Woman: Problems of Exclusion in Feminist Thought* (Boston: Beacon Press, 1988).

98. E.g., Angela Harris, "Race and Essentialism in Legal Theory," *Stanford Law Review* 42 (1990): 581–616.

99. On protecting the particular virtues of the public and private realms, see Elshtain (1981), pp. 217–218, 331–353. On the mutual interpenetration of the spheres, see Okin (1989), pp. 124–133; Young (1987), p. 74; Benhabib (1987), p. 177, n. 12; and MacKinnon (1989), p. 120.

100. See Dietz (1985) and (1987).

101. Aristotle, much of whose work rested on categorization, distinguished relatively sharply between a family, a village, and a polis. The political begins at the polis, which Aristotle described as having reached full self-sufficiency (*Politics* 1252b), existing for the sake of a good life (1252b), exemplifying justice (1253a), demanding a common place of residence, (1260b), and being composed of different kinds of men (1261a). The interdependence of different elements distinguishes a polis from a military alliance or a tribe (1261a), and by implication, from a village and household.

Yet Aristotle may not have drawn as sharp a line regarding the nature of the "political" as some subsequent commentators assume. Careful in his classifications, and sensitive not only to sharp demarcations but to the variety of "mixed" states and continua that occur in nature, Aristotle might have believed that elements of the political existed even in the household, and certainly in the village, although those elements were not fully developed until the polis itself. He pointed out, for example, that every polis has "itself the same quality as the earlier associations from which it grew" (1252b), and argued that association in language and the ability to declare what is just and unjust "makes a family and a polis" (1253a). By explicitly including a family with the polis in the process of perceiving and speaking about justice, Aristotle may have suggested that the two are parts of a continuum rather than radically separate.

102. In some philosophic readings, neither innateness nor efficiency is automatically good. Nor does innateness or efficiency automatically trump other goods. Societies work hard and often successfully to reduce or eliminate the effects of many innate impulses, such as the impulse to defecate spontaneously. Societies may also decide against implementing certain efficient ways of functioning, such as plantation slavery, on the grounds that these forms of efficiency are incompatible with other social ideals.

103. The terms "minimalist" and "maximalist" derive from the work of Catharine R. Stimpson, e.g., "Knowing Women," the Marjorie Smart Memorial Lecture, St. Hilda's College, University of Melbourne, August 1990. For divisions in the women's movement on this issue, see Ann Snitow, "Gender Diary," in Marianne Hirsch and Evelyn Fox Keller, eds., *Conflicts in Feminism* (New York: Routledge, 1990).

104. Robin West, "Jurisprudence and Gender," *University of Chicago Law Review* 55 (1988): 1–72, comes close to making a claim for innateness when she says that "women, uniquely, are physically and materially 'connected' to those human beings when the human beings are fetuses and then infants. Women are more empathic to the lives of others because women are physically tied to the lives of others in a way that men are not" (p. 21). West states the "connection thesis" as follows: "Women are actually or potentially materially connected to other human life. Men aren't. This material fact has existential consequences" (p. 14). West also somewhat exaggerates the evidence of gender difference by writing, "According to the vast literature on difference now being developed by cultural feminists, women's cognitive development, literary sensibility, aesthetic taste and psychological development, no less than our anatomy, are all fundamentally different from men's, and are different in the same way: unlike men, we view ourselves as connected to, not separate from, the other" (p. 17). Or, "Intimacy is not something which women fight to become capable of. We just do it. It is ridiculously easy. It is also, I suspect, qualitatively beyond the pale of male effort" (p. 40). In her conclusion West modifies her emphasis on biology by saying that "material biology does not *mandate* existential value: men *can* connect to other human life. . . . *Biology is destiny only to the extent of*

our ignorance" (p. 71, emphases in original), but her stress throughout on "material" and "physical" connection, and her use of phrases like "fundamentally" and "qualitatively beyond the pale of ... effort" make the differences sound insurmountable.

105. My own experience suggests that the differences between college-educated men and women in the United States today are no greater than the differences between college-educated residents of France and the United States. I have found no systematic comparison, across different norms or behaviors, of the size of gender differences to the size of class or other cultural differences. Janet Shibley Hyde's recent study, demonstrating that gender differences in cognitive abilities are generally not large and differences in social behavior depend greatly on context, implies that comparisons of the size of gender differences with the size of class or other cultural differences are rare or non-existent. Janet Shibley Hyde, "Meta-Analysis and the Psychology of Gender Differences," *Signs* 16 (1990): 5–73, esp. 63–64, 72.

106. Community may be valued both as an end in itself and as a means to other ends. When community is at least in part a means, clarity about ends allows us to look for ways of achieving those ends with lower costs. Communities cohering through interdependence, for example, allow more individuality than communities cohering through sameness (Emile Durkheim, *The Division of Labor in Society* [1893], trans. George Simpson [New York: Free Press, 1964]); chosen communities with easy exit allow individuality than "given" communities with non-voluntary obligations (Friedman [1989]). Evaluating these alternatives requires asking what aspects of community different kinds of people most value, and why.

107. Benjamin Zablocki, *The Joyful Community* (Baltimore: Penguin, 1971).

14

FEMINISM AND DEMOCRATIC COMMUNITY REVISITED

CAROL C. GOULD

What contribution can feminist theory make to the conception of a democratic community? In recent years, feminists have drawn on women's experiences as the basis for a reconstructed political theory. They have sought to revise or replace the models of contract, or of the marketplace, or of formal justice with alternative models derived from the relations of care and mothering and from women's experiences of inequality and domination.[1] Some feminist theorists have also put in question what they regard as a prevailing Western model of rationality, sometimes characterized as logocentric, which they see as underlying the political conceptions. But there have been few attempts to articulate the connection between feminism and the important part of political philosophy that may be characterized as democratic theory.

In this context, Jane Mansbridge, in her chapter "Feminism and Democratic Community," offers a useful and detailed summary of the feminist literature focussing on two central contributions that bear on the concept of democratic community: namely, feminism's sensitivity to the phenomenon of unequal power, and the distinctive emphasis on the dimension of care and commonality that derives in part from the experience of mothering. She advances a perceptive critique of gratuitous gendering and of gender coding. She also points to the need for a notion of democracy as not simply atomistic or adversarial, which is a theme she has developed at length in her earlier work. Her present chapter, therefore, provides a point of entry for an analysis of the contributions that feminist theory can make to democracy and of some of the limitations of the contemporary debate.

One general difficulty in Mansbridge's account arises because despite the close analysis of unequal power, care, and other relevant aspects of women's experiences, she does not yet make explicit how these concepts contribute to a theory of democratic community. Perhaps how these forms of women's experience would enrich democratic theory is evident, and maybe a tacit understanding of all this is implied by her account. But it seems to me that after offering rich materials for such an interpretation, Mansbridge stops short and fails to proceed to the conceptual articulation of the transformations feminism can make in democratic theory. Here, I wish to explore some of the contributions that feminist theorizing concerning the care perspective and the critique of domination can make to democratic theory and to the concept of democratic community in particular. However, I wish to be more critical than Mansbridge about the limits of the mothering/familial model for politics.

Democracy and Democratic Community

To assess the feminist contributions to democratic theory, it will be helpful to operate with a basic normative conception of democracy to which these ideas can be shown to be relevant. It is no longer necessary, however, to hark back to the classical liberal theory of democracy to show how it ought to be transformed. Such a development has already taken place, in diverse but related ways, in the work of recent theorists like C. B. Macpherson, Carole Pateman, Jane Mansbridge, and Benjamin Barber.[2] In this context, I prefer to make use of the construction of the transformed theory of democracy that I develop in my book *Rethinking Democracy*,[3] particularly because it already reflects the contribution of feminist themes to some of the basic political norms. In fact, it was an early and ongoing concern with the critique of domination, with the idea of individual and gender difference in the critique of abstract universality, and with the nature of social relations—all of these partly defined in feminist terms, as well as in contexts of social theory more generally— that led to my conviction about the central importance of democratic theory in critical social philosophy.[4]

To put it briefly, the central constitutive idea of the conception of democracy that I develop is that of equal rights of participation in decision making about common projects and common activities. This equal right is grounded in equal positive freedom, that is, an equal right to the conditions of self-development. Positive freedom goes beyond negative freedom as freedom from constraint in focussing on access to, or the availability of, means or conditions for exercising agency and effecting one's choices, and through this enabling the differentiated development of individuals. I argue that individuals have prima facie equal rights to the conditions of such self-development on the grounds of their equal agency as human beings, however differently each exercises it. This requires reciprocal recognition by each agent of the other's equal agency. One of the main conditions for self-development is common or joint activity in which people act together to achieve shared ends. Therefore, in contexts of common activity, the principle of equal positive freedom entails equal rights to participate in decision making about common activity and its ends, because otherwise some would be deciding for others about the course of their agency and would be denying them the exercise of their freedom as self-development. But equal rights to participate in decision making concerning the common activities is precisely the core of democracy. Further, because these contexts of common activities oriented to shared ends are characteristic not only of political institutions but also of economic and social ones more generally, it follows that democratic decision making is required in these contexts as well.

As to the communal nature of democracy, we may say that democracy presupposes community in a minimal sense, namely, that agents in a democratic institution have a common interest in shared ends, in pursuit of which their cooperation is voluntary and not merely constrained by law or habit, or effected by coercion. That is, democratic community is constituted by the decisions of agents to engage in the determination of shared ends and free cooperation toward these ends. But I would like to maintain a distinction between a democratic community in this sense and the more organic and tradition- or culture-defined notions of community implied by Tonnies' concept of *Gemeinschaft* or by contemporary communitarian ideas. The issue of whether social relations of care or mutual concern or support are requirements of a democratic community needs further analysis and bears directly on the impact of feminism on the concept of democratic community.

BEYOND DOMINATION: WOMEN'S EXPERIENCE AND DEMOCRATIC COMMUNITY

A major area of women's experience that is clearly relevant to democratic community is domination. This presumably is what Mansbridge refers to in her discussion of women's experience of unequal power. But unequal power is one thing and domination another. Though this may be a minor point of difference, there would seem to be a distinction between having less or greater power than another to effect one's ends and exercising power over another for one's ends. For example, we may say that a parent has more power than the child, but it does not follow by virtue of this alone that the parent stands in a relation of domination toward the child. Unequal power is a necessary but not a sufficient condition for domination.

Mansbridge's account has the advantage of generality and objectivity in describing the inequalities in power between men and women in various contexts. But a description of unequal power omits reference to the social relations of domination between men and women in personal contexts or through the functioning of institutions. Domination, as distinguished from coercion on the one hand and unequal power on the other, involves control or delimitation of the actions of another through control over the conditions of action, objective or subjective. Such domination is not necessarily fully conscious or deliberate, and may be implicit in the way certain social institutions or customs operate. Of course, many of the relations between men and women are not characterized by domination, but it remains a serious problem nonetheless, which tends to be slighted if described only in terms of inequalities of power.

The critique of domination presupposes a norm of equal freedom and a requirement of reciprocal recognition of equal agency. That is, individuals have equal rights to exercise their agency in the development of their capacities and the pursuit of long-term projects. This entails a prima facie equal right to the conditions for such activity and requires recognition by others of these rights.[5] Though this much follows directly from the critique of domination, what may be less obvious is how this critique bears on the requirement for democracy. Equal agency, presupposed by the critique of domination, entails in general an equal right of self-determination of one's activity, within the constraints of respect for these equal rights of others. And where one's activity is a common and shared, as it would be in a polity, or in economic or social institutions, it entails an equal right to participate in joint decision making concerning this activity. But this is in effect the requirement for democracy. If, by contrast, others determine the range or direction of one's activity, or control the conditions necessary for carrying out that activity, whether this activity is individual or shared as in the institutional contexts of social, economic, or political life, then this is, in one degree or another, a case of domination in the exercise of unequal power. It may in a certain sense seem obvious that the critique of domination, of which women's experience is a paradigmatic case, maps on to an institutional requirement for democracy, but the intrinsic relation between these concepts is not often articulated.

These implications for democracy of the norm of equal freedom implicit in the critique of domination also bear on the question of individual rights, that is, on the protection of individuals from interference with their liberties or from domination, either by other individuals or by the community as a whole. And it also suggests the need for certain positive rights. For if individuals are to be equally free, their basic freedom of choice needs to be protected by civil liberties and political rights from undue interference; and their power to effect their choices needs to be supported by positive rights to the conditions for their agency.

This view conflicts with the position recently taken by some feminists that rights-based theories of ethics and politics are misguided and ought to be replaced by theories based on caring and particular obligations. A care perspective, they argue, emerges from women's experience, in contrast to the rights and justice perspective held to be drawn from men's experience in the public sphere. Whatever the merits of this emphasis on care, which I consider shortly, I would argue that some conception of equal rights is both implicit in the critique of domination and essential to the justification of democracy. In this way, preservation or further development of an approach that includes rights should not be abandoned by feminist theorists. Such an approach to rights may well need to be developed beyond traditional liberal conceptions. Parenthetically, Jane Mansbridge may be similarly concerned with the rights of individuals when she proposes that women's sensitivity to the experience of unequal power suggests the need for protections of individuals, or as she puts it, individual interest, against the power of a community, though she seems to shy away from the language of rights.

Likewise, the principle of equal positive freedom, which is implied in the critique of domination, constitutes a principle of distributive justice, namely, that individuals have prima facie equal rights to the conditions necessary for their differentiated self-development. Thus, justice, which has been denigrated as the male gender-coded value in social and political theory, may itself be seen to have a source in the critique of domination that grows out of women's experience.

This interpretation supports not only a norm of equal rights but one of reciprocity as well. By reciprocity I mean a relation characterized by a shared understanding and free agreement that the actions of each individual with respect to the other(s) are equivalent. However, the form of reciprocity that I have in mind goes beyond what I have called instrumental reciprocity or what has been characterized by others as return for benefit done or as "tit for tat." This is the externalized form of a relation stripped of its richer aspects. Rather, the reciprocity that I believe grows out of the feminist critique of domination is an intentional relation of reciprocal recognition in which each recognizes the other as free and self-developing, hence as unique.[6]

This mode of reciprocity is most obviously applicable to face-to-face relations among individuals. But something like this may also be seen to be an essential feature of a democratic decision process in which each agent affords the other reciprocal recognition as a free and distinctive individual, and in which their differences are respected. Respect for differences may take two correlative forms: First, those individual differences that are irrelevant to the decision process—typically, in political contexts, race, sex, religion, and so forth—are respected by being treated as indifferent to it and therefore as not subject to discrimination; and second, those individual differences that *are* relevant to the decision process, that is, differences in judgments or beliefs, are respected by affording full freedom of such difference in the deliberative and decision procedure.[7]

The relation of reciprocity is most obviously characteristic of participatory democratic processes. But it applies to other modes of democratic deliberation and decision making as well. In representative contexts, recognition of equal political rights and liberties—voting, eligibility for office, free speech, and so forth—entails tacit, if not explicit, recognition by each citizen of the other's equal rights. However, I wish to distinguish this sort of reciprocity from that which is sometimes adduced of the care and mothering relation. This latter is a more problematic sense of reciprocity for politics, as I note later.

These reflections bear on the import of the feminist critique of domination, and of what Mansbridge refers to as women's experience of unequal power, for questions of individual freedom and rights. Some feminists, however, have criticized such an emphasis as implying an atomistic conception of individuals,[8] which in turn suggests an adversarial model of democracy. But this interpretation of freedom and equal rights seems to me mistaken. And it would be a further mistake to suggest that an emphasis on individual freedom and equal rights entails an atomistic conception of democracy. In fact, the slide from individual freedom and rights to atomic or abstract individualism may derive from a kind of dichotomous thinking that sees individuals and relations, or again justice and care, as mutually exclusive categories rather than as closely related aspects of a complex social reality. By contrast, I have argued that the basic entities that make up social life should be construed as individuals-in-relations or social individuals;[9] and that justice and care are complementary, rather than conflicting frameworks.[10] Moreover, emphasis on individual freedom and equal rights, when so understood, certainly does not entail an atomistic or adversarial conception of democracy, but in fact is entirely congruent with the concept of democratic community.

The concept of democratic community goes beyond the traditional and thinner notion of democracy as simply a matter of political representation and equal voting rights. This is most often understood as a mediation of individual differences or interests, that is, a fair method of adjudicating among them. Although it is compatible with a notion of a common interest, at least in an aggregative sense, and presupposes a minimal procedural common interest in this method of decision making itself, liberal democratic theory stops short of a notion of community. By contrast, the very notion of equal rights of participation in shared decision making concerning common activity connotes a common interest in the common activity, as well as in the process of decision making concerning that activity. In effect, if unequal power and domination are to be replaced by a norm of equal freedom, or power, and shared authority, then relations among the individuals engaged in this process are just those relations that constitute a community, namely, reciprocal recognition and respect for individual difference and freely joined cooperation toward common ends. In this sense too, then, one consequence of thinking through the contribution of women's experience in the context of the critique of domination and of unequal power is a notion of democracy as involving community and not merely a mediation of differences.

Is Care an Adequate Model of Democratic Community?

The second major domain of women's experience that has increasingly been adduced as a normative model for ethics and politics is that of care, especially as it relates to the practice of mothering.[11] Care is held to encompass a range of characteristic dispositions, such as concern for the other not out of duty or obligation but out of feeling or sympathy; attention or attentiveness; sensitivity to the needs of others, and more strongly, taking the others' interests as equal to or more important than one's own; concern for the growth and enhancement of the other; and an orientation to the common interest of the family or of those who are close or related to one. These feelings and dispositions are directed to particular others rather than universally, and so contrast with traditional notions of universal and impartial principles and obligations. Although some of the feminist literature associates these characteristics exclusively with a gender-defined experience of mothering, some feminists, including Mansbridge, rightly see these features as not exclusively gender-related—and therefore I would say perhaps better characterized as related to parenting—although it is clear that the culturally dominant expression of these traits has heretofore been identified with the role and experience of women.

There is a presumption that these experiences lend support to notions of community and hence to a richer conception of democracy. The question is how to interpret these dispositions of caring and attentiveness and the concern with the common interest of the family for the case of democracy. In one sense this seems obvious: These ways of expressing concern for others and for their needs that characterize the relation of care in intimate personal relations and in certain familial relations would seem to match the democratic community's requirement for relations of reciprocity and especially for reciprocal respect, though not all relations of care are reciprocal, as I discuss below. Further, the notion of a common interest seems to be easily extrapolated from the commonality of family feeling to a larger polity or community.

Indeed, the elements of what I have called democratic personality include just such features as a disposition to reciprocity, and receptivity or attentiveness to the views of others.[12] In addition, a shared or common interest both provides the context for democratic decision making and is elaborated in the process of deliberation.[13] I think that the experience of caring and concern that is characteristically taken to belong to women facilitates an awareness of common interest that is fundamental to the possibility of a democratic community. In addition, I also believe that the typical concern for providing for the specific needs of others associated with mothering or parenting or with family relations more generally can usefully be imported into the larger democratic community in terms of a focus on meeting the differentiated needs of individuals and not simply protecting their negative liberties. Thus, care in this context translates into responsiveness to the particular needs and interests of individuals or groups instead of treating them all in the very same way. It also connotes a concern for providing the economic and social means for the development of individuals and not only refraining from impeding their choices. So far so good.

However, the notion of care as a model for democratic community has serious limitations. But to deal with them, I think it important to draw some distinctions in the concept of care that have been overlooked in the feminist discussion. In the recent literature, the idea of care seems to be drawn mainly from two sources or models, which are most often blended together. However, important differences exist between them, even though they are related. The first of these sources is mothering or parenting, in which care manifests itself largely as nurturance or concern for the vulnerable child and for its development. Care in this sense of nurturance is nonreciprocal, because in this relation, the parent takes care of the young child but, at this stage at least, the child is not in a position reciprocally to take care of the parent, even though they reciprocally care *about* each other and reciprocally adjust their responses to each other. The child is initially utterly dependent on the parent and the parent provides for, teaches, and has responsibility for the child. Of course, as Virginia Held points out, the mothering relation is aimed at raising an equal in the child so that the relation with the child becomes reciprocal with maturation;[14] and it is already reciprocal in that parent and child love each other. But *qua* mothering or parenting, the care is nonreciprocal. A somewhat related context of nonreciprocal relation is care for others who are vulnerable or dependent by virtue of their weakness, illness, or deprivation. Here, common models are nursing and welfare.

The nonreciprocal relation of care as nurturance may be characterized as a case of benign nonreciprocity by contrast with what we might call malignant nonreciprocity. The latter refers to non-reciprocal relations of domination or exploitation, in which one controls the actions of another and thus inhibits the other's freedom or benefits at the other's expense.

The second main source for the feminist concept of care is that of love or intimate personal relation, which entails, ideally, a reciprocal or mutual concern of each for the other. Feminist theorists have most often interpreted this as involving mutuality, in a sense that connotes not only reciprocal recognition of the individuality of the other and respect for the other's needs, but beyond this, enhancement by each of the other, by altruistic actions. The distinction between the two models of care based on these two rather different sources, mothering and love, has largely been disregarded in the literature. But it remains a significant distinction between a nonreciprocal and a reciprocal relation.

Where care involves a reciprocal relation, as in the case of love or intimate personal connection, we need a further distinction between the strong case of mutuality, as a relation in which each individual consciously undertakes to enhance the other, and the more minimal model of care involved in social reciprocity or the reciprocity of respect. In this latter type of reciprocity, each recognizes the distinctive individuality of the other and has concern for the differences in the other's needs, and for their satisfaction. We have a relation of sympathy or understanding of the other but not yet the active engagement in enhancing the other that characterizes mutuality. A relation of reciprocal sympathy and understanding, or concern for the other, is clearly a feature of the relation of love or indeed of friendship. But it may also characterize a social relation among members of a community who are neither lovers nor friends. For example, among members of a tribal or ethnic or political community, there may be relations of such reciprocal sympathy, as a type of care.

In addition to the two sources for the conception of care, the maternal and the love relation, one should mention a third source for this concept in the feminist literature. This is the family as a model of common concern or a common good that relates all of the members to each other.[15] In addition to caring for each other, as in the case of love, on this model they are bound by a common interest in the well-being of the family unit that is not identical with the care they have for each other as individuals. In such a case, we may speak of cooperative reciprocity as a relation among individuals engaged in activities toward common ends. It is easy to see how such a familial model could be interpreted for political community. The family metaphor is commonplace in the history of political thought, though most often with a patriarchal interpretation, the King or the State as Father.

The limitations on the extension of the concept of care to the democratic community can be seen from this account of the various models of care. The maternal or parental model has obvious limitations in any extrapolation to political or institutional contexts of democratic communities. Even though it includes elements of reciprocity, parenting is more fundamentally a nonreciprocal relation. A democratic community, by contrast, is based on reciprocal relations among equals who share authority by virtue of their equal rights to participate in decision making. This is not to say that the elements of personal care that characterize both parenting and care for the indigent or ill are irrelevant to democratic community. On the contrary, concern for specific needs and individual differences is one of the features that marks off democratic community from a society of abstract equality.

Another limitation of the maternal or parental model is the particularism and exclusivity that are characteristic of the caring concern for the child in the family. Though appropriate in that context, it can hardly provide a model for the democratic community, because in this case fairness requires equal rights and equal consideration of interests, independent of any particular feelings of care for given individuals. In fact, it is an acknowledged violation of democratic equality to act on the basis of favoritism, or of special interests, or to permit personal alliances to violate requirements of fairness. The same limitation holds for the model of love or intimate personal connection, as well as for the model of the family, which are characterized by particularism and exclusivity of care.

Yet it should be granted that the domain of politics, like those of the economy and social life, has its own modes of exclusivity and particularism, some warranted and some not. For example, citizenship itself is an exclusionary category, at least as states are now constituted. And the criteria of membership in social institutions more generally is a live issue in contemporary political and social debate. Similarly, ethnicity connotes not only belonging but exclusion as well. Nonetheless, at the political/institutional level, membership or exclusion ought not to be on the basis of personal feelings that are relevant in the contexts of care. Similarly, universality and equality are norms for politics in the context of law and rights in ways that are inappropriate for the domain of personal relations.

The models of loving care and of the family in their extrapolation to political or other institutional contexts have the further problem that it would be misplaced or wrong to require in a democratic community that people act toward others out of feelings of love or even affection, or that they aim at the enhancement of particular others. Such mutuality is appropriate in interpersonal relations of love, family, or in the case of friendship, but cannot be expected or normatively required at an institutional level. It may be observed that the models of both mothering and intimate personal connection display the same problem as does the friendship model of democracy that has so often been drawn on,[16] namely, the problem of attempting to extrapolate what is appropriate for a two-person relation to institutional relations. More generally, I suggest that a norm like mutuality that is fully appropriate as an ethical desideratum in certain relations among individuals does not map onto the political level as an appropriate value, where instead we need to speak of the value of reciprocity, along with freedom, equality, and democracy. Further, the more complex norm of care cannot be simply taken over whole into political or institutional contexts of democracy. This does not rule out that certain personal relations and traits of character, as well as certain specifically ethical norms, may themselves be conditions for the development of democratic community. Additionally, there may well be specific forms of family or personal relations, for example, shared childraising between parents, that are more conducive to democratic community than are other arrangements.

Despite these limitations, some features of these models of care can usefully be extrapolated to the larger context of democratic community. We may point to three relevant aspects: First, the concern for the specific individuality and differences of the other that is involved in social reciprocity or the reciprocity of respect. This type of reciprocity is, as we have seen, a prime feature of democratic community. It expresses a relation of care inasmuch as it involves a sympathetic understanding of the perspective of the other and the other's concrete individuality. In deliberation or decision making in politics, or the workplace, social relations of this sort help to distinguish a democratic community from the merely procedural form of decisions by voting. However, reciprocal concern does not either presuppose or require that the individuals have any personal affection for each other. We are speaking of what we might call political feelings rather than personal sentiments or even moral feelings.

A second type of care that relates to democratic community, whether in politics, the economy, or social life more generally, is that involved in cooperative reciprocity. In this case, the concern that individuals have for each other is defined by their participation in a common activity oriented to shared ends, or to what they take to be a common good. The care in this case is therefore aimed at the achievement of this good that in turn requires their concern for each other's participation in this common activity and concern about their own responsibility for the joint undertaking.

The third type of political or social care is concern for the vulnerable that we have characterized as a benign form of nonreciprocity. In a democratic community, this concern expresses itself in support of and participation in those programs that provide for the welfare of the sick, the aged, the unemployed, and the otherwise dependent members of the community. Here, as in mothering, the aim of care is the elimination where possible of the conditions of dependence.

We have considered the contributions that the perspective of care makes to the concept of democratic community, and also the limitations of this perspective displayed in attempts to extrapolate it to the political/institutional level. However, other aspects of women's experience, in the contexts of mothering, love, and family life, must be recognized as negative and as potentially having a distorting effect on the concepts of care and democratic community. First, as Mansbridge observes, the ideal model of the caring mother, concerned with the good of the child, is not always realized in practice, for the relation is sometimes marked by domination or even abuse. Likewise, care in family relations between men and women is sometimes distorted by the subordination of the interests or the personality of one to the other. In consequence, women's experience may generate indifference to or even embarassment over the exercise of effective power in social or political contexts, as if it were exclusively a male prerogative and therefore to be eschewed. This leads to a distortion of the idea of democratic community, where in fact the proper uses of power have an important place, and where effectiveness in reaching goals is as central as concern for others.

Another negative element in women's experience tends to be left out of discussion in some uncritical or romanticized accounts of care. In our culture there is a tendency to overlook the degree to which women are socialized to adopt the prevailing norms of competitive and possessive individualism, which may well describe contexts of the family and mothering, as well as work. Consumerism and self-seeking, antagonistic attitudes toward others, including other women or families, are not absent from women's contemporary experience. Where women act in these ways, whether at home or at work, it is not simply that they are emulating men, as it is frequently suggested, but these modes may be part of their own upbringing as well.

Moreover, it would be a mistake to focus the import of women's experience for democratic community exclusively on the domains of mothering, love, or family. This would make it appear that the context of work and of social engagement outside these personal relations is not a distinctive source of women's experience that is relevant to the concept of democratic community or indeed to the model of caring itself.

Beyond this, I suggest that the exclusive association of the model of care with women's experience overlooks the degree to which caring is also a deep feature of human experience generally. One is reminded of the early Heidegger's view that the Being of Dasein is care.[17] The term "care" obviously has wider connotations than the more limited notion of maternal concern. This has been noted by some feminists who distinguish different connotations of the term.[18] A further analysis of the concept, and the various concrete caring relations in the experience of men as well as of women, would lead to a more nuanced view of care, while recognizing the centrality of parenting and love.

In an earlier essay, I proposed that what was needed was what I called "political androgyny," that is, an importation into the public domain of politics, economics, and social life of the range of capacities, concerns, and values deriving from women's historical experience, as a corrective for the predominance in public life of historically male concerns and values.[19] What is needed is a synthesis of these two, which would integrate considerations of care with those of justice, and of individuality with those of community. Here, I have tried to suggest some of these mediations. The gendering of these concepts, though historically important (as well as in most ways historically unfortunate) is incidental to their normative content. Nonetheless, only through an explicit study of women's experience that is the main source of the norm of care itself, can we realize the full depth of the concept and work out its relations to the concepts of justice, power, and democratic community.

One consequence of my analysis is that the conception of a democratic community cannot involve a reduction to a set of personal relations nor should it be understood in terms of a holistic or organic community imposed on a set of indifferent individuals. Instead, I propose that democratic community is constituted by what I have called individuals-in-relations, who reciprocally recognize each other, share some ends, and take themselves to be members of the community. Further, in a democratic community, this same joint intentionality constitutes what comes to be represented as the common interest, but that is the beginning of another story.

NOTES

1. Cf., for example, Virginia Held, "Non-Contractual Society: A Feminist View," in M. Hanen and K. Nielsen, eds., *Science, Morality and Feminist Theory* (Calgary: University of Calgary Press, 1987); Sara Ruddick, *Maternal Thinking* (Boston: Beacon Press, 1989); and Iris M. Young, *Justice and the Politics of Difference* (Princeton: Princeton University Press, 1990).

2. C. B. Macpherson, *Democratic Theory: Essays in Retrieval* (Oxford: Oxford University Press, 1973); Carole Pateman, *Participation and Democratic Theory* (Cambridge: Cambridge University Press, 1970); Jane Mansbridge, *Beyond Adversary Democracy* (New York: Basic Books, 1980); Benjamin Barber, *Strong Democracy* (Berkeley: University of California Press, 1984).

3. Carol C. Gould, *Rethinking Democracy: Freedom and Social Co-operation in Politics, Economy, and Society* (Cambridge: Cambridge University Press, 1988).

4. Cf. Carol C. Gould, "The Woman Question: Philosophy of Liberation and the Liberation of Philosophy," in C. Gould and M. W. Wartofsky, eds., *Women and Philosophy: Toward a Theory of Liberation* (New York: G. P. Putnam's, 1976); and *Marx's Social Ontology: Individuality and Community in Marx's Theory of Social Reality* (Cambridge: MIT Press, 1978).

5. Cf. Gould, *Rethinking Democracy*, chap. 1.

6. Carol C. Gould, "Beyond Causality in the Social Sciences: Reciprocity as a Model of Non-Exploitative Social Relations," in R. S. Cohen and M. W. Wartofsky, eds., *Epistemology, Methodology and the Social Sciences: Boston Studies in the Philosophy of Science*, vol. 71 (Boston and Dordrecht: D. Reidel, 1983), pp. 53–88; and Gould, *Rethinking Democracy*, pp. 71–80.

7. Cases in which there have been inequalities on the basis of, for example, race or sex, may require that these differences be taken into account to insure equality, that is, to insure that they are really indifferent. In a somewhat related way, differences in individual need may be relevant in decisions about individuals, because taking account of individual differences in these contexts is required to assure equality of opportunity or equal access to the conditions of self-development.

8. See, for example, Carol Gilligan, "Moral Orientation and Moral Development," in E. F. Kittay and D. T. Meyers, eds., *Women and Moral Theory* (Totowa: Rowman and Littlefield, 1987), pp. 19–33.

9. Gould, *Rethinking Democracy*, chap. 2; and *Marx's Social Ontology*, chap. 1.

10. Cf. Carol C. Gould, "Philosophical Dichotomies and Feminist Thought: Towards a Critical Feminism," in H. Nagl, ed., *Feministische Philosophie*, Wiener Reihe, Band 4 (Vienna: R. Oldenbourg Verlag, 1990), pp. 184–190.

11. Cf., for example, Held, "Non-Contractual Society"; Sara Ruddick, *Maternal Thinking;* Carol Gilligan, *In a Different Voice* (Cambridge: Harvard University Press, 1982); Nel Noddings, *Caring: A Feminine Approach to Ethics and Moral Education* (Berkeley: University of California Press, 1984); and the essays in Kittay and Meyers, eds., *Women and Moral Theory.* This is also considered by Mansbridge in chapter 13 in this volume.

12. Gould, *Rethinking Democracy,* chap. 10.

13. Cf. Carol C. Gould, "On the Conception of the Common Interest: Between Procedure and Substance," in M. Kelly, ed., *Hermeneutics and Critical Theory in Ethics and Politics* (Cambridge: MIT Press, 1990), pp. 253–273.

14. Held, "Non-Contractual Society," p. 131.

15. By family here, I do not exclusively mean family by marriage or in terms of blood relations.

16. Most recently by Jacques Derrida, "The Politics of Friendship," *Journal of Philosophy*, LXXXV, 12 (1988): 632–645.

17. Martin Heidegger, *Being and Time,* tr. by J. Macquarrie and E. Robinson (New York: Harper and Row, 1962), pp. 225–273.

18. Cf. Joan C. Tronto, "Women and Caring: What Can Feminists Learn about Morality from Caring?" in A. M. Jaggar and S. R. Bordo, eds., *Gender/Body/Knowledge* (New Brunswick: Rutgers University Press, 1984), pp. 172–187; and Noddings, *Caring.*

19. Carol C. Gould, "Private Rights and Public Virtues: Women, the Family and Democracy," in C. Gould, ed., *Beyond Domination: New Perspectives on Women and Philosophy* (Totowa: Rowman and Allanheld, 1984), pp. 3–18.

15

POLITICAL THEORY AND THE AIMS OF FEMINISM

DAVID A. J. RICHARDS

Jane Mansbridge brings to our attention a literature she calls feminist, largely but not always quite recent, which she examines from the perspective of its possible contribution to the theoretical and practical discourse of democratic community. Her sympathetic yet critical review of this literature communicates a wide range of diverse views, probes their connections with classical themes in political philosophy (continuities with Aristotle, self-conscious discontinuities with Kant), and suggests how some of these views illuminate the discourse on democratic community. Her review of the literature is notably more extensive than her constructive claims, and I therefore look further into the constructive fertility for political theory of the views she has presented.

Mansbridge suggests that this literature offers us three kinds of contributions to the discourse of democratic community: First, it offers and analyzes the experience of good mothering as a generative model for ethical and political virtue in general, a model of Aristotelian as opposed to Kantian virtue; second, it analyzes the experience of gender subjugation as a way of rendering visible and articulate forms of unjustifiable inequality that would otherwise be brutally suppressed, as they have traditionally been; and third, an empirical literature on the experience and reality of gender differences suggests a politically malign social construction of gender differences that she calls "gratuitous gendering." I offer some comments on each of these points, and, in conclusion, explore some constructive views of my own on the larger issue of Mansbridge's chapter in this volume, namely, political theory and the aims of feminism.

1. MOTHERING AS ETHICAL-POLITICAL MODEL

Mansbridge reviews an extensive and diverse literature on this issue, but gives special salience to some of the literature's explicit or implicit claim that the moral experience of mothering gives us good reason to believe that neither contract nor justice exhaust the moral categories relevant to political morality more generally. It therefore affords a further good reason to resist a Kantian political morality of respect for human rights. The argument for these claims centers on the moral phenomenology of mothering that, on this view of it, acknowledges moral claims that are non-contractual and not naturally articulated as claims of justice. Rather, they are seen as expressions of attentive empathic concern and love for the web of dependent personal relations in which one finds oneself embedded. The centrality of love, not the emotionally etiolated claims of Kantian conscientiousness, to the moral experience of these relations suggests further the inadequacy of Kantian ethics and politics. The literature that Mansbridge reviews has a number of illuminating implications for political morality, but the implications on which Mansbridge focuses are not among them.

First, the suggestion that moral theorists like Kant and those influenced by him suppose that moral claims are exhausted by contract and justice is inaccurate. Observing a distinction similar to Hume's between the natural and artificial virtues, Kant had separate theories for our natural duties as persons and our institutional duties as members of communities.[1] The experience of moral obligation in mothering, to the extent it is distinct from contract and justice, fits within the moral theory of our natural duties, among which may be our duties to our dependent offspring.[2]

Second, moral and constitutional feminist theorists have become increasingly preoccupied in the late twentieth century with the issue of reproductive autonomy as a right to be guaranteed to women as a minimal requirement of their emancipation. Perhaps this was a right women always had, but the contraceptive and reproductive technologies of modern science have rendered political claims on behalf of this right more urgent and more credible than ever before. To the extent that we recognize and vindicate this right as central to feminism, it must perforce change, although not entirely supplant, more traditional conceptions of the moral experience of mothering along the two dimensions that the traditional moral model of mothering ignores, namely, reasonable choice and the just distribution of individual and collective responsibilities of sexuality and child rearing. The right of reproductive autonomy took its place among our basic political and constitutional rights because it secured a greater measure of reasonable freedom in undertaking the responsibilities of mothering and because it more justly accorded women a kind of freedom to be sexual but not reproductive that had traditionally been central to masculine perquisites. The moral and political discourse central to modern feminism cannot either coherently or safely immunize the moral experience of mothering from the discourse of contract and justice in the way that Mansbridge suggests it might and should. Indeed, if Susan Okin is correct that the just distribution of responsibilities in child rearing is the central feminist issue of justice for Americans today,[3] then nothing can be more important than to insist that the experience of mothering become part of our discourse about rights and justice.

Third, the moral experience of mothering does suggest that Kant's rigoristic theory of conscientious moral worth, namely, action from abstract principle freed from all personal feeling and attachment, cannot be right. That fact is confirmed by much of the rest of our moral experience as well. Kant's theory of moral worth may be wrong, perhaps inhumanly so; and his related claims about women's inferior moral experience, which Mansbridge quotes, are reasonably judged to be unacceptable by many modern Kantians like myself. But it does not follow, as Mansbridge appears to suppose, that the logical structure of a valid moral belief must not, on examination, exhibit a principled character along the lines of Kant's universalizability requirement of treating persons as ends and never exclusively as means. Kant confuses an argument about the logical structure of moral belief with the theory of moral motivation, but the issues are independent and separable. Once we separate them, we may grant the moral integrity and value of moral actions based on personal feeling and attachment, and still understand the moral evaluation of those actions to require appeal to universalizable principles.

Fourth, there are good reasons, grounded on a feminist ethical and political morality, to insist that almost any traditional argument about men's and women's roles be subjected to such ethical testing precisely because women's claims to equal treatment as persons have been so often denigrated, denied, and degraded. It would be a mistake to suggest that even the most intellectually powerful and humane contemporary theory of justice along such Kantian lines, that of John Rawls,[4] has been adequate to these issues. As Jane English earlier[5] and Susan Okin later[6] made clear, it has been largely myopic on these issues. And the exploration of women's experience in general and of their experience of mothering in particular may be central to the articulation of such better arguments of justice at various levels.

Harriet Beecher Stowe's brilliant use of the experience of mothering makes my point; she thus appeals to moral heart over rationalizing pro-slavery intellect in order to make clear to her antebellum audience, in a way no other account of the facts of slavery did, the moral evil of slavery.[7] We see such appeals as prophetic *moral* arguments because they give us a better, more impartial understanding of our culpable failures to treat persons as persons. Stowe enables us feelingly to see the moral enormity of the unjust deprivation of basic human rights in intimate family life inflicted by the forcible separations of slaves from their spouses, parents, children, and so on, separations legitimated by the institution of American slavery.[8]

Reflection on women's experience also may stimulate deeper insight into fundamental ethical ideals of respect for free moral personality and the public reasonableness of political power. Moral philosophy may, for example, have phobically ignored the early formation of moral personality in relation to other persons and the insight into moral personality that reflection on that process may yield for moral and political philosophy.[9] And, a similar distortion in liberal political philosophy may have led to a defective understanding of what is required for political power over women to be legitimate.

2. Subordination and Democracy

Much feminist literature explores women's experience of unjust subjugation, and Mansbridge rightly brings to our attention the fertility of this literature for larger questions of democratic community and our culpable failures to realize such community. The analogy to race has, of course, been a central historical feature of feminist discourse in America and Britain, which began to articulate its distinctive claims on the basis of the pivotal role of increasingly active women in the abolitionist movement.[10] John Stuart Mill understandably took the abolition of slavery as his analogy in understanding and rectifying the subjection of women.[11] Mansbridge's analysis of recent literature suggests the continuing importance of this theme to rendering articulate forms of unjust subjugation that have remained politically invisible for much too long. If so, we need more, not less, integration of such perspectives with theories of justice, which is my point.

3. Gratuitous Gendering

Both Mansbridge's discussion of the empirical literature on gender differences and her constructive theory of gratuitous gendering are helpful. However, we need to be more skeptical than Mansbridge is inclined to be about the kind of contribution that the literature on mothering should and does make to both feminist justice and to the creation of a more just democratic community. That literature often celebrates gender-coded conceptions of parenting, morality, and responsibility in ways that should worry us in light of Mansbridge's discussion of gratuitous gendering. Such moral experience may itself be the consequence of an unjust social and political construction of gender and, for that reason, a crippling form of false consciousness. One thinks, in this connection, not only of De Beauvoir's worries about women's traditional moral consciousness,[12] but of Ann Douglas's devastating portrait of the debasement of American women's standards of critical moral thought in the nineteenth century by an overpowering moral sentimentality about woman's higher and purer morality in their role as asexual mothers and wives in the Victorian family.[13] As the recent literature on slavery and racism in America makes clear,[14] even unjustly oppressed groups are never wholly manipulated, victimized, or crushed. Forms of religious and family life may creatively foster self-respect even within barbarously unjust constraints and lay the foundations for later forms of moral protest and even leadership; for example, Martin Luther King was a constitutional leader of the American people in understanding the meaning of the Reconstruction Amendments.[15] We need, then, a critical account of those forms of the moral experience of women as an oppressed group that are valuably emancipating and those that are not, and the moral experience cannot itself be self-validating but must be subjected to some independent ethical testing. In light of Mansbridge on gratuitous gendering, I am more skeptical than she is about the critical value of a moral experience that appears sometimes to glory in its immunity from such testing.

Mansbridge acknowledges this problem and claims to solve it by offering two criteria: first, whether a proposed moral model gives us a possible critique of itself; and second, whether the ideal leads to more abuse than other ideals. But her application of the criteria to the maternal model of morality draws on moral criteria extrinsic to the model, namely, the proper criticism of forms of the model, patriarchy and bad mothering, on grounds of the unjust suppression of equality and individuality. Precisely because the model is justly subject to such criticisms in light of independent moral criteria, we should find it problematic to give fundamental weight to its alleged moral virtues, some of which, for example, its celebration of feeling and particularity, may self-blind it to such just demands.

4. FEMINISM AND DEMOCRATIC COMMUNITY

Mansbridge takes as her theme the contribution that various forms of feminist analysis make to the discourse of democratic community. Her central constructive emphasis is on the ways in which the distinctively feminist discourse of caring, co-operation, and distrust of hierarchy suggest practical and theoretical virtues. These virtues enhance both the practice and understanding of a democratic community of deliberative discourse among equals about justice and the common good rather than an adversarial competition among interest groups. She makes many of these claims eloquently and well in service of a model of a democratic community of fraternal principle that I find attractive.

Mansbridge's constructive view of these matters is, however, unduly circumscribed by her understanding of these issues solely in the terms of community. In fact, another aspect of the just claims of both classical and contemporary feminism is central to women's claims, as moral persons, to their rights of moral independence against communities viciously hostile to such rights. Sexism, like racism, is a crime against intelligence in the name of historically powerful communities of thought and practice that have allowed no space for the equal participation of women, as free and reasonable beings, in the deliberative discourse about justice and public and personal good in their communities; and Aristotle, we should decidedly not forget, offered perhaps the most influential philosophical rationalization of these morally corrupt attitudes.[16] If this is so, feminists in general and Mansbridge in particular should worry more than they do about any moral and political theory of women's issues, such as communitarianism, that tends to distort the whole range of critical discourse. They ignore the costs of appealing to Aristotelian community as the governing ideal rather than the equally important ideals of moral independence, individuality, and self-respecting autonomy. Perhaps no group has been morally more unjustly victimized by the unjust claims of community morality than women; accordingly, feminists should worry more about attempts to align political feminism with the traditional tools of their oppression.

Democratic community is, on my view of it, a moral, political, and constitutional ideal of a polity committed to the justification of the power of the community on terms of equality along two dimensions: respect for equal rights and equal weight for all human interests in pursuit of the public good. Women have been unjustly treated along both dimensions: They have been deprived of basic rights and their interests have not been accorded the weight due them in pursuit of the public interest. Many of these injustices cut so deeply into the fabric of the common sense borne of our common cultural traditions that they remain invisible to us. The critical insights of feminist thinkers often crucially articulate these injustices, and—giving them a name and voice—better advance the cause of democratic community. Certainly, both Mansbridge and the literature she reviews confirm the contribution of feminism to democratic community. But they do so not, as they sometimes appear to suppose, by invoking a new and superior model of ethics and political morality, but by showing us convincingly how our political and constitutional values of equal respect for persons have, both in theory and in practice, failed to accord women their due.

NOTES

1. For works that suggest some such distinction, see Immanuel Kant, *The Metaphysical Elements of Justice,* John Ladd trans. (Indianapolis: Bobbs-Merrill, 1965); Immanuel Kant, *The Metaphysical Principles of Virtue,* James Ellington trans. (Indianapolis: Bobbs-Merrill, 1964).

2. Kant observes that "parents have a natural duty to educate their children." Immanuel Kant, *The Metaphysical Elements of Justice,* at p. 99.

3. See Susan Moller Okin, *Justice, Gender, and the Family* (New York: Basic Books, 1989).

4. See John Rawls, *A Theory of Justice* (Cambridge: Harvard University Press, 1971).

5. See Jane English, "Justice Between Generations," *Philosophical Studies* 31, no. 2 (1977), 95.

6. See Susan Moller Okin, *Justice, Gender, and the Family.*

7. See, for such appeals to the experience of mothers, Harriet Beecher Stowe, *Uncle Tom's Cabin; or, Life Among the Lowly,* Ann Douglas ed. (New York: Penguin, 1981), at pp. 90–91, 105, 153–54, 623–24.

8. "The best available evidence...discloses that about one in six (or seven) slave marriages were ended by force or sale." Herbert G. Gutman, *The Black Family in Slavery and Freedom 1750–1925* (New York: Vintage Books, 1976), at p. 318.

9. See, for a suggestive account along these lines, Annette Baier, "Cartesian Persons," in her *Postures of the Mind: Essays on Mind and Morals* (London: Methuen, 1985), at pp. 74–92. For commentary on the utility of such insights, see, in general, Lorraine Code, *What Can She Know?: Feminist Theory and the Construction of Knowledge* (Ithaca: Cornell University Press, 1991).

10. See, for example, Ellen Carol DuBois, *Feminism and Suffrage: The Emergence of an Independent Women's Movement in America 1848–1869* (Ithaca: Cornell University Press, 1978).

11. See, in general, John Stuart Mill, *The Subjection of Women,* in John Stuart Mill and Harriet Taylor Mill, *Essays on Sex Equality*, Alice S. Rossi ed. (Chicago: University of Chicago Press, 1970), at pp. 125–242.

12. See, in general, Simone de Beauvoir, *The Second Sex,* H. M. Parshley trans. (New York: Vintage Books, 1952).

13. See, in general, Ann Douglas, *The Feminization of American Culture* (New York: Knopf, 1977).

14. See, for a notable example of this genre, Eugene D. Genovese, *Roll, Jordan, Roll: The World the Slaves Made* (New York: Vintage Books, 1976).

15. See, in general, Taylor Branch, *Parting the Waters: Martin Luther King and the Civil Rights Movement 1954–63* (London: Papermac, 1990).

16. See, for a good general perspective, David Brion Davis, *The Problem of Slavery in Western Culture* (Ithaca: Cornell University Press, 1966), at pp. 69–72.

INDEX

434

Government (*continued*)
  restriction of political freedoms by,
  136
Government intervention in
  economy, 98, 259, 266, 267, 278–
  79; coercive, 275–77; costs of,
  276–77; in Egypt, 322; failure of
  rational persuasion to prevent,
  267–75
Government regulation, 9; and
  identity, 175
Great Britain, 267, 278; economic
  mobilization, 262–63
Greed, 62
Green, T. H., 91, 92, 93, 94, 95, 116,
  117, 118
Griswold v. Connecticut, 123
Group defamation, 220
Group membership, social meaning
  of, 343
Group process in feminist
  movement, 289
Group representation in feminist
  organizations, 302–3, 304, 307
Group voice, 304
Groups, 4, 15–40, 168; competitive
  status of, 340; consensus in, 374;
  defined, 19–22; democracy within,
  32–39; domination/subordination
  relations in, 344; hypostatizing,
  119; and individuals, 21–22;
  irreducible plurality of, 20–21;
  minority/majority, 303; particular
  interests of, 28; private democratic,
  36–39; relations among, 29–32;
  role of, in democracy, 24–32; rules
  of access in, 24–27; structureless,
  289–94
Guardianship, 278
"Guatemala Guerrilla" organizing, 287
Guilt, 54, 64; in Mill, 94; as weapon,
  301, 303
Gutman, Amy, 7–8, 126–60

Habermas, Jürgen, 106, 171
Hansen, Karen, 291

Harding, Sandra, 382 n. 32
Hartsock, Nancy, 361
Hayden, Casey, 284
Hayek, Friedrich von, 5
Hegel, G. W. F., 45, 67, 94, 102
Heidegger, Martin, 411
Held, Virginia, 352, 383 n. 39, 405
Herland (Gilman), 349
Heteronomy, 172; autonomy and,
  169–70
Hierocratic regime, 23
Hillary, George A., Jr., 377 n. 12
Hirschmann, Nancy, 354, 355
Hobbes, Thomas, 6, 48, 49, 52, 64,
  104, 108, 118, 354
Hobhouse, L. T., 91, 95, 96, 97–98
Holism, 100, 118; and political
  ideology, 116–17
Holist-individualist argument, 98–99,
  100–101, 115, 118
Home (the), 6; democracy in, 72–73
Hook, Sidney, 56–57
House Internal Security Committee,
  245
House Un-American Activities
  Committee, 244–45
Hoyt, Edwin P., 242
Hoyt, Olga G., 242
al-Hudeibi, Hassan, 317
al-Hudeibi, Maamoun, 334 n. 52
Human beings, 45, 48–53; in
  normative theory, 48, 54–55, 56,
  60; relations among, 59–60, 119–
  20; standard starting point for, 60
Human experience, caring in, 411
Human interests, equal weight for, in
  democratic community, 421. *See
  also* Interests
Human life: as a game, 59–60; as
  rational pursuit of interests under
  constraints, 58
Human nature, 5–6, 48, 99, 106,
  156; in Aristotle, 100; open-ended,
  105
Human relations: gender in, 346;
  models of, 369

438   *Index*